Dedicated to
James D. Van Trump,
co-founder of the
Pittsburgh History & Landmarks Foundation,
who has devoted his life to recording
the landmark buildings of Allegheny County

LANDMARK ARCHITECTURE
PITTSBURGH AND ALLEGHENY COUNTY

TEXT BY

WALTER C. KIDNEY

PITTSBURGH HISTORY & LANDMARKS FOUNDATION
PITTSBURGH, 1985

Published by the
Pittsburgh History & Landmarks Foundation
450 The Landmarks Building, One Station Square, Pittsburgh, PA 15219
Copyright © 1985, Pittsburgh History & Landmarks Foundation
Manufactured in the United States of America

Author
Walter C. Kidney

Project Director, Editor
Louise King Ferguson

Editor, Photographer
Martin Aurand

Library of Congress Catalog Card Number: 85-62177
ISBN 0-916670-09-0

ACKNOWLEDGMENTS

The author and editors are grateful to Ellis L. Schmidlapp, president of Landmarks Design Associates, Architects, who reviewed the text for the essay and guide, and to the following people who reviewed the essay and offered valuable suggestions:

Edward K. Muller, Department of History, University of Pittsburgh
George Swetnam, historian
William F. Trimble, editor, The Historical Society of Western Pennsylvania
James D. Van Trump, vice-president emeritus of the Pittsburgh History & Landmarks Foundation

We are indebted to Clyde Hare, photographer, who patiently worked with us, searching through his photographs of Pittsburgh to find the most appropriate views for this publication and offering valuable suggestions from the inception of the project. We also thank Frank J. Kurtik, photo archivist with the University of Pittsburgh, and Maria Zini, head of the Pennsylvania Division, Carnegie Library of Pittsburgh, for their assistance in helping us select and obtain many of the historic photographs for this publication.

ALLEGHENY COUNTY SURVEY

This publication is based on the results of a comprehensive historic sites survey of Allegheny County conducted by the Pittsburgh History & Landmarks Foundation staff from 1979 through 1984. We are pleased to acknowledge the following staff members who were involved in the survey project:

Martin Aurand
Eliza Smith Brown
Bill Bylewski
Laurie Cain
Laura Coffey
Peta Harrington Cole
Kate Crouch
Lu Schleck Donnelly
David Kahley
Steven Kibert
Amy Machemer

Patricia McLaughlin
James Miller
Catherine Mourkas
Jan Murdock
Terry A. Necciai
Robert Ritter
John Sandor
Christina Mann Schmidlapp
Jean Slominski
William Stevenson

We also thank the many individuals throughout Allegheny County who volunteered their time and talent to work with our staff on the survey.

The Allegheny County Survey was generously supported by the following contributors:

Pennsylvania Historical and Museum Commission with funding from
the National Park Service, United States Department of the Interior
Allegheny County Department of Development
Fisher Charitable Trust
Vira I. Heinz Fund of the Pittsburgh Foundation
Richard King Mellon Foundation
Pittsburgh History & Landmarks Foundation general fund

Landmark Architecture: Pittsburgh and Allegheny County was typeset in Paladium by Cold Comp with Times Roman chapter headings, and was printed on 80 lb. Vintage Velvet text by Hoechstetter Printing Company, Inc. The publication was designed by Thomas S. Stevenson, Jr. of Landmarks Design Associates, with assistance from Greg Pytlik, Jean Hodak, Daryl Bruno, and David Seaman.

CONTRIBUTORS

The Pittsburgh History & Landmarks Foundation gratefully acknowledges the following for contributing to the publication of *Landmark Architecture: Pittsburgh and Allegheny County.*

PATRONS

Alcoa Foundation
Alfred Pope Brooks
The Hillman Foundation, Inc.
Mr. & Mrs. Henry P. Hoffstot, Jr.
The Hunt Foundation
Katherine Mabis McKenna Foundation, Inc.
Richard King Mellon Foundation

DONORS

Mr. & Mrs. Charles C. Arensberg
Meredith M. Armstrong
L. D. Astorino & Associates, Ltd.
Martin and Joann Aurand
Fred C. Babcock
Mrs. Kenneth S. Boesel
Mr. & Mrs. Charles H. Booth, Jr.
J. Judson Brooks
Carl Wood Brown
Mrs. James H. Childs, Jr.
Mr. & Mrs. Wm. Howard Colbert
Frederic L. Cook
Kathleen Casey Craig
Pat Davin
Mr. & Mrs. John P. Davis, Jr.
Mr. & Mrs. Robert J. Dodds III
George C. Dorman
Willa McCormac Dunn
Arthur J. Edmunds
Mr. & Mrs. Richard D. Edwards
Virginia A. Elliott
Mr. & Mrs. Sanford B. Ferguson
Mrs. James A. Fisher
The Emery Garlock Family
Councilman Richard E. Givens
Helen Pittock Green
Andrew J. Griest
Mr. & Mrs. J. Blaine Griffith, Jr.
Dr. & Mrs. Clifford C. Ham
John H. Hill
Wayne K. Homren
Mrs. Ira Hurwick
IKM SGE, Architects & Engineers
William J. and Mildred M. Johnston
Mrs. B. F. Jones 3rd
Tasso Katselas, Architect/Planner
Mr. & Mrs. William C. King
Landmarks Design Associates, Inc.
Edward B. Lee, Jr.
Chester LeMaistre
Sonia and Aaron Levinson Philanthropic Fund
Richard L. Linder

Arthur Lubetz Associates
Mrs. Harold F. Lyke
Dorothy K. Lynch
Grant McCargo
Shirley A. McMaster
Mr. & Mrs. Edward A. Montgomery, Jr.
Mr. & Mrs. Wm. H. Moreland
Mr. & Mrs. J. L. Murdy
Mrs. Thomas J. Murrin
Mrs. Hugh G. Nevin
E. C. Quick
Marirose and John Radelet
Mrs. Cleveland D. Rea
Reid & Stuhldreher, P.C.
Senator James A. Romanelli, 43rd District
Mrs. Sidney M. Ruffin
Mr. & Mrs. Ellis L. Schmidlapp
Glen Alan Schultz, A.I.A.
Shaughnessy Associates
Stephanie G. Sladek
Mrs. Steven J. Smith
G. Whitney Snyder
Milan and Sylvia Spanovich
Bob Spear
Thomas S. Stevenson, Jr.
Thomas A. Streever/Donna Marshall
Dorothy M. Suckling
Mr. & Mrs. James B. Summers, Jr.
Mrs. Rose S. Tarasi
Dr. & Mrs. Donald E. Thomas
Professor Franklin K. B. Toker
Dr. & Mrs. Albert C. Van Dusen
Congressman Doug Walgren
Mr. & Mrs. James M. Walton
Helen M. Wilson
Mary Wohleber
Robert F. Wohleber
Mr. & Mrs. C. Holmes Wolfe, Jr.
George H. Yeckel
Mr. & Mrs. Arthur P. Ziegler
Arthur P. Ziegler, Jr.

ADDITIONAL SUPPORT

The research and writing of *Landmark Architecture: Pittsburgh and Allegheny County* was supported in part by the contributions of more than 350 trustees, members, friends, private foundations, and businesses who contributed to the Pittsburgh History & Landmarks Foundation Capital Campaign.

The printing of the publication was made possible in part by the Revolving Fund for Education which was established in 1984 through a generous grant from the Claude Worthington Benedum Foundation.

Revenues from Station Square, a mixed-use development of the Pittsburgh History & Landmarks Foundation, have also been utilized to underwrite the cost of this publication.

ILLUSTRATION SOURCES

CONTENTS

PROLOGUE

Why do we want to "save" what we think is interesting in Pittsburgh's architectural heritage? We know that Job said: "Some remove the landmarks . . . they turn the needy out of the way; the poor of the earth hide themselves together." We know that Marcus Aurelius prescribed a law decreeing the loss of a hand for mutilating or destroying a landmark. We are reminded that F. W. J. Schelling described architecture as "music in space, as it were a frozen music [*erstarrte Musik*]." These conceptions have found their modern counterparts in zoning laws, city planning commissions, and organizations such as the National Trust and our own Pittsburgh History & Landmarks Foundation. Preservation has come of age in our country.

Age has its beauty too, as we all know who have traveled through Europe and Asia and seen its ancient monuments:

The soul's dark cottage battered and decayed
Lets in new light through chinks that
Time hath made.

But why Pittsburgh? This is not Paris or Salamanca, Venice or Stockholm. Here we have no Parthenon, Coliseum, or Westminster Abbey. But Pittsburgh is our city, unique in all the world. We were born or transplanted here. We know its hills, its fine rivers and sweeping valleys; many of us are familiar with its Hartford Streets, its Rhine Streets, its Grandview Avenues, its mills, its parks, and yes, its cemeteries, Allegheny and Homewood. And we know its architects too, from Latrobe and Chislett to Richardson and Hornbostel, Scheibler, Janssen, and Stotz, and down to our present-day leaders in the field.

We can see its past in the Mexican War Streets and old Manchester, in Shadyside, the South Hills, and Lawrenceville. We can see its future in the ever-changing skyline of the Golden Triangle, and in the vitality of Oakland and many of our neighborhoods. We think it has a host of fascinating vistas and quiet streets. We do not apologize that Pittsburgh is our home. We are proud of this city and region.

This book is an attempt to capture some of that unique essence and make a record of it.

Charles Covert Arensberg,
Chairman of the Board
Pittsburgh History & Landmarks Foundation

PREFACE

Of all the fine arts, consider how architecture is the one closest to us every day, in our personal lives as well as in the wider social scene. From birth to death, it is mostly in buildings that we work, eat, sleep, worship, shop, experience illness and recovery, entertain ourselves and others. And consciously or not, our spirits, minds, and bodies react to and take shape from these buildings.

Creating these structures is always more or less a community effort, involving money, people, time, materials, and often political actions or even conflict. The success or failure of the architect's work has a social effect, leaving some imprint on the patterns of human life.

All around us stand our architectural works — the new, the older, and still yet older, all with stories to tell. Here in our city there is nothing else like the fun and satisfaction of finding, studying, preserving, adapting, and *using* our architectural heritage.

Why should it be surprising that so much of the old is so good? It isn't to me. Every time has something worth keeping.

Of course, this special enjoyment needs to be passed on and shared by a written record — and here it is.

We Pittsburghers are fortunate to have these faithful recorders: Jamie Van Trump, Walter Kidney, Charles Arensberg, Arthur Ziegler, and others working with them to bring us this precious gift — our past in architecture.

Richard Dilworth Edwards,
Vice-Chairman and Trustee
Pittsburgh History & Landmarks Foundation

THE POPLAR AND THE AILANTHUS

ARCHITECTURE IN AN INDUSTRIAL REGION

Author's Note

Pittsburgh, the seat and principal city of Allegheny County, was founded in 1758. Thus, it is notably newer than Nieuw Amsterdam (1625), Boston (1630), Charleston (1680), and Philadelphia (1682). Yet after 1800 it was largely in the American architectural mainstream, keeping pace — more or less — with innovations elsewhere.

The following essay is a brief history of Allegheny County architecture, taking into account national trends in architecture as well as our own special circumstances in order to provide a context by which the reader can more fully appreciate the significance of individual buildings and sites.

Our notable early buildings were constructed throughout the county. But from the advent of the Victorian period around 1840, this essay focuses largely on Pittsburgh. This may seem unfair to the county as a whole, but reflects our history. Money that was made in commerce and industry throughout the county came largely to Pittsburgh, where an ample part of it was converted into office buildings, mansions, and public institutions. Pittsburgh continually expanded, besides, absorbing neighboring cities, towns, suburbs, and farms, and built and rebuilt within its growing boundaries to become the county's economic, social, and architectural heart.

More than 150 photographs in this section illustrate our architectural history. Many of these form a "Lost Allegheny County," a roll-call of significant buildings and scenes that have long since passed. We have lost much that was handsome, dramatic, or intimately familiar, and our architectural history would not be complete without recognition of these notable landmarks. This essay also includes buildings of the last 50 years, buildings under probation now that in time may come to be seen as true landmarks of our region. Finally, buildings are illustrated that are not outstanding in themselves but are so characteristic of this area that without them a local inhabitant would feel that something was being overlooked.

A selection of the most historically significant extant buildings and sites found throughout Allegheny County is illustrated in the guide section which follows the essay. ■

3

The Allegheny River Valley at the Pittsburgh Point.

THE TERRAIN

We in Allegheny County live in a terrain of hills and ravines, with occasional plateaus and river plains and much rolling country; a place that has been difficult to build on and frustrating to travel, yet one with remarkable natural beauty and grandeur.

The county is very roughly trisected by three rivers: the Allegheny coming in from the northeast, the Monongahela from the south and east, and the Ohio formed by their confluence at the Pittsburgh Point, flowing at first northwest. River elevation at the Point is 710 feet above sea level, and hill elevations in the county can be nearly 700 feet higher. Indeed, the crest of Mount Washington, opposite the Point and only 1,000 feet from the Monongahela shore, is almost 400 feet higher. Other bluffs and hills crowd close to the rivers in many places, reducing the areas of river plain to almost nothing.

For nearly two-and-a-half centuries, man has scraped and scratched at this primitive terrain, building roads on its slopes, bridging its voids, tunneling its hills, filling in its shallower depressions. But despite all this activity, the nature of the terrain is essentially unchanged. Many hilltop views in the county are dramatic for their vistas along ancient river valleys, up among the hills and over a landscape that is still basically an ancient river delta, eroded by rivers that took nearly their present courses in the Ice Ages that ended 12,000 years ago.

In such a landscape engineering naturally is a major presence. The county, and Pittsburgh especially, has been called a museum of bridges. We have had none of the swing and lift bridges needed over navigable rivers in flatter country, but we have had most of the other types, including one or two rarities and several that were very advanced in their time. Some of our bridges, especially those of the late nineteenth century, were grotesques by any aesthetic standard, but much of what we see today is the handsome

legacy of a massive bridge-building campaign by
the County, begun in the early 1920s and concluded a decade later: bridges of progressive
design, clean in their lines, with modest architectural touches in a Classical or Modernistic manner.
Most of these bridges, recently repaired, are good
for a few years more.

On the other hand, we have lost several striking ones, and three early works by John Augustus
Roebling, who later designed the Brooklyn Bridge.
A German immigrant living in Saxonburg in
Butler County, the great engineer began manufac-
ture of the first wire cable in America in 1841. This
he applied to suspension bridges, first in 1845 in
an aqueduct across the Allegheny for the Pennsylvania Canal — an especially tricky problem —
then in 1846 to replace the Smithfield Street
Bridge which burned in the Great Fire of 1845, and
finally in the second Sixth Street Bridge of 1859.

Less frequent than the bridges, less conspicuous in the landscape, but striking nonetheless are the great Victorian retaining walls that
appear here and there where the right-of-way for
a street or railroad has been cut from a hillside.
Until the 1900s, like bridge piers and abutments
of the time, these were typically made of massive,
rugged-textured, roughly squared stones, which
if the stonecutters were on piecework might have
their personal symbols scratched on the surfaces.
Such walls, which may be 50 feet high and
hundreds of feet in length, made of the local

*Crossing the rivers: John Augustus Roebling's Sixth Street Bridge
over the Allegheny (above) and, from a century later, the Fort Pitt
Bridge over the Monongahela (below).*

Until 1970, the Point and the Manchester Bridges met at the Pittsburgh Point (left). The Point Bridge of 1927 is in the foreground. (Both gone.) Below are the Allegheny River bridges to and from the Golden Triangle.

yellow-gray sandstone turned a soft black under the Pittsburgh soot, are impressive in their rugged texture, their perceptible mass. The distinctive Romanesque of Henry Hobson Richardson, once it appeared in downtown Pittsburgh in the Courthouse and Jail (1884–88), was imitated in churches and commercial buildings for a decade, perhaps because it was simply a refinement of the raw engineering masonry that the city had known for years.

Tunnels have, by their very nature, been less conspicuous, and the portals visible from downtown Pittsburgh have been masked with modern boxy structures that reveal nothing of their essential nature as holes drilled into steep hillsides. Of our 20 or more inclines of the past, though, two are still to be seen. Half-cable car, half-elevator, the inclines once hoisted passengers, and even wagons and teams, up various of our steep slopes. The two survivors, the Monongahela and the Duquesne Heights Inclines, still carry passengers up Mount Washington on frail-looking structures of girders and bents. The Duquesne Incline uses its original cars of 1877, with their Eastlake interiors. The alternatives to incline travel on such slopes were long heaven-storming roads such as Mount Washington's East Sycamore Street (nicknamed the Burma Road) or flights of public steps, hundreds of them sometimes, of rotting wood or flaking concrete that simply went straight up with the occasional small mercy of a landing or that joggled from side to side to make contact with scattered houses.

A retaining wall along Carson Street in 1930 (above) and public steps on the North Side in 1951 (below). Opposite, the vehicle-carrying Knoxville Incline in the 1950s. (Gone.)

8

The Pittsburgh of legend. This fiery nocturne by the Monongahela shows, in its most heroic mode, our region as the world imagines it. By day, other and less colorful elements would elaborate the scene: rust, black paint, mud, weeds, and a gray river, with smoke and steam rising from complicated constructions of steel and concrete. Yet this Pittsburgh is disappearing today. The industrial fires and the industrial plants themselves are withdrawing from the scene. And, as the next pages show, some of our industry has always been out in the country, away from the towns and the rivers.

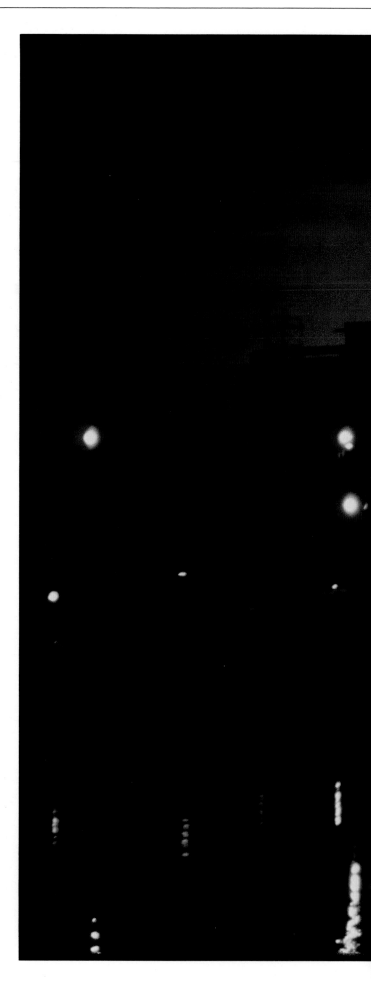

And of course, the engineering presence in the Pittsburgh area has been felt very strongly in the industrial plants strewn along the river shores and in the inland valleys, wherever the river boat or the railroad could go. The steel mills — huge, complex, mysterious, sullen black and brown, emitting fire, smoke, and steam — are still in many people's eyes the very symbol of the region. Less spectacular installations have come, though, and sometimes gone, in the valleys. We of Allegheny County have built boats, smelted and fabricated iron and steel, manufactured glass and aluminum, made electrical equipment, refined petroleum, canned food, and generated electricity. Here and there on our uplands, too, are the surface structures of coal mines and oil wells.

We are still living down one consequence of this industrial activity: our reputation as a region that has cared exclusively for manufactures and money, and nothing at all for the amenities, public ones especially, that make for a good, well-rounded life. The famous smoke, which until four decades ago rose from fires of bituminous coal all over the region, has dwindled to nearly nothing. The rivers, once so polluted, have been greatly cleaned and fish have returned. But for a century and a half we were truly careless of how we were living. Our grimly casual environment had its grand spectacles of fire and clouds, and there were places where nature was left alone and trees and shrubs grew wild, but travelers to Pittsburgh used to greet their first sight with comments — many of them published — of disgust and anguish. Recent observations, those since the 1950s, have been quite different. Even today they retain the pleasant air of discovery with which journalists who first investigated the Pittsburgh Renaissance praised our attainment of civilization at last.

Other forms of the region's industrial presence: counterclockwise from the top, a coal mine headframe in Penn Hills Township, an oil well in South Fayette Township, a coal tipple in Forward Township, and brick kilns in Jefferson Borough. Opposite, above: kilns in East Deer Township for manufacturing ceramic nozzles for the steel industry.

The Pennsylvania Railroad approaches to Union Station in the late 1950s (below).

In architecture, we have not been a particularly creative, or even tasteful, city. We have had creative architects; to mention two from the past, the native Frederick G. Scheibler, Jr. and the New Yorker Henry Hornbostel, who gradually became one of us. We have also had architects who, if not particularly innovative, have applied existing architectural styles with taste and intelligence: Benno Janssen and Ingham & Boyd did first-rate work in the Eclectic period early in this century. But it has been a long-standing lament of Pittsburgh architects that the really outstanding commissions so often go to out-of-towners who are either in fashion or deemed more competent to handle a specific problem. Thus, the Courthouse and Jail are exotics, designed in Brookline, Massachusetts, and faced in Massachusetts granite. Union Station and the Frick, Oliver, and Koppers Buildings were designed in Chicago; the Cathedral of Learning, Heinz Chapel, and First Presbyterian Church, in Philadelphia; Carnegie Institute of Technology, the University of Pittsburgh hillside campus, the Mellon Bank, Gulf Building, Alcoa Building, U.S. Steel Building, Equibank Building, One Oxford Centre, One Mellon Bank Center, and PPG Place, in New York; and the East Liberty Presbyterian and Calvary Episcopal Churches, in Boston. The one prestigious building type that has regularly gone to Pittsburgh architects is the mansion — George Orth, Alden & Harlow, and Janssen & Cocken did well in this area — but when the very rich of the past retired to New York, as several did, they left Pittsburgh architects behind. Henry Clay Frick and Henry Phipps, partners of steel entrepreneur Andrew Carnegie, used well-known New York architects for their New York homes, and Charles Schwab hired a Frenchman.

Perhaps this part of the state has been too busy and distracted to develop a way of life in which good architecture, not exceptionally but as a normal occurrence, is produced. Philadelphia, Boston, and New York have grown as commercial centers, less violent to their environments than the Pittsburgh-area industrial towns, more tightly built up, and with more private and corporate clients who could afford and knew and cared enough to demand good architecture. The Boston and Philadelphia areas, with their gentlemanly mercantile, manufacturing, and professional classes, have been especially creative with houses, while New York, architecturally a rather dim city until the 1880s, then developed a colorful, varied architecture for business and the social life.

Somehow, such creativity has never happened around Pittsburgh in a big way, and most of our architects and builders never developed the sensitive eye for proportion and detailing needed to transform their works, whether simple or elaborate, from collections of features into something integrated and alive.

Of our buildings generally, the greatest praise we can give is that they do not quarrel with our landscape when seen from afar. The building type most often seen in Allegheny County is the free-standing single-family house, and groupings of these, serrating the skyline of a hill, clinging to a distant slope, or riding the edges of a street that dips and rises with the land, dramatize the contours of the terrain and its great scale. They animate the space, reveal it as inhabited, and articulate the surfaces, otherwise winter-gray or summer-green with trees and shrubs, with their little white, cream, or red cubical forms. On the plateaus and river plains, where brick is more common than frame, they fall in orderly red rows, with the contrast here and there of a church, a school, a store, or an industrial building. So often of no account when seen up close, they become from afar the low-keyed brushstrokes on an Impressionistic canvas.

The real glory of the region, in fact, is its wonderful spaces, the vivid contours of the land and the sense of distance they create. From Mount Washington you can look out toward the South Side Flats, 400 feet down and a mile-and-a-half away, still appearing like an independent town, but a town seen in some peculiar dream perspective hardly credible in a waking state; then look outwards toward the hill that rises behind, crowded with minute houses like little white granules and see, behind the hip of land they occupy, a colossal silver cloud of steam rising from a steel mill hidden in the valley beyond. Or walk, again on Mount Washington, down a colorless commercial street toward a void, with the tops of skyscrapers appearing strangely beyond its edge, and distant hilltops far beyond those; then look up and through a great red-and-white radio tower that rises, a little uncannily, from a lot by the street, and feel that one is inhabiting the sky rather than the earth. Or look out over the city at twilight, when the sun is just down, and see the shapes of buildings and hills begin to fade, tiny lights begin to glow, far away to the horizon, and get a poignant sense of human settlement, how it is spread wide but thin over the huge bulk of the earth. ◼

Houses on the hills, and a view from Mt. Washington of the South Side Flats and Slopes.

The Point at nightfall, 1985. Here the beginning of Fort Pitt in 1759 (opposite) coincided with the beginnings of Pittsburgh, the oldest town in Allegheny County.

Fort Pitt, from a plan of the 1950s by Charles Morse Stotz. Later discoveries have shown that the names of the Grenadier and Flag Bastions should be switched. The shoreline is that of the mid-eighteenth century. (Gone, except for the Blockhouse and some foundations.)

SETTLEMENT

The first notable work of architecture in the Pittsburgh region came immediately after the British took firm hold of the Pittsburgh Point in November 1758. This was Fort Pitt, successor to the abortive Fort Prince George, the weak French Fort Duquesne, and the temporary Mercer's Fort. These had been vulnerable affairs of logs and dirt, but Fort Pitt was the most elaborate British fort in North America: a full-blooded Baroque installation with bastions, casemates for munitions and stores, a moat, profiled counterscarps, ravelins, outerworks, and a glacis. The pentagonal fort itself was over two acres within the walls, and had masonry quarters for the officers and good frame barracks for the men. The whole fort occupied 17 acres. The bastions facing inland and the curtain walls between them were revetted in brick, and the remainder of the work was of dirt carefully profiled and sodded. Harry Gordon, a resident engineer captain, may have been the designer, but the skilled workmen were brought in specially from Eastern Pennsylvania. So was the machinery for a sawmill to cut the timbers; erected on Sawmill Run a mile down the Ohio River, it brought the Machine Age to Pittsburgh almost at its very start.

Begun in 1759 and finished in 1761, the fort had only a moment of perfection. Floods in 1762 and 1763 washed away much of its dirt defensive work, creating a tense situation during the uprising of the Indian tribes under Pontiac in the latter year. To strengthen the riverward defenses so weakened, five redoubts for sharpshooters were built in 1764; Bouquet's Redoubt, the so-called Blockhouse, is all that remains of the fort aside from some of its foundation masonry, and indeed of the eighteenth century in downtown Pittsburgh. Soon after, maintaining the fort seemed pointless to the military, which began to sell its building materials in 1772. Some repairs were made during the Revolution, and a vestigial garrison was kept on until 1792, but the fort

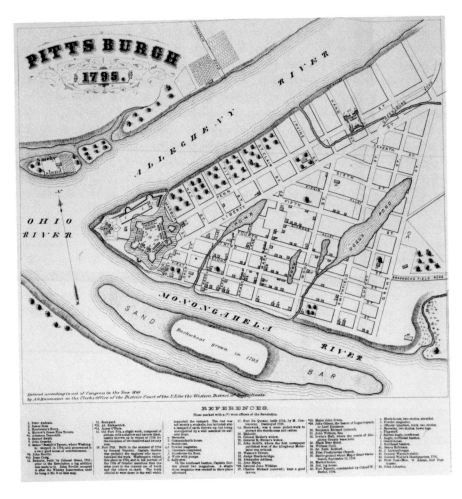

The Woods-Vickroy plan (right) as reproduced in 1876, showing a Fort Duquesne that had wholly ceased to exist in 1795 and a Fort Pitt of which only a few traces remained. In the actual plan, the grids went all the way to the Point. In 1788, David Redick surveyed the land across the Allegheny River from Pittsburgh (opposite page) for the seat of the newly created Allegheny County. Allegheny Town is shown with its surrounding Commons and agricultural "out-lots."

gradually faded away, and in a few years even its form and location were locally forgotten.

Shortly after the building of Fort Pitt, Pittsburgh saw its first essays in landscape design and town planning. The 10-acre, trapezoidal King's Gardens were basically utilitarian, a place for growing the fruits and vegetables the garrison needed to avoid scurvy, but were intended also as an ornamental layout with promenades. An earlier design with 77 little plots may not have been executed, while it does seem that a later one with radial walks was.

In 1764, Colonel John Campbell took advantage of the destruction of civilian shelters around Fort Pitt in preparation for the Indian siege to lay out the tiny settlement of Pittsburgh in an orderly fashion. He planned a four-block grid, now bounded by Stanwix and Market Streets, Fort Pitt Boulevard, and the Boulevard of the Allies.

In 1784, the Penn family, no longer Proprietors of Pennsylvania but with extensive manors — areas of private property — in Southwestern Pennsylvania, commissioned George Woods and Thomas Vickroy to survey what is now the Golden Triangle so that it could be sold.

Woods and Vickroy extended the Campbell grid, though varying the dimensions of the blocks for no apparent reason, so that most of the triangular city plan had streets parallel or perpendicular to the Monongahela River. However, a two-block strip by the Allegheny was laid out with reference to *that* river, its inland edge being Liberty Street, the road to the Northern Liberties on the Allegheny plain just outside town. Liberty Street was thus like a seam joining two pieces of tartan, each with its own undeviating pattern, and the junction was marked by peculiar triangular and trapezoidal blocks and awkward traffic intersections that remain after two centuries. In the whole plan there was only one public square, the marketplace then called the Diamond — a Scotch-Irish term for such a space — and now called Market Square; this was at an intersection of Market Street and the downtown section of Forbes Avenue, then called Diamond Alley.

The first civilian shelters around Fort Pitt, erected for traders and workmen, shared none of the technical sophistication of the fort itself. They were rough, bark-clad huts and log cabins, none of which survives. From the pioneer days in

18

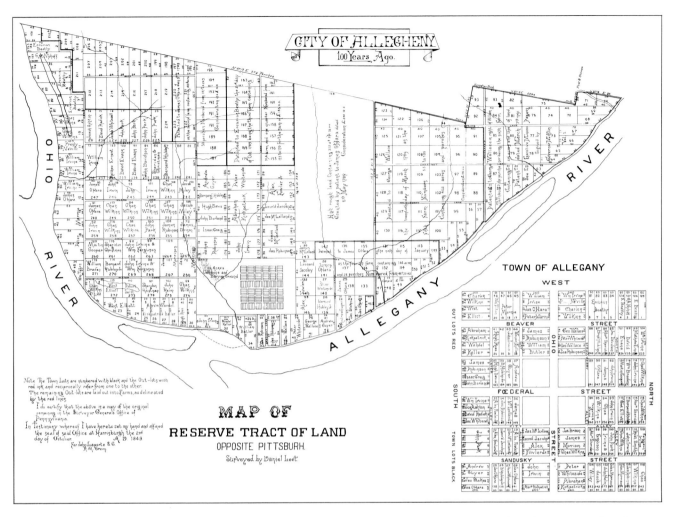

MAP OF
RESERVE TRACT OF LAND
OPPOSITE PITTSBURH.
Surveyed by Daniel Leet

Allegheny County we have only their successors, the more refined log houses that were built on into the early part of the nineteenth century.

A log cabin was a crib of logs, left round and with only enough notching to lock them together, quite possibly without a chimney and with the only openings the doorway and a smoke hole in the roof. A log house, on the other hand, was as finished a product as an ax, an adze, and a few other rough carpenter's tools could shape. The logs were squared and notched at the corners so that each had a gable-shaped upper edge and a corresponding indentation on the lower edge. The spaces between the logs were chinked with a mixture of clay and stone. Chimneys might be of piled-up logs or sticks with a heavy clay lining, but later on were more likely of massive fieldstone, possibly with jambs and lintels of regularly cut stones. Windows were very likely of oiled paper or merely shuttered openings until after 1800, when locally made window glass was available, and the roof — nails in the eighteenth century were hand-made and expensive — would probably be of planks, clapboards, or shakes held down with horizontal poles.

Typically in demand at first was a log house of one full story with a loft, and later a two-storied house; such a house, with not too much replanning, could serve as a tavern, a store, a school, or even a pioneer courthouse. A church was usually square, but could be built for a fairly large congregation in a blunt cruciform shape, each arm of the cross being one standard log in length. The image of the cross was not important — it was even a drawback in a Protestant culture — but it was useful for structural reasons, and brought the congregation close to the pulpit about which the service centered. This plan was later repeated in masonry churches, and a number of Pittsburgh churches of the end of the nineteenth century recalled pioneer days in their layouts, probably without their congregations being aware of the fact.

These simple log buildings could have been developed into a versatile local architecture of long duration under different conditions. Switzerland, Scandinavia, Finland, and Russia have had log-building traditions equal to the production of large farmhouses, town houses, storehouses, churches, and even mansions. Often the logs were exposed

The Trax house, begun in 1806, in South Park Township (above) and the Fulton house of 1830 in Upper St. Clair Township (below).

but decorated with carved and painted trim of cut-out boards and with shingles, but sometimes too they were concealed behind board siding that served as extra insulation — our pioneers sometimes used clapboards for this purpose too — and as a smoother finish to which fashionable detailing was applied. The log tradition went on into this century, and in Russia there are exposed-log houses with Art Nouveau detailing.

In Southwestern Pennsylvania, such a developed tradition did not occur. Once trees were cleared for farmland, logs had to be fetched from further away, and brick clay and stone were present as rival materials. The population were settlers, busy starting a new life and coming from areas that had passed beyond the bark-hut-and-log-cabin stage long before into one of masonry or frame-and-clapboard, and they had not the cultural background, the time, the tools, or the skills to evolve a folk architecture based on logs. Later generations might look at the log house, with its picturesque unevenness of line, its grays and gray-browns that toned in so well with the browns, greens, and spots of color of the pioneer's

garden and the somber green or brown of the hills beyond, and enjoy the picture. And the log house, well maintained, could be quite comfortable. But toward 1785, with conditions in Southwestern Pennsylvania beginning to become stable, log architecture began to be supplanted by the Georgian building tradition from the East and the South.

20

GEORGIAN SIMPLICITY

In its simplest form, that used increasingly in Southwestern Pennsylvania between 1785 and 1830, the Georgian manner of designing a building was simple, easy, and obvious: so obvious that even today, if a child draws a house, the house is apt to be Georgian. It was a synthesis of three elements: the natural tendency of humans to make an object symmetrical if it is easy to do and if there is no special reason to do otherwise; the practice in the Italian Renaissance of designing house facades with rather widely and evenly spaced windows, uniform on any one story; and the sliding-sash window, a Dutch invention of the seventeenth century that eliminated the mullions and transoms that subdivided the medieval casement window, thus making a neater contrast between the solid and void areas of a facade. These elements were synthesized in England at the end of the seventeenth century, and from 1710 were present in America as the basis of a tradition that lasted, despite rivalry from styles with different compositional bases, for two-and-a-half centuries.

Essentially, a Georgian building is a combination of rectangles topped by triangles. The perimeter on the ground is a rectangle, easy to lay out, easy to frame with wooden sills or define in masonry, easy to fit into a standard building lot. Walls rise sheer to the eaves, and the roof is usually of the easily framed gabled sort. A house will usually have an ell, a rear wing at right angles to its main body, and may have a front or side porch, but all these are distinct elements, all rectangular in plan and elevation save for the gable areas. The geometry is clear and simple: no buttresses, no bay windows, no turrets, no fancy compositions of roof planes.

On the front, the doorway is normally at the center, though not where this is impractical. The windows, of uniform dimensions on each floor, are symmetrically disposed, and are three or four

"The Meadows," the James Ross house of 1820 in O'Hara Township. Georgian simplicity prevails in the simple geometry and sparing decoration. (Gone.)

The 1800-period doorway of the Ferree house in O'Hara Township (above) is skilled in execution if not in design. The same delicate tooling appeared in a mantelpiece (below) of c. 1820 once in the Allegheny Arsenal.

feet wide and about twice as high: the two-to-one ratio is a good Classical proportion for an opening, and a window so dimensioned allows the sliding sashes to be easily handled. Aside from the simple moldings of the window frames, ornament is confined to the doorway, the cornice, and the dormers if any. Basically, this is ornamented construction, relying on good proportion, a nice use of decorative accents, and the attractiveness of local building materials for its effectiveness. The Allen-Raisner house in Forward Township survives as an example of this Georgian building practice in its form, proportions, use of materials, and Classical doorway with a rare surviving fanlight.

The builder of a Georgian house need not be a man of any talent or learning; in the overall design he has tradition to guide him, and in decorative detailing he has design manuals, originally from England but after 1800 compiled in America, which show him specimens of doorways, mantelpieces, cornices, and decorative woodwork of all sorts. In Southwestern Pennsylvania the builder is inclined not to keep his library up to date, so that a doorway normal in Philadelphia in the 1780s or 1790s may turn up on a house or church of this region in the 1810s or 1820s.

In one respect the local builder, like others of the Georgian period, is apt to cheat a little. The main front gets the full Georgian treatment, but the other sides of the building may not. The front has regularly disposed openings, but those elsewhere are put wherever expedient; the front has ashlar while the other sides are of rubble, or brick laid in the elegant but expensive Flemish bond while the rest of the building is in the easier but less attractive common bond.

Regional traditions had some influence over the specific ways in which the Georgian formula was realized in Southwestern Pennsylvania. Everyone was more or less of a newcomer, and a builder or client brought his own customs and prejudices regarding construction and planning with him. Many of the early settlers south of the Ohio were Virginians — the exact boundary between Pennsylvania and Virginia was not surveyed until 1784, and Virginia had long claimed the whole region — and the original part of the Presley Neville house in Collier Township, for instance, is regarded as a Virginia house for a former Virginian. Stone was naturally used more often than brick at first, but it was also the preferred material of the Eastern Pennsylvania rural

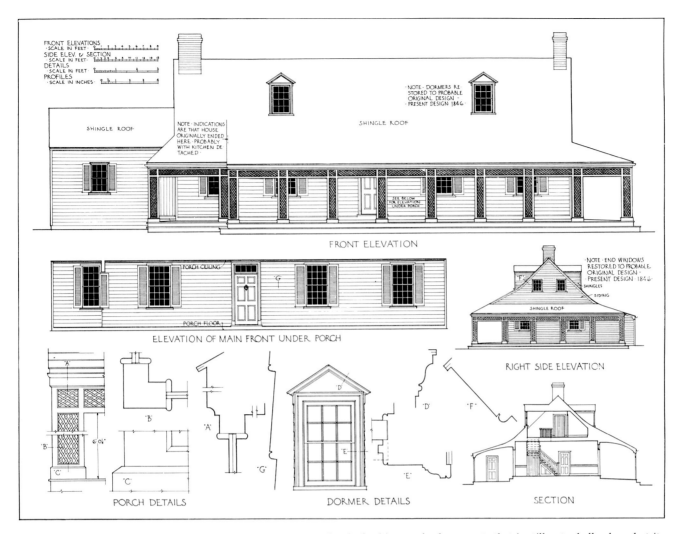

The Presley Neville house in Collier Township, begun in 1785, has had a history of enlargements that is still not wholly clear, but its rather steep main roof suggests Virginian building practice.

areas from which some settlers had come. Any given design, especially for a house, might indicate the builder's habits, the owner's preference, or a compromise.

Charles Morse Stotz, director of the Western Pennsylvania Architectural Survey of the early 1930s, was able to cite some examples of houses in the western third of the state whose original owners' varied places of origin were known, and demonstrate that similar houses were common there. As Allegheny and its surrounding counties were officially pronounced part of Pennsylvania just at the time when the Georgian building tradition was coming into use in the region, it may be natural that most of our earliest house architecture in that tradition resembles either the typical Eastern Pennsylvania farmhouse, a cube of masonry with chimneys flush with its end walls but often with a cornice that projects in a way that suggests a pediment, or a city row house that might have been imitated from a builder's guide with plain side walls. Had the region gone to

Virginia, and Virginians been encouraged to go on settling here, we might have had a domestic architecture of prominent and dormered rather than unobtrusive, undormered roofs, of sheltering porches rather than unsheltered doorways, of more frame and brick construction and less stone, and perhaps those big, tapered, exposed end chimneys often found on the gable walls of Colonial Virginia houses.

Behind this new Georgian architecture lay a more advanced technology than Southwestern Pennsylvania had thus far known. To apply the builder's skills there had to be chisels to cut mortises, planes to make true surfaces and moldings, gouges to form delicate reeding and fluting for mantelpieces and doorframes, lathes to turn balusters, lime for mortar and plaster, good brick clay, the right kind of sand for clear window glass and the right kind of heat-resistant clay for the pots that melted the sand, and iron for door hardware and the nails that secured shingles and siding.

Trade and industry had to be organized, then, and money and leisure accumulated before thoughts of going beyond log houses and log churches could be entertained. Around 1785 these conditions had begun to be met in Southwestern Pennsylvania, though in 1800 Pittsburgh was still primarily a town of log houses. It was only around 1800 that the region was able to make its own window glass or produce cheap enough nails to shingle a roof economically. By 1816, when Pittsburgh was promoted from its 1794 status of borough to that of city, it had at least one handsome three-story brick house row, and the former King's Gardens site, remote from the commercial activity along the Monongahela River, had become a fashionable quarter.

The grandest architectural work of Allegheny County at this time was its first Courthouse, erected on the Pittsburgh Diamond and finished in 1799. This was a square building, hip-roofed and with a central belfry that terminated in a spire. There were two one-story wings. The doorways, the cornice, the belfry, and the interiors had carved decorative woodwork, though which Classical orders were used is uncertain. The windows were capped with the conspicuous flat arches of stone that Georgian builders in the Eastern Seaboard cities often used for decorative effect. In front of the Courthouse were two quadrants of brick-pillared open market sheds, and straight sheds eventually flanked the Courthouse itself. Such a building easily dominated the

The Fahnestock house of c. 1830, formerly on Penn Avenue near the Point of Pittsburgh (above), had a Bostonian-looking recessed doorway. This section of Penn Avenue retained an early nineteenth-century look into the 1890s (below).

town's early, unambitious skyline, but by the 1830s it was regarded as worn out and a disgrace to the city. In 1841 it was replaced in its role of Courthouse, and demolished in 1852.

The first architect to practice in Southwestern Pennsylvania was probably Adam Wilson, an Englishman hired around 1801 by the ironmaster Isaac Meason to build his country mansion "Mount Braddock," which still survives in Fayette County. The first architect to practice in Allegheny County was very probably Benjamin Henry Latrobe (1764–1820), that brilliant, optimistic, often-disappointed Englishman who came to Pittsburgh in 1813 to supervise steamboat construction for Robert Fulton. Fulton, as greedy as he was bold, eased Latrobe out of his interest in the venture as soon as the boat-building operation was well under way, and Latrobe found himself and his family stranded. He had fought the typical package-deal system of the time in Philadelphia, by which a builder supplied the design he then executed, in favor of one in which the architect, a professional designer, supplied the plans and supervised their execution by the builder. In Pittsburgh, Latrobe compromised: as architect-contractor, he produced an indoor circus, several houses, a warehouse, and additions to the First Presbyterian Church. The church, built in 1802 on land donated by the Penns for religious purposes, was to a typical Georgian formula, a brick rectangle with arched windows. Latrobe added two blunt transepts to increase its capacity and two

The First Presbyterian Church (above; gone) as enlarged by Benjamin Henry Latrobe. Pittsburgh in 1817, as this sketch shows (below), was still dominated by the first Courthouse, which was painted from memory (bottom) after its demolition in 1852.

25

simple but handsome porches of wood at interior angles of the cross-shaped plan. The plan itself was of course like that of the large log churches of the day.

Latrobe's name is also associated with the Allegheny Arsenal, begun in Lawrenceville in 1814, but how far he can be credited with what was actually built is unknown. Certainly, his careful drawings, some of which survive, are different from the executed work in important ways. Of the very little that is left, Latrobe's biographer Talbot Hamlin suggests that the powder magazine in Arsenal Park is the sort of thing Latrobe *might* have designed. Latrobe's role in designing the Arsenal is obscured too by his recommendation to the Army of Thomas Pope, a visionary young engineer who may have done some of the design work.

After Latrobe left Pittsburgh at the end of 1814, Allegheny County appears to have had no professional architects for nearly two decades. Log construction gave way to frame, stone, and brick, and builders continued to erect simple rectangular buildings whose ornamentation might or might not reflect current trends back east. The Georgian tradition was to prove remarkably hardy. The ornamentation of future styles — Greek Revival, Italianate, even Gothic — might cling to the facades of farmhouses and city houses like froth, but the places they clung to were the traditional Georgian places: the doorways, the cornices, and

The central building of the Allegheny Arsenal as designed by Benjamin Henry Latrobe (below) and as built (above; gone).

the dormers, and in those later years quite often to the window heads as well. In most buildings the walls remained unadorned, penetrated at regular intervals by sliding-sash windows, just as before. Even in the late nineteenth and early twentieth centuries, when ostentation and a compulsive picturesqueness dominated the fronts of buildings, the less-visible sides might reflect the neat and sober Georgian practice, and the sliding-sash window has never been wholly given up. Around 1930, before air-conditioning, a Modernistic skyscraper still breathed through windows basically identical with those of a Colonial farmhouse, and their limited widths helped determine the spacing of its dynamic verticals.

THE STYLES

The detailing so far applied to the Georgian buildings of Southwestern Pennsylvania had been derived, however remotely, from ancient Rome and a millennium-and-a-half of additions to and variations on Roman forms for artistic and practical reasons. This design practice was only in retrospect a series of styles.

Benjamin Latrobe, however, in his Philadelphia days in the 1790s had applied Gothic detailing to a house and a Grecian Ionic temple front to a bank, breaking with the evolutionary pattern to introduce something consciously different: a style, a distinctive vocabulary of ornamental detail and large-scale composition that could be more or less closely labeled. The use of such a style had obvious temptations: greater artistic freedom; novelty for both the designer and his client; an air of cosmopolitanism; and the opportunity, if the style adopted were to shape the whole building, not its separate decorative features, of creating a showpiece in the community.

A well-chosen style was also the striking of an attitude, a means of saying something about the institution or family housed behind the exotic ornamentation. Latrobe had designed the Arsenal buildings in a stripped-down, avant-garde Classical manner without military allusions, but the central building of the Arsenal as built was furnished with symbolic battlements, though these may have been added afterwards. When William Strickland and John Haviland, two Philadelphia architects, successively designed (in 1820) and later remodeled the Western Penitentiary on the West Common of Allegheny, they gave the administration block the air of a castle — though a castle as remodeled by some eighteenth-century gentleman who wanted the feudal look but with big modern windows. Castles were used to keep people in as well as out, and short round towers and battlements seemed like a good expression of a prison.

The Western Penitentiary as shown in an English engraving of 1839. The penitentiary was the first American building type to draw international interest. (Gone.)

27

Trinity Church, from Hopkins' Essay on Gothic Architecture *(1836), which he addressed especially to clergymen who might want to be their own architects. (Gone.)*

The Western University of Pennsylvania building of 1830, in a painting by Russell Smith. (Gone.)

When the brilliant and versatile John Henry Hopkins (1792–1868) became rector of Trinity Episcopal Church, his congregation worshiped in the individualistic but not especially ecclesiastical-looking "Round Church" of 1808, an octagon with a round-headed window in each side. The next year, 1824, Hopkins built a Tudor Gothic church to his own design to replace it, complete with tower, buttresses, battlements, and a ceiling painted — by Hopkins himself — in imitation of fan vaulting. The plan was the old-fashioned meeting-house one, a simple rectangular hall with raised side galleries, but the added medieval elements recalled church tradition. The Catholics, very possibly in a spirit of rivalry, built between 1829 and 1834 their own Gothic church in brick, the first St. Paul's Cathedral at Fifth Avenue and Grant Street.

In the future, speaking very generally, Gothic and other medieval styles were to express tradition in the English-speaking world, while an expanding range of Classical and quasi-Classical styles were to suggest enlightenment, cosmopolitanism, worldly sophistication, and indeed almost any quality expressible in a look of order and elegance. In 1819 the Pittsburgh Academy of 1787 became the Western University of Pennsylvania,

and in 1830 built for itself with conscious dignity. Essentially, its new building was a big Georgian structure of the simplest sort, but its ground floor was treated as a rusticated basement whose central three bays broke forward to allow a four-columned, pedimented portico in Grecian Ionic to stand against its plain upper walls; a cupola on a podium rose above the hipped roof. Neither the design formula — a Palladian one quite familiar in England and occasionally used on the Eastern Seaboard — nor the Grecian order may have been used for the first time in the Pittsburgh area, but they do reflect a new desire, not merely to ornament a building but to turn the building itself into an ornament. From a practical viewpoint the applied portico and the broad podium of the cupola were worse than useless, complicating the roof system, but a dignified gesture took priority. The building had an architect-designed look, but which architect is not known.

Two other city buildings of the 1830s should be mentioned. The Branch Bank of the United States, as it was in 1832, was essentially a big Georgian house, but it had a Grecian Doric portico and a parapet whose raised, bluntly pointed central part hinted at a pediment. Much Greek Revival had this applied character; the big but unpretentious Coltart house that stood in Oakland until the 1970s had a similar front porch of Grecian columns, made of wood but dimensioned for stone, and the Thomas Wilson Shaw house in Shaler Township still does. On the other hand, John Haviland's 1833 design for the Pittsburgh Theater seems not to have been particularly Greek at all: a vague sketch, all we have of its first condition, shows a rusticated, arched ground floor with five rectangular windows, and possibly a pediment, above. This seems a little plain for a 1,200-seat theater, Pittsburgh's most ambitious to date, but by the time the facade was accurately depicted a particularly dreary false front in Italianate had replaced the upper part.

The Branch Bank of the United States, from a painting of 1832 by Russell Smith. (Gone.)

The Coltart house in 1843 (below), shortly before its demolition in 1974. The road front, on the opposite side, had a rather heavy Ionic porch. The view at bottom shows the south side of Fifth Avenue between Wood and Smithfield Streets in 1840; the Pittsburgh Theater is second from the right.

29

Not long after this public architecture began to appear, individuals began to show the aspirations to grandeur that their counterparts on the Eastern Seaboard had been revealing for quite a while. The latter-day form of the Georgian style that we now call Federal was already loosening up at the time when Greek Revival began to appear. Instead of a narrow front door with a fanlight, a builder might supply a broad doorway with sidelights flanking the door itself and an overdoor light above. As a Federal house on the North Side, visible from East Ohio and Chestnut Streets, shows, the rooms might even be lighted by broad three-part windows rather than the standard pairs of narrow eighteenth-century ones. Two other extant Federal houses, the Nicholas Way house in Edgeworth and the Lightner house in Shaler Township, go further still by extending pedimented porches, like gestures of welcome, to the tops of high entrance steps. Both houses are otherwise rather plain and not especially large, but their raised main floors and the porches themselves give them an air of Palladian elegance.

A Federal house at East Ohio and Chestnut Streets (above) survives as the ell of a later building. The Allegheny Institute and Mission Church of 1849 (below; gone) was typical of Greek Revival buildings of some pretense in its use of brick pilasters and paneling. Very basic Greek Revival is shown in the Morning Post Buildings of c. 1840 (below, right; gone).

The Greek Revival, as it was being developed back east, suggested even more obvious effects. True, "Picnic House," the best-remembered house of the time that was built on what is now Stanton Heights around 1835 for Mary Croghan Schenley, was big but not especially imposing: its grandeur was inside, and the ballroom and vestibule, decorated by Mordecai van Horn of Philadelphia and now preserved in the Cathedral of Learning of the University of Pittsburgh, still

attest that it was considerable. But "Woodlawn," the Samuel Church house in Allegheny, used the temple-like compositional formula of the time, and Judge William Wilkins' "Homewood," in the East End, had an imposing front with a tall Doric portico and wing pavilions. (Behind the pompous facade of 1835, though, the exterior was utterly bare.) Even a town house built directly on the street and deprived of such a rhetorical device as a portico could make a good appearance. The John Shoenberger house of c. 1847, demolished for Gateway Center in downtown Pittsburgh but

The ballroom of "Picnic House" (above); "Woodlawn" of 1833 (left); and "Homewood" (below). (Houses gone; ballroom preserved.)

31

defaced some years before, had an imposing doorway between two Bostonian-looking bow windows, rich grilles in the windows of its frieze, and a parapet in the advanced Classical taste — rather old-fashioned in 1847 — of Regency England. Inside, like "Picnic House," it had its ballroom, its fine Grecian plasterwork.

The first architect to make a career in the Pittsburgh area may have been John Behan, an architect and civil engineer, in the early 1820s. The first one whose work is known, however, is John Chislett (1800–1869), an Englishman who had studied in the elegant city of Bath and who is known to have been practicing in Pittsburgh in 1833. It is just possible that he had designed the Western University of Pennsylvania's building of three years before, and because of the very peculiarly English character of the Shoenberger house parapet, one wonders if that may not have been his as well. There is a possibility too that Chislett designed the Third Presbyterian Church

The Shoenberger house (below). John Chislett's Bank of Pittsburgh (opposite page, above) and the second Courthouse (opposite, below). (All gone.)

of 1833, though a sketch shows an Ionic entablature handled so clumsily that one is disposed to doubt it. That Chislett knew Grecian Ionic thoroughly is evident in his Bank of Pittsburgh of 1835, formerly downtown on Fourth Avenue. That he was far from a clumsy designer is proven by the now-gone Shoenberger summer villa in Lawrenceville, Burke's Building still on Fourth Avenue, the Butler Street gateway of Allegheny Cemetery, and that cemetery's Romantic layout of winding roads, at once picturesque and practical for a hillside site. Chislett's biggest work, though not necessarily his best, was the second Courthouse, built in 1841 on the site of the present one. Its Doric portico and domed cupola gave it the imposing character expected of the courthouse of a thriving county, and beneath the cupola was a rotunda 60 feet in diameter and 80 feet high inside. Sited on a Grant's Hill much higher than it is now, it dominated the city from 1841 to 1882, when it burned.

Pittsburgh as shown in a lithograph of 1859 by William Schuchman, with the second Courthouse and the towers of St. Paul's Cathedral dominating the skyline. To the left is Allegheny, and vignettes show the nearby towns of Manchester and Birmingham.

THE MID-VICTORIAN AGE

Let us pause while we have a quick look around Allegheny County — the year is 1850 — and take note of what is there and what — sometimes surprisingly — is not.

Technology had come to the rivers, and the Western River packet, which originated at Pittsburgh in 1811, had matured into a sometimes-beautiful, sometimes-dangerous device for moving people and goods west and south. The push towing of barges, which today dominates the rivers, was still in the experimental stage, but coal boats from the mines along the Monongahela drifted down that short and winding river, which a private company was canalizing. The U.S. Army Corps of Engineers had accepted responsibility for the Ohio River in 1824, but its channel-scouring and snag-pulling did little to maintain a navigable amount of water in the river, which might run nearly dry in the summer. Great timber rafts floated down to Pittsburgh from ravaged forests up the Allegheny, and the old-fashioned flatboat, an unpropelled floating box, still was making its slow way down the Ohio on trading voyages as it had been doing for a half-century.

There were no railroads! The first, the Ohio & Pennsylvania, was to come in 1851 with Allegheny as its terminus; through train service to Philadelphia, on the Pennsylvania Railroad, in 1852; and to Chicago, on the Pittsburgh, Fort Wayne & Chicago Railroad, in 1858. Travelers from the East arrived either by the Pennsylvania Turnpike, a good macadam road of carefully compacted stone since 1820, or over the State's canal-railroad system, completed in 1834. In Allegheny County, the Canal had required two notable engineering works: an aqueduct between Pittsburgh and Allegheny, built as a wooden covered bridge in 1829 then replaced by Roebling's suspension structure in 1845, and a tunnel under Grant's Hill to the Monongahela, where junction with the Chesapeake & Ohio Canal was anticipated but never made.

The Pittsburgh, Fort Wayne & Chicago Railroad bridge over the Allegheny River, probably built in 1857: a lattice truss of wrought iron replaced the original wooden bridge. (Gone.)

Until the Indians were subdued permanently in the 1790s, settlement north of the Allegheny was inhibited while that south of the Monongahela, much of it by Virginians, had been going on steadily from the 1760s. By 1850 a network of roads — dirt, plank, and macadam — had developed in both directions. Pittsburgh, between rivers, needed bridges as well for the northern and southern trade. The first Smithfield Street Bridge of 1818, crossing the Monongahela River, was a conventional covered bridge by Lewis Wernwag, whose wooden ''Colossus'' at Philadelphia had the greatest arch span ever built at that time: 340 feet. After the Great Fire in 1845, this first Smithfield Street Bridge had been replaced by one of Roebling's suspension bridges. The Allegheny River had first been crossed in 1819 at St. Clair (Sixth) Street with a covered bridge by a builder named Lothrop. Other Pittsburgh engineering works were less interesting, albeit useful: the filling-in of four ponds that inconsiderately lay across the Woods-Vickroy street grid; the digging of a reservoir in the late 1820s where the Frick Building is now; and successive lowerings of the miserably steep Grant's Hill Hump, which between the 1830s and 1913 came down 60 feet.

From the 149 people of 1760, Pittsburgh had grown to a population of 47,000 in 1850. Its rival Allegheny now had 21,000. Birmingham and East Birmingham, boroughs now in the South Side Flats, were busy iron- and glass-manufacturing centers. Lawrenceville was growing around the Arsenal. Some other river and canal towns were of varying importance. The Penn Salt Company was building an early company town, Natrona, in Harrison Township. On the other hand, Sewickley and East Liberty were farm villages, the East End and South Hills were very thinly settled, and some manufacturing towns of the future, like Homestead, Wilmerding, and East Pittsburgh, did not exist.

The dense Pittsburgh smoke had already been noted in the 1790s and by 1850 was quite thick. Iron was processed in and around Pittsburgh, but oddly enough not smelted here; the unfinished product came from stone blast furnaces close to ore deposits and charcoal sources in other Western Pennsylvania counties. Aside from an abortive furnace in Shadyside in the 1790s, the first furnace within the present city limits would come in 1859, shortly after ironmaking technology replaced charcoal with coke, an oven-refined form of coal. Glass, much of it of high quality, was a major industry. Coal was mined within sight of town from the interior of Coal Hill, presently called Mount Washington. Boat-building and engine-building were quite important, from Elizabeth up the Monongahela to Shousetown down the Ohio. On the other hand, petroleum — which was to boom a decade later and make Pittsburgh briefly a refining center — was of no importance; electrical equipment, aside from the six-year-old telegraph, was almost without economic significance anywhere; aluminum was a rare product of the laboratory; natural gas went unused. All these were later to become elements of the region's economic base.

In 1850, Greek Revival was being either abandoned or undergoing a mutation. The temple form, which could be cheaply sketched out with pilasters, offered an easy formula for construction of pretense, but Greek Revival at its best was a lucid, balanced, tasteful, but undeniably rather standardized style. After a while, as with

Lewis Wernwag's Smithfield Street Bridge after a flood in 1832 (above; gone). The Union Bridge of 1874 (left): a wooden bridge from the Point to Allegheny that lasted until 1907. Below, the Point Bridge across the Monongahela River, built between 1875 and 1877 to designs by Edward Hemberle. The stiffening trusses over the catenaries were very unusual. (Gone.)

Georgian architecture before and Modern architecture in the late 1960s, people began to wish for something different.

The Mid-Victorian architect was typically trained through apprenticeship, untraveled and unschooled unless he had immigrated from Europe. He was catering to increasingly style-conscious clients, and to help him adapt foreign styles — *never* American styles of the past — to modern requirements and resources, he had to rely on paintings, prints, book illustrations, and perhaps an occasional photograph. He might subscribe to foreign architectural magazines too; there were no American ones.

He might enlarge his income and disseminate the new styles by authoring pattern books, intended for builders and building owners in places deprived of architectural services. These offered plans, elevations, ornamental details, structural drawings, capsulated architectural histories, and advice on interior decoration and sound building practice: any or all of these in a given pattern book.

Mid-Victorian architecture, whatever its style, tended to have a hard look. It was executed in materials to which machinery and craftsmanship gave an unwavering perfection: bright red brick, yellow-gray sandstone, cast iron, and machine-cut lumber were typical locally, and in the best

work all were geometrically regular and carefully surfaced. The architect, and the builder following a pattern book, thought in edges defining surfaces rather than materials with characteristic densities, colors, and textures. While the building might be histrionically decorated in a style that expressed something of the building's purpose, it was still executed in plain Victorian materials, sash with two panes or even one big pane, under a flat roof perhaps, and the architect's fancy was weirdly counterpointed with the drab common sense of the basic structure.

Mid-Victorian architecture, so recently despised, has not yet had a comprehensive history, and we have much to learn about it. Our historians have gone so far, though, as to label one of its major design idioms the Italianate. Certainly there was a polymorphous design idiom, which made its first mild appearances in the United States in the 1830s and developed around 1850, that owed much to Renaissance Italy, even more to Baroque Italy, and something to Romantic British fantasies about Italy. It had the advantage of being a good all-purpose style, capable of sweet simplicity, capable of the wildest ostentation. A Cubical Tuscan villa's elementary geometry might be gently disrupted by no more than a delicate verandah and a flaring cornice whose widely spaced brackets were sawn in fan-

The 270-foot cabin of the Mississippi River packet Great Republic, *1867 (below). The hull was built at Shousetown and the boat was completed at Pittsburgh with joiner work by Charles Gearing. The decorative style, as was often the case, was a mixture of Italianate and Gothic. Right, the sparely Italianate Second Presbyterian Church of the 1850s at Penn Avenue and Eighth Street. (Gone.)*

The heavily Italianate Exchange National Bank of c. 1870. (Gone.)

tastic curves. Yet a bank might present an appearance of sinister luxury, cornices with richly modeled, close-spaced brackets above tall, narrow windows that seemed to stare. A fashionable store building might take on the air of a palace, Renaissance or Baroque window frames jostling one another as if tempting you to speculate on the sumptuous contents, but even a humble store might add wooden brackets to its fascia and frame its display windows to suggest archways. Of the grandest commercial architecture of the time little remains, but the cast-iron fronts at 805 and 927 Liberty Avenue show the open yet ornate character it had.

The arrival of the Italianate in America has been reasonably well documented; we know something about our early Italian villas and our first imitations of Renaissance palazzi. Yet it is tempting, too, to see one strain of the new manner as a sprouting as it were of the Greek Revival. The Shoenberger house for instance was generally Greek Revival, yet it had heavier detail, and more of it, than was standard. To put consoles under a lintel that once simply rested on the wall masonry, to sink narrow panels into a normally flat pilaster and decorate their ends with honeysuckle ornament: such things showed a desire for novelty and lavishness, and this Greek Revival gone to seed blended with the conscious Italianisms.

Liberty Hall, 1858, at Penn and Ellsworth Avenues. (Gone.)

Commonplace Italianate: George Hardy's drugstore in Crafton (left) and small commercial buildings on Penn Avenue in East Liberty (below). (All gone.)

The First National Bank of 1871 at Fifth Avenue and Wood Street. The mansard roof burned in a fire of about 1880, and the Second Empire building ended its days as an Italianate one.

One Mid-Victorian style, which arrived on the heels of the Italianate, was more label than substance. What historians call the Second Empire style in actual practice usually entailed appending a mansard roof to an otherwise Italianate design. The mansard roof, a double-pitched roof with a very steep lower slope, was devised in Paris to increase usable attic-level floor space. It had sophisticated connotations, being from Paris, and was useful in lessening the apparent height of a tall building while giving it a strong terminal feature.

Other styles of the time have never been labeled. There is, for instance, a brick vernacular, a little like the simplest Italian Romanesque and similar to a Central European manner of the 1840s called the Rundbogenstil (Round-Arch Style). Of course, round arches were not necessary. Applied to churches it often included Gothic arches, and industrial applications might use segmental arches or flat-headed openings. It was, in fact, used for industrial buildings and churches alike, as shown by St. Michael the Archangel on the South Side slopes and the Westinghouse plant in Wilmerding. In this style the wall was visibly divided into piers and panels. The piers presumably supported the building's principal beams and trusses while the panels, set in from the faces of the piers, excluded the weather. At the top of the wall, corbeling that might be plain or fancy supported the last few courses, which ran in a straight line beneath the roof. Such a style, whose decorative detailing was of standard brick and well within the competence of a Victorian bricklayer, was inexpensive and stately, and allowed for fantasy. In industrial architecture it lasted until after 1900, when the reinforced-concrete frame replaced it.

Above, the quasi-Romanesque Allegheny Market House of 1863. (Gone.) The First Baptist Church of 1867 on Ross Street (left) was designed by David Gendell of Philadelphia in true Romanesque. (Gone.) The Irish Block of 1886 by John Barr (below) dramatizes bare masonry construction with brick in contrasting colors.

Toward 1880, another style, again as yet unlabeled, appeared. The French theorist Eugène-Emmanuel Viollet-le-Duc had been arguing for a rational treatment of construction and planning, and had much to say on the technique of building in masonry. Perhaps this is why the elements of masonry construction, exposed, even dramatized, became the basis of a style. At 820 Liberty Avenue for instance, the spanning of wide voids with segmental arches is the main architectural theme. In the Irish Block at Tenth Street and Penn Avenue, red and yellow brick express the function of the arch and the stratified nature of masonry in a facade with an odd harsh beauty.

43

The Gothic style of this period was a more studied and elaborate affair, at least when budgeting permitted, than heretofore. The Singer house in Wilkinsburg and the much-smaller "Heathside Cottage" overlooking the North Side survive to show the rich decoration sometimes used on secular Gothic. Church congregations, too, had greater ambitions than previously.

As early as 1846, St. Philomena's Roman Catholic Church, built in what is now the Strip district, displayed a novel feature in American church architecture, the clerestory. The raising of the nave windows above the roof level of the adjoining aisles was standard in medieval architecture of course, but at the time perhaps only Trinity Church in New York had such a feature in America. The architect of St. Philomena's was probably Robert Cary Long, well-known in Baltimore.

In 1851 the Episcopalians of Pittsburgh had a clerestory to boast of too, and in a more polished work. The Episcopal Church had been under pressure for some time from Ecclesiological Societies in England and New York to build in English Gothic of authentic design, and John Notman of Philadelphia had demonstrated, in St. Mark's in that city, that he had mastered its forms. (Notman, Scottish born, was a good, stylistically versatile architect. He had used, if not introduced, the Italian Villa idiom in its earliest days, and probably introduced from England the urban, palazzo-like variety of Italianate. He also designed in Romanesque, Baroque, Moorish, and Chinese at various times.) His design for St. Peter's, on Grant Street at Fifth Avenue in downtown Pittsburgh, was so admired that 50 years later, when the site was to be cleared for the Frick Building, the church was moved stone by stone to Oakland, where it still stands at Forbes and Craft Avenues.

The year St. Peter's was begun, St. Paul's across Fifth Avenue burned, and the Catholics contemplated a more ambitious cathedral. Thomas Walsh of New York may have supplied the actual design, but the architect who saw to its realization was Charles Bartberger, who at this time was also serving as architect for the large and handsome First Presbyterian Church on Wood Street. St. Paul's, as built between 1853 and 1870, was an awkward church, too diffused in its elements. Its two high spires joined with the Courthouse dome near by in dominating the city, but did so more effectively than they did the cathedral's own spreading mass. The cathedral lasted until the early 1900s, when it was demolished.

St. Philomena's, in the Strip district (top). The second St. Paul's Cathedral, begun in 1853 (above). The First Presbyterian Church of 1851, facing Wood Street (right). (All gone.)

If the church favored Gothic or the brick Romanesque, government held to a Classical range of styles that was notably more subdued than the commercial architecture of the city. Pittsburgh's City Hall of 1854, built in the Diamond along with a quietly Italianate market hall, was an essay in tall archways, quite plain. In 1872 this was replaced as City Hall by a new building at Smithfield Street and Virgin Alley (Oliver Avenue) which was more ornate in its Italianate facades and had a tower with a grandiose mansard roof, yet was still overall a rather sober building. The Post Office and Custom House next to it, begun in 1853 under the direction of the federal architect Ammi Burnham Young, looked almost like a work of eighteenth-century England, stone-fronted and quietly elegant. Allegheny's City Hall of 1864, which replaced the very modest Early Federal "town house" of 1834, was an austere essay in arches, pediments, and pilasters by the immigrant Charles Antoine Colomb Gengembre.

Market Street in the early 1890s, looking north. The City Hall of 1854 is to the right. (Gone.)

The City Hall of 1872 (left), by Joseph W. Kerr, with the Post Office and Custom House to its left. Below is the Allegheny City Hall. (All gone.)

Apart from a curious Neo-Baroque station in Allegheny, railroads also favored quiet architecture. The 644-foot Duquesne Depot of 1854 — actually on the site of Fort Pitt — was a respectable work in the brick industrial vernacular. The second Union Station, completed in 1865 on the site of the present one, was fronted with a Renaissance loggia and was crowned by an eagle between two pediments, but otherwise had simple brick fronts with arched windows. Commuter stations along the Pennsylvania main lines were usually simple, cottage-like affairs.

School architecture was also inclined to be plain. A number of Mid-Victorian schools, usually no longer used as such, survive — the former Morse School on the South Side is an example — and others are remembered from the not-too-distant past. The Greek Revival schools, big boxes with pilasters, were replaced by three-story brick edifices which, despite the architectural styles sparingly used in their entrances, had a Georgian gravity about them as a result of the characteristic forward break in their center bays and their tall, regularly spaced windows. Their appearance suggested a specialized and rather genteel industry: here, they seemed to say, educated children are produced.

The Duquesne Depot (above), shown in use as a festival hall during the Pittsburgh Centennial celebration of 1858. Below, the second Union Station by Collins & Autenreith of Philadelphia, built in 1865 and destroyed in the Railroad Strike of 1877. Central High School stands in the background. (All gone.)

The South School of 1841 (above left), shown around 1910 with the Allegheny County Mortuary in its original location. To the left, the Italianate Central High School of 1871, by Barr & Moser. Below, Soho School, built in 1870. (Schools gone.)

The home was less likely than any other building type to be predictable as to style. Perhaps it was too important and too personal a thing to be readily typecast. Its associations for the inhabitants and its appearance to the public were apt to be serious matters, and a good house was, in fact, the symbol of what man in this busy century was striving for. It was a refuge from the disorderly world and a sign of respectability, or even eminence, attained. The middle class might be content with substantial brick city houses in close-packed rows, still Georgian in form though fashionable in decoration, but roads over the hills, the railroads, horsecar lines, and eventually inclines, invited escape from the disorder of the smoky city, where stray pigs roamed the streets as late as 1860. Some wealthy families might go only as far as Allegheny, where they settled on Ridge Avenue and nearby streets and built with great pomp into the 1900s, but others wanted the open spaces of Oakland, East Liberty, Edgewood,

Irwin Avenue in Allegheny, the present Brighton Road, in the early 1890s (top right). Cupolas and mansard roofs on Ridge Avenue, North Side, in the 1950s (right). Below, the Italianate G. W. Hailman house of 1864 in East Liberty, enlarged around 1890 as the Kenmawr Hotel. (Gone.)

The A. A. Carrier house (left) was one of the numerous Bellefield works of Isaac Hobbs of Philadelphia. Built around 1870, it had the typical echelon arrangement of an Italian villa though its tower was mansarded. The Second Empire B. F. Jones house (below) also appears in the Irwin Avenue view on the opposite page. (Both gone.)

A lithograph by William Schuchman of Evergreen Hamlet in the 1850s with the schoolhouse (gone) and the Shinn-Beall house.

and the Sewickley area, where their Italian villas that suggested civilized leisure, their steep-roofed Gothic cottages and houses that suggested shelter for the essential man, could be seen in the round, set among trees and flowers. Evergreen Hamlet in Ross Township still retains four of the five houses from its beginnings in 1851: two in a very simple Italianate, two in Gothic. Of these, three are clad in the vertical board-and-batten construction that not only gives their walls a fine play of light and shadow but acknowledges that these are simple affairs of wood. "Heathside Cottage" in Fineview, though built of brick and more ornate, has a similar message: Here we take our quiet leisure, content to view the bustling world from a distance. ■

The Philadelphian Frank Furness built at least three of his brash, gritty works in Pittsburgh. Here is the Farmers Deposit National Bank c. 1885. (Gone.)

NEW IDEAS

After the Civil War the architects of the United States began to have a new sense of themselves as professionals. The American Institute of Architects, founded in 1857, started at last to become an effective national organization, and other professional associations, national, regional, and local, came into being. Furthermore, between the late 1860s and 1890, American architectural schools, journals, exhibitions, traveling fellowships, and a whole apparatus in fact arose to educate the architect, represent him to the public, discipline him, and put him in systematic contact with his colleagues. Not least, architectural publishing continued to develop, and with it forms of graphic reproduction that gave the architect a better idea of architecture he could not see for himself and that allowed him to publish his own designs.

Furthermore, the public became more interested in architecture, more receptive to new ideas, more demanding to some extent. The Centennial Exhibition in Philadelphia exposed visitors to new design trends in England, the art of Japan, and the Colonial arts of America itself, all suggesting something more relaxed and charming than the heavy yet rather stark kinds of architecture and furnishing with which they had been living.

The result was a time of experimentation in the big cities, particularly in Boston and Philadelphia, particularly in domestic architecture. In the office of Henry Hobson Richardson — which had moved to Brookline, a town wholly surrounded by Boston, in 1874 — these experiments had been going on even before the Centennial, as they had in a few other offices.

A time was to come when the artistic literacy that the new architects were acquiring would turn all too easily into literalism, the mere imitation of historic styles once vital and evolving, but in the 1870s and 1880s the new sense of what American architecture might be was still fresh: architects were hunting down old forms, inventing new ones, examining the potential for color, texture, and pattern in fieldstone, brick, shingles, contrasting woods, terra cotta, even combinations like stucco inlaid with pebbles and broken glass. Modern attempts have been made to identify styles in this period: Queen Anne, so labeled in its time, which evoked Merrie England indiscriminately over a several-century range with a little of Old Japan thrown in; the Colonial Revival, our home-grown Queen Anne and with no more formal discipline than its English counterpart; Eastlake, a hard-looking style of chamfered and incised wood that had begun as a reform in furniture; the Shingle Style, with its sophisticated shaping of roofs and walls; Richardson Romanesque, emphasizing the mass and texture of masonry; and a variety of other manners, blurred at the edges, never labeled and probably never to be labeled.

Before H. H. Richardson presented his revised design — the first was too expensive — for Emmanuel Episcopal Church in Allegheny, there may have been homes reflecting this new architecture in Pittsburgh. Emmanuel was begun in 1885, and Eastlake's *Hints on Household Taste*, the book that introduced the American public to some of the new ideas, had been published in Boston 12 years

"Lyndhurst," the East End home of Mrs. William Kendall Thaw (below), as it was in the mid-1920s after remodeling and additions. The original house was a work of the late 1880s in a quasi-medieval style, possibly by a family friend, Theophilus Parsons Chandler of Philadelphia. (Gone.) The Post Office and Federal Court House on Smithfield Street (right) was designed under the direction of James G. Hill, federal Supervising Architect, and built between 1881 and 1891. On the pediments are the "Ladies of Stone" groups of statuary saved by the Pittsburgh History & Landmarks Foundation when the Post Office was demolished in 1966.

Like Hill's Post Office, the four competitors for the County Buildings commission placed towers at the centers of the principal fronts and pavilions at the corners of their courthouses. Below is W. W. Boyington's submission. At bottom are the County Buildings around 1890, with the Jail in its original form.

before. Yet as far as is known this little church, the ''Bake Oven'' that still stands at Allegheny and West North Avenues, was the first completed building in which some of the new thinking appeared locally. It was very much a composition in masses of material, not lines on paper. On paper it looks a little stupid in fact; you have to see the rock-faced stone sills, the patterns in the brickwork bonding, the thickness of the window and entrance arches to get the effect.

Richardson, a sick man and a busy man, at first ignored the invitation in 1883 to compete for the County Buildings — the new Courthouse to replace John Chislett's on the same Grant Street site, which had burned the year before, and a new Jail. When he agreed he produced a plan of such lucidity that it won against even the well-rendered submission of Elijah Myers, a champion job-getter whose wins included the capitols of Michigan, Texas, and Colorado. The County Commissioners had specified soot-resistant granite for the street

fronts, and Richardson claimed that he had detailed these fronts with Pittsburgh's special atmospheric problems in mind. Yet he used his customary rock-faced masonry, with passages of the delicate Byzantine carving he enjoyed, and we can take his soot-repelling claim about as seriously as we do his rationalization of his superb tower — the last of a series of lovingly studied towers throughout his career — as the intake for a sort of air-conditioning system.

The rugged stonework, the delicate carving, the big round arches, and the steep, mountainous roofs that rose above the walls had a prompt local impact. Richardson Romanesque, in the 1880s and later, was like lightning: you could only wonder over where it chose to strike. New York and Philadelphia, for instance, were almost immune. Boston, Chicago, St. Paul, and many others were not, and Richardsonian influence even spread to Finland and the Netherlands. Pittsburgh was very much under the influence of Richardson, not only because of the County Buildings but also because of the commercial buildings, academic buildings, railroad stations, and libraries he had designed for New England. Through the early 1890s little that was conspicuous in our architecture was being designed in a way wholly free from his influence. His successors, Shepley, Rutan & Coolidge, maintained his standards if not his creativity at the Shadyside Presbyterian Church. Longfellow, Alden & Harlow — Frank Alden from Richardson's office

The Courthouse interiors (below) combined elaborate oaken joinery with exposed construction. (Altered.) The Romanesque style swiftly became fashionable in the Pittsburgh area. Some of its applications were informed and suave, as in the Freemason's Hall of 1888 (right, above) by Shepley, Rutan & Coolidge; many others were at least competent, as in the Western University of Pennsylvania (right, middle), built on Perry Hilltop in 1890 to designs by James T. Steen; and still others merely crude, as in the Shadyside car barn of the Duquesne Traction Company, 1890 (right, below). (All gone.)

The Exposition Buildings, built near the Point in 1889 (above). The overall style was Romanesque, but Mechanical Hall (right) was like French exposition architecture of the time, a mixture of iron-and-glass rationalism and fancy decoration. (Both gone.) Below, a store building on Jacksonia Street imitates Richardsonian masonry in pressed sheet metal.

had been assigned to supervise construction of the County Buildings — adapted his Romanesque to a more classicizing form in the Duquesne Club downtown and went even further in the Carnegie Institute in Oakland. On the other hand, ordinary builders solemnly vulgarized Richardson Romanesque in the house rows of Shadyside and Allegheny with mock-towers and rugged stone-work four inches thick.

And even a sandstone facing a few inches thick was an unnecessarily expensive way of getting a Richardsonian effect. As a store on the North Side shows, a builder could have his rugged masonry stamped out of sheet metal. Later, when Richardson's Romanesque was completely out of fashion, his characteristic textures were to live on in the rock-faced concrete block that forms many a backyard garage or rural house, and underlies many a South Hills porch.

In ordinary middle-class house design, under the influence of Romanesque and the picturesque new domestic styles, Georgian simplicity was finally banished, at least from the street front. The basic shape of the house might perforce be a simple box if it were a unit of a close-packed row, but the front was available for picturesque surface treatment; bay windows dressed up to imitate

Houses in Hazelwood dating from about 1890 (above), showing mixtures of Romanesque, Shingle Style, and Colonial Revival forms. Below, Soho Curve at the entrance to Oakland, c. 1890, with the cable cars of the Pittsburgh Traction Company. On the hill is the Ursuline Young Ladies' Academy. (Gone.)

towers, uninhabitably small turrets, false gables masking flat roofs, deep front porches, changes in facing material from level to level, and broad parlor windows with upper panels of stained glass distracted the mind from this essential plainness. Where there was space around the house the perimeter could be varied with towers, bays, porches, and wings, and the skyline varied with complicated roofs and bristling chimneys. At 5960 Alder Street in Shadyside is a remarkably successful example from the 1890 period, but less-happy examples could be found in many places. Inside such houses were complementary details, ingenious screens of profiled spindles, complexities of paneling, complicated mantelpieces.

There was a demand in this area for the kinds of houses in open settings that had caused the new domestic styles to be devised. The Pennsylvania and other railroads were proving favorable to the development of commuter suburbs, and two cable-car lines to East Liberty opened in 1888 to cut the fair-weather trip from nearly two hours by horsecar to perhaps half that time. Furthermore, with new industrial plants opening in the Monongahela and Turtle Creek Valleys, there was a demand for good executive housing not too far away. The most elegant housing seemed to accompany the steam railroad or flock, at a discreet distance, around heavy industry. Inclines did not have the magic touch, nor did the electric trolley, which was promoted by fantastic numbers of local companies in the 1890s. These were the carriers of the classes with enough money to own their homes, but the homes were generally plain.

The picturesque architecture of the 1890 period was unlikely, locally, to be very creative or sensitive. The mannerisms and ornamental trademarks of Queen Anne and the other domestic manners of the day were imported and applied without much sense of the telling effect that a very simple composition could have, or on the other hand of the potential in a tall roof whose planes, folded, cut back, or extended like an origami in shingles, could effectively *be* the architecture of a house. A local and national vice throughout the Victorian period was the assumption that architecture consisted of ornamental features, and that their coordination in the overall composition of a building, a perception of where to put them and how many of them to use, was of lesser importance.

This was very conspicuously true in some of the tall buildings that rose in Pittsburgh. The business district of a Victorian city had reason to build tall. Commercial buildings on a downtown street like Liberty Avenue might be 25 or 30 feet wide and 100 feet deep, obtaining much of their light and all of their ventilation from the windows at the ends. The best space for sales, administration, manufacturing, or rental was that closest to the windows, and the height of many Liberty Avenue fronts shows that such space was in demand. Business offices communicated by face-to-face contact, messengers, telegraph companies whose wires made cat's cradles over the streets, and only eventually by telephone. There was reason, then, to concentrate business space in a small area of town, and thus to pile floor on floor. The Mid-Victorian city, however, held to a maximum level of five stories until the elevator became a practical means of taking people higher; when it did, the skyline rose with it. The metal skeleton frame, eliminating the need for space-consuming solid masonry, soon after gave the final encouragement.

Without much warning, architects who had been thinking of five stories of habitable space at

Many people lived in the respectable anonymity suggested by the buildings to the left: little frame houses in McKeesport with cheap ornamentation and large parlor windows (top) and solid row houses in Manchester (middle). After 1900, they might live in apartment houses like this one in Bellevue (bottom). The YMCA (below) formerly at Penn Avenue and Seventh Street was a work of 1883 by James T. Steen, a rare local use of Queen Anne. (Gone.)

the utmost were being required to design for 10, or 15, or 20, or more. Sometimes a facade on a new building might be a high, narrow slice of the block front. Sometimes it was a square, an acre in extent. All too often, even in Chicago where the skyscraper was largely developed, an architect reacted by applying a little of this and a little of that to various levels of the facade and devising some picturesque feature for its middle, its ends, or an exposed corner as a distraction from its great expanse and its level skyline.

This futile attempt to make architectural conversation all the way up and across inflated facades was countered in the 1890s by the more Classical conception of the tall building as a column, with a base, a shaft, and a capital. This was actually, despite its fatuous sound, a very sensible approach. The base would ordinarily be shops, banking rooms, restaurants, spaces that the public would visit in large numbers and that were often on two levels. Giving these a special expression was natural enough and would create a distinct composition that passers-by could easily take in. The shaft would contain the majority of the office spaces, manifested in an abstract pattern of windows of no special interest, and could be treated rather plainly. The capital would be a decorated terminal feature, speaking for the building as a whole, announcing it on the skyline, and would include the last few office stories, any service spaces at the top, and a climactic cornice.

The first skeleton-framed building in Pittsburgh was the Carnegie Building, named in honor of Thomas, brother of Andrew Carnegie, and built between 1893 and 1895. Longfellow, Alden & Harlow approached the new problem calmly, applying the same simple Quattrocento style that they were currently using at the Carnegie Institute in Oakland. If the results were not an expression of steel they at least had visual unity. The same was true in the more florid Park Building of 1896, designed by the New York architect George Browne Post and still standing on Smithfield Street. After this there was a retrogression. The Peoples Savings Bank Building, the Farmers Deposit National Bank Building, the Arrott Building, the Standard Life Building, and a number of other downtown highrises of the 1900 period were spread over with decorative detailing, encouraged by the new availability of terra cotta, so that visual coherence was lost. The excesses went on for a few fitful years, but by 1905 simplicity — though not unadorned — had returned and would remain.

The tall business building gave the architect unprecedented problems. The Chronicle-Telegraph Building of the late 1880s illustrates the uneasy bedding-down of fantasy and drab common sense that often resulted. (Gone.)

The Westinghouse Building of 1889 at Penn Avenue and Ninth Street (left) was of solid masonry. The steel-framed Carnegie Building (below, left) had a much lighter, more open expression. (Both gone.) Below, Alden & Harlow coped, or failed to cope, with the compositional problem of the Farmers National Deposit Bank by dividing its tall facade into a multitude of sections. (Refaced.)

Two local offices were prominent in this period toward the end of the nineteenth century. One was Longfellow, Alden & Harlow, organized in 1887, which had branches in Boston and Pittsburgh. New Englanders all, the partners brought a great deal of taste, if not brilliance, to their early work, applying Richardsonian motifs sensibly; then evolved out of Romanesque, as other architects of the 1890s were doing, into a Renaissance style that seemed more appropriate, with its smooth surfaces, its sparing applications of ornament, and its simple geometry, to the architecture of a big modern city. Longfellow, in charge of the Boston office, resigned in 1896, and the style of the new firm of Alden & Harlow began to coarsen, as if contact with Boston had been a steadying influence. The Peoples Savings Bank Building and the Farmers Deposit National Bank Building (now refaced) represent Alden & Harlow's skyscraper designs a decade after the Carnegie Building, while the Forbes Avenue section of the Carnegie Institute, begun in 1903, is interesting in its own lavish way but lacks the quiet charm of the original part that was designed in 1891. Alden & Harlow remained popular through the 1900s though, not least for the personal architecture of the rich: the mansions of the Carnegie

The library entrance of the Carnegie Institute (above) in its original state. The Carnegie Institute, around 1900, with the original towers and exposed hemicycle of the Music Hall (bottom; altered and enlarged).

partners Alexander Peacock and Thomas Lovejoy,
the Byers-Lyon house which remains on Ridge
Avenue in Allegheny, and the sprawling Tudor
mansion of Richard Beatty Mellon in the East End,
begun in 1909, were some of the truly outstanding houses of the Pittsburgh area.

Their contemporary Frederick John Osterling
(1865–1934) was quite as successful, though he
seldom approached Longfellow, Alden & Harlow
in polish. Artistically he was at his best in
Romanesque, though he was uneven in all of the
several styles he used. The Times (now the
Magee) Building of 1892 is a handsome Romanesque work in granite located on Fourth Avenue,
yet his Morgue of 1901 is a stale dish of leftovers
from the adjacent County Buildings. Called on to
expand the Jail he repeated Richardson's detailing meticulously, then disgraced himself by pro-
posing to heighten the Courthouse by two stories.
His Bellefield Presbyterian Church of 1887 was

The drawing room of "Rowanlea," the mansion of Alexander Rolland Peacock, designed in 1901 by Alden & Harlow and decorated by Duryea & Potter. (Gone.)

Two mansion remodelings of the early 1890s by Frederick J. Osterling: ''Greenlawn,'' the house of H. J. Heinz (right; gone), and ''Clayton,'' the house of Henry Clay Frick (below).

Gothic of a very awkward sort, but the Union Arcade building of 1915 downtown is very suave indeed. The Washington County Courthouse and the Arrott Building in downtown Pittsburgh are heavy and rich — but not very coherent — Classicism, impossible to praise if judged with a coolly tasteful eye yet somehow so generous in their ornamentation as to be very likeable buildings. He, too, had his East End mansion commissions: ''Greenlawn,'' the home of H. J. Heinz which was demolished in 1924, and the enlargement of ''Clayton'' for Henry Clay Frick. ■

ECLECTICISM

The increase of architectural professionalism in the late nineteenth century had local results, as might be expected. The local chapter of the American Institute of Architects was founded in 1891 and the Pittsburgh Architectural Club in 1896, with formal incorporation in 1901. The Carnegie Technical Schools, founded in 1900 and today a component of Carnegie-Mellon University, began teaching architecture in 1905, at a time when they had just begun to build for themselves. From 1886 to 1919 a good local professional magazine, *The Builder,* was published.

By 1900 the trend among American architects was decidedly away from experimentation in most building types. The knowledge of historic and contemporary architecture acquired through education here and abroad, through travel, through well-illustrated architectural publications, and through well-reproduced photographs encouraged architects to develop a sense of how the architecture they admired had really been composed: how its distinct elements were proportioned to each other; what materials, with what textures and in what colors, were employed; where decorative details were used, and to what extent. Mid-Victorian architecture now seemed mere barbarism, its originality the product of a totally deplorable ignorance.

Aside from a few architects who were consciously searching for a "modern" way of designing, American architects between 1890 and 1930 can be loosely categorized as Eclectics. Though vastly more informed, they retained the Victorian sense of a given architectural style as appropriate to certain institutions of society; indeed, with more styles in their repertoire, they surpassed the Victorians in this way. The old, free-wheeling Classical styles, Italianate and Second Empire, were echoed in new all-purpose Classical manners which, like those of the Victorian period, were at the service of business, cultural institutions, and private wealth. This new Classical

Drawing by Edward J. Weber for the title page of a Pittsburgh Architectural Club yearbook. The 1907 exhibition included many examples of advanced architecture in the United States and Europe as well as conventional work by local Eclectics.

The Bank of Pittsburgh, 1895, by George B. Post of New York. (Gone.)

architecture came in shades of intensity, so to speak: at one extreme, cool austerity in the Grecian Doric order; in the middle range, that quite often employed around 1900, overall compositional restraint but with passages of florid ornament; and at the opposite extreme, the Beaux-Arts style, a rather overfed version of the Second Empire, mansard roofs and all. A house or a secondary school was likely to be Georgian or Tudor; Georgian was another good multi-purpose style, and both styles had strong associations with Anglo-Saxon culture. A school at the college level, on the other hand, was often Classical. A church would normally be Gothic or Georgian. A non-traditional building — a factory, an automobile dealership, or a skyscraper for instance — might appear in any style, including one made up for the occasion. Theaters were likewise institutions at large among the styles, places where the architect's roaming fancy might inspire that of the audience.

A knowing eye can usually place a building of the Eclectic period within its proper decade. There are differences in proportion, in the subordination of the details to the whole composition, in materials, colors, all kinds of subtle things, and it would be wrong to say that in the 1890s the experimentation of two decades was suddenly replaced by a knowing, dedicated imitativeness. Rather, it is as if the profession were self-consciously maturing, acquiring taste, learning to do things right at last, and thus coming closer in visual effect to the ''precedents'' of the past insofar as modern building programs and the increasingly versatile resources of the building industry permitted.

Above, the interior of the Diamond National Bank, c. 1910, by MacClure & Spahr. The Second National Bank of Allegheny, c. 1900 (left), was on Federal Street. The Logan Armory of 1911 (below, left) by the William G. Wilkins Company, stood at O'Hara and Thackeray Streets until the 1960s. "Grandview" (below, right), the Phipps-Braun house on Warwick Terrace, was begun in 1901 to designs by J. Edward Keirn. (All gone.)

The Nixon Theatre (right) opened in 1902. The work of T. H. Marshall of Chicago, it was considered an exemplary playhouse, and was one of Pittsburgh's rare Beaux-Arts designs. (Gone.) St. Margaret's Hospital (below) was a work of the early 1890s by the New Yorker Ernest Flagg. (Exterior unrecognizable.) The 1905 entrance to Luna Park at Baum Boulevard and Craig Street (below, right) was routinely Classical beneath its fantastic cresting. (Gone.)

The Fort Wayne Station of 1906 in Allegheny was a work of the Philadelphia architects Price & McLanahan. Much of their work was innovative, but here the style was Dutch Renaissance. (Gone.)

The Wabash Terminal, Pittsburgh's largest Beaux-Arts building (left), was completed in 1904 to designs by Theodore C. Link of St. Louis. The Loyal Order of Moose Building (below) was an unusually late work in Beaux-Arts. It dated from 1915 and was designed by U. J. L. Peoples. (Both gone.)

Built on Baum Boulevard in 1913, the small shelter to the right is claimed to be the world's first drive-in gasoline station. The Mellon Securities Company (below) was a Florentine Renaissance remodeling of an old printing plant, designed in the mid-1930s by Roy Hoffman. (Both gone.)

Colonial Revival houses on Baum Boulevard, photographed in the 1930s.

Thus, Queen Anne's touches of not-too-serious nostalgia disappeared and Tudor's more scholarly quaintness took their place. The Colonial Revival, which began as a cheerfully sloppy style, as loosely organized as the Queen Anne, turned in the 1890s into a style of boxy simplicity — though with big front windows of un-Georgian dimensions — under high roofs and with heavy trim imitated from the homes of the Yankee rich of a century before; then the florid detail contracted, the proportions became more carefully studied, and the tasteful and discreet Neo-Georgian emerged. The Shingle Style, at its best as much abstract sculpture as architecture, was tamed into a rustic manner in which the shingled wall surfaces became neutral backgrounds for decorative trim. Richardson Romanesque as a church style was out of date after the mid-1890s, and a rather dumpy Gothic with bluntly pointed arches replaced it. This in turn was banished from high-style religion, along with pictorial stained glass, by Ralph Adams Cram and others who felt that it was simply not good enough. These architects produced a new, rather synthetic Gothic that was intended as a creative development rather than a mere imitation. Cram testified to his beliefs three times in Pittsburgh — Calvary Episcopal Church in Shadyside, Holy Rosary Roman Catholic Church in Homewood, and the East Liberty Presbyterian Church — and

his partner Bertram Grosvenor Goodhue did so as well in the First Baptist Church in Oakland. All of these churches are standing today.

This trend toward a more polished architecture was accompanied locally by a radical change in architectural materials and colors. The Mid-Victorian city had been a place of bright red brick that the soot would soon dim and yellow-gray sandstone that would become a rich, velvety black — frankly, an improvement over the original color. Richardson's County Buildings, faced in pale pinkish-gray granite, not only towered over the low-built streets around but were startlingly light, and while most of the new Romanesque buildings were faced in sandstone, others too used gray granite; this dignified, soot-resistant stone was to have a certain popularity until 1910. Granite's major rival in downtown architecture from the late 1890s was terra cotta. Shaping granite, carving it especially, was an affair of brute force, while terra cotta, beginning as refined mud, could be modeled to the heart's desire. The 1890s, struggling with the tall-building problem, returning tentatively to Classical architecture after a period when Romantic picturesqueness had prevailed, welcomed such an ornamental resource. Until a little after 1900 the tendency was to use it floridly and in strong reds and ochres. Then, rather suddenly, the color sense changed, and by 1905 terra cotta was apt to be white or cream or some other nearly white hue and kept on in this way until the end of its popularity in Pittsburgh for major buildings, around 1920. At that time, as part of a general trend toward restrained simplicity, the off-white, fine-grained limestone took its place in prestige architecture though terra cotta remained popular in ordinary commercial architecture into the 1930s. Sandstone declined rapidly in favor; its last great applications in the Pittsburgh area were in the Soldiers' and Sailors' Memorial in Oakland, designed in 1907, and the extension of the Carnegie Institute, finished in 1907; the original section had been designed for sandstone in 1891.

By 1900 brick was no longer necessarily a bright-red material, hard-surfaced and set in thin joints of white mortar. The mortar itself might be dyed red, black, or even purple, and the brick was available or becoming available in buff, golden-brown, warm gray, cream, or white. Toward 1910 "tapestry" brick came on the market, artificially roughened and offered in a large variety of water-color shades so that a house wall needed no longer appear as a hard, unyielding mass but could become a pictorial element matching the grass and the informal plantings of flowers from which it rose. Around 1915 raked mortar joints, accenting the individual bricks, had a vogue.

It was curious, indeed: Around 1910, business and institutional architecture was tending toward simplicity — not starkness, not a total divestiture of ornamental detail, but rather a greater dominance of detail by a simple building mass clad in light-colored materials. At the same time, in domestic architecture, a compulsive pictur-esqueness was rather likely to prevail — gables, chimneys, loggias, patches of half-timber, a variety of window shapes, no two bays of a house alike — and the materials tended to be so textured and colored as to obscure the geometry of the house. Then in the 1920s things started to reverse themselves; red and brown brick became accept-able in business and institutional architecture, while houses tended to become simpler in form.

At the end of the 1920s a way of designing that is sometimes vaguely called Moderne began to appear in the Pittsburgh area. There had been free styles in the 1900s of course, ad hoc combina-tions of decorative forms invented for specific projects like Highland Towers in Shadyside or the Oakland Turnverein; but Moderne was a less per-sonal, less temporary manner, evolved since the early 1920s by a number of architects. Stylistic labels are still uncertain — as is often the case, the

styles were named after they passed into history — but it is possible to speak of two varieties of Moderne: Art Deco and Modernistic. Art Deco — a term invented in the 1960s — is the earlier and more sensuous variety, delicately ornamented, sumptuous in its materials, using color as an expressive means. Modernistic on the other hand is simpler, more geometrical in its form, less detailed or hardly detailed at all, and sober in its color scheme. On this basis of distinc-tion between the two styles, the Koppers Building in downtown Pittsburgh, with its external chateau roof, its interior decorative bronzework and colorful veined marbles, is Art Deco, while the Western State Psychiatric Hospital in Oakland, blocky and full of plain, unrelieved verticals, is Modernistic.

Both styles were additions to the repertoire of the Eclectics rather than radical approaches to twentieth-century architecture such as the Modernists were attempting. Art Deco and Modernistic dressed the steel frame of the skyscraper rather than expressed it, imposing ver-ticals on what was really a cage of columns and girders framing horizontal rectangles, and their appeal was in the feeling of Progress their non-traditional detailing evoked. For a large philistine part of the public in the Eclectic period, architec-ture was an affair of manners and dress, and for a business building, a smart shop, or a festive in-terior like the Urban Room at the William Penn Hotel in downtown Pittsburgh, Moderne was per-missible wear. It was not encouraged for domestic

The ceiling of the Urban Room in the William Penn Hotel, decorated in 1929 by the New York architect Joseph Urban.

use, and Swan Acres, built in the late 1930s in Ross Township, was quite unusual for the time in its departures from tradition.

Several architectural offices were of great importance locally in the Eclectic period. As it happens, the two that come first chronologically were in other cities.

D. H. Burnham & Co. of Chicago was a very large office for its time, famous and influential. Daniel Hudson Burnham (1846–1912), its principal, was not so much an architect as a master organizer. Given an area of swampy shore by Lake Michigan, he had realized the plans for the World's Columbian Exposition of 1893 in all their enormous detail. He devised master plans for Washington, Chicago, San Francisco, and Manila. Furthermore, his office specialized in business buildings, and between 1898 and 1910 it provided Pittsburgh with the present Union Station, the

In 1901 the Burnham office replaced a fire-ruined section of the Exposition Buildings with a new one (above). Below is the first section of the same office's building for the First National Bank of Pittsburgh, built in 1909; in 1912, twenty-two office floors in the same Quattrocento style were added on top. (Both gone.)

The Liberty Theatre in East Liberty, 1915, by Henry Hornbostel (right; gone). Below, Hornbostel's 1908 competition design for the Western University of Pennsylvania.

Drawing by Frederick G. Scheibler, Jr. of an unidentified apartment complex.

Frick Building, the McCreery department store (now 300 Sixth Avenue), the Frick Annex (now the Allegheny Building), the Oliver Building, the Highland Building in East Liberty, and 10 others. This was a large body of work, much of it very conspicuous, and the evolution of Pittsburgh business architecture toward lightness and simplicity was in part the evolution of design in Burnham's own office.

Henry Hornbostel (1867–1961) was a partner in the New York firm of Palmer & Hornbostel when he won the 1904 competition for the master plan of the Carnegie Technical Schools. Beginning with this excellent start, he proceeded, for the next two decades, to establish almost an architectural domain in an Oakland-Shadyside area a mile across. In 1906 he began Rodef Shalom Temple on Fifth Avenue, using some of the earliest polychrome terra cotta. In 1907 he won the Soldiers' and Sailors' Memorial competition. In 1908 he won the competition for the new Schenley Farms campus of the Western University of Pennsylvania (immediately renamed the University of Pittsburgh). In 1915 he designed the U.S. Bureau of Mines building, in 1922 the Schenley Apartments, in 1923 the University Club, all in Oakland, and in 1925 the Smithfield United Church downtown. He was a collaborator, and quite possibly the dominant one, on designs for the Webster Hall hotel in Oakland and the City-County Building and Grant Building downtown. In New York, he was architect for the Manhattan, Williamsburg, Queensboro, and Hell Gate Bridges, all but the first realized to his plans and all but the Williamsburg in connection with the engineer Gustav Lindenthal, who had designed Pittsburgh's third and present Smithfield Street Bridge, that of 1881.

A successful man, then, and a colorful one in dress and conduct, Hornbostel was an architect in the Romantic vein even as Frank Lloyd Wright was to be. His style tended to be very loosely Classical, though in general effect rather than detail, with a freshness of imagination that gives it the cheerful pompousness of Beaux-Arts without the Beaux-Arts vice of overloading the essential fabric of a building. Much remains in the Oakland-Shadyside area to show the genial power of Hornbostel's work, although his Carnegie Tech plan was never wholly realized, and one building, State Hall built in 1909, has been lost of the very few erected to his designs on the Pitt campus. Hornbostel should have his monograph one day.

A native architect, Frederick Gustavus Scheibler, Jr. (1872–1958), remains our outstanding Modernist. Yet "Modernist" has to be qualified. He was rather like the better-known San Franciscan Bernard Maybeck, original yet committed to no theory, capable of simple but well-reasoned design yet capable too of being whimsical, even pixyish, at times. Whether he wanted it that way or not, his work consisted almost wholly of modest East End houses and apartment buildings. His grandest works were only medium-sized: the simple but finely crafted Highland Towers on the edge of Shadyside and the picturesque Old Heidelberg near the eastern border of the city. He was not a complete original: his designs reflect progressive trends in Central and Eastern Europe, and very possibly a little of Frank Lloyd Wright and other Prairie School architects who were concerned with geometry in the composition and decoration of buildings. Yet he was not following in their footsteps; he was walking alongside, perhaps one pace behind.

Two other Pittsburgh architectural offices had something of the same originality. One was that of Titus De Bobula, who around 1905 produced a series of remarkable designs for churches and other buildings, influenced most likely by the Floreale, the rather chunky Italian version of Art Nouveau. At least three De Bobula designs were executed: St. John's Greek Catholic Church and rectory in Munhall, the First Hungarian Reformed Church in Hazelwood, and the St. Peter and Paul Ukrainian Orthodox Greek Catholic Church in Carnegie. In addition, a Greek Catholic church formerly on the South Side, seen in an old photograph, has very much a De Bobula look. Nothing, however, is known of him aside from these few facts. Kiehnel & Elliott, though by no means fully committed Modernists, were broadly Eclectic enough to depart from tradition in at least a little of their work; the Oakland Turnverein building, at O'Hara and Thackeray Streets, is certainly non-traditional, mildly influenced by the Modernism of Chicago.

Benno Janssen (1874–1964) was not basically an original architect, but he was a highly intelligent one: not a creator but a first-rate appreciator. His two partnerships, Janssen & Abbott (1906) and later Janssen & Cocken (1922), displayed a sensitivity and polish in any style they adopted that no out-of-town office could have surpassed, and in institutional, business, and domestic architecture they did very well from the mid-1900s through the early 1930s. The Janssen offices had a tendency to use either a Classical style, as they did in a series of institutional buildings in Oakland from the Pittsburgh Athletic Association, begun in 1909, through the Mellon Institute, begun in 1931, or a more Romantic range of manners that were modeled, with increasing freedom, on English and French rural architecture. An early house at Schenley Farms, designed around 1907, is not especially better than other houses of the time in its application of half-timbering and other standard domestic motifs, but in the 1920s, at the Longue Vue Country Club in Penn Hills and "La Tourelle," the Fox Chapel home of Edgar J. Kaufmann, specific styles were sublimated into generalized Old World expressions, and the carefully chosen materials, notably fieldstone, were displayed unhelped and unhindered by large amounts of decorative detailing. Like most Eclectics, Janssen ventured into other styles from time to time. In 1925 the Shelton Hotel in New York, a red-brick Romanesque mass by Arthur Loomis Harmon that terminated effectively

Design for a Greek Catholic church by Titus De Bobula (above), illustrated in the Pittsburgh Architectural Club yearbook for 1905. The Greek Catholic church formerly on Sterling Street on the South Side (below) was probably by De Bobula.

without the use of cornices or pinnacles, seemed to show a new solution to the tall-building problem, and Janssen emulated its redness, its closed character, and its slightly joggled skyline in the Keystone Athletic Club — now the dormitory of Point Park College — and the annex to the Duquesne Club, both in downtown Pittsburgh. Called on to remodel the ground-floor sales area of Kaufmann's department store in 1930 he even used Modernistic in black glass and silvery metal work, set off by the simple shapes and mild coloration of a mural group by Boardman Robinson.

Franklin Felix Nicola (1859-1938) was not an architect, but his Bellefield and Schenley Farms development companies transformed a large area in Oakland and provided the setting for much of the city's best architecture. In 1897, much of the land close to the newly completed Carnegie Institute was still rural, in the hands of the absentee Schenley family and the O'Hara family. Close to the narrow St. Pierre Ravine, over which the entrance to Schenley Park passed, Nicola pur-

The Janssen & Cocken interior remodeling of Kaufmann's ground floor (gone) with the Robinson murals in the background.

The Oakland Civic Center and Schenley Farms development in 1924 (above). Forbes Field shortly after its opening in 1909 (left, gone.)

On the opposite page, a bridge by Stanley L. Roush on the Mount Washington Road (presently, P. J. McArdle Roadway), 1928. (Gone.)

chased a cornfield. The next year the Hotel Schenley, glamorous and set in landscaped grounds, was in operation on the site. This was the time of the City Beautiful movement, and Nicola soon developed the vision of a new Civic Center on the Oakland plateau, away from downtown, away from the riverside industry, gathering institutions in an impressive architectural group and with a select residential neighborhood near by. In 1905 he bought 103 acres of land from the Schenley estate and adjacent rising land from the O'Haras and began to sell it with outstanding success. The Western University of Pennsylvania bought the 32-acre hillside site for which Hornbostel was named architect in 1908; the County built the Soldiers' and Sailors' Memorial; and the Pittsburgh Athletic Association, the Masons, the Shriners, the University Club, and several other institutions and businesses built on Nicola land. One of the most important structures was Forbes Field, the now-gone baseball stadium of 1909; the players, like the performers who sang, soloed, and acted at the Shriners' Syria Mosque, stayed at the Hotel Schenley.

The Schenley Farms residential development, tree-planted, without utility poles, and featuring one-of-a-kind houses built to very high standards, was so successful that around 1910 Nicola was able to solicit, and receive, a bookful of letters from the area's very solid residents praising the beauty and the order of their neighborhood.

In 1922 the Bellefield Company began construction of the 235-suite Schenley Apartments beside the hotel; these opened the next year, and included Nicola's own spacious apartment. A conspicuous void in his holdings was Frick Acres, overlooked by the hotel, but when the University of Pittsburgh gave up on its hillside plan and began the absurd but beautiful Cathedral of Learning, 535 feet high, in the middle of the land, the Civic Center got a focus beyond all anticipation. After the 1920s, trouble came for Nicola. In 1933 he was in litigation with the County over the sale of a Fifth Avenue block, just east of Masonic Temple, for a new Town Hall; in fact, the lot was not built on until the 1950s. When Nicola died in 1938, he had a little over two thousand dollars.

Ingham & Boyd, like the Janssen firms, was an intelligent office, not creative but tasteful. The Historical Society of Western Pennsylvania, built in Schenley Farms in 1912, was delicate Italian Renaissance, the nearby Board of Education building gracious High Renaissance, and the Buhl Planetarium of 1939 on the North Side a work in the compromise Classicism of the time that attempted to combine tradition and modernity. Chatham Village on Mt. Washington shows Ingham & Boyd using a quasi-Georgian style, much less radical than the site plan designed by Stein and Wright of New York, but appropriate to its purpose of creating a neighborhood of good homes.

Finally, Stanley Lawson Roush (1885–1946) deserves mention. As first City, then County Architect, he was an accompanist more often than a soloist, providing architectural detail for bridge projects and other public works, yet always with a sensitive eye. In the portals of the Armstrong

Tunnel, uptown, and the Corliss Street Tunnel in Esplen he designed with power; but when he had the not-very-thankful task of lowering the entrances of the Courthouse he supplied new doorframes in a bland 1920s Romanesque that neither rivaled Richardson's architecture nor showed fear of it. His adjacent County Office Building was never built to the full anticipated height, but what was built is creditable. The exterior expresses masonry, not steel, and the lobby inside is cinematic historical romance, but it is nonetheless a very pleasant building to look at.

The First World War had the usual deadening effect of war on culture, and left the Pittsburgh Architectural Club in a state of torpor. Before the war the P.A.C., like other American architectural clubs, had held exhibitions of current local work and work of interest from elsewhere, and had published well-illustrated, historically valuable exhibition catalogues that were also club yearbooks. These were never resumed after the war, but in 1920 *Charette* began publication with the explicit purpose of bringing the P.A.C. back to life and continued as its organ until 1971. It began modestly — for most of 1923 it did not publish at all — but took on new features and ended as a slick publication, well-illustrated, full of professional news, recording from 1956 the region's architectural history through the writings of James D. Van Trump.

Old volumes of *Charette* offer a way of taking the pulse of the profession a half-century ago. Members' new work went tactfully unmentioned except for an occasional word of praise, but there were occasional controversies over the work of out-of-towners: the Cathedral of Learning for instance, and a Squirrel Hill house by Goodhue. Movies and even music were reviewed, professional advice given, and an interest in old Western Pennsylvania architecture revealed in both words and sketches. A new club headquarters, opened on Liberty Avenue in 1927, was touted as a lunch place. Toward 1930 the question of "modern" architecture — is there such a thing, should there be such a thing, what form should it take? — broke out from time to time. Then, the Depression. This was the age of the Babbitts, the joiners who knew the occasions for solemnity but otherwise went in for heavy kidding around; and as architects lost work the frequent facetiousness of *Charette's* prose, supplemented by doggerel verse, became more resolute. The journal took on a more social tone, reporting parties and picnics of architects who had not much else to do but spoiling the note

A Charette *cover of 1924, showing a side entrance to the Courthouse in its original condition; the upper part of the archway was later filled in for extra office space.*

A sketch by Charles Morse Stotz from the early 1930s, made near the Point. A note says, "Nice chimneys, well detailed shutters." The house is now gone.

of fun in brief passages that urged architects to pay at least part of their dues or announced meetings of unemployed draftsmen.

Old architects have looked back on this time with some nostalgia. From fretting over large commissions that were going out of town, from contemplating an Architects' Building in 1928, they were reduced to consoling each other in misfortune, and in misery they found a new companionship. It was a relief though in 1932, when the Buhl Foundation made a grant for the Western Pennsylvania Architectural Survey that gave some of them jobs and made possible a historical undertaking many architects had long thought important. Under the direction of Charles Morse Stotz, a devoted student of early Western Pennsylvania architecture, the Survey team recorded architecture before 1860 through field notes and the fine draftsmanship of the period. Much of the photography was by Luke Swank, the self-taught Johnstowner who had recently become famous. In the Survey book of 1936, *The Early Architecture of Western Pennsylvania*, Stotz praises Swank's dedication to the work.

With the Depression, Eclecticism ended as a really effective movement in local architecture; the resumption of widespread building activity after 15 years of depression and war found Modernism triumphant in a community dedicated to self-renewal.

The Triangle in June, 1906. The city is evolving in a piecemeal way. Its skyline rises, but crudities of the past survive as well. The freight station in the foreground, for instance, will occupy the northern end of Grant Street until 1929.

THE SEARCH FOR ORDER

We last paused in 1850 for an overview of Allegheny County, just before important industrial and urban development took place. Here is another pause, and the year is 1907. In 1907, among other things:

The Pittsburgh Survey, sponsored by the Charities Publication Committee in New York and concerned local citizens, and largely financed by the Russell Sage Foundation, examined the Pittsburgh way of life. Most of the published findings made very unpleasant reading.

A reluctant city of Allegheny (1900 population 130,000) was annexed by Pittsburgh (322,000), and its old areas became the North Side. The State Legislature had ordained that a majority of the combined vote should determine the annexation issue.

The old Union Bridge between the Point and Allegheny came down, to the relief of steamboat operators. However, the Sixteenth and Forty-third Street Bridges remained as low-built wooden covered bridges crossing the Allegheny River, the latter until 1924.

The expanded Carnegie Institute was rededicated, and Pittsburgh acquired three sizeable parks: a government donation of land from the Arsenal, long a dead letter, in Lawrenceville, and the two major Allegheny parks, the Commons of 1867 and Riverview Park of 1894.

The Pittsburgh filter beds were about to start operation near Aspinwall. Heretofore, the municipal water had been totally untreated, and every well-equipped house had its own filter. As treated water came to successive parts of the city, the incidence of typhoid, the nation's highest, declined dramatically.

Downtown Pittsburgh was flooded. The Chamber of Commerce appointed a Flood Commission to study the problem and make recommendations, but the 1936 flood was to be even worse, six feet high in Wood Street.

Furthermore, since 1850:

What had been a handful of close but separate industrial towns, surrounded by farms, woods, and villages, had changed notably. Homestead, Braddock, Swissvale, and the little boroughs of the Turtle Creek Valley had come into being or been altered out of recognition to serve heavy industry. Iron was smelted in and near Pittsburgh, and steel, a specialty commodity in 1850, was now the principal product. Important, too, were glass, electrical equipment, and increasingly, aluminum, with coal, coke, and natural gas as industrial fuels. Aside from glass and coal, none of these commodities had been industrially significant in the county in 1850. Coal mining had increased as a local industry because of the use of coke in iron smelting and the demands of railroads, steamboats, and powerhouses. Mine structures and "patches," miners' settlements of small uniform houses, could be found in many scattered parts of the county where there had once been only farms. Petroleum had come and gone, but during the Oil Boom of the 1860s and even later, Pittsburgh had been the world's greatest oil-refining center.

The Baltimore & Ohio Railroad had entered Pittsburgh in 1871, and the Pittsburgh & Lake Erie Railroad in 1879, to break the near-monopoly of the Pennsylvania Railroad and its system of leased trackage; the foredoomed Wabash-Pittsburgh Terminal Railway had followed in 1904. All four

The heart of Allegheny, now the North Side, in 1911, with Diamond (or Ober) Park in the foreground and the Carnegie Library beyond (opposite, above). Urban renewal has replaced the park, but the library has survived. The Forty-third Street Bridge of 1870 (opposite, below) crossed the Allegheny River until 1924. The Baltimore & Ohio railroad station of 1888, at the Triangle entrance to the Smithfield Street Bridge (below; gone), by the individualistic Philadelphian Frank Furness. At bottom, the Pittsburgh & Lake Erie Railroad terminal, at the opposite end of the bridge, as it was in 1923.

East Liberty Station, by Furness & Hewitt of Philadelphia (below; gone). At bottom, the Monongahela Wharf around 1910, with the Wabash railroad bridge in the background. Opposite, the Smithfield Street Bridge after it was widened (toward the right) in 1889.

railroads had impressive passenger stations in or near the Triangle, and the Pennsylvania had built a handsome station at East Liberty in 1906.

On the rivers, packet service was dwindling, though it would survive until the early 1930s. Push towing was thriving, and the Monongahela River Consolidated Coal and Coke Company (the "Combine") owned two-thirds of all the tonnage of any kind on the whole Western River system. On land the Pittsburgh Railways Company had restored order after the trolley mania of the 1890s, which had seen the incorporation of over 200 companies in and around Pittsburgh. The South Hills Tunnel, opened in 1904, had allowed the Pittsburgh Railways Company to spread its tracks over the city's hilltop neighborhoods south of the Monongahela and start development of suburbs miles away to the south. The West Penn system,

beginning in 1904, was building and buying up interurban trolley lines, and in this year of 1907 two interurban lines from Pittsburgh to Butler and New Castle opened, giving new communications to the rural areas of the North Hills. The trolley gave ordinary people a mobility they had not had before, and entrepreneurs, some of them trolley-company owners, hastened to give them destinations: the Highland Park Zoo was endowed with the trolley-riding public in mind; Kennywood Park and other amusement parks lured them; so did such diverse developments along the right-of-way as camp-meeting grounds and dance halls. Macadam, plank, and dirt roads gave private traffic communications of mixed quality, but the automobile was beginning to be taken seriously enough to create a demand for better routes and surfaces.

Despite its reputation for grim endeavor, Allegheny County had some extremely pleasant quarters. Sewickley, down the Ohio River, had developed from a farm village to a comfortable riverside suburb, with its neighbors Edgeworth and Sewickley Heights attaining not only comfort but elegance. Ridge Avenue on the North Side, the old home of wealth, was to receive a few more great houses — the last in 1911 — and the other Millionaire's Row, on Fifth Avenue in Shadyside, had good years ahead of it as well. Schenley Farms was building, Shadyside was fairly well built-up already, and the remainder of the sprawling East End was under development. The Pennsylvania Railroad, until the hills of the Monongahela Valley came in sight, passed through one comfortable neighborhood after another on its way to Philadelphia.

The remainder of the Pennsylvania's eastward route in Allegheny County was bleak. Henry L. Mencken, in "The Libido for the Ugly" (1927), wrote, "From East Liberty to Greensburg . . . there was not one [house] in sight from the train that did not insult and lacerate the eye." Most of the Pittsburgh Survey had to do with conditions of work and life in such a setting: "the incredible amount of overwork by everybody, reaching its extreme in the twelve-hour shift for seven days a week in the steel mills and the railway switchyards"; the conclusion that "never before has a great community applied what it had so meagerly to the rational purposes of human life."

There was grandeur in the fires of the steel mills, the organ tone of the river steamboat whistle, the exhaust beat of the laboring locomotive, but there was also billowing smoke from furnaces, steamboats, locomotives, and domestic fires in quantities hard to conceive these days. The coke ovens gave off a powerful rotten-egg stench. The rivers ran with the raw sewage, industrial wastes, and mine runoff that gave water-drinking its air of suicide. Workers, quite often unskilled, inarticulate in English, and generally in a poor or non-existent bargaining position, crowded together in shabby houses and shanties with whatever vermin cared to join them. The laborers found consolation, and a little color in their lives, in churches where their languages were spoken and to which they contributed money, even work, for construction and decoration. Above the gray little houses rose the Catholic spires and the Orthodox onion domes as visual relief from the drabness of the streets and a reminder of something more meaningful than the daily grind.

The state of things on Sylvan Avenue, Hazelwood, in 1907 (below). A hilltop neighborhood in the northeastern part of Pittsburgh in 1929 (bottom). Industrial smoke over the Strip on a July afternoon in 1906 (opposite).

90

Thus it was that Pittsburgh and its county plodded through the first half of the twentieth century without much coherent, over-all improvement. There were improvements in detail, many of them: some large and splendid, some minute but welcome. Nicola's growing Civic Center in Oakland was complemented by the Cathedral of Learning, the Heinz Chapel, and palatial institutional buildings in the adjoining Bellefield area, while the old villas on the Oakland hillside yielded to a widespread Medical Center associated with the University of Pittsburgh. Downtown the skyline continued to rise, and the ziggurat that topped the 582-foot Gulf Building in 1932 was to dominate the Triangle for 38 years. Churches such as Calvary Episcopal and East Liberty Presbyterian, residential constructions such as Chatham Village and the Schenley Apartments, gave some Pittsburghers at least an experience of light and gracious places such as the Victorian city had not known. In Squirrel Hill and the East End neighborhoods, Colonial, Tudor, and houses of a more rustic character filled up the lots into which old farms and woods had been divided, each with its entourage of trees, hedges, flowers, and lawns. The South Hills was now fully open to settlement,

its absolute dependency on the trolley lines ended with the opening of the Liberty Tubes in 1924 and the Liberty Bridge in 1928. Here and there a monument was erected, a new and handsome bridge replaced an old, awkward one, or a stately row of Lombardy poplars dignified a property.

Yet the county as a whole was quietly aging in its building stock and casual as ever in its infrastructure. Pittsburgh especially appeared as a casual city, with its scattered bursts of magnificence amid so much that seemed a matter of chance. If a tree were to be its symbol, the elegant poplar was less appropriate than the ungainly but vital ailanthus, which grew wherever a little earth was left undisturbed. Hillside streets might progress from Belgian block to dirt to wild nature in a hundred yards, and off such streets the crazy wooden steps, or their concrete replacements, threaded together precariously sited houses, with their tumbledown sheds and fences. Wooden poles, hung with electric cables like strangling jungle vines, extended steel arms that held lightbulbs over the intersections of streets fantastically named in an effort to give them identities. Often, in a neighborhood, there was an illusion that time had stopped in 1900 or

Expansion eastward: duplexes, c. 1920, on Forward Avenue in Squirrel Hill (opposite). The mail-order suburban house: this house in Dorseyville, O'Hara Township (right) was built in the late 1920s from a kit supplied by Sears Roebuck. The South Hills in the automobile period (bottom): the south end of the Liberty Tubes in 1932.

On the opposite page, a North Side scene of the 1930s photographed by Luke Swank.

1920; once completed, the neighborhoods seemed to be immutable. In fact, though, they *were* changing. Masonry was getting dirty. Paint was darkening, cracking, then flaking away. Rotted porch posts were being replaced by brick piers, and drop siding was being covered by Insulbric. Where once there were trimmed hedges, the ailanthus was growing.

The industrial presence was still strong, and to be unaware of it was merely to have succeeded, for a time, in escaping it. The audience of an "Evening in Old Vienna" concert in Syria Mosque emerged to the faint sulphur smell of coal smoke and the flicker of Bessemer fires reflected off the clouds. The hoarse whistles of steam locomotives and towboats could be heard in the night. The grandeur and the gloom had a compelling effect on artists: John Kane's optimistic primitives; Luke Swank's moody studies of old, dusty neighborhoods in hazy sunlight; Samuel Rosenberg's forlorn houses and heroic perspectives; Harry Scheuch's sad figures in humble streets.

The casual city was a place with the incongruous, possibly ironical, contrasts a social commentator might desire: the superb institutional tower rising beyond shabby-genteel housing, the clip-clop as the huckster's wagon, lantern swinging, passed the aristocratic apartment complex. We can look back, we who knew that city, deplore much of it from our experience of it, deplore it even more because we feel we ought to. But there are features of it that we miss, and perhaps most of all the many works of architecture that, with the broader vision that we now have, we might have saved, returned to full life, and now be enjoying.

If Allegheny County was a disorganized place during these times, it was not because nobody cared; it was more that those who did care met an inertia that was insurmountable for years.

The county was a mosaic of towns, boroughs, and townships, each acting by itself and usually not effectively. The Olmsted report of 1910 was to complain about bad local maps; officials were incompetent even to measure their territories. Since officials, with some exceptions, were also unwilling or unable to do anything effective about the problems — which, apart from working conditions, centered on public health, housing, poverty, recreation, traffic, and visual amenity — business and professional people united unofficially in frustrated attempts to improve things. In vain, there was talk of "Greater Pittsburgh," the whole county united as a municipality. Private attempts were made to supply necessary housing: the greatest success came only in 1932 in Chatham Village on Mt. Washington, which demonstrated that capitalism could supply very good middle-class housing, but found no emulation. Other groups attempted to unite the charities, to pressure officials to enact or enforce laws promoting public health, with no great success. These private groups contained eminent people; yet in this connection their political influence was wavering, and critics have remarked on a region where industry was organized with supreme efficiency and all else was chaos.

In 1910, Frederick Law Olmsted, son of the famous landscape architect, submitted a report on the investigation that he and a team of consultants had made for the Pittsburgh Civic Commission. Typically for the time, it concentrated on circulation, public squares, and park and recreation areas, citing European precedents as ways to make them efficient and beautiful. A few of its recommendations were: a Triangle lined with tree-shaded river walks above commercial quays, leading to a landscaped Point; Forbes Street and Penn Avenue as major arteries eastward from town; a grand plaza under the Bluff, with a big new City Hall and access to the new South Hills Bridge the motorists wanted. Outside the Triangle, traffic and recreation were major preoccupations. The South Hills Bridge was to lead to a tunnel that would rise to Warrington Avenue and Haberman Street, from which traffic would be distributed over the hilltops. The Boulevard of the Allies was anticipated from Soho eastward. Formal planning near the Carnegie Institute, close to Nicola's developments, was proposed. In addition the Olmsted report advocated public control of the steep slopes and neighborhood parks. Some of these ideas were to be realized in the future, some not.

The first great triumph in public projects was the Pittsburgh park system. When the completion of the Courthouse and the County centennial were celebrated in 1888, the pale granite tower rose over a city that had no parks aside from very small ones. There were wild slopes for children to scramble on, river banks beyond the railroad tracks for swimmers and boat-watchers, but almost no formal provision of places for what relaxation the industrial life allowed. In 1889, though, the City's new director of the Department

The Phipps Conservatory in Schenley Park in the early 1890s (right), showing the original entrance pavilion. The Casino (below) was a skating rink at the Oakland entrance to Schenley Park; it burned in 1896.

of Public Works, Edward Manning Bigelow (1850–1916), helped persuade Mary Croghan Schenley, who had long been living in England, to donate 300 acres of her Oakland farmland for a park. In the same year Bigelow persuaded the City Council to reserve park land around the Herron Hill and Highland Reservoirs. Over the next few years Bigelow, assisted from 1896 by the landscape architect William Falconer, laid out his new parks. In 1890 Andrew Carnegie, who had begun his famous library donations at Braddock in 1888, repeated his offer of 1881 to the City of library, museum, art museum, and concert hall under one roof. This was now accepted, and in 1892 the Carnegie Institute was begun at the entrance to Schenley Park. The Carnegie partner Henry Phipps had donated a conservatory to the Allegheny Commons in 1888 and was now persuaded to give the new park an even bigger one. The donation of the Zoo gave Highland Park a similar attraction.

But what Pittsburgh needed was comprehensive planning, and that came slowly. The City Planning Commission of 1911 was official but,

aside from a veto power over registration of new plats submitted by developers, it had only advisory powers. The Municipal Art Commission of the same year was almost as ineffective, with a veto power limited to City art purchases and building designs. The Art Commission did have two conspicuous successes in the 1920s, though. It backed the city's first zoning law, passed in 1923. Before this time it was theoretically possible for incompatible land uses to be packed together in one area, regardless of property values and amenity, and for a building to rise to infinite height regardless of the effect on natural light and air — this was still a time when, for ventilation, you opened a window. The zoning law regulated these matters. Again in the mid-1920s, the Art Commission exercised its influence by deciding that the new Sixth, Seventh, and Ninth Street Bridges across the Allegheny River should be of the suspension type. The County engineers obligingly used a new German system, imposed by site conditions, that forced them to build the bridges as cantilevers, then convert them to suspension bridges.

These "Three Sisters" were part of a massive series of bridge-building campaigns begun in 1924 by the Allegheny County Department of Public Works and finished in the late 1930s by the Depression-period Allegheny County Authority. American civil engineering has had a reputation for conservatism: yet the Three Sisters had only one predecessor in the world; the hangers of the West End Bridge were among the earliest pre-stressed structural members in the United States; the 460-foot center span of the Westinghouse Bridge was the nation's greatest for a concrete arch; and the Wichert truss of the Homestead High-Level Bridge was a new and clever expedient of the pre-computer period to obviate unknowable stresses in a continuous structural member passing over more than two points of support.

Not only were these bridges progressive: they were handsome, in ways that previous bridges had not been. The Liberty Bridge might appear to the uninitiated as a pair of arches rather than the cantilever bridge it really is, but most of the County's bridges were clean and straightforward expressions of a structural system, modestly decorated perhaps with architectural work by Stanley Roush and in some cases with the sculpture of Frank Vittor. Much of the actual design was by George S. Richardson, who came to the County as draftsman in 1924 and became Chief Bridge Design Engineer in 1932.

The most notable figure in Pittsburgh's complicated planning history was Frederick Bigger (1881–1963). Starting out in private architectural practice, he went on from 1914 to posts in the Municipal Art Commission, the Citizens' Committee on the City Plan, and the City Planning Commission, whose chairman he was from 1924 to 1954. Meanwhile he worked for other organizations. His work for the Citizens' Committee led in 1920–23 to six reports, well-known at the time, on playgrounds, streets, public transportation, parks, railroads, and waterways. He was a steady advocate of comprehensive planning under firm government control. Often frustrated, sometimes resentful of outsiders who were applauded for saying what he had been saying all the time, he still had the consolation of knowing that many people believed him right.

Despite all the inertia, it was becoming clear that fundamental reforms were necessary. It was a matter of finding the right time and the right people to define the reforms, implement them, and get the public to support them. The time came in the mid-1940s with the Renaissance. ■

The George Westinghouse Bridge across Turtle Creek Valley, shown here under construction, was one of the most remarkable works of great County bridge-building campaigns of the 1920s and 1930s.

The Blockhouse roof peeps shyly over elevated grounds (far right center), as its old enemy the Pennsylvania freight terminal is demolished and Gateway Center rises.

RENAISSANCE

Because the first architectural consequences of the Pittsburgh Renaissance came only around 1950, people tend to forget that it began some years earlier.

In 1939 yet another planning study of Pittsburgh took place. Robert Moses, New York City's famous Commissioner of Parks and Parkways, was hired by the Regional Planning Association — the Citizens' Committee on the City Plan, of many years' existence, under a new name — to study traffic conditions. Moses' recommendations were not carried out in detail, and some Pittsburghers said that he was merely suggesting things that they had been urging for years. Moses, however, had the benefit of a national reputation, and his report had at least the advantage of putting all the recommendations, whoever they may have been, in a single place. The Moses report created an impetus that survived the War.

Another genuine advance came in 1941, thanks to public agitation that caused Pittsburgh to pass a smoke-control ordinance that was, at last, taken seriously. It was a performance specification: whatever fuel you burn, whatever you burn it in, and for whatever purpose you burn it — no smoke over a certain low level. There were objections: the law implied new furnace equipment, new locomotives for the railroads, less business for the local coal industry. And the War delayed things. But industry was made to conform in 1946 and homes a year later. In 1947 the State Legislature imposed smoke abatement on the whole county.

For once business and government were united on what needed to be done. The Republican capitalist Richard King Mellon and the Democratic political leader David Leo Lawrence, both very powerful, joined forces for the good of the city. Being who they were, they could between them make almost anyone listen to their ideas. They were backed by the Allegheny Conference on Community Development, an organization of

concerned business and community leaders of the sort that Pittsburgh had had for 50 years, but that under the new circumstances was unusually effective.

Renaissance as an architectural phenomenon began in 1950. That year, demolition started of everything west of Stanwix and Ferry Streets save for the Blockhouse, the Public Safety Building that later disappeared, and the well-maintained, architecturally inoffensive Pittsburgh Press Building. On the first area cleared, the Equitable Life Assurance Society of New York started the first three units of Gateway Center. In 1949, Mellon Square, a raised public park over an underground garage, had been announced near the middle of the Triangle, and shortly thereafter new buildings on the Square were announced for Alcoa — which had been thinking of leaving town — and United States Steel. The architectural Renaissance went on from these beginnings and reached its eventual symbolic climax in August 1974, when the 150-foot jet of the Point State Park fountain first rose.

The Point was a symbol of Pittsburgh, and had thus been a subject for improvement proposals for years. George Washington himself had noted its suitability as a location for a fort in 1753, and forts had indeed arisen there as the British and French empires clashed. The Ohio River that began there led westward and southward, and from the great early days of flatboat emigration until mid-century when the railroads were built it was *the* way to get to the huge Louisiana Territory and the southern portions of the Northwest Territory. Even later, when the city was a rail and industrial center, nothing within its boundaries had quite the specific symbolic value of the Point: no public square, no railroad station, no industrial plant, no skyscraper, not even the Courthouse. Yet until 1970 the Point was merely a little diamond of land in the shadow of two elevated bridge approaches, a place where a few workers from nearby buildings lunched and napped on nice days, and looked down weedy banks at tied-up boats: a typical piece of the casual city of the past.

In 1900 the Pittsburgh Architectural Club published a wishful plan for a reformed Triangle that showed a park at the Point. In 1914, Edward H. Bennett, Burnham's partner in the famous 1909 Commercial Club plan for Chicago, was brought in by the Municipal Art Commission to make landscaping recommendations. In 1930 there was talk of a civic center and a monumental light-house, in the late 1930s agitation for a Washington Memorial National Park, and at various other times other proposals. Around 1950, Frank Vittor, the monumental sculptor whose public-works commissions were numerous, displayed a model of his masterpiece: a hundred-foot stainless-steel statue of Joe Magarac, the legendary steelworker. Under each hand was to be a Bessemer converter, pouring water into a third Bessemer at Magarac's feet; no mandate to erect this came from the people.

Of the Point projects that were never realized, the most famous were the two of 1945 that Edgar Jonas Kaufmann, the public-spirited department-store owner, included among his many commis-

The Point in 1915 (opposite). What to do about the Point? One unknown designer in 1916 suggested a memorial to William Pitt (above). Edward H. Bennett proposed a less grandiose scheme in 1914 (below).

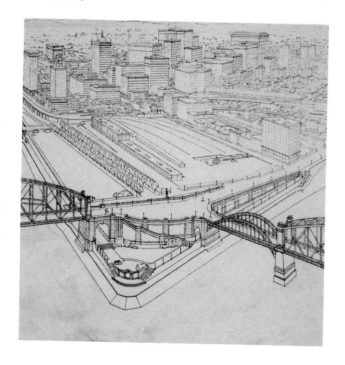

What to do about the Point? Frank Vittor's Magarac fountain (below) and Frank Lloyd Wright's cultural and entertainment center (bottom) were two other ideas.

sions to Frank Lloyd Wright. A detail of the Wright legend is disparaging comments about Pittsburgh ("it would be cheaper to abandon it"; his advice to make the Triangle a park-like setting for the County Buildings; his characterization of the Cathedral of Learning as "the biggest keep-off-the-grass sign in the world"), but he put his fertile imagination enthusiastically to work on these two grandiose schemes. The larger contained a megastructure, based in plan on automobile access to all parts and in structure on the reinforced-concrete cantilever, that would contain almost every cultural, entertainment, and commercial facility a city would need, along with two bridges and a 500-foot tower. To visiting civic leaders Wright was vague about cost — 200 million dollars, perhaps — and the stunned visitors persuaded Kaufmann not to release the plans; they were not exhibited for several years.

The aim of the Renaissance in its physical development was to throw off the dirty rags of the past and put on clean and bright new clothing. Lawrence, reminiscing in the early 1960s, said, "The town has no worship of landmarks. Instead, it takes its pleasure in the swing of the headache ball and the crash of falling brick." This was demonstrably true. While the Blockhouse was saved, and even the gingkoes the D.A.R. had planted around it were tolerated in the new Point State Park landscaping, the Shoenberger house and all other buildings within the Gateway Center area — the Pittsburgh Press Building alone excepted — were eventually demolished. The first

ALLEGHENY RIVER

MONONGAHELA RIVER

102

swing of the headache ball, duly celebrated on May 18, 1950, was against a house believed to be 103 years old. Perhaps nothing in the demolition area was in a redeemable state by then, but the next few years saw as well the destruction of the Post Office on Smithfield Street, Burnham's First National Bank, the Nixon Theatre, almost everything on the Lower Hill, and almost everything in the original Allegheny Town within the Commons, with more impending at one time or another.

In 1954 it looked as if even the Jail, the county's one building of international fame, might go. Conrad Hilton was considering the site, and the County Commissioners seemed willing to sell it. The Jail had been in intermittent danger for 30 years. Businessmen of the 1920s saw it as a gloomy entrance feature for the Triangle, and in 1924 the County Planning Commission had talked of removing it, while the next year saw publication of a plan for its replacement by a traffic circle and a small park. Architects and art-loving citizens protested — the Eclectics saw H. H. Richardson as that rare entity, a *good* Victorian architect — and the local American Institute of Architects chapter produced a plan that showed the Jail, with Osterling's additions of the 1900s removed, converted to a Hall of Records. There was one flaw with their otherwise-attractive idea: the wall of the jail yard had been extended by Osterling, though as everywhere else with complete fidelity to Richardson's detailing, and this was taken as a pretext for removing it altogether; a rendering

The A.I.A. proposal (below) for the Jail, returned to its original cell-block configuration but without walls or chimney. The fountain in Point State Park (bottom).

shows the Jail building, minus wall, standing monastically calm in an Old World garden. Yet of all the Jail's features, the wall has been the most greatly admired, and without it Richardson's work would have been very notably diminished.

As it happened, inertia as well as public protest has stopped any attempts to destroy the Jail. The question of where to put the County's prisoners was insurmountable until the mid-1980s, when an auxiliary jail was constructed. Yet threats to the existence of Richardson's masterpiece continued, latterly on humanitarian grounds.

Demolition has been only a part of the violence done to the older architectural scene since 1950. Building owners in search of a bright new image gave the Jenkins Arcade of 1912 — now entirely gone — a sort of cummerbund of gold-anodized aluminum and swaddled the Pittsburgh Press Building, a handsome piece of 1920s Romanesque, in patterned brown sheet metal. The Farmers Deposit National Bank, admittedly no masterpiece but a familiar sight, was also enveloped in sheet metal. This was quite a sheet-metal period. At the Carnegie Institute, gray sheet metal replaced the old bronze cheneau of masks that had invigorated the roofline.

If it was not *quite* true, in the 1950s and 1960s, that New — anything new — equaled Good, it was very nearly true that Old equaled Bad. A fad arose for modernizing old houses. In a masonry neighborhood like Shadyside, the procedure was to take off the porch, patch up the scars more or less, and paint everything else gray or beige or pale green. Or impart a Californian touch, with pebbles instead of grass and dark-stained boards applied to the Victorian walls to convey the effect of an elegant shack. In neighborhoods with simple frame houses, the South Side Flats for instance, the old wooden siding was covered with aluminum made to imitate wooden siding, and a metal awning was extended over steps that were covered with indoor-outdoor carpeting when that became available. Faced with large Victorian windows — the early Modernists had ritually deplored the gloom of Victorian interiors — a landlord's response was to fill in their openings around cheap new sash to a half or a quarter of their original area. With energy-conservation policies of the 1970s, dropped ceilings became popular; houses and institutional buildings alike developed a half-blind look, and generous headroom was treated as a frivolity of the reckless past, now abjured.

To these individual efforts were added urban-renewal projects, some fully realized such as Gateway Center, some aborted partway through, and some merely proposed. "Urban renewal" — rebuilding from scratch, with particular attention to optimum automobile circulation, at least minimum housing standards, commercial and industrial development, and a certain amount of civic display — was of course quite common in the 1950s and 1960s all over the country. Its theories and formulas seemed to offer an obvious way out of all the muddle and squalor of the past. The Lower Hill was almost totally cleared for the Civic Arena, which was built, apartment houses that were only partly built, and a big and showy Center for the Arts, which was never built. East Liberty and Mount Lebanon were cutely street-furnished in their commercial centers, and East Liberty got a new traffic pattern that failed to work. The North Side north of the Commons was replanned in the 1950s as almost wholly cleared for new housing and a few institutional buildings, and highway engineers working on the road system in the area proposed a viaduct that would cross West Park 15 feet from the ground. Manchester and Allegheny West were under similar threats. In the 1960s, Junction Hollow, the unkempt but majestic ravine that separates the Carnegie Institute from Carnegie-Mellon University, was planned to be filled to overflowing with a half-dozen or more levels of utilitarian space.

The things done and the things proposed were in part necessary reforms, in part the results of an attitude of revulsion toward the past. Aside from a few colorful recollections and surviving amenities, the past seemed expendable. Most of it was perceived as disgusting; there was no apparent way of or reason for using its buildings for modern purposes; and the new business and professional blood the region wanted to attract would not care about the local past anyway. One official in the 1960s wanted to mask the Jones & Laughlin blast furnaces by the Parkway East as bad for Pittsburgh's new image.

Reaction against this prevailing utilitarian, tidy-minded attitude came already in the 1960s. The Pittsburgh History & Landmarks Foundation, founded in 1964 by Charles Covert Arensberg, Barbara Hoffstot, James D. Van Trump, and Arthur P. Ziegler, Jr., set out to demonstrate that a practical approach to historic preservation could save individual old buildings and entire neighborhoods: not merely the architecture of the neighborhoods but the usefulness of their buildings and

The Lower Hill in the early 1950s, before urban-renewal clearance.

The Lower Hill in the early 1960s, after completion of the Civic Arena.

the morale of those who used them. Historic preservation, at that time, was emerging from its museum and touristic phase and concerning itself more with the everyday world, and Landmarks was one of the early organizations to think of those who would actually use preserved buildings as homes, stores, places for ordinary purposes: the people who would have to find the buildings convenient, take pride in them, and care for them. Landmarks made a policy of conferring with and selling preservation to citizens' groups and individuals who were trying to improve their homes and their neighborhoods, often on very slender means.

For its first 15 years Landmarks concentrated on physical matters and public advocacy: saving the Post Office of the former city of Allegheny, which became its own headquarters between 1971 and 1984; purchasing and restoring North Side and South Side houses as examples to property owners and signs of better times to neighborhood dwellers; arranging for design-consultation services; establishing a community museum and offering it as a repository for historic artifacts; and rescuing endangered landmark buildings such as the Neville house. At the same time, Landmarks publicized historic preservation; a Van Trump-Ziegler survey of 1965–67 resulted in *Landmark Architecture of Allegheny County*, the predecessor to this book, while the "Stones of Pittsburgh" series of booklets explored individual buildings and building groups.

In the mid-1970s, Landmarks turned its attention to commercial revitalization on a large scale with the Pittsburgh & Lake Erie Railroad terminal complex. Beginning modestly in a crowded industrial district in 1879, the P&LE had by 1930 taken over almost the whole south shore area on the Monongahela opposite the Triangle, but by the mid-1960s had so dispersed or lessened its services that conventional urban-renewal schemes were being prepared for the land. Landmarks saw in the P&LE site a chance to demonstrate its ideas of historic preservation as an integral feature of urban development and to test the validity of its principles of urban design, its belief in the potential of then-unused waterfronts, and its faith in a quality Pittsburgh consumer market. In 1976 Landmarks reached an agreement with the railroad that has resulted in the development of Station Square, a business, retail, and cultural center that is planned to cover 43 acres. The five historic railroad buildings have been saved and adapted for new uses, and new buildings have

The Langenheim house on Liverpool Street in Manchester, as it was when the Pittsburgh History & Landmarks Foundation received it for preservation and eventual restoration.

107

Tustin Street, Soho, in the late 1950s.

been constructed. The project, a daring departure from official planning at the time, was initially funded by The Allegheny Foundation, a Scaife family charitable trust.

By 1980 historic preservation was established as a sound method for urban rehabilitation and supported by many segments of the community. Therefore, Landmarks realized that it could turn its attention to education, in a broad sense, as a principal means to accomplish preservation. Through publications, architectural surveys and nominations to the National Register of Historic Places, tours, lectures, and educational programs for students and teachers, Landmarks now presents local history and the significance of historic preservation to the public, while using its revolving fund to support neighborhood groups in undertaking preservation projects.

Historic preservation has been a sort of Counter-Renaissance, not because the dusty city that Luke Swank knew is one that preservationists wish to keep frozen in time but because the progressives of the Renaissance too often ignored what was good about this city's past. They failed to see, certainly, that to break the continuity of a neighborhood's visible history, to sponge away whole streets of buildings, risks diminishing the inhabitants' sense of — their right, even, of sensing — who they are and what they are part of. If they are moved about arbitrarily, old associations are broken up, old friendships, old patterns of living. And how about the old architecture, considered purely as art? Has it perhaps touches of humanity in its detailing, perhaps concessions to human dignity in its deviations from the utilitarian, perhaps more positive visual effect in its color and texture, not to be found in what might replace it? Renaissance brought order, and a prosperity demonstrated in a way that attracted more prosperity, but it was not the most sensitive way of reshaping a city. It had to work fast, and there were penalties inherent in such speed. ■

A panel of the Alcoa Building going up, 1951.

MODERN ARCHITECTURE

Major Eclectic buildings continued to rise during the Depression: the Gulf Building, the Mellon Institute, the East Liberty Presbyterian Church, the Cathedral of Learning, the Heinz Chapel, the Buhl Planetarium, and the Florentine institutions of the Medical Center that were replacing the old villas on the Oakland hillside. These were sensational additions to the architecture of Pittsburgh, yet nothing was to follow. Eclecticism seemed to have exhausted itself with these last great efforts, and when the Renaissance built, it built in ways that had to be considered Modern.

The decline of Eclecticism was certainly due in part to its demand for expensive materials and workmanship at a time when money was hard to come by, followed by war years when both manpower and the supply of materials were subject to higher priorities. But there was a nationwide feeling, as well, that Eclecticism had simply gone too far. Engineers, contractors, artists, craftsmen, and suppliers had become used to catering to the architect's fantasies, his whims, even. If he demanded the delivery of 62 monolithic columns 42 feet high — the Mellon Institute — an indulgent patron might allow it. If he and his client dreamed of a 535-foot skyscraper with a richly detailed, tapering silhouette of Gothic masonry — the Cathedral of Learning — their dream could be realized. If he wanted gnarled bricks in a wall, or stucco troweled to a certain quaint texture, or ragged-edged slates on a roof, he got them. The visual effect of a building was too often dependent on historic associations, too often an affair of make-believe; there was too wide a deviation, too often, between the appearance of a building and the realities of the civilization in which it was built, the purpose for which it was built, and the system by which it was built. The architect seemed sometimes like a sportsman who, inept at polo, insisted on playing it by the rules of croquet. Toward 1930 some architects became restless, tried

109

to be "modern" at least in solving specifically modern architectural problems; then broke out into open controversy, with the extremists declaring that *all* building programs should be executed in a style explicitly of the twentieth century. Compromises were attempted, often in a stripped-down Classical manner with sculpture that was greatly simplified though not banished. This short-lived manner gave the impression of an Old Guard retreat rather than the result of positive artistic conviction, and Henry-Russell Hitchcock and Philip Johnson seemed to state a clearer case in *The International Style* of 1932: "The current style sets a high but not impossible standard for decoration: better none at all unless it be good. The principle is aristocratic rather than puritanical."

Now that the Modern-Eclectic controversy of five decades ago, a war of religion at the time, has died down, we can look at Eclectic architecture with a less committed eye, smile at the excesses but enjoy and admire the many real accomplishments, the solidity and amplitude and fine taste so often to be found. First-class construction and workmanship were among the best to be found at any period of history — the Cathedral of Learning can stand for 300 years — and the ornament, even when sedulously copied from some "precedent" found in the architect's library, at least conveys the assurance that what you see was built by and for human beings: an assurance that the mute architecture of more recent times has seldom bothered to impart.

If we were to sum up the history of American architecture, we might be tempted to an epigram, sweeping but with some truth in it. In the Georgian period we had an architecture, simple and tasteful; after 1830 we had a hundred years of, not so much architecture as pictures of architecture, appearances and reality increasingly at odds; and since 1930 we have had, not so much architecture as illustrations of theories about architecture.

Certainly, the Modernist polemics of 1930 and later attempted to establish an *a priori* basis for the exclusive use of a "modern" architecture, whatever form it might take, regardless of individual preference. The polemics had a Germanic sternness in asserting the claim that History, in modern times manifested in The Machine, demanded a new architecture. There was a touch of French rationalism, insisting on direct responses to practical requirements. And above all there was a moralistic Anglo-Saxon quality, an insistence on truth: truth to modern civilization, truth to the building program, truth to construction: a building must be honest. Despite Hitchcock and Johnson, there *was* a puritanical quality to the polemics; Modern architecture was being sold like Filboid Studge, the breakfast food in Saki's story that the Edwardian public bought, not because it was delicious — it was not — not because it was nourishing even, but because they had somehow been convinced that it was their duty to eat it.

And yet, in a time when Frank Lloyd Wright, Mies van der Rohe, Louis Kahn, Bruce Goff, and Eero Saarinen were all active on the national scene, it was very nearly impossible to characterize Modern architecture with any objectivity; perhaps the only thing they and their less-famous colleagues had in common was the non-use of historically derived decorative forms. This specific abstention may be the one and only hard basis for a definition of Modern architecture, and a very unsatisfactory one it is. Beyond this we wander into a realm of more vague associations with flat roofs, steel frames exposed or suggested, great sheets of glass, no ornament of *any* kind, not much color or texture, and similar features characteristic of most Modernists but not all.

Certainly, the Modern architecture in which the Pittsburgh Renaissance was manifested showed no particular unity of expression, and individual buildings suggested indecision rather than artistic liberation. Some of the works, by Pittsburghers and outsiders both, were boxes covered by unbroken ruled verticals of metal or stone, while others attempted more arbitrary surface modulations. Some architects used no color at all, while others attempted visual hedonism in a smoke-free city with blue panels that eventually faded, or expressed "Golden Triangle" literalistically in sheet metal with a dull golden sheen. Of all the buildings that symbolized the Renaissance, the Alcoa Building by Harrison & Abramovitz was the one positive artistic success; faced with aluminum panels pierced with windows whose gaskets required them to be rounded at the corners, it had the air of a suave work of industrial design.

In 1970, Harrison & Abramovitz followed its Alcoa Building essay in aluminum with another headquarters building displaying the company product. The United States Steel Building was given an exposed frame and curtain walls of weathering steel. But most downtown architecture in the 1960s and 1970s was more standardized, more in the manner of Ludwig Mies van der Rohe, who was actually represented in Pittsburgh

The Alcoa Building, 1951-53 (left). A more primitive Modern architecture appeared a decade earlier in the temporary USO building in front of Union Station (below, left). Victor G. Tilbrook's Forbes Substation (below) is late Modernistic from 1953, using two tones and contrasting bonds of brick to decorate otherwise-plain walls.

111

At 841 feet, the U.S. Steel Building (right), built to designs by Harrison & Abramovitz between 1968 and 1970, is the tallest in the Pittsburgh area. Its exposed steel frame is the basis of its design. The same is true of the Central Blood Bank (below) of 1968 by Curry, Martin & Highberger; the brick section is decorated with similar steelwork imitated in trompe-l'oeil.

European Modern architects who settled in the United States sometimes designed for this region. To the left, the Richard King Mellon Hall of Science at Duquesne University by Ludwig Mies van der Rohe, 1968. Below, a house on Woodland Road in Squirrel Hill by Walter Gropius and Marcel Breuer, 1939.

by Mellon Hall at Duquesne University, or of that corporate favorite Skidmore, Owings & Merrill, designers of the downtown YWCA, the Equibank Building, and the Research Building at the Heinz plant on the North Side. Meant for business, this colorless architecture suggested, in fact, an oversize business suit: sumptuous in material perhaps but conservative in cut, devoid of individualism, making no damaging personal revelations. At times the business suit was worn, so to speak, with a hand-painted necktie: arbitrary contrasts of material, peculiar roof structures, facings odd in color or texture. These efforts at marginal individualism were so patently uninspired that the public simply ignored them.

Away from the business districts a less rigorous Modernism prevailed, and in fact in house and church design a greatly enfeebled Eclecticism often carried on, powerless to live, powerless to die. Very rarely had these last Eclectic works the sense of proportion that might have given them life, or the air of material solidity that their detailing required to be effective. As to the Modern works, some were plain and rather sullen, while architects of the more ambitious ones tried gesture after gesture, facing after facing, to distinguish them from the others lined up along the highway or the commercial street. Church design of the period revealed a certain anguish, the combined strains of somehow looking like a

113

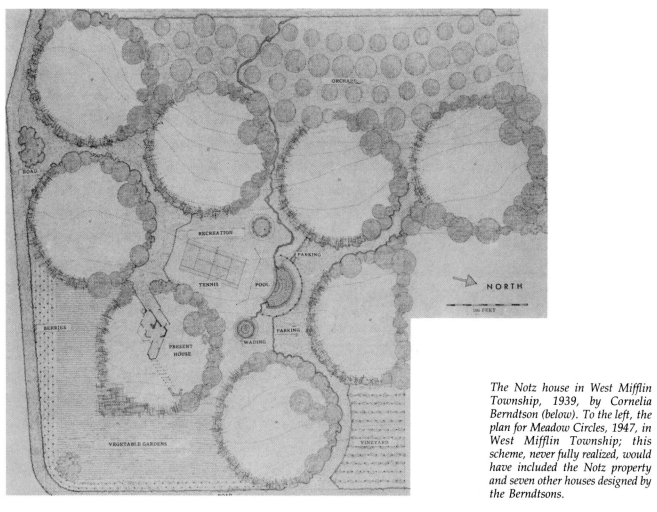

The Notz house in West Mifflin Township, 1939, by Cornelia Berndtson (below). To the left, the plan for Meadow Circles, 1947, in West Mifflin Township; this scheme, never fully realized, would have included the Notz property and seven other houses designed by the Berndtsons.

church while abstaining from Federal porticoes and Gothic arches, of being in synch with the dynamic, skeptical present, and of course of building on budget. House design revealed an ambivalence between modernity and homeyness, but typically ended up with lots of plate glass, a certain amount of unpainted wood, a roof with a token amount of pitch, and some sort of chimney, preferably of stone.

Of our local Modernists, Frederick G. Scheibler, Jr. excepted, the outstanding figures are Peter Berndtson (1909–1972) and to a lesser degree his wife Cornelia, both students of Frank Lloyd Wright around 1940. Their houses are on the Usonian pattern that Wright had developed a few years before, with strong and often unconventional geometrical systems as bases for their plans, an interplay between hovering eaves and emphatic chimneys, and a use of earth materials — brick especially — and unpainted wood. Berndtson is remembered as a man of strong convictions, and one who insisted on the most scrupulous execution of his designs. Certainly, of all the local work under strong or tenuous Wrightian influence, his reveals and imparts the most conviction.

The Abraam Steinberg house in Squirrel Hill, 1951, by Peter Berndtson.

The skyline of the Golden Triangle, 1985.

THE PRESENT

In 1985, Pittsburgh and its surrounding area are undergoing economic changes whose outcome is still unknown. The Triangle is dominated by the 841-foot United States Steel Building on Grant Street. Two other tall buildings — One Mellon Bank Center and One Oxford Centre — have risen more recently on the street, deferential in their designs to, yet far overtopping, the Courthouse tower that once dominated the scene. Down by Market Square, the eye is caught by the 680-foot glass tower and auxiliary buildings of PPG Place, somewhat ethereal in effect because of their reflective faceted glazing and many pinnacles. There is an apparently insatiable demand for office space; still other business buildings are to rise, and the brave expression Renaissance II has been heard for several years.

The white-collar presence is strong and the industrial presence is fading. Gourmet restaurants come, and sometimes go again. More and more formless houses are built on the hilltops and in the valleys of centerless suburbs. The Patton Township of 1950 has long since become Monroeville, in all its commercial glory. On the other hand, the Jones & Laughlin furnaces below Oakland went cold in 1979 and were torn down in 1983. The industrial fires once visible from far away have been contained or extinguished, and can hardly be seen any more. Steam has long since given way to diesel on the railroads and the rivers, and for that matter the 15-barge tows of coal that overtaxed the river locks as late as 1980 no longer appear. The water is fairly pure again; pleasure boating, and even fishing, are popular.

The economic situation is disturbing. United States Steel has found it expedient to sell its building although its headquarters remain, and Gulf Oil, merged with the San Francisco-based Chevron Oil, has left its old Pittsburgh headquarters; thus, the two tallest Pittsburgh buildings of their times, named after their industrial owners,

117

Station Square (below), the former Pittsburgh & Lake Erie Railroad terminal, is the largest single historic-preservation project in Pittsburgh. The Grand Concourse restaurant (left) occupies the former passenger rooms. One advantage of Modern architecture is that it often allows you to see old architecture twice (opposite).

have rather sad associations today. However, finance thrives; Mellon Bank Center now consists of three buildings, one of them the grand old Union Arcade which is being partially restored.

Historic preservation has caught on, partly because of two decades of effort by the Pittsburgh History & Landmarks Foundation, partly because preservationists everywhere have secured tax advantages for the rehabilitation of buildings meeting standards of the National Register of Historic Places. Long-ignored commercial buildings on Liberty Avenue, First Avenue, and elsewhere are being brought back to the original condition on their facades, while architects have expended creative effort on their dark, massively constructed interiors. The Classical lobby of Grosvenor Atterbury's Fulton Building has been transformed, a little to its surprise, into the Mirage discotheque, while the Shovel Transfer Warehouse at Station Square has become Commerce Court, with a towering Hi-Tech atrium. Mansions and near-mansions have become apartment buildings, and new paint and repaired cornices on smaller houses in many places show a renewed respect for their qualities, and perhaps also a new appreciation of the neighborhoods where they stand.

There are still large, challenging old buildings, though, buildings that would be missed, silently awaiting constructive plans and committed capital. Union Station is one; Amtrak camps in a tiny

section of its huge, otherwise-deserted space while the terra cotta deteriorates. Others of comparable size and smaller ones, such as churches without congregations, are still waiting for developers to find ways of using their difficult spaces.

The growing interest in historic preservation doubtless owes something to a growing discontent with Modern architecture. It is surely fair to judge an artistic style or movement by its average productions as well as its outstanding ones, and to do so here is to cast an eye over blank acres of glass, concrete, granite, acoustical tile, and contract carpeting, scaleless and featureless, a Barmecide feast after the old promises of a Radiant City. The reasoning of the polemics often seemed impeccable, and so did the argument, used earlier in the century in connection with every art, that the possibilities of the medium had not been exhausted, that there were further delights to be found. But in Modern architecture, these delights have, very largely, not appeared. We may wonder if there is to be cold, gray, and very possibly dirty concrete for eternity, and balustrades of planks on steel uprights, and bricks of no positive color, and never a carving, turning, or molding.

Indeed, the ordinary person has probably regarded Modern architecture of the usual sort with passive acceptance rather than pleasure or pride; emerged from his play-it-cool office building to take refuge in the soothing silliness of a theme restaurant; aspired to a house with a

119

vague Colonial air about it; chosen to marry at the Heinz Chapel rather than in a 1960s church attempting relevance. Perhaps Williamsburg, Beacon Hill, and Old Economy, a few miles down the Ohio River, draw tourists not because their orderly streets are quaint but because there the eye is nourished with amenities no longer produced: building forms that are simple but eloquent, good proportions, little ornamental touches that lighten the compositions, bricks that are positively red. Historic preservation has doubtless struck such a responsive chord because it values these typical Georgian features and the more lavish ones of later times. A small minority of the buildings preservationists have attempted to save have been masterpieces or historic shrines, but in most there is rather the appeal of some bygone architect's or builder's attempt to please. The results can be ridiculous, but better that, perhaps, than the muteness of what might be built in their place.

The first American attacks on Modern architecture to find any public response came in the late 1950s, and by the mid-1960s deviations from the tidy mainstream of Modernism had begun to be quite wide-ranging. A while later, critics began to use the term Post-Modernism: a term not too satisfactory because the prefix seemed to deny it any central idea of its own. Perhaps there was not one, indeed; perhaps, just as Modernism may boil down to abstention from historic ornament, Post-Modernism may boil down to a rejection of the neat utilitarian package typical of Modernism — any rejection, though *typical* of the new trend is allusion to the architectural past: a few Corinthian columns, perhaps, or the glazed lunette gables of the Crystal Palace. Post-Modernism, indeed, has been like Queen Anne in its raids on history and its witty and unconventional displays of the spoils. It seems almost a point of honor for Post-Modern architects not to use these bygone motifs correctly, perhaps because to do so would make them Eclectics, perhaps because these old forms, combined with new ones, are leading them toward a new sort of Baroque: a free and venturesome architecture, part of whose arsenal of motifs is literate allusion to the older and more codified styles, with all their traditional associations.

Thus far, around Pittsburgh, we have seen only a little Post-Modernism, though in Arthur Lubetz Associates and L. P. Perfido Associates we have two sensitive offices whose work can be called Post-Modern. PPG Place, though it follows

Number 357 North Craig Street (below) was built in 1982 to house its architects, Arthur Lubetz Associates, and office tenants. Bellefonte Place (bottom) was also built in 1982 to designs by L. P. Perfido Associates.

Two neighbors in the Woodland Road area of Squirrel Hill by well-known offices: Venturi, Rauch & Scott Brown of Philadelphia (left) and Richard Meier & Partners of New York (below). Both are untypical of the neighborhood, perhaps a little too much so.

a very Modern glass-box formula, is probably to be called Post-Modern as well; Philip Johnson deviated from the usual business-building formula at least by *terminating* his buildings, outlining them vividly against the sky with 231 pinnacles, and by angling the glass in plan so as to create a faceted effect.

For a guess, Post-Modernism is a transitory manner, not to last long, just as Queen Anne was. Its strength lies in an amount of creative intelligence that is not often to be found; it is not easy to imitate, and on that basis may discredit itself as it *is* imitated. Furthermore, as construction much of it looks frail, and where it deteriorates it also discredits the movement. Finally, like Eclecticism, it deviates so far from a direct response to specifiable architectural programs as to raise the question whether something simpler might not create architecture of at least equal beauty. It may be a Baroque that leads to a Neo-Classical reaction. Yet at the very least it is freeing us of the rectitudes of a half-century, and for that we must be grateful.

A fish-eye lens captures PPG Place.

Two different Pittsburghs: the Triangle as seen from the South Side.

124

Epilogue

Bring to mind some good, long-held memories: Skies, tea-colored or purple in the west. The long, loud rasp of cicadas. The chirp of birds echoing between close-set walls. A house where time seemed to have eased to a halt around 1920. The bite of a winter evening when the streetcar was a long time coming. Lombardy poplars in a row on a hilltop. Quiet front-porch conversations, walks around the block, lamplight through the leaves. The smell of rain on cement, and the lindens turning up their gray-green leaves. Lighted windows seen through heavy rain. Ailanthus trees, and the pungent smell of their bruised leaves. Far away, the shouts of children beneath the white bulb of a streetlight in a dusty, weed-grown alley.

Oddly significant moments of one's life occur in such concrete circumstances, which themselves may sound meaningless. A building, a neighborhood paved in a certain way, lighted in a certain way, built up in a certain way, can be the occasion of such a personal moment in spite of itself, in a way beyond the possible calculations of an architect or planner. Such a professional has to concern himself with the public role of his work: its value as art, its provision of amenity, its performance as a thing to be used. So must the critics and the academics who study and report on it; the purely personal eludes them, and they comment in terms their public will understand.

Yet to a certain extent those familiar with a neighborhood or a city share the same experiences, which nature, geography, history, society, and the constructions of man together provide: the unacknowledged institutions of a community, which make it unique and whose inertia under forces of change keep it the same place in people's minds even as it is altered in detail.

Historic preservation has been a source of such inertia, keeping widespread destruction from occurring in neighborhoods where good architecture might have been replaced by bad architecture or by mere paved-over vacancy. But there is a sad aspect to the very triumphs of the preservationists: a tacit public confession that we cannot expect much of the building arts today. Handsome, charming, witty, sensitive buildings are being designed — but will we see them erected on our street? We think not, and we cling to what we have. Yet old buildings *will* decay and new ones *will* be built.

In the Georgian period, architecture did not fall below a certain level. The building programs were simple and demanded no extraordinary dimensions. Building materials were limited, and so were constructional techniques. Neither designer nor client felt any compulsion to demonstrate originality. Tradition assured orderly design, and builder's manuals provided ideas for woodwork. Ornamentation and moldings, which imparted graceful touches and articulation to the building, enlivened the work. Our circumstances are much more complicated, and our opportunity to perpetrate aesthetic disasters much, much greater.

The same people who have supported historic preservation should find a means of intervening in design in the years to come: create a public demand, backed by informed ideas from architects and builders, for an architecture suited to the places where we live and the associations they have accumulated. This suggestion does not imply the imposition of a range of historic styles as happens in some preservation districts; unless modern demands are met with modern resources, with only limited artistic modification, the results will be unconvincing, shallow, and painfully artificial. Rather, it is made in the hope that the Modern architecture we have in time to come will be a positive contribution, a thing from our own time that we can be proud of and that will add to, not be a subtraction from, what the past has left us.

What the past has left us: simple buildings graced with art glass (right, above) or fancy woodwork, (right), and elegant, architect-designed buildings such as the Allegheny Post Office (opposite, above) and the Margaret Morrison College (opposite, below) at Carnegie-Mellon University.

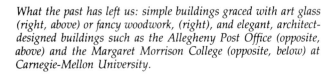

Houses and churches: Liverpool Street, Manchester (below) and Polish Hill (opposite).

A GUIDE TO THE
LANDMARK ARCHITECTURE
OF
ALLEGHENY COUNTY

Author's Note

The following guide is based on a five-year survey of Allegheny County conducted by the Pittsburgh History & Landmarks Foundation. The survey was an unprecedented effort to record the historic resources of the county. With funding support from the Pennsylvania Historical and Museum Commission, Allegheny County Department of Development, Richard King Mellon Foundation, Fisher Charitable Trust, Vira I. Heinz Fund of the Pittsburgh Foundation, and the Pittsburgh History & Landmarks Foundation, our staff canvassed the county, seeking buildings, bridges, monuments — any construction of historical interest with a permanent site — to identify, describe, photograph, research, and evaluate. From Allegheny County's more than two centuries of permanent habitation and 728 square miles, over 6,000 significant historic resources were recorded.

The Allegheny County Survey has provided a valuable data base for historians, preservationists, and planners. It has added greatly to our awareness and knowledge of the county's historical patterns and individual resources, and has prompted historic landmark designations. The survey files are accessible to the public.

The 468 historical architectural resources discussed and illustrated in the guide are a carefully chosen high-quality sampling of the resources identified by the survey. They date from the years before 1940, times remote enough from the present to allow for an evaluation of enduring significance. Some of them are old friends, well known to historians and the public. Others are new discoveries, fresh and surprising. Some are the best examples of types found in relative abundance. Others are one-of-a-kind items. All should be preserved as important elements of our heritage. But this is only a sampling. Thousands of additional properties that were included in the survey, and even thousands which were not, are also of value and are worthy of preservation, respect, and care.

The guide is organized in a sequence of geographically based chapters. These correspond to groupings of major neighborhoods and sections of Pittsburgh and regions of the county. Resources with individual entries are identified first by their historic name, then by later or common names. Some areas with high concentrations of significant resources are acknowledged by introductory paragraphs followed by individual entries for each distinct significant resource. Other areas, where the significance of individual resources is less distinct, are addressed by a single entry that includes discussion and illustration of the best representative resources.

Some entries conclude with notations indicating historic landmark designation. Three different designation programs are noted:

National Historic Landmark designation acknowledges nationally significant properties, and is the highest possible recognition. National Historic Landmarks are designated by the Secretary of the United States Department of the Interior.

The National Register of Historic Places is the official listing of the nation's historic resources worthy of preservation. Nomination of a property or district for inclusion on the National Register requires thorough documentation of its outstanding local, state, or national significance, and final approval by state and federal government agencies. Designation provides nationwide recognition; a measure of protection from harm by state and federally supported projects; and in some cases, eligibility for rehabilitation incentives.

The Pittsburgh History & Landmarks Foundation awards a Landmarks plaque to architecturally significant historic resources in Allegheny County. An owner must apply to Landmarks' Historic Designations Committee for such a plaque. If a plaque is awarded, the owner must bear the cost. A plaque does not guarantee protection of a property; it identifies it as a significant element of our local architectural heritage.

Designation under any of these programs implies superior worth; but lack of designation does not necessarily imply inferiority. Many eligible properties still await designation. Designations are noted as of 1984.

The architectural resources of Allegheny County are worthy of identification and preservation because their recognition helps us better understand the history, culture, and enduring significance of this region, and furthers our enjoyment of the communities in which we live.

History made visible: the rising skyline of the Triangle as seen from Station Square.

134

THE ORIGINAL PITTSBURGH

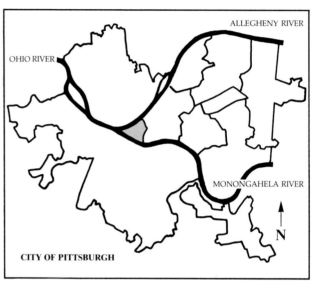

ALLEGHENY RIVER

OHIO RIVER

MONONGAHELA RIVER

N

CITY OF PITTSBURGH

Pittsburghers speak of their central business district, without any braggadocio these days, as the Golden Triangle. The apex of the triangle is the westward-facing Point, the Forks of the Ohio land fought for by the British, French, and Indians in the eighteenth century. The sides of the triangle are the Allegheny River to the north and the Monongahela River to the south. The base of the triangle to the east is less clearly defined, but lies at the foot of rising land a little beyond Grant Street, the outer limit of the Pittsburgh that George Woods and Thomas Vickroy surveyed for the Penn family in 1784.

The Woods-Vickroy plan, with its two street grids intersecting awkwardly at Liberty Avenue, was imposed upon a terrain which included ponds and the Hump, a spur of the hills that rise east of the Triangle. The ponds were quickly filled and forgotten, but the abstract street grid clashed for many years with the reality of the Hump. Bit by bit, beginning in the 1830s, the Hump was lowered, and existing buildings rode high above the streets. Between 1911 and 1913, a massive campaign was launched and the Hump was completely conquered at last, brought down a total of 60 feet from its primitive state.

Of eighteenth-century Pittsburgh, aside from the plan, very little remains. The Blockhouse, Bouquet's Redoubt, stands among the gingkoes in Point State Park, and there are a few foundations of Fort Pitt near by. Of the nineteenth century prior to the Fire of 1845, there is only one building left for certain, the Greek Revival Burke's Building of 1836. A few simple buildings erected soon after the Fire remain in the 100 block of Market Street and in other places.

To a casual eye, the Triangle's history seems to start in the Mid-Victorian period. On Fort Pitt Boulevard, the old Water Street that once overlooked the steep pavement of the Monongahela Wharf, a few warehouses, stores, and business buildings from 1850 and after remain. Liberty Avenue has a large concentration of Victorian commercial architecture too, including Mid-Victorian cast-iron fronts and Late Victorian masonry fronts, much taller, in the fashionable styles of the 1880s and 1890s. Penn Avenue, beyond Liberty, continues in time where Liberty leaves off with an array of turn-of-the-century commercial buildings.

Commercial development was accompanied by financial growth, although regional industrialization provided much of the new capital. Fourth Avenue west of Smithfield Street became a street of banks and financial offices: low-rise banking rooms and early high-rise office towers formed a catalogue of the possible varieties of architectural pretense.

But when Pittsburgh built large, it tended to do so in the Grant Street corridor. The Courthouse tower, which dominated the Triangle in the 1890s, was matched in height by the Frick Building in 1901. The Union Arcade and William Penn Hotel of the 1910s each filled an entire block. And corporate skyscrapers followed.

A view from across the Monongahela River reveals the Triangle's architectural history in the most vivid way. Higher and newer buildings rise above and behind their predecessors, piling up toward the center of the Triangle and Grant Street to the east, raising the skyline from the modest 50 feet or so of the Mid-Victorian pre-elevator buildings to the 841 feet of the U.S. Steel Building.

Among the close-built streets are special places, places that invite pause or leave a vivid impression. Mellon Square, a 1949 gift of the Mellons, offers not only popular public space but a vantage point for seeing some of the city's best architecture. The Courthouse Park is smaller and more relaxed, with H. H. Richardson's beautiful towers as a permanent display around the landscaped courtyard. Market Square, the old Diamond of 1784 that was the only original public space, lives on in pointed contrast with the new square of PPG Place, a half-block away: the first a bit raffish and haphazard; the other consciously elegant, every inch a work of design.

The Triangle once had a boatyard, foundries, and an assortment of rail lines with three stations. Tiny houses still cluster at Strawberry and Montour Ways. But zoning in 1923, Renaissance in 1950, and two centuries of continuous urban growth and change have transformed the Triangle generally into a compact retail and white-collar office district. And the work of building and rebuilding goes on. ▪

The marble and bronze lobby of the Arrott Building is one of downtown's many dramatic public interiors.

The Blockhouse (Bouquet's Redoubt)
Point State Park
1764

No shot has ever been fired in military anger at or from this, the sole eighteenth-century building left in downtown Pittsburgh. It was built with four other redoubts to secure the western portions of Fort Pitt after extensive flood damage. In its brick walls are two sill-like members of squared logs, pierced with loopholes for sharpshooters.

If the Blockhouse has escaped war, peacetime has occasionally been dangerous to it. The great fort itself and the other redoubts disappeared as their land and their materials were absorbed by the growing city. The Blockhouse itself was converted into part of a dwelling, which when painted by Russell Smith in 1832 was decidedly slummy; it was here, however, that the newspaper publisher and early Pittsburgh historian Neville B. Craig was born. Later in the century it was a peculiar enclave in a Pennsylvania Railroad freight terminal, vaguely known but not especially cherished as a souvenir of the past and intended for demolition as the terminal expanded. In 1894, Mary Croghan Schenley gave the Blockhouse to the Daughters of the American Revolution, whose Fort Pitt Society restored it and has maintained it ever since. It is open, free to the public, and remains independent of the State's nearby Fort Pitt Museum.

National Historic Landmark; National Register

St. Mary of Mercy Church (Roman Catholic)
Stanwix Street and Third Avenue
William P. Hutchins, architect, 1936

A church in a built-up downtown area presents a challenging design problem. It must hold its own with taller buildings, and conventional gables, steep roofs, and spires are apt to be dwarfed and made of little account. At St. Mary's, the architect erected two red brick walls at the property line, cutting deep window openings into them, setting their upper sections back a few inches over a course of limestone, and breaking up the surface lightly with other devices. The tower at the corner is isolated from neighboring buildings and is kept low, with a simple, strong shape. A deep slot in the wall separates the church visibly from its parish house, and the latter has a stringcourse and an elaborate fretted band of stone to reduce its apparent height. The simplicity and strength of the resulting design maintains the dignity of the church regardless of what may be built around it. Its vivid red looks good, indeed, alongside the steely gray glass of PPG Place. Inside, the church is simple and auditorium-like, with a diagonal axis toward the altar.

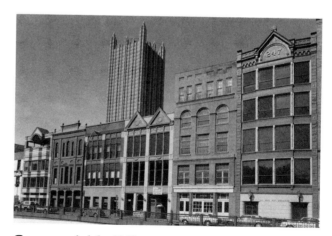

Commercial buildings
211-47 Fort Pitt Boulevard

This commercial row is in many respects as it was when Fort Pitt Boulevard was Water Street and these Victorian fronts overlooked a sloping, roughly paved embankment at whose edge wharfboats lay and packets and towboats tied up. This is the city's most tangible reminder of its old days as a diversified river port, with passengers, crates, and barrels coming in and out as well as coal and steel products moving past. A view of the Triangle from across the river begins with these relatively low buildings, then moves inland, finding ever-higher buildings as it moves further away, and thus reads the history of the Triangle itself over almost a century and a half.

It is curious too that a look at these waterfront facades from left to right recapitulates the history of our commercial Victorian architecture almost perfectly. The building farthest left, Number 211, is in the very simplest Greek Revival, a reconstruction from shortly after the Fire of 1845. Number 231 is an elegant Italianate front of the 1860s, intact save for the original capitals under its entablature. Numbers 235 and 239 were once twin facades in the Queen Anne style of the 1880s, a style not commonly associated with business architecture. Number 243 seems to match the burly image of a waterfront building more closely: Richardson Romanesque of around 1890, down to the shallow detailing of its sturdy cast-iron piers. Number 247, with its large, slightly bowed windows and its crowning sheet-metal pediment, can simply be called Late Victorian, its date and style not to be clearly established.

Conestoga Building
Wood Street and Fort Pitt Boulevard
Longfellow, Alden & Harlow (Boston and Pittsburgh), architects, 1890

Of stone, brown terra cotta, and golden-brown brick, this is a sumptuously detailed, carefully studied building by the architectural firm that would soon be designing the first part of the Carnegie Institute. The loss of the cornice is a pity with everything else intact. This is still traditional bearing-wall construction, and the outer structure is visibly divided into solid piers and screen walls of spandrels, mullions, and transoms set slightly back. The admirable care that was taken with details can easily be seen in the ground-floor openings. Not only do little corbels project to give token support to the lintels and help maintain the continuity of the masonry, but the edges of the corbels are carefully rounded in some parts and left sharp in others: an almost-invisible detail that adds a touch of life, a refinement of a refinement.

Hartje Building (presently, West Penn Building)
Wood Street and First Avenue
Charles Bickel, architect, 1906–07

Here the steel frame is decorated yet not disguised; seen in outline, indeed, the building has a rather ladder-like appearance. The lush spandrel and frieze ornament and the heavy cornice are a little old-fashioned for the late 1900s, although the contemporary Machesney (Benedum-Trees) Building has such features too. At the top is a shallow-pitched copper roof.

Engine Company Number One and Engine Companies Number Nineteen and Thirty
344 Boulevard of the Allies
Richard Neff, architect, 1900; remodeled, 1926

A broad segmental arch covering the portal for the fire engines is stabilized visually by two blunt semi-obelisks. The rear on First Avenue is simpler but intended equally to please, with its Roman brick upper story and delicate wooden cornice. This is a survivor from a time when a work of governmental architecture was expected to be an ornament to its surroundings and to represent government itself in a dignified manner.

Firehouse
112 Smithfield Street, 408 Boulevard of the Allies
C. 1905

Built as a firehouse, this is unusual in having a Beaux-Arts style, specifically a kind of Rococo with a little Art Nouveau detailing in the windows: quite a departure from the usual sober municipal architecture, though the heavy cornice with the City arms seems to reprove the mild frivolity below. The plan is L-shaped, and there is a narrower front on the Boulevard of the Allies. Number 112 has not been used as a firehouse for many years; there is an older and still-functioning one a half-block away. Rather, it has been used for commerce, and now houses a movie-maker, an art gallery, and an architect's office.

Pittsburgh has not had much Beaux-Arts architecture, and the Triangle has lost almost all of the little that once existed there; that these pleasant facades have survived almost unchanged is all the more welcome.

Hartley-Rose Building
425 First Avenue
Janssen & Abbott, architects, 1907

Now remodeled as an office building, this loft structure of masonry and timber was built as a factory and warehouse for the Hartley-Rose Belting Company, manufacturers of the belting that drove pre-electrified industrial machinery. Its cheerful urbanity was wasted for many years on a street that was hardly more than a seldom-visited alley, and it is pleasant to see it appreciated and part of a reviving section of town.

National Register

139

Smithfield Street Bridge
Monongahela River at Smithfield Street
Gustav Lindenthal, engineer, 1881–83; widened,
1889, 1911; Stanley L. Roush, architect for portals,
c. 1915

This, one of the oldest bridges in the county, is also one of
the most remarkable. It has two 360-foot main spans of the
rare lenticular-truss type, in which the upper chord, an arch
thrusting outward, is combined with a lower chord in the
form of a catenary, pulling inward. The two forces cancel
each other out, and, with the aid of diagonal bracing to
counteract moving off-center loads, they have been doing
so for more than a century. The product of a time when
welded construction was unknown and structural members
in bridges had to be fairly light, the Smithfield Street Bridge
has a typical Victorian limberness, quivering beneath the
loads of crossing traffic.

The downstream part of the bridge is the original. The
upstream side was added in 1889, then widened to match
the first part in 1911, and the City Architect Stanley L. Roush
then replaced the ponderous cast-iron portals with light,
rather witty, quasi-Gothic ones. In a 1933 reconstruction the
original steel floor members were replaced with aluminum,
an early structural use of the material that adapted the bridge
for heavier traffic loads by reducing its dead weight. In the
late 1970s the trusses were examined and reinforced. Yet the
original eyebars of the catenaries still bear the stamp
"Kloman patent process 1881." In 1984 the upper chords of
the downstream trusses were outlined in lights by Station
Square and the City.

The bridge is the third on the site, successor to others also
by distinguished engineers. Lewis Wernwag built the original
Smithfield Street Bridge in 1818, the first river bridge in Pittsburgh, and John Augustus Roebling built the second in 1846.

The present bridge has been designated a National Historic
Civil Engineering Landmark by the American Society of Civil
Engineers.

National Historic Landmark; National Register; Landmarks plaque.

Fourth Avenue

Fourth Avenue, between Market and Smithfield Streets, retains much of its turn-of-the-century image as Pittsburgh's "Wall Street," a street of financial institutions. Banks and trust companies first came to this street in 1835 with the Bank of Pittsburgh and arrived in increasing numbers in the late Victorian period when oil, iron, and steel made Pittsburgh a great industrial city and industrial capital spurred financial growth. The oldest bank building on the narrow street is now the Dollar Savings Bank's 1871 building, but there are numerous others, large and aloof, small and aggressive, which together form an intense historic streetscape.

One curiosity of the street is notable at a distance: a historic skyline of early skyscrapers of almost equal dimensions, evenly spaced along the avenue — the Machesney Building (now Benedum-Trees), Investment Building, and Arrott Building — and their near neighbors the Peoples Savings Bank Building and the Union National Bank Building. The architecture that these buildings display at 20 stories is only a hint of that which lines the street below.

Burke's Building
209 Fourth Avenue
John Chislett, architect, 1836

This is the oldest business building in the Triangle, fortunately spared by the Fire of 1845. It is a small but very polished work by an English-trained architect who had begun practice in Pittsburgh in 1833. Its boxy form is apparent, but both the forward break of the central bay, a sort of token pavilion, and the moldings and rustication that cross the facade show the professional touch, an enlivening of a plain front with contrasting verticals and horizontals. The wreaths on the doorway frieze are unusual in American Greek Revival architecture, probably a borrowing from Napoleonic France. The Grecian Doric doorway, and indeed the whole front, is of stone; this was obviously intended to be a first-class building. Of the interior detailing nothing significant is left, but a recent exterior restoration has reproduced the window sash.

Built by Robert and Andrew Burke, the Burke's Building housed a bank at one point in its history.

National Register; Landmarks plaque

Machesney Building (presently, Benedum-Trees Building)
221 Fourth Avenue
Thomas H. Scott, architect, 1905

Here is a skyscraper still evolving out of Victorian elaboration into a more modern simplicity. The base-shaft-capital formula is in effect, with a three-story Corinthian colonnade, piers rising sheer and almost unadorned above a transitional story, and an elaborate conclusion with balcony and cornice jutting boldly. The whole composition is realized in light-colored granite and white brick and terra cotta. The choice of materials is in a contemporary 1905 spirit, but the elaborate ornament of the spandrels and the heaviness of the uppermost part are carry-overs from the recent past. Inside, the lobby is a remarkable and enjoyable sight; though a mere corridor without the spaciousness of many office-building lobbies of the time, it has decoration in marble, bronze, and plaster in high concentration, little altered since the beginning.

The building was erected for Haynes Allen Machesney but was bought in 1913 by Michael Late Benedum and his partner Joseph Clifton Trees, oil speculators and principals of the Benedum-Trees Oil Company. It has been a favorite location for stockbrokers.

Landmarks plaque

Centennial Building
241 Fourth Avenue
1876

The upper stories of this front have a delicacy unusual in Mid-Victorian architecture. Flat surfaces advance from the wall plane, but are themselves incised, so that though the whole composition is of sandstone there is a cameo-like effect of layer upon layer of material, cut away to produce the design. The ground floor, remodeled at least twice, is still at odds with the original Victorian work though its present state shows an attempt at harmony. Since the third story is more delicate than the second, the ground floor should probably be the sturdiest-looking of all, stylistically in contrast with the Italianate treatment above but with a reduced amount of decorative detailing and a maintenance of the original rhythm of openings. The front, one of a dwindling number of Mid-Victorian commercial fronts downtown, deserves such thoughtful treatment.

Arrott Building
Fourth Avenue and Wood Street
Frederick J. Osterling, architect, 1901–02; Edward B. Lee, architect for remodeling of lower facades, 1928

Osterling's design manner was a heavy one, best suited to Romanesque, and when he did a Classical work, the results were likely to be rich and ponderous. Here he tackled the skyscraper problem, using the reasonable base-shaft-capital formula. The base is rather thin in effect, but is given impressive depth by the great recessed archway of the entrance, executed in gray granite. Above this, the shaft shows the common inability of the turn-of-the-century architect to let any part of a building go unadorned; there is a balcony, and bands of white terra cotta and brown brick stress the horizontals, even though this is a tall and rather narrow building. The capital is the best element of the three, with its tall arcades that some have compared to Venetian palace architecture, its massive cornice, and its crowning cheneau.

Within the entrance arch is a lobby, tall, narrow, a little clumsy in overall design, but rich to the eye and full of character. Ornamental bronze and heavily veined marble inlaid with Cosmati mosaic borders create an effect hard to describe. It is as if someone should descend that rather steep stair, hand trailing along the richly worked balustrade, pause by the newel-post lamp on its four Ionic columns, and say something portentous, possibly reproachful.

Commercial buildings
411, 413, and 417 Wood Street
1876; 1883 (refaced c. 1905); c. 1875, respectively

Three curious buildings of equal height stand side by side, illustrating Victorian fashions in small-scale commercial architecture. Number 411, built in 1876, is Mid-Victorian Gothic executed in cold, white marble. As with many Victorian commercial buildings, its center is accented as if to pull the eye as far as possible away from other buildings. Its contemporary, Number 417, unusual for the time, attempts Florentine Gothic, with rusticated walls; it used to have Italian-looking split battlements too. Number 413, much newer as refaced, takes advantage of its greater width to display a broadly proportioned North Italian Renaissance front of Roman brick and dark terra cotta, lavish in its decoration.

The Forbes Avenue front of the Colonial Trust

The Bank Center
317 Forbes Avenue, 414 Wood Street, and 307–17 Fourth Avenue
1893-1926; remodeled, 1976

The Bank Center is a commercial complex adapted from a cluster of financial buildings. The nucleus is the T-shaped Colonial Trust Company, much of whose interior is still visible though the space has been filled in, in large part, by new construction. It has similar granite-and-sandstone entrances, pedimented, Corinthian, and with florid Baroque cartouches, on Forbes and Fourth Avenues; for both, the date was 1902 and the architect Frederick J. Osterling. In 1925–26, Osterling added a Greek Ionic entrance on Wood Street.

At the corner of Wood and Fourth is another element, the 15-story Peoples Savings Bank Building of 1901-02 by Alden & Harlow. Here, above a three-story base of pale pink granite, vehemently rusticated, rises a brick-and-terra-cotta shaft, heavily ornamented and rusticated at its openings, entirely of a deep red. Much of the terra-cotta rustication had to be

Peoples Savings Bank Building

143

chopped out in the early 1960s and replaced with brick, so the tower now has a curious peanut-brittle look. Press C. Dowler extended the rustication of the lower floors along Wood Street in 1926, using composition stone, a colored and textured cement, not granite.

Next to the Peoples Savings Bank Building on Fourth Avenue is the Freehold Realty Building of 1893, unchanged except for its groundfloor window and its parapet, and next to that the Commercial National Bank Building of 1897, whose original big arch, springing from the beltcourses at the sides, is now gone. Features to see inside include the vast stained-glass ceilings, the marble geometrical stair inside the Forbes Avenue entrance, and the marble stair in the Peoples Savings Bank Building lobby.

Union National Bank Building
Fourth Avenue and Wood Street
MacClure & Spahr, architects, 1906

The simple design of this formidable bank-plus-skyscraper of gray granite is quite up-to-date in its elimination of detail — if anything, a little ahead of common practice in the mid-1900s — yet it has a corner entrance of the sort common in Mid-Victorian banks, as if an old tradition were being recalled. The entrance is emphasized, not with a burst of ornament as it would have been 30 years before, but by making the whole corner of the building a quarter-round. The banking room, though much remodeled, is impressive still, with its green marble columns and ceilings with silver-dollar motifs.

Industrial Bank (later, Stock Exchange Building)
333 Fourth Avenue
Charles M. Bartberger, architect, 1903

The exaggeratedly large arch with a dwarf colonnade above suggests some Neoclassical work of early in the previous century in Germany or Italy. A banking room with an office floor above provides a rationale for the composition, and doubtless the architect wanted as well to help a small bank building make a big impression on a street that was lined with banks.

Two adjoining bank buildings on Fourth Avenue have been annexed. The one next door began as the Commonwealth Trust Company, and its building permit was issued on the same day as that for the Union National Bank, April 30, 1906. There was a race to complete the two buildings, which Union won. The Commonwealth banking room retains some gorgeous cast-bronze railings by Frederick J. Osterling, its architect.

Union Trust Company (later, Lawyer's Title Building)
337 Fourth Avenue
D. H. Burnham & Co. (Chicago), architects, 1898

This was the first Pittsburgh work by the Burnham office. The combination of a cool and correct Grecian Doric temple front with big, florid acroteria on the pediment and the wall behind is typical for the 1900 period. Classicists would produce a simple academic facade or interior, then add bursts of sculptured ornament, intricate metal railings, or great surfaces of heavily veined marble as if some Victorian urge to decorate things would be denied no longer. At the time that this building was going up, Burnham was beginning the design of Union Station.

Landmarks plaque

Fidelity Trust Company Building
341 Fourth Avenue
James T. Steen, architect, 1888–89

A decidedly thin-looking front of Richardson Romanesque. Its best elements are the low-built doorways, with little red granite nook shafts in contrast to the prevailing gray granite, and the triple windows of the uppermost floors. The bronze grillework of the doorways is handsome in its own right, though an addition.

The building is very important in context. It provides a transition in scale between the smaller buildings to the west and the Pittsburgh Bank for Savings to the east, and relates well to the Richardson Romanesque Times Building across the street.

Pittsburgh Bank for Savings (presently, Standard Life Building)
Smithfield Street and Fourth Avenue
Alden & Harlow, architects, 1902–03

The busy rustications and banding, and the strong ochre terra cotta and red brick of the upper stories are typical of a transitional phase in skyscraper design. The architects still hesitated to make their building "a proud and soaring thing," as Louis Sullivan had been recommending, and included insistent horizontals to fight its rise and heavy masonry detailing at the top and bottom to deny the lightness of its construction. Of the original ground floor only one granite doorframe remains; each front originally had a screen of Doric columns with heavy bands around them that added still more horizontality and massiveness.

The composition, like that of the Peoples Savings Bank Building at the other end of the block, was probably intended not so much to address the compositional problem of the skyscraper as to state that this particular bank was the peer of the others on Fourth Avenue, with capital to spend on solid, dignified display.

Times Building (presently, Magee Building)
346 Fourth Avenue
Frederick J. Osterling, architect, 1892

This is one of Osterling's most successful buildings, a Richardson Romanesque work that is massive in the way that suited his talent best and assured in its detailing. Both the Fourth and Third Avenue fronts are handsome, though different. The interior corridor running the length of the building has recently been half-restored, half-remodeled, with a strong color scheme and re-use of the old decoration. The cast-bronze frames that fill the Fourth Avenue arches, one Rococo, one Classical, are later but vivid features.

The building was erected for the *Pittsburgh Times,* a newspaper whose principal owner was the noted local politician Christopher Lyman Magee.

Commercial building
Smithfield Street and Third Avenue
Frederick J. Osterling, architect, 1890

This small Richardson Romanesque office building once contained the Marine National Bank. The broad front arch on Smithfield Street is a reconstruction; there were two arches here originally. Osterling had less wall space to work with than in his almost-contemporary Times Building around the corner, and designed a rather open, airy structure rather than aiming for monumentality. In the Times Building he included sculptured heads and leaf ornament; here, his detailing is more spare, but a gargoyle dragon enlivens the corner.

Dollar Savings Bank
348 Fourth Avenue
Isaac Hobbs & Sons (Philadelphia), architects, 1868–71; James T. Steen, architect for additions, 1906

Hobbs designed the sort of "Victorian" architecture the public had in mind 40 or 50 years ago, when the word "Victorian" was automatically followed by the word "monstrosity." But at the time when he was designing this bank, Hobbs was a favorite of home-builders in the Bellefield section of Oakland, and certainly not because he was seen as a creator of monstrous designs. Nor did the Dollar Savings Bank, a mutual bank run for the benefit of its thrifty working-class depositors, wish to intimidate them. The fantastic front of Connecticut brownstone, with its Baroque display of Composite columns and curved corners, suggested rather solidity, dignity, wealth to spend. The recumbant lions by Max Kohler seem to guard the bank, yet they are not aggressive lions; James D. Van Trump is of the opinion that they are "hearth-rug champions . . . the Noble Animals so dear to Victorian sentimentality [with] a gemütlich dignity, a cozy grandeur that is entirely charming."
National Register

Diamond Building (later, Dravo Building)
Fifth and Liberty Avenues
MacClure & Spahr, architects, c. 1905

This medium-sized office building fills out an oddly shaped site. Like many buildings of its time it is a gray-and-white essay in the base-shaft-capital formula, here with one slight touch of color in a green bronze cheneau on the cornice.

Though never one of the star performers on our architectural scene, it is a nice solid design, a handsome building of the sort that people enjoy without pausing to study. It punctuates a major intersection quite effectively, with a mass that dominates the immediate area.

Buhl Building
Fifth Avenue and Market Street
Janssen & Abbott, architects, c. 1913

This is a little gem of a building, clad in blue-and-creamy-white terra cotta thickly decorated with Renaissance motifs. The color contrast recalls Italian sgraffito work, in which an outer layer of stucco is cut away while still fresh to reveal, scratchboard fashion, an inner layer in a contrasting hue. The ground floor has been altered in a Moderne manner.

This was a downtown speculation of Franklin F. Nicola, the developer of the Schenley Farms area of Oakland.

National Register

Grand Opera House (later, Warner Theatre; presently, Warner Centre)
336 Fifth Avenue
MacClure & Spahr, architects, 1906; reconstructed, 1983–85

Only the terra-cotta facade and Fifth Avenue lobby remain of a legitimate theater built in 1906, burned in 1917, reconstructed for movies and vaudeville by the movie-house specialist C. Howard Crane (Detroit) in 1918, and gutted in 1983 for a commercial development. After all this, a curious feature is still to be noted: sockets in the upper windows for the light bulbs that once outlined the facade. This device, popular in theaters in the early twentieth century, was also used to outline the arches of the grandiose cab shelter at Union Station.

The facade is now restored, including its bulb sockets and the big Warner Theatre sign (which now reads "Warner Centre"); but a large office and retail building now lies behind, and presents a Modern glass-box front to Forbes Avenue.

Penn Theatre (presently, Heinz Hall)
Sixth Street and Penn Avenue
Rapp & Rapp (Chicago), architects, 1925–26; remodeled, 1970–71

In the late 1960s the Pittsburgh Symphony was due to move out of its old home at Syria Mosque in Oakland. Yet its promised new concert hall in the showy Center for the Arts, planned for the Lower Hill urban-renewal area, had not been started (and never was). To give the Symphony temporary space, the Heinz Endowment bought the old Penn Theatre, which, like many of the silent-movie theaters, had stage space. As the hope of the cultural display case on the Hill was deferred still further, and as interested parties stressed the advantages of a concert hall in the center of the city, the temporary expedient became the permanent plan. Shop space became a lobby; the old entrance became a huge foyer window; and broad office windows above were partly filled in, in a rather Viennese Baroque style. The last maker of architectural terra cotta in the United States was commissioned to match the warm off-white of the original facing, and did an almost-perfect job.

Inside, the richly decorated auditorium, originally meant to be dark, was lightened in tones of cream, red, and gold, and Verner S. Purnell of Sewickley painted huge gray-gold trophies in a Neo-Baroque manner. The old spaces outside the auditorium were adapted to intermission crowds, presenting a spectacle of real marble, fake marble, glossy ceramics, and chandeliers.

The popularity of Heinz Hall led to its facilities being overtaxed, and another grand movie house of the 1920s, the Stanley Theatre, is currently being adapted to meet the demand for performing space.

Fulton Building
Sixth Street and Fort Duquesne Boulevard
Grosvenor Atterbury (New York), architect, 1906

Like some other Pittsburgh industrialists, Henry Phipps, a partner of Andrew Carnegie, became interested in downtown real estate and made his mark on one part of the Triangle with a close-set group of buildings. The architect he chose for the three office buildings he erected was the New Yorker Grosvenor Atterbury, a mildly experimental architect best remembered for the half-Modern, half-quaint station square of Forest Hills Gardens, a Long Island suburb. The Manufacturers Building, gone now, was the location of the once-famous Pittsburgh Natatorium, a health establishment centered around a grandly vaulted swimming bath. The Fulton Building, still extant, and the Bessemer Building, demolished around 1964, were buildings of roughly similar design that once framed the Sixth Street entrance to the Triangle from Pittsburgh's rival city of Allegheny, the present North Side.

The general design of the Fulton Building follows the common base-shaft-capital formula of skyscraper composition, yet the capital is understated: tiled-roofed corner pavilions of somewhat Mediterranean character with arcades between, mostly clad in patinaed bronze. The dramatic feature of the building is in the middle of the shaft, facing north: a tall, cavernous archway opening into an interior light court of the kind that once allowed offices at the center of the building to have air. It is said to have worked very satisfactorily in the days before air conditioning.

The semi-Classical marble lobby, with its grand stair, has been converted to a discotheque without much permanent impairment, but the main entrance to the building is now through a new and less-spacious passage. An original side entrance off Sixth Street leads to the old Gayety Theatre, now the Fulton Theater.

149

Gayety Theatre (presently, Fulton Theater)
602 Fort Duquesne Boulevard
Dodge & Morrison (New York), architects, 1903–04

The gayety has departed. The original entrance, while this was a legitimate theater, appears to have been on the Fort Duquesne Boulevard front, but a nearly blank wall now replaces it. Like the adjacent Fulton Building and the vanished Bessemer Building, this was a real-estate speculation of Henry Phipps. Presently it is the Fulton Theater auditorium and is entered through the Fulton Building.

Sixth Street Bridge

Sixth, Seventh, and Ninth Street Bridges
Allegheny River
Vernon R. Covell, T. J. Wilkerson, A. D. Nutter, and H. E. Dodge of the Allegheny County Department of Public Works, engineers; Stanley L. Roush, architect; 1925–28

In the early 1920s the County wanted to replace three adjoining Victorian bridges whose appearances ranged from the drab to the grotesque. The Municipal Art Commission had a right to decide on the form of bridges within Pittsburgh, and in this case opted for identical suspension bridges.

The catenary of a suspension bridge — the down-curved part from which all else hangs — is usually secured at its ends by anchorages, which are simply heavy weights. Local conditions prevented the six anchorages normally needed for three such bridges, so the engineers looked to Germany and the one self-anchored suspension bridge in existence; instead of weights holding the ends of the catenaries *down*, a rigid girder in the German bridge held them *apart*, with the same result. But to construct such a bridge, it proved expedient to use old-fashioned, clumsy catenaries of eyebars, bolted together joint by joint, instead of the standard wire cables that could be much more easily built up on a single initial strand passed between the shores. Until the catenaries were complete, in fact, the bridges had to be built as cantilever trusses, with struts that were later removed. In brief, a lot of fuss and corresponding expense to build a type of bridge that looked nice but was inappropriate on the site. But the Municipal Art Commission was vindicated in the long run; the American Institute of Steel Construction awarded the Sixth Street Bridge, the last to be completed, a beauty prize in 1929.

The Sixth Street Bridge is 884 feet long, the center span being exactly half that length.

Century Building
120 Seventh Street
Rutan & Russell, architects, 1906–07

This is a fairly tall mid-block office building of early in the century, its exterior somewhat modified with a 1940-period Modernistic entrance. Like much commercial architecture of its time, the greater part of the street front is treated as an arcade enclosing window areas treated in a contrasting way. Here, the structure is faced in matte white or near-white materials, while the solids around the windows are in glossy bronze-green terra cotta that creates a miniature architecture within the major architecture of the building frame.

Meyer, Jonasson & Company department store
606 Liberty Avenue
MacClure & Spahr, architects, 1909–10

Built as the Meyer, Jonasson & Co. department store, this building has the large window area and cream-colored terra-cotta facing common to department stores in the early twentieth century. Where it differs from Gimbels or Kaufmann's, which also have these characteristics, is in its style, a mixture of Beaux-Arts and Art Nouveau that was probably intended to impart an air of Parisian smartness. The facades form an obtuse angle because Oliver Avenue, now terminated a block away, used to meet Liberty Avenue at this point. The exterior was restored in the early 1980s, with the original false roof, serving as a cornice, reproduced.

Stanley Theatre (presently, Benedum Center for the Performing Arts)
Seventh Street and Penn Avenue
Hoffman-Henon Company (Philadelphia), architects, 1926–27; remodeled, 1985–86

Heinz Hall, opened in 1971, has proven such a success that it has not been able to handle all the business offered it.

Further space has been needed, and fortunately it is available at the old Stanley, another grand movie house of the 1920s. At the time of writing, this theater, which like other large movie houses was built with live performances in mind as well as films, is being adapted for opera, light opera, and ballet. It will retain its original capacity of 2,800, but its old stagehouse volume will be tripled, and a six-story annex on Liberty Avenue will contain two stage-sized rehearsal halls, one of them available as a theater. A description of the project says that there will be "more usable backstage floorspace than [at] New York's Metropolitan Opera House."

The exterior and interior decoration will be preserved. The style is a general Classical one, with details that suggest both late Georgian England and Napoleonic France. Outside, the building is mild in expression, faced with off-white terra cotta and pale-tan brick; inside, the colors are dark and varied, and the detailing is rich.

Keenan Building (presently, Midtown Towers)
Liberty Avenue and Seventh Street
Thomas Hannah, architect, 1907

Col. Thomas J. Keenan, Jr. was the chief owner of the *Penny Press*, founded in 1885, that survives as the *Pittsburgh Press*. A man with an eye for publicity, he erected a skyscraper visible down Sixth Avenue with an almost-unique climactic feature: a reinforced-concrete dome clad in shiny copper-finish tiles that was originally surmounted by a globe, which in its turn was surmounted by an eagle poised for flight. The great dome was surrounded by four smaller domes, each with a flagstaff. Now that globe, eagle, and staffs are gone, the effect suggests a Prussian general with four aides, still a remarkable terminal feature for a tall building. Originally, the terra cotta of the lower part of the building contained 10 medallions of Pittsburgh worthies and Pennsylvania politicians, but several of these have yielded to weathering.

The dome once housed the Baird Studio, the elegantly furnished workplace of a fashionable photographer.

151

Commercial buildings
Penn-Liberty

Liberty Avenue marks the edge of a narrow street grid of the 1784 Woods-Vickroy plan that was laid out with reference to the Allegheny River. By the end of the nineteenth century, Liberty and its parallel street Penn Avenue were very largely commercial, intensely busy streets where stores and loft buildings were closely ranged with Italianate walkups alongside the much taller Romanesque and Renaissance buildings of the elevator period. Until 1905, a railroad freight line ran down the center of Liberty Avenue, and long after that interurban trolleys continued to mingle with local street railways.

811 Liberty Avenue

927-29 Liberty Avenue

In recent years this area has been a mixture of the forgotten and the unrespectable. But it is now in transition with the rehabilitation of many old buildings. Of the buildings that have been restored or may hope to be restored under the new conditions, the oldest are four walkup iron-fronted structures of c. 1870, which have almost a small-town look. Numbers 805–07 and 927–29 Liberty Avenue appear to be made from the same molds; a founder's mark on the former pair names the Anderson & Phillips foundry once on Water Street, the present Fort Pitt Boulevard. The style is Mid-Victorian Italianate, though the ornament in sunken panels in the pilasters is Rococo.

Number 811 Liberty Avenue appears to be from the 1880s, an elongated Queen Anne building that begins rather plain but becomes fancier and fancier as it rises, until it terminates in a flourish above the sixth story with a pediment and a pair of shell motifs. Its contemporary across the street, Number 820 from 1881, is altogether a tougher building, prominent skewbacks resisting the thrust of wide flat and segmental arches beneath a heavy, elaborate parapet. The whole facade seems, with its distribution of forces and its slender supports, to be trying to tear itself apart, yet to be holding together out of some mysterious inner strength. This dramatic exercise serves the practical function, of course, of letting the very maximum of light and air into the building.

820 Liberty Avenue

Triangle Building

The Triangle Building at 926-34 Liberty Avenue, built in 1884, is much calmer in tone despite its floridly Gothic ground floor. (The two top stories are additions.) In fact, it makes rather gracious use of one of the peculiar bits of land casually created by the Woods-Vickroy plan; with nothing to gain in usable space from acute angles, it squares and rounds them off and appears as a firm, solid shape that is accented by courses of stonework. The architect was Andrew Peebles, who just at this time was entered as a competitor for the County Buildings. He never submitted designs, and we may wonder what they would have looked like: Gothic again, perhaps?

Finally, there are two store buildings by the busy architect Charles Bickel, about 20 years apart. The Ewart Building at 925 Liberty Avenue, built in 1891 for a wholesale grocer, is Richardson Romanesque and once was one of three Romanesque fronts that stood side by side. Having an alley alongside, it was not quite so pressed for light and air as most other Liberty Avenue stores, and the architect made the main

Ewart Building

915 Penn Avenue

facade a little more massive than those of some of the others. Still, there is plenty of window space. In 1984–85 the building was cleaned and restored, and the cast-iron mullions of the lower two floors were painted a yellow-gray to match the sandstone above. The Ewart Building was of masonry and timber; around 1910 the architect, at 915 Penn Avenue, produced a counterpart in steel clad in terra cotta. For the most part his building was plain, open, and generally matter-of-fact, almost a frank expression of the structural cage. But he arched his uppermost windows very slightly, then set off his white surfaces with thin verticals of ultramarine, very strikingly, and concluded in the fashionable manner of the time with a flaring cornice.

Third National Bank (presently, Bell Savings and Loan Association of Bellevue)
Wood Street and Oliver Avenue
D. H. Burnham & Co. (Chicago), with Alden & Harlow, architects, 1903

This dignified little bank is an essay in gray tones of stone, terra cotta, and Roman brick; the last of these materials is now concealed. A voluptuous modern banking-room interior is in complete contrast to the simple facades.

153

German National Bank (presently, Granite Building)
Sixth Avenue and Wood Street
Bickel & Brennan, architects, 1889–90

The old German National Bank has lost its large-scaled ground-floor arcade, a unifying element that the overall composition misses greatly; yet its profusion of ornament has an interest of its own, with the doorway an especially pleasant feature. Together with its much more restrained neighbor the Duquesne Club, it forms an element of one of the very handsomest architectural groups in the city.

The bank, founded in 1860, was intended primarily for the German community and thus, like other banks of the Victorian period, was created to meet the needs of a specific class of customers. Presumably a customer could transact his business in German if need be: a real consideration in a period of massive immigration.

Duquesne Club
325 Sixth Avenue
Longfellow, Alden & Harlow (Boston and Pittsburgh), architects, 1887–89; Alden & Harlow, architects for addition to main front, 1902; Janssen & Cocken, architects for tower addition, 1930–31

The Duquesne Club, founded in 1873, is famous as a wealthy, conservative institution, traditionally the club of leading industrialists and businessmen. In choosing Longfellow, Alden & Harlow to design their new home, they may have seemed bold, for the firm was quite new. Yet Frank Alden had been assigned by H. H. Richardson to supervise construction of the County Buildings, and the firm may thus have borrowed some glamour from the recently dead master, a brilliant architect who was known also to be a gentleman. Certainly, the original part of the club has a simple dignity that rewarded their expectations. The doorway, now a window, is fully Romanesque, but the remainder is almost Classical in its symmetry, its gently textured brownstone walls, and its balustrade emphasizing a level roofline. Furthermore, the bay windows that allow observation of the passing world from an elevated and rather private vantage point must have struck the clubmen as entirely right. The office went on from this good beginning to design the homes of the wealthy for two decades.

The addition to the club along the street continues the Romanesque style, and so does the residential tower to the rear in different terms. In this last, Janssen & Cocken produced a variation of their Keystone Athletic Club, built in 1928: a red-brick Romanesque with shallow, simple detailing that neither celebrates its steel frame nor explicitly denies it, that neither wastes expensive ornamentation on a back-alley perspective nor ungraciously denies the passer-through a little architecture to look at.

Landmarks plaque

154

church was built, though here the detailing is more elaborate and historically correct. Inside, the walls are made up of small, rock-faced stones, so that the rather exiguous light breaks over them in a rippling texture. Arched trusses cased in heavily molded woodwork run the *length* of the nave to support the roof purlins over the gallery fronts. What seems to be a very shallow apse, paneled in wood, behind the minister's desk sometimes parts, like the doors of an old dirigible hangar, to reveal a chapel-like space with three tiers of Sunday-school rooms on each side of a great "east" window.

The stained glass is notable. The nave windows, all but one, are by the Tiffany Studios and in a technique never used by Tiffany before: paint on grayish glass, backed by a layer of opalescent glass. The "east" window beyond the Sunday-school rooms is a Tree of Jesse — a genealogy of Christ — by Clayton & Bell of London. The most famous window cannot be seen from the inside: the "west" window by William Willett, concealed almost from the beginning by an organ. The pulpit was an early addition to a design by Charles Bickel.

First Presbyterian Church
320 Sixth Avenue
Theophilus Parsons Chandler (Philadelphia), architect, 1903–05

Like the adjoining Trinity Cathedral, this church stands on former property of the Penn family that was donated in 1787 for religious purposes. The previous church of 1851 was on approximately the same site, but fronted on Wood Street; the present arrangement is more impressive, with the two church fronts side by side on their terraced grounds.

Behind a cathedral-like front in thirteenth- and fourteenth-century English Gothic stands a church on the old-fashioned meeting-house model, a rectangular preaching space with raised side galleries. This is very much the way the earlier

Trinity Cathedral (Episcopal)
322 Sixth Avenue
Gordon W. Lloyd (Detroit), architect, 1870–71; Carpenter & Crocker, architects for parish house, c. 1907

Gordon Lloyd was a successful Detroit architect who designed in a variety of styles. Here he used a long-standing favorite of the Episcopal Church, the Decorated Gothic of early fourteenth-century England.

Despite a fire in 1969 and some rearrangement for liturgical

155

reasons, the interior retains much of its Mid-Victorian character. The ceiling is a ribbed wagon roof, a pointed arch in form, painted pale blue. Accent colors on moldings are a warm gray. Much of the 1871 glass is still in place, along with glass from John Henry Hopkins' church of 1824. The pulpit of 1922 by Bertram Goodhue is one of those finely wrought decorative designs of which he was a master; its style is generally fifteenth-century but with no specific national character.

Trinity has a historic churchyard, with some of the oldest graves in Pittsburgh set among grass and trees.

Landmarks plaque

Henry W. Oliver Building
Smithfield Street and Oliver Avenue
D. H. Burnham & Co. (Chicago), 1908–10

Comparison with the Frick Building of the early 1900s is inevitable. Both have main fronts of about the same size; both have an E-shaped plan, with light courts to the rear; both are Classical in detail and follow the base-shaft-capital elevation scheme of the early twentieth-century skyscraper; both have very high interior lobbies with rich bronzework against simple white marble; both have memorials to their developers; and both were designed by the same office.

The differences are, primarily, due to the facing materials used. The Frick Building is rather like our image of the man himself, gentlemanly in bearing but made of steel and granite; and granite is best adapted to simple effects. The Oliver Building, above its base, is faced in the much more facile terra cotta, easily molded or modeled and thus encouraging floridity. And yet the facade is generally restrained, breaking out only in its capital into a pilastered arcade with a broad and delicate cornice, the handsomest that survives in the city, to crown everything.

Lamp brackets in the lobby.

To contrive a rivalry between the two buildings is futile; there is much to enjoy in each. Frick is a shade heavier in effect, less genial, but it also has more art and more space overhead in its lobbies.

The Oliver Building offers one extra pleasure, though, because of its unique situation: the pleasure of wondering over how good an architectural neighbor it is with the very different Trinity Cathedral. The secret is in the radicalism of the contrast. The cathedral is Gothic, blackened by Pittsburgh soot so that all its rich details are subordinated to a great shape that terminates in the grand gesture of the spire. The spire rises against a sheer gray-and-cream wall regularly perforated with windows not too much larger than those of a house, creating a broken but not restless pattern. The spire comes nowhere near the level of the office building's cornice; its scale is nonetheless greater than that of the office building facade. It is a big thing against a background of small things whose number no one will bother to count. Neither building disparages the other; they are in contiguous, different, but compatible worlds.

Henry W. Oliver, with interests in railroads, iron specialties, and mining — he is best remembered for early development of the Lake Superior iron mines — was also interested in downtown real estate. He had contemplated this building before his death in 1904, and his estate went on to build it and name it in his memory. After his death the City renamed Virgin Alley, which passes one end of the building, as another memorial in his honor.

156

Detail before remodeling

Park Building
Fifth Avenue and Smithfield Street
George B. Post (New York), architect, c. 1896

This is probably the oldest extant skeleton-framed building in Pittsburgh, the work of a New York architect who had a large commercial practice. The materials are gray-brown brick and terra cotta, with a gray granite rusticated base. Time has been both kind and unkind to the building: the crouching atlantes, figures of Atlas, beneath the cornice remain with not very much damage, but an expediency-oriented remodeling of the 1960s stripped away decorative ironwork that graced every window, altered window proportions, and filled in the spaces within the tall arches in a cheap and flimsy-looking way. Inside, the surfaces of the old elevator lobby were covered or destroyed, though to a knowing eye the odd horseshoe plan of the space still suggests an 1890s office building plan, meant to cram as many one-room offices as possible into the available space.

In 1985 the sad condition was partly reversed, when destroyed exterior stonework at the base of the building was partly restored and discordant shopfronts were replaced with candidly modern ones to a more unified design.

David Edgar Park, for whom the structure was built, was one of the earliest steel manufacturers, a vice-president of the Park Steel Company and a banker. His brother William was a partner in the speculation.

Kaufmann's department store
Fifth Avenue and Smithfield Street
Charles Bickel, architect, 1898; Janssen & Abbott, architects for addition, 1913; additions and alterations

The first section of 1898, at Forbes Avenue and Smithfield Street, is a rather clumsy design by Charles Bickel, architect of the Granite and the West Penn Buildings. To this, in 1913, Janssen & Abbott added a larger section in the manner typical of the time: cream-colored terra cotta with faint Renaissance relief decoration and plenty of window space. A distinguished ground-floor redecoration of 1930 by Janssen & Cocken, Moderne white metal and black glass, is now gone, but its decorative metal door pulls and heating grilles survive, while its Boardman Robinson murals on canvas are now owned by the Pittsburgh History & Landmarks Foundation. Three of these are installed in the Sheraton at Station Square.

The clock at the corner of Fifth Avenue and Smithfield Street is a familiar downtown landmark, a popular meeting place.

Edgar Jonas Kaufmann is still remembered as a public-spirited citizen and as the owner of "Fallingwater" in Fayette County, one of his numerous commissions to Frank Lloyd Wright.

Landmarks plaque

157

Mellon Bank
Fifth Avenue and Smithfield Street
Trowbridge & Livingston (New York), architects;
E. P. Mellon, associate architect; 1923–24

In a way this is the architectural equivalent of the rich lady's simple but expensive dress. In the gray granite exterior there is no ostentation, just dignity and self-respect. But: in an area of tall buildings, this is only four stories high; this place of money casually throws away the rentals from 15 to 20 possible stories of upper office space. Inside there is nothing flamboyant about the banking room, 62 feet high, lined with beige marble and with marble Ionic columns with gilded capitals.

Thomas Mellon, born to an Irish farming couple, came to the United States at the age of six, and eventually became a lawyer and a judge. Retiring at the age of 56, he founded the private banking house of T. Mellon & Sons in 1869. This became the Mellon National Bank in 1902, and has continued to grow. Mellon Bank Center consists of three buildings adjoining the Mellon Bank itself, and most of their office space is used by the company for administering the huge organization. The Mellon family is famous for its philanthropies, which have had spectacular architectural consequences such as the East Liberty Presbyterian Church, the Mellon Institute, and the National Gallery in Washington.

Landmarks plaque

German Evangelical Protestant Church (later, Smithfield Congregational Church; presently, Smithfield United Church)
620 Smithfield Street
Henry Hornbostel, architect, 1925–26

Here, Hornbostel was designing a new church for a congregation of long existence, one of the recipients of land from the Penn family in 1787. He chose to design in Gothic, even though he was a Classicist by inclination; perhaps he felt that only Gothic expressed the Christian religion properly, or perhaps he wanted the challenge of using the style effectively among tall downtown buildings.

In its massing the church is broad and bulky, not too different in its proportions from his Beaux-Arts designs of the past. And the Gothic exterior, examined in detail, is literally superficial, a perceptible application of a stone veneer and panels of composition-stone ornament to a steel frame. The style is quite eclectic, with a small "e": a Tudor arch at the entrance and plaster fan vaults inside suggest England, but the square tower with one belfry arch per side between solid corners looks Italian, while the intricate tracery of the decorative panels and the openwork spire have a fifteenth-century German feeling. The spire represents a very early architectural use of aluminum; City officials refused permission to build the whole spire of the material as planned, but the panels are cast aluminum supported by a steel frame.

Inside, the church has an 18-foot rose window from an earlier church of 1875 and stained-glass windows that depict historical scenes in the life of the church and Pittsburgh.

Landmarks plaque

Harvard, Yale, Princeton Club group
William Penn Place and Strawberry Way
C. 1890; Edward B. Lee, architect for remodeling, 1930

Development in 1930 converted what had begun as workers' row housing in a little residential court into the Harvard, Yale, Princeton Club on one side and into offices on the other. Two Romanesque columns from a demolished building at Princeton terminate the view into the courtyard. The rose window of the Smithfield United Church makes an impressive backdrop ornament to this picturesque, retiring little scene in the middle of the city.

Houses
Strawberry and Montour Ways
C. 1850

A fragment of Old Pittsburgh has somehow remained between Sixth and Seventh Avenues and Grant and Smithfield Streets. Jostled by such proud neighbors as Bell Telephone, Alcoa, the First Lutheran Church, and the Smithfield United Church, three tiny old houses manage to survive in company with their not-too-different neighbor the Harvard, Yale, Princeton Club. Except as survivors they are not remarkable, but there is drama in the contrast of scale and elaboration they provide with so much that is bigger and newer. Looking uphill along Strawberry Way, the visitor sees the U.S. Steel Building of 1970 in a particularly dramatic perspective.

the little street. The crowning feature of the post-Osterling construction is a limestone Ionic colonnade with a frieze of strigil ornament into which octagonal panels of marble are set: little noticed, but one of the handsomest Classical compositions in Pittsburgh.

Bell Telephone Company
Seventh Avenue and William Penn Place
Frederick J. Osterling, architect, c. 1890; Alden &
Harlow, architects for addition, 1905; James T.
Windrim (Philadelphia), architect for additions,
1915, 1923, 1931

There are two distinct parts to this building, Osterling's red-brick Romanesque and Windrim's multiphase annex. Of the whole complex, what appears to be the last part is the best. A one-story covered walk on Strawberry Way, with shallow vaults in green-and-cream Guastavino tile and limestone piers, is not only a handsome space in itself but frames the view of the old and tiny houses opposite and creates an appreciable relationship between the tall building above and

Chamber of Commerce Building
Seventh Avenue and Smithfield Street
Edward B. Lee and James Piper, architects,
1916–17

One of the interesting aspects of Eclecticism is the sense of the stylistically appropriate that seems to have guided its architects. Here is a Chamber of Commerce building, and a rather tall building as well. It was quite common for a tall business-oriented building to be in a Classical or Gothic style, yet by 1915 it was not absolutely necessary; a free, *ad hoc* manner was acceptable too, even a decade before Art Deco was imported to give the occasional experiments some sort of orientation. On the other hand, a Chamber of Commerce had an institutional character, which usually implied a Classical treatment.

Our architects chose innovation, and the greater part of their building is a matter-of-fact fabric executed in red brick — strong color was beginning to return to fashion in city architecture — with a decorative terra-cotta top that included false gables to enliven the skyline. The lowermost floors, however, include a very stylized Ionic colonnade, so that there is at least a touch of Classicism in the composition.

Fort Wayne Bridge, Pennsylvania Railroad
Allegheny River east of Eleventh Street
Pennsylvania Railroad engineers, 1901–04; raised, 1918

This is a double-decked railroad bridge with a variation of the Pennsylvania truss, invented for the railroad, in the main span. This truss is a development of the Pratt truss for the purpose of withstanding the heavy, off-center, moving loads of trains. A Pratt truss consists of upper and lower horizontal chords, the upper one in compression, the lower one in tension, with posts supporting the upper chord and diagonals in tension hanging from the heads of the posts and supporting the feet of posts closer to the center of the truss: essentially, a beam with all the non-essential parts left out. The bridge was made three tracks wide, but only two tracks ever existed on each of the decks, and highway construction on the North Side has cut off access to the lower deck.

The bridge was raised in 1918, probably to give clearance for steamboats; the extent of the raising is clearly shown in the concrete tops to the original stone piers.

National Register

Union Station
Grant Street and Liberty Avenue
D. H. Burnham & Co. (Chicago), architects, 1898–1903

Theoretically, the Pennsylvania Railroad went no further west than Pittsburgh; yet that did not stop it from leasing other railroads that did do so, such as the Pittsburgh, Fort Wayne & Chicago Railway and the Pittsburgh, Cincinnati & St. Louis Railway, and running its own trains over their tracks. Hence, at Pittsburgh, it had a "union station," where these and other "Pennsylvania Lines" converged. The present station is the fourth of these.

The initial design was relatively modest, both in the office block with its ground-floor passenger and baggage spaces

Pendentive ornament from rotunda dome.

161

and in the shelter for the cabs' turning circle; but the tower grew on paper while the cab shelter evolved into a 1900 architectural student's dream, the fantastic Beaux-Arts "rotunda" that we see today. The scheme was executed in buff terra cotta with matching brick in the office tower; the color was suited to both the taste of the 1890s and the station's exposure to billows of locomotive smoke. The ornamentation was French in flavor, like the rotunda itself: urns, heads, leaf ornament, in florid episodes here and there. Inside the rotunda, on pendentives beneath the skylit central dome, four women's heads smiled over tablets naming four destinations of the Pennsylvania Railroad. Originally, the arches of the rotunda were outlined in light bulbs. The waiting room was lined with green marble and white terra cotta, and skylit from an internal courtyard. To the rear was a "balloon" trainshed, a barrel vault of steel 556 feet long and 258 feet wide.

The trainshed was demolished in the 1940s, and passenger service diminished. The railroad merged with the New York Central, tried to diversify, then went bankrupt. Long-distance buses used the rotunda as a Pittsburgh station — and were able to drive under its *little* arches, so large is its scale. Railroad personnel left, and the office tower stood empty. Amtrak ran a passenger service, but camped out in a minor space behind the station building. In 1979 the Pittsburgh History & Landmarks Foundation developed a feasible plan for a 300-room hotel — the new Convention Center was to be only two blocks away — but the City favored another site and a new hotel. Terra cotta deteriorated; snow fencing kept the public at a safe distance from the high walls. The rotunda's round skylight wore a shabby nightcap of tarpaulin to keep the weather out. Options to purchase were granted, then extended. Finally, in early 1985, a plan to convert the station into apartments offered some hope that this historic building, whose rotunda especially adds to the vigor of the city scene, could be returned to life.

National Register

Grant Street

The easternmost street of the Golden Triangle, the original Pittsburgh that Woods and Vickroy carved from the manor of the Penn family, is Grant Street, which over two centuries has made an unsteady march toward grandeur. A spur of Grant's Hill, the notorious Hump that was finally tamed in 1913, originally raised it near its center to an inconvenient degree. In the late nineteenth century it was terminated at Seventh Avenue so that the Pennsylvania Railroad could build a freight terminal near Union Station. A street, then, which passed Richardson's Courthouse, the City-County Building, the Frick Building, the Union Arcade, the William Penn Hotel, the Grant Building, and ultimately the Koppers Building dead-ended in a shed full of boxcars.

But the erection of these buildings and later ones, and restoration of the street's full length in 1929 marked progress toward fulfillment of Grant Street's potential. Now, with its concentrations of major historic buildings and modern skyscrapers, and work begun to reconstruct the street in boulevard fashion, Grant Street is downtown Pittsburgh's showplace thoroughfare.

Federal Reserve Bank of Cleveland
717 Grant Street
Walker & Weeks (Cleveland), architects; Henry Hornbostel and Eric Fisher Wood, associate architects; 1930-31; additions

Walker & Weeks had a rather heavy repertoire of Classical and Art Deco forms, with which they designed many of the prominent buildings of Cleveland; the most familiar of their works there is probably Severance Hall, home of the Cleveland Symphony. Here, white Georgia marble and decorative aluminum, now black, form a dignified Art Deco exterior with the aid of the sculptor Henry Hering.

Situated between the prominent Gulf Building and the big and banal Moorhead Federal Building, the Federal Reserve Bank is little noticed, yet it is a very agreeable work.

Gulf Building
Seventh Avenue and Grant Street
Trowbridge & Livingston (New York), architects;
E. P. Mellon, associate architect; 1930–32

In the late 1920s Grant Street was extended northward over what had long been a freight yard, and valuable building land became available. On one parcel of this, opposite the new Koppers Building, the Gulf Oil Company built a 44-story tower that would be the tallest building in Pittsburgh until 1970.

The architects were Trowbridge & Livingston, who had designed the main Mellon Bank. They went down 90 feet to find a proper footing for their great tower — Allegheny River water lay under the site — then raised it in a sober Modernistic manner that began and ended with allusions to Classical architecture: a colossal doorway with a 50-ton granite entablature on Seventh Avenue and a limestone stepped-back pyramidal top that recalled the Mausoleum at Halicarnassus. The treatment in between followed a skyscraper formula quite common at the time, the verticals of the steel skeleton emphasized, the horizontals suppressed. Such verticality said Steel to the public in 1930, yet the architects somehow made the building exterior an expression of stone, giving the facing of the tower and its base a high relief and softened outline proper to massive construction.

The interior, with its dark marble, is more simple and serious than that of the Koppers Building across the street; the two buildings, contemporaries, are indeed conceived in two different spirits.

The top was long covered with neon tubes in the Gulf corporate colors of orange and blue that predicted the weather: steady blue, precipitation and rising temperatures; flashing blue, precipitation and falling temperatures; steady orange, clear and rising temperatures; flashing orange, clear and falling temperatures. Today, only a light in the uppermost lantern predicts the weather.

As a result of the Gulf/Chevron merger initiated in 1984, the Gulf Building was sold to New York developers for rental office space.

Landmarks plaque

Koppers Building
Seventh Avenue and Grant Street
Graham, Anderson, Probst & White (Chicago), architects, 1928

Here, the successor firm of D. H. Burnham & Co., which had designed so many business buildings for the Triangle, created an Art Deco skyscraper, the sort that imparted a progressive image. Such an image went well enough with the client's business. Heinrich Koppers, in 1908, had invented a by-product coke oven, one that captured wastes so that they could be utilized rather than releasing them to the air, where they were worse than useless. He had moved his business to Pittsburgh in 1915 and entered into the production of coke, coking equipment, illuminating gas, and chemicals.

The limestone facing of the building, like the tall lobby spaces inside with their colored marbles and ornamented bronzework, suggests a cool urbanity remote from industrial toil; business took itself very seriously in the 1920s and was very much on its dignity. Yet a little quiet humor crept into the design, with or without management's approval. The crowning chateau roof, being made of copper, can be taken as a pun, while the downstairs mailbox is a doll's-house version of the whole building, roof included.

Though the present lighting is too cold to do them justice, the lobby spaces are among the very best Art Deco works in Pittsburgh, restrained in overall design but rich in detail and full of quiet color.

Landmarks plaque

First Lutheran Church
615 Grant Street
Andrew Peebles, architect, 1887–88

When this church was built, Grant Street still had the air of a small-town Main Street, with the new Courthouse and St. Paul's Cathedral by far its most imposing objects. A picturesque cluster of steep-roofed Gothic elements and a 170-foot spired tower had still, for a brief while, a chance to dominate the immediate area. But the fairly tall buildings made possible by the elevator were already rising, and now of course the church is overlooked on all sides. Inside are several attractive objects: an altarpiece in the fifteenth-century Italian Renaissance style with mosaics, the Tiffany *Good Shepherd* window, and a font in the form of a kneeling angel with a basin, a copy of one at Copenhagen by Bertil Thorvaldsen.

Landmarks plaque

William Penn Hotel
Grant Street and Sixth Avenue
Janssen & Abbott, architects, 1914–16; Janssen & Cocken, architects for enlargement, 1928–29

The hotel stands just north of the Union Arcade, and its older part, overlooking Mellon Square, is one of Frick's ventures in real estate. By the time it was designed, the big-city hotel had attained the form exemplified here, an adaptation of the base-shaft-capital formula. The base is clad in warm off-white terra cotta and designed in a generalized eighteenth-century Classical manner. The shaft is plain and of warm red brick, with broader areas of wall surface than tall office buildings needed. The capital reintroduces the terra cotta against a background of the brick, and terminates with a cornice and a parapet. Deep light courts allow the maximum number of guest rooms to have natural ventilation and some sort of outdoor view. The choice of red brick for the greater part of the building — becoming typical of hotel design at the time — may have been intended to impart a domestic feeling, a warmth not found in the impersonal surfaces of business structures. Soon, business buildings like the Chamber of Commerce Building, under design around 1915, were to revert to color for their upper walls as well, as if they too had come to seem too cold and monotonous with their perpetual grays and whites.

The 1928 addition carried on in the spirit of the original, with highly decorated public interiors that were mansion-like, but genially so, on the lower floors and on the seventeenth floor as well. On the latter is a remarkable exception to the Classical spirit that prevails: the Urban Room of 1929, the ultimate in smartness at the time, designed by the New York architect Joseph Urban who was best known for the Ziegfeld Theater. This Art Deco interior of maroon, black, and gold is now restored, though its painted decorations could not be brought back fully to their original state. The public rooms were sensitively redecorated in the late 1970s, and many of the guest suites have been enlarged to keep the hotel competitive with newer ones.

Landmarks plaque

Union Arcade (later, Union Trust Building; presently, Two Mellon Bank Center)
Grant Street and Fifth Avenue
Frederick J. Osterling, architect, 1915–17

All of Henry Clay Frick's building speculations in the Triangle were first-class, but here he was persuaded to build something not only solid but lyrical. Though he was just moving into his New York mansion, a very polished work by New York architects, he chose the Pittsburgher who had remodeled his East End house "Clayton" two decades before to construct this new work. Osterling, in his turn, consulted Pierre A. Liesch, a native of Luxembourg, on the general design. Liesch suggested the building substantially as it is, but Osterling carried the scheme to Frick with the roof eliminated. Frick, in turn, went to his interior decorator Charles Allom and his art consultant Joseph Duveen, both eminent men, who said that the building would be even better with a prominent roof. Liesch was no longer working for the office, but Osterling supervised the working-out of the details of the design with a lightness of touch quite unusual for him.

The style is Flemish Gothic of the period around 1500, its ornament executed primarily in stone-colored and white terra cotta. There was probably inspiration from the similar Gothic of the Woolworth Building in New York, then the tallest building in the world. The relatively low skyline and the delicate lines disguise the fact that this is a spacious building, and a tough one. Inside was space for 240 shops, facing two four-story open arcade spaces, and about 700 offices. The office floors were built with a strength remarkable today, intended for loads of at least 150 pounds per square foot since tenants were apt to bring in massive iron safes and locate them as they pleased.

The tall arcade spaces were floored in in 1923, when the Union Trust Company remodeled the building, and some of the openings into the great central well, 10 stories high, were blocked. Otherwise, though, the building has been treated with great respect. Four street entrances, now as originally, meet at this dramatic central space beneath a stained-glass dome. Semi-gloss white terra-cotta walls line the public spaces instead of Pittsburgh's habitual white marble, but gorgeous bronze fixtures still play off against their more neutral surfaces. Above the entrances are windows of leaded glass with colored inserts, and the vestibules are covered with vaults of colored mosaic.

At the time of writing the building is under partial restoration. The arcade spaces will not be reopened, and four interior courts are being filled with floor and mechanical space, but old decorative work, inside and out, is being replaced. When the work is done, the Union Arcade will have a brightness and freshness of effect.

National Register; Landmarks plaque

A penthouse.

The central court, with its stained-glass dome.

Frick Building
Grant Street and Fifth Avenue
D. H. Burnham & Co. (Chicago), architects,
1901–02

Henry Clay Frick made a number of major real-estate investments that resulted in construction of a close-set group of buildings in the Grant Street area: the Frick Building, Frick Annex, Union Arcade, and the first part of the William Penn Hotel. In the Frick Building, the earliest of these, he created a personal monument and the location of his own office.

The tall new building that was finished in 1902 put an end to the 14-year dominance of the Pittsburgh skyline by the Courthouse directly across the street. It also occasioned the removal of St. Peter's Episcopal Church, stone by stone, to its present site in Oakland. The steelwork and sturdy granite facing, hauled to the site by horse and wagon, rose with remarkable speed to reveal a simplicity of skyscraper design quite unusual in Pittsburgh. Inside, its corridors of simple white marble with ornate bronze fittings were once again a little severe for the early 1900s, though certainly no one could call them meager, and two lions by Alexander Phimister Proctor and John La Farge's windows *Fortune on Her Wheel* — Dame Fortune as a unicyclist — gave these spaces a special distinction. To these was added a memorial bust by Malvina Hoffman after Frick's death. When the Grant's Hill Hump was lowered between 1911 and 1913 the already spacious ground-floor lobby and corridor system was made even more so by lowering it to give an entire story of extra height.

When built, the Frick Building had several peculiarities that are now gone: hydraulic elevator machinery and a generating plant in the basement, washrooms for the whole building

on the tenth floor, and the very spacious rooms of the Union Club on the twenty-first floor. One reminder of the past survives in the main corridor in four bronze telephone booths with an operator's space between each pair; in this corridor there were once three telegraph offices as well.

National Register; Landmarks plaque

Allegheny County Courthouse and Jail (the County Buildings)
Courthouse, Grant Street and Fifth Avenue;
Jail, Ross Street and Fifth Avenue
Henry Hobson Richardson (Brookline, Mass.),
architect, 1884–88; Frederick J. Osterling, architect
for Jail alterations, 1904; Stanley L. Roush, architect for Courthouse entry alterations, 1928

The "County Buildings" that H. H. Richardson started in 1884 but never lived to see completed are the county's only architectural works of international fame. The Jail especially will have a place in any comprehensive history of Modern architecture. Richardson's designs were chosen over those of his competitors because of the lucidity of his planning, but architects and architecture-lovers have found much else to admire according to their personal preferences. The Modernists admire the undecorated arches of the Jail and the Courthouse courtyard and the apparently simple but actually subtle walls of the Jail, with their tapered surfaces and their use of smaller stones over larger ones to convey a sense of mass. The Eclectics admired these things too, but also the masonry textures, the carving, the mountainous roofs, and the towers, dominated by the great tower — slender yet strong, solid when seen from some angles, diaphanous when seen from others — that was once the most prominent object in the city.

Richardson might have been indifferent, amused, or mildly annoyed at attempts to conscript him as a Modernist. His schooling at the Parisian Ecole des Beaux-Arts had trained him to think clearly about an architectural problem, and he was certainly concerned to eliminate inefficiencies of plan and fussy detailing. Yet he was no tidy-minded utilitarian, opposed to ornament. The Courthouse tower is one big ornament, despite its rationalization as an air-conditioning intake; he had been designing towers for a decade and a half, and this was the biggest and most refined of all, one of the world's great towers. The Italian Romanesque lions by the Grant Street doorways are attributed to no sculptor but are splendid pieces, and the guiding spirit in their carving may well have been Richardson's. The carved leaf ornament of the Courthouse, inside and out, has a crispness yet a

167

Grant Street entrances to the Courthouse.

The Jail with the Bridge of Sighs to the Courthouse on the left.

lushness that is in harmony with both the rugged granite of the exterior and the interior's fine-grained limestone. The Courthouse main stair is a set of variations on the theme of the arch, with arches in massive repose, arches leaping, and arches lightly skipping from one slender shaft to another. The "Bridge of Sighs" over Ross Street between the Courthouse and Jail is itself a very dramatic use of the arch.

At times both the Courthouse and the Jail have been threatened, but their most visible features have always been ardently defended and alterations have been mild. The lowering of the Hump in 1913 and the widening of Grant Street in 1927 forced the lengthening-downward of the Courthouse entrances; in the case of the Grant Street entrances the County Architect Stanley L. Roush designed inoffensive new doorways with ironwork by Samuel Yellin, leading to a basement vestibule-and-stair system covered by Guastavino tile vaulting. In the 1900s Frederick J. Osterling was commissioned to expand the Jail and copied Richardson's wall system meticulously while adding a round tower at Fifth and Ross in something of the original spirit.

In the Courthouse courtyard, long a parking lot, there is now a park with trees, shrubs, and benches, very popular in the summer. This came into being as a joint project of the County and the Pittsburgh History & Landmarks Foundation, with the aid of a grant from the Sarah Scaife Foundation.

National Historic Landmark; National Register; Landmarks plaque

168

City-County Building
Grant Street and Forbes Avenue
Edward B. Lee, with Palmer, Hornbostel & Jones, architects, 1915–17

There was a trend, early in the twentieth century, toward making public administrative buildings look somewhat like ordinary business buildings. The sheer growth of public services may have imposed an architecture of little windows, and perhaps there was as well an official desire to hint that public affairs were being handled in a businesslike manner. Yet a certain monumentality had to survive when the towers, pavilions, and mountainous roofs of the older public architecture were swept away. At the City-County Building, too, the greatly respected Courthouse was to be a neighbor. The architects designed a big Classical box, recalling neither the massing nor the style of the Courthouse. Yet they repeated its Grant and Ross Street portal scheme, three at one end, one at the other, on a colossal scale, and used gray granite again, albeit in a smooth not a rugged form.

Inside, as at the Courthouse, was a light court, but through it the architects put an airy Classical corridor of great windows and bronze columns, a composition more light and charming than the frowning exterior allows you to guess.

The Grant Street archways under the allegorical sculptures of Charles Keck open from a vast vaulted porch, whose space, surprisingly, is exhilarating, not oppressive. The building's glum exterior, in fact, is totally misleading. The whole place shows an attempt to reconcile a modern nononsense attitude with Classical dignity, to play off episodes of lavish ornament like the sculptured elevator doors and subtleties such as contrasts of matte and polished granite against a prevailing rational simplicity. This is a sort of Modernism, but one, you might say, that has conversation, not the mute thing we have had to get used to in the last few decades.

Landmarks plaque

the early 1980s, the old sash was replaced with single panes of reflective glass, so that the void-solid relationship was changed. Once, under the setting sun, the brickwork had a bronzy glow when seen from afar; now it is the windows that gleam. The most flamboyant feature of the early days survives, however: a neon-covered beacon tower that spells out **P-I-T-T-S-B-U-R-G-H** in Morse. Like the Empire State Building's dirigible mast, this had pretensions to usefulness in the developing technology of aviation; and it may be that, in the days before radio navigation, it really did help aviators to tell where they were.

The original lobby is gone, but a Post-Modern renovation of the mid-1980s has created an honorable substitute in an interior of pink and cream marble, set in panels in a way that has a Classical feeling.

Grant Building
Grant Street and Fourth Avenue
Henry Hornbostel and Eric Fisher Wood, architects, 1927–30

The Grant Building, as we see it today, has undergone several modifications. Hornbostel's initial Beaux-Arts treatment was first simplified into a trendy but quiet Modernistic, executed in bronze-colored brick and buff-colored cast stone over a base of dark Swedish granite. Later, pinnacles that rose above the stepped-back parapets were cut off short. In

County Office Building
Forbes Avenue and Ross Street
Stanley L. Roush, architect, 1929–31

Roush, the County Architect who had recently acquitted himself well in altering the Courthouse entrances, had here the problem of adding a new neighbor to the Courthouse and Jail, directly across the street from the City-County Building. What we see is the first phase of a building campaign for a structure nine stories taller. Outside, a Romanesque arcade with polished granite columns on the two more conspicuous fronts opens up the limestone wall; above, the same heavy and conservative Modernistic found on the contemporary Gulf Building takes over. Inside, in the public corridor off Forbes Avenue, antiquity as seen through the lens of 1920s Hollywood prevails: the dark stone walls, the groin vaults, and the ironwork call for a parade of halberdiers or adventurers crossing swords, not engineers going to their offices or property owners on their way to dispute assessments.

Allegheny County Mortuary
604 Fourth Avenue
Frederick J. Osterling, architect, 1901–03; moved,
1928

Here are H. H. Richardson's County Buildings in lugubriously amusing caricature, by the architect who on the one hand enlarged the Jail with faithful adherence to Richardson's detailing and materials and on the other proposed to heighten the Courthouse, very awkwardly, by two stories. The dormers imitate those of the Courthouse. The rear tower imitates that over the Jail end of the Bridge of Sighs. And the entrance portal is copied from the rear entrance of the Courthouse, the impost blocks included. The little monsters carved on these last are at least quite appropriate in this place; they seem to say, with Poe, "That the play is the tragedy, 'Man,' And its hero, the conqueror Worm."

Jones & Laughlin Building (presently, John Robin Civic Building)
200 Ross Street
MacClure & Spahr, architects, 1907

This Tudor Gothic office building was built as the headquarters of a steel company. It seems almost penitential of J&L to have raised a building faced in sandstone and highly textured brick that the smoke from its plant, two miles away, would quickly help to darken. Now cleaned, the rich medium red of the brick makes a beautiful appearance in its contrast with the pale-brown sandstone trim.

The Jones & Laughlin Steel Corporation traces its origins back to 1852 and the Jones & Lauth ironworks, and in the year of this building's construction had a plant that extended down the Monongahela on both sides. On the north side of the river, it went for two-and-a-half miles from the Eliza furnaces at the foot of Oakland to the coke ovens at Hazelwood. Ann furnace, one of the Eliza group, was the last blast furnace to operate in Pittsburgh. When it shut down in 1979, it ended 120 years of iron smelting in the city.

Memorial Columns, Boulevard of the Allies
Boulevard of the Allies and Grant Street
Frank Vittor, sculptor, 1921–22

The downtown conversion of Second Avenue into the Boulevard of the Allies did not create a grand avenue; the street was merely widened northward, and the results even today suggest the aftermath of a street widening: one side old and haphazard, the other side of a single later period but otherwise with nothing much in common among its components. At Grant Street, though, where the Boulevard rises to go along the side of the Bluff, a statement of its memorial function was inserted in the exiguous spaces at the edges of the ramp. Twin Doric columns of granite rise from pedestals carved with Liberty heads, patriotic symbols, and dedicatory inscriptions. Above, American eagles clutch globes. A row of iron bollards leads away from each column. The columns, hardly noticed from speeding cars, are scrutable to pedestrians only at the cost of a certain amount of mortal danger.

Liberty Bridge
Monongahela River between the Boulevard of the Allies and the Liberty Tunnels
George S. Richardson of the Allegheny County Department of Public Works, engineer, 1926–28

The Liberty Bridge, a direct automobile link between town and the new Liberty Tubes, was as useful in opening parts of the South Hills to development as the trolley tunnel to South Hills Junction had been two decades before. The bridge had been sought by motorists for two decades, and opening day was celebrated with a mile-long procession of cars.

The 450-foot main spans suggest arches, but this is a deception. This is in fact a rather complicated cantilever bridge. Its main portion rests on three piers, and in the pre-computer days when it was designed, calculation of the possible forces acting on a continuous bridge truss with more than two supports was practically impossible. The continuity therefore was deliberately broken up into two cantilever structures, each calculable, and a "suspended span," an ordinary truss, was hinged to cantilever arms extending into the northern main span from both structures. In 1982 the deck and ornamental parts of the bridge were reconstructed, so that the bridge has not quite its original appearance.

Panhandle Division Bridge, Pennsylvania Railroad
Monongahela River west of Liberty Bridge
1903

Two camelback Pratt trusses and one Pennsylvania truss of 351-foot span once served to bring Pennsylvania Railroad trains from the south shore of the Monongahela into town. The trains went underground at Forbes Avenue, following the approximate route of the old Pennsylvania Canal, and saw daylight again just before reaching Union Station. The

bridge is now used by the Light Rail Transit line from the South Hills; one branch of this follows the old rail route all the way and ends by the East Busway at Union Station.

The bridge marks the approximate location of the mouth of Suke's Run in Pipetown, the area where some of the earliest Western River steamers were built and where the Pennsylvania Canal emerged from its tunnel under Grant's Hill.

Old Allegheny and the new North Side — in all its density and diversity — from Perry Hilltop.

OLD ALLEGHENY

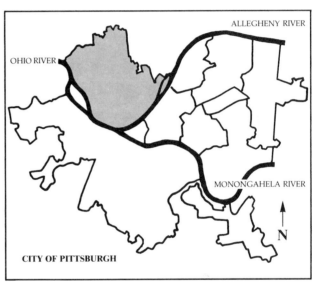

ALLEGHENY RIVER

OHIO RIVER

MONONGAHELA RIVER

N

CITY OF PITTSBURGH

Directly across the Allegheny River from the Triangle lies Pittsburgh's North Side, which until annexation in 1907 was the independent city of Allegheny. The original Allegheny Town had been surveyed by David Redick in 1788 as a square of blocks and streets a third of a mile on a side, surrounded by grazing commons that were themselves surrounded by "out-lots" for agriculture. Allegheny Town was to be the seat of the new Allegheny County, created in 1788, but since the town existed for many years only as a plan, Pittsburgh became at first the temporary, then the permanent, county seat. Thus began more than a century of inter-city rivalry.

It was only around 1810, when the Indian menace was long past, that industry and a sizeable residential population moved north of the Triangle. After this, development was rapid. The first bridge to Allegheny opened in 1819. The Pennsylvania Canal made Allegheny a terminus in 1829, as did the Ohio & Pennsylvania Railroad in 1851. In 1867 the Commons, muddy and unused, were laid out as a handsome Victorian park. In 1889, H. J. Heinz moved his plant down

Decorative woodwork, a North Side specialty.

the river from Sharpsburg to Allegheny, strengthening an economic base that was already well-founded.

The original town soon became too small, and the out-lots were developed, parcel by parcel, with houses. Neighborhoods, each with its own distinct character, ringed the perimeter of the Commons and gradually climbed the steep hillsides to the north. The Anglo-Saxons tended to stay in the old Allegheny Town within the Commons, but the Germans settled to the east in Dutchtown on the plain and on Troy Hill further east still, and the Irish and Scotch-Irish settled west of the Commons. They lived in homes that ranged from back-alley houses in Dutchtown to grandiose mansions on Ridge Avenue. It is apparent that many of them lived quite comfortably because their neighborhoods became rich displays of Victorian residential architecture. Dutchtown and the Mexican War Streets were developed with collections of large houses facing the Commons and interesting but more modest, close-set housing behind. The streets of Allegheny West were lined with substantial houses to the north of the Ridge Avenue mansions. Manchester, laid out in 1832, merged with Allegheny in 1867 and developed as a solid bourgeois neighborhood with architectural fantasies in red brick. Perry Hilltop and Fineview, high above the river plain, acquired Romantic villas and expansive views.

More modest houses clustered on other hilltops and hillsides, reached by inclines and public stairs, or were strung along narrow valleys. Annexations of new neighborhoods quadrupled the area of Redick's original survey, out-lots included, prior to 1873, and Allegheny's population passed 100,000 by the turn of the century.

The new century, however, saw Allegheny's own annexation in 1907 and subsequent decline. There was still a distinct sense of the new North Side as a separate place; its crossroads of Ohio and Federal Streets retained very much the look of a town center with a towered Carnegie Library, a City Hall that was eventually replaced by the Buhl Planetarium, a Post Office, a market hall, a park, and the respected Boggs & Buhl department store. Yet the North Side, as the years passed, took on the air of a respectable lady alone with memories in a dusty parlor, or latterly, even, of an old pensioner sitting exhausted on an unkempt front porch. In the 1930s, Luke Swank photographed the North Side and revealed poetry in century-old houses and streets on hazy mornings, but a North Side survey of 1951 found no romance in housing that was 41 percent slum and six-tenths of a percent fully satisfactory.

Conventional urban renewal was the planners' obvious answer, sweeping and theoretically humane. Almost everything north of the Commons was to go, to be replaced by garden apartments of uniform design. The original Allegheny Town was to be stripped of all existing housing, as well as the Post Office and market hall, and a shopping mall and new housing were to be built. Much of Manchester and most of the river shore area were to be cleared; so was the East Street Valley, which was to contain an expressway.

Some of these plans have been realized, some not. The old crossroads is now merely an intersection of walkways. The market hall and Boggs & Buhl are gone. The shopping mall and apartment and business slabs dominate the former Allegheny Town. The shore area is largely cleared and partially redeveloped, and the East Street houses are gone as construction finally begins on the planned expressway.

On the other hand, the Post Office has been a museum since 1971, and for 13 years was the home of the Pittsburgh History & Landmarks Foundation, which saved it. Landmarks, neighborhood organizations, and private citizens have worked to rehabilitate large portions of the Mexican War Streets, Manchester, Allegheny West, and Dutchtown. Other neighborhoods are displaying renewed pride and revitalization. Today, the big, heterogeneous North Side is in some quarters a place of emptiness, decay, and impersonal architecture. But it is also a place of charm and warmth with Victorian streets returned or returning to their old well-being. ■

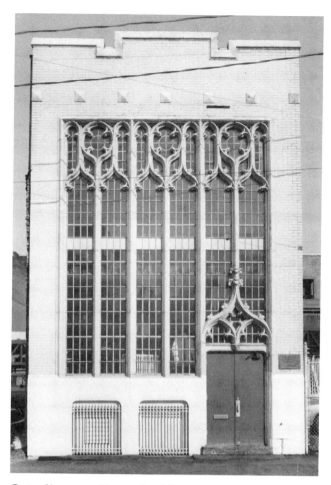

Warehouse
Sandusky and Isabella Streets, North Shore
C. 1900, 1910

This warehouse, now adapted for use as an office and retail building, is actually the product of two building campaigns and two technologies. One side is heavy masonry and timber; the other, steel frame of a later date. The in-and-out surface of rock-faced rusticated stonework on the ground floor is uncommon and quite effective. The bold corbeled cornice suggests machicolations, which allowed defenders of medieval fortifications to drop rocks and other deadly objects on besiegers. The general appearance is one of impressive strength, suitable to a warehouse.

Osterling studio and office
228 Isabella Street, North Shore
Frederick J. Osterling, architect for facade, 1917

Osterling's father had owned the original Victorian building on this site and an adjacent area on which he had a lumber yard. Osterling's reconstruction of 1917 for his own offices included this facade, whose light Gothic detailing recalled his recent triumph, the Union Arcade downtown.

In the main, the facade has a strength and decisiveness, together with a lightness not usually associated with Osterling's work. The great window, which includes a doorway, is divided into three compartments, defined by mullions that rise sheer to the molding that frames the whole opening. The first impression is Venetian but the tracery itself is more French, with its ogee curves for the door head and the heads of the main window compartments. The parapet, with its battlemented silhouette, is a fairly common feature of the early twentieth century, a device for masking an uninteresting flat roof and giving an interesting skyline. The original doors, too, must have been decorative.

Architects of this time usually rented their personal working space, or incorporated space for themselves into larger commissions. An independent building housing an architect's studio and office and built to his design is a rarity.

Frick & Lindsay Building (presently, Volkwein Building)
Sandusky and General Robinson Streets, North Shore
C. 1913

Faced for its entire height in cream-colored terra cotta, Volkwein's displays a cheerful, charming style that is partly Beaux-Arts, partly one of those improvised Modern manners

175

that architects used on commercial and industrial work around 1910. Insofar as there is a philosophy in such a way of designing, it recalls the attitude of the Queen Anne period: anything is all right if it looks good. Here the architect accepted the discipline of a steel frame and the need for big, broad windows, and applied his decoration to good effect. The absence of the original cornice may actually improve the silhouette.

Volkwein's, a well-known Pittsburgh music store, has occupied the building since the mid-1960s. Previously it belonged to the Frick & Lindsay Company, dealers in machinery. Despite the rather delicate exterior, this is a very strong structure.

St. Peter's Church (Roman Catholic)
West Ohio Street and Arch Street,
Allegheny Center
Andrew Peebles, architect, 1872–74

With its large, intricately traceried windows, St. Peter's presents an impressive front to a major avenue of the former city of Allegheny. This was even more the case when a tall spire rose above the gables of the tower. For the 1870s, and for Catholic churches especially, this was in fact a very polished design. The side walls, high because there is no clerestory, suggest a Protestant meeting-house plan, however, rather than that of a Catholic church. Following a fire, some reconstruction work occurred in 1886-88. Behind the chancel is a picturesque rectory of 1876, unfortunately with some of its ornamental work cut away.

Landmarks plaque

Allegheny Post Office (later, the Old Post Office Museum; presently, the Pittsburgh Children's Museum)
Allegheny Square, Allegheny Center
William Martin Aiken of the U.S. Treasury Department (Washington, D.C.), architect, 1894–97

This was once the central Post Office of an independent city, one of the buildings that gave a monumental character to its major crossroads. Yet unlike many later buildings of government, its formality of character was kept within the human scale. Its arched windows are ample but not yawning voids, and its Early Italian Renaissance wall treatment is delicate and crisply cut in pale-gray granite, evincing not the slightest intention of overwhelming the public for whose use it was intended. It was designed, obviously, to maintain the dignity of government but without presenting government as a superhuman, alien power. The central domed space inside is surprisingly tall, mosque-like, a little overawing perhaps, but in Post Office days the public caught only glimpses of it through wickets in the wooden screen that restricted them to outer corridors.

It is curious to know that the plan was a standard one that could be clothed in other styles. At Clarksville, Tennessee, for instance, it is interpreted in French Renaissance, with a big chateau roof in place of the dome that looks so right in Pittsburgh.

In the late 1960s the Post Office was destined to disappear in the Allegheny Center urban-renewal clearance, but the Pittsburgh History & Landmarks Foundation, then only a half-decade old, was able to acquire it intact after a year-long struggle. The remodeling at the time included opening the central space to the public, installing a new stair and office mezzanine, and making other alterations in which artifacts saved from the nearby Henry W. Oliver mansion and other demolished Allegheny County structures were built into the construction. The remodeled building was returned to use in 1971 as a community museum and as offices for Landmarks itself.

In 1974 a garden court, designed by the Foundation, was opened. It has artifacts from demolished Pittsburgh buildings built into and set within its Belgian-block walls. Its proudest display is Charles Keck's portal sculptures of 1915 from the Manchester Bridge.

In 1983 the Pittsburgh Children's Museum opened in the lower gallery, and in 1985 it expanded its operation, leasing the entire building and grounds from the Pittsburgh History & Landmarks Foundation.

National Register; Landmarks plaque

Buhl Planetarium and Institute of Popular Science (presently, Buhl Science Center)
Allegheny Square, Allegheny Center
Ingham, Pratt & Boyd, architects, 1939

One of the most polished architectural firms in the city, especially good at Classical design, had here the task of creating a windowless building with institutional dignity at what was at the time a busy, noisy intersection. Science was the theme and the climactic feature was the round auditorium, where the ant-like Zeiss planetarium machine projected the stars on the dome above.

Outside, a sparing use of rustication and six pieces of sculpture by Sidney Waugh in the simplified, high-relief style favored in the 1930s mitigate the utter plainness of the basic shell. Around back, the taller, copper-domed octagon of the Planetarium varies the perimeter and skyline. Inside, a gorgeous application of various marbles to the walls creates a resonant public gallery, dominated by the silvery Foucault pendulum whose serene passes over a compass rose illustrate the rotation of the earth.

Henry Buhl, Jr. was an Allegheny merchant who entered a partnership with Russell Boggs in 1869. The Boggs & Buhl department store, which survived the conversion of Allegheny into the North Side and remained a Pittsburgh institution, in fact faced the Planetarium until its closure in 1958. The Buhl Foundation, founded at the time of Henry Buhl's death in 1928, advanced money for Chatham Village, funded the Western Pennsylvania Architectural Survey in the early 1930s, and gave the Planetarium to the City.

Allegheny Library (presently, Carnegie Library of Pittsburgh, Allegheny Regional Branch)
Allegheny Square, Allegheny Center
Smithmeyer & Pelz (Washington, D.C.), architects, 1888–89

This was the second Carnegie Library commissioned, finished a few months sooner than the one at Braddock. It was designed by the architects who had created the controversial plan for the Library of Congress shortly before. The Library interior is generally modernized now, and the adjacent Carnegie Hall, the auditorium where the evangelist Kathryn Kuhlman held services for many years, is now a theater. In general, despite rock-faced granite exteriors, the building has a rather thin effect. There are some excellent finials though: an urn on the Library tower, a lyre on the Carnegie Hall gable, and a splendid flourishing plant in copper on the Library's hip roof.

In front of the library Andrew Carnegie commissioned a monument, with Daniel Chester French as sculptor and Henry Bacon as architect, erected to a man to whom he felt a personal debt of gratitude. Colonel James Anderson, an iron manufacturer who died in 1861, had taken a friendly interest in the boys who worked in the offices and industrial plants, and who, like the young Carnegie, ran through the streets delivering messages. He opened his extensive private library to the ambitious ones — and Carnegie was definitely one of those — to allow them a chance at the knowledge they would need to succeed in life. In 1850 Anderson put his library on an institutional basis, making it the first public library in Allegheny, and eventually his collection went to the City.

Carnegie himself followed Anderson's example in a massive way. Beginning at Braddock and his native Scottish town of Dunfermline in 1888, he and the foundations he established donated 2,811 library buildings all over the world, especially where English was spoken, at a cost of 50 million dollars.

The Anderson Monument stood at the foot of the library tower, facing the very crossroads of Allegheny, from 1904 until the late 1960s. Anderson's bust looked out on the scene

177

814-16 Cedar Avenue

from a Grecian stela of granite; at his feet was seated a statue of a workman who has lain down his hammer and is reading. During urban renewal in the 1960s the monument was dispersed; Bacon's architecture was destroyed, Anderson moved inside the library, and the workman stayed outside. In the mid-1980s, a proposal to reconstruct the entire monument was under consideration.

National Register; Landmarks plaque

Commercial buildings and houses
Dutchtown

East of the Commons lies Dutchtown, the area where the German-speaking peoples settled, as newcomers arrived in Allegheny early in the nineteenth century and overflowed the original little Allegheny Town.

East Ohio Street, the Butler Turnpike of 1830, developed as the main commercial street of Dutchtown, with impressively decorated Victorian facades rising above the shopfronts two or three stories. Many of these remain, seldom cared for, a reproach to the visual chaos below. The lively perspective of these fronts is interrupted, though, by demolitions and especially by the clearances of the years around 1970 for the East Street Valley Expressway — as yet not built. The Hollander Building of 1888 at Number 413 is one of the most impressive of these commercial buildings, with a front in the Queen Anne style. The bricklayer has been hard at work here, showing his skill at paneling and corbeling, and

910 Cedar Avenue

using terra-cotta panels of leaf ornament here and there to offset the geometry of his own inventions. The building was purchased in 1985 by a neighborhood development consortium for restoration, with the aid of a loan from the Pittsburgh History & Landmarks Foundation.

The residential showplace of Dutchtown is Cedar Avenue, facing the East Common, especially the part north of East Ohio Street. As was the case with North Avenue, the view of a handsome park stimulated good residential construction in the Mid- and Late-Victorian periods. Numbers 814 and 816 stand out, partly because of their pointed roofs, terracotta decorative panels, and leaded glass, partly because they look a little alien to the Pittsburgh-area. The shallow projecting bays with chamfers are more characteristic of Washington, D.C.; might a Washington builder have supplied the design? Number 910 is odd too in another way,

Hollander Building (left)

with its emphatic lintels and lumps of carving that give it a big-boned look; these contrast with extremely thin moldings that pursue their own independent courses on the facade, while a split round arch and two wavy metal star medallions further the effect of brash individualism. A commercial building of about 1890 on Fifth Avenue in the Uptown area shows these same traits, suggesting that an interesting Pittsburgh architect is waiting to be discovered.

Avery, Lockhart, and Pressley Streets, narrow passages lined with good Late Victorian houses, comprise a rather quaint quarter of Dutchtown which is just beginning to experience rehabilitation activity.

National Register District

St. Mary's Church (Roman Catholic)
Pressley and Nash Streets, Dutchtown
Father John Stibiel, designer, 1853–54

The plain though harmonious exterior of this large church, which looks Neoclassical because of its semicircular windows, disguises the elaboration within. There, barrel vaults meet at a crossing dome 30 feet in diameter. The vaults themselves are supported on Corinthian columns crowned by entablatures of an unorthodox and so to speak homemade appearance. To these original details were added murals in 1882 by M. Lambart of New York, 12 Austrian stained-glass windows in 1912, and a three-manual Gottfried organ. An entrance vestibule was added c. 1900.

The towers were once topped by flamboyant onion domes that differed radically in mood from the placid masonry below to add a touch of Central European Baroque, and only the lunettes of the side windows were originally glazed, allegedly to prevent vandalism by anti-Catholic "Know-Nothings."

The adjoining Priory of 1888 is more restless than the church, built in a stone-and-brick medieval manner that owes something to Richardson Romanesque.

At the time of writing, the property is no longer used for church purposes. A developer hopes to use the church itself as a public hall; the existing decorative work is to be retained in place. The Priory is to become a small bed-and-breakfast hotel.

National Register District

Latimer School
Tripoli and James Streets, Dutchtown
Frederick C. Sauer, architect, 1898

This many-windowed school is built of yellow-gray brick and sandstone trim that has darkened in the Pittsburgh air. Its Tripoli Street entrance, with a tower above, is impressive, but more impressive still is the chimney that rises on the side: a square, solid tapering stack rising toward a deep ornamental termination, contrasting its solid mass against an open facade that by comparison looks delicate. There is a sort of

barbaric energy about the chimney as it breaks the symmetry of the composition that is oddly pleasing to see.

In early 1985 there was a plan to convert the school into apartments.

National Register District

Allegheny General Hospital
East North and Cedar Avenues, Central North Side
York & Sawyer (New York), architects, 1928–30

York & Sawyer were well known in the 1920s as bank and hospital specialists, and specialized as well in two styles, fifteenth-century Italian Renaissance and Italian Romanesque. The latter is used here in a suave composition typical of the architects. The facing is white brick, set off with granite colonettes that are red and gray alternately and terra-cotta cornices and capitals that are yellow, blue, and green. The gentle colors against the prevailing cold white are very effective.

The 17-story tower is the most conspicuous element of the North Side as seen from a distance, more so even than the vast but dark-hued Heinz plant. It terminates the northern end of Cedar Avenue and marks the northeast corner of the Commons in a way that makes it seem especially to belong.

Major hospital functions have been assumed by the modern building seen in the background, but the original structure remains in use housing clinics, offices, and a visitors' center with overnight facilities for patient families.

Engine Company Number Three
Arch and Jacksonia Streets, Central North Side
1877

The style of this red brick and sandstone firehouse is indeterminate though the banding of the arches has a medieval Italian air that is doubtless due indirectly to the propagandizing of John Ruskin, the British critic and social reformer of this same period who advocated Italian Gothic

as a style for the architecture of his own time. The overall composition, though, suggests the Italian Villa style, the tower — which once had an open cupola — being placed at the exact center of the front. This placement is unusual; most firehouses, whose towers are used for hanging hoses to dry, have them to one side.

It is to be hoped that the firehouse, unused at the time of writing, will be imaginatively adapted for new purposes.

Orphan Asylum of Pittsburgh and Allegheny (later, Allegheny Widows' Home)
306–22 North Taylor Avenue and 1319–27 Sherman Avenue, Mexican War Streets
John Chislett, architect, 1838; additions, c. 1873

The principal element of this institutional complex, three stories high, was built in 1838 to house the Orphan Asylum of Pittsburgh and Allegheny. The design, a very simple one in the Grecian Doric order, was donated to the charity by John Chislett, the English-born architect who had begun practice in Pittsburgh about five years before. The Asylum and Burke's Building in the Triangle are, as far as we know, the only extant works in the Greek Revival by Chislett, and this is one of his five extant works of any description.

Built for 30 orphans, the Asylum became overcrowded and was vacated in 1866, at which time the Allegheny Widows' Home Association moved in. In 1872, the City of Allegheny decided to extend Taylor Avenue through the Widows' Home property, a measure that obliged removal of part of the Asylum building. The City's compensation and the loss of floor space stimulated the Widows' Home to build simple row houses, of a Greek Revival character, along the adjacent streets and in the yard area behind.

In the early 1980s, the entire complex was rehabilitated and externally restored, and the row-house plans were revised to make the courtyard, not the street, the principal means of access.

National Register District

Houses
Mexican War Streets

Just north of the West Commons is a 27-acre area whose street names allude to places and people of the Mexican War. The war had just ended when the district, part of Allegheny's original out-lots, was laid out in 1848 by General William Robinson as the Buena Vista Extension.

In the next 50 years the land was very largely built up, houses and a few commercial establishments side by side with no front or side yards, and only occasionally with porches, in the streets behind the more spaciously sited houses that faced West North Avenue and the Commons. For the most part the houses were rather small and unpretentious, simple Italianate being quite typical as a style, though Gothic, Romanesque, and turn-of-the-century Classical were to be found as well.

1245-47 Monterey Street

Numbers 1245–47 Monterey Street, a residential block with a corner shop, is unusually large for a building in the Mexican War Streets. Its handsome but unassuming Italianate detailing of c. 1870 is shared by adjacent row houses. The contemporary Gothic treatment of 1213 Resaca Place, on the other hand, is unique. The front, which is now somewhat remodeled, has angular detailing and added decorative

1213 Resaca Place

1215-29 Buena Vista

features that distinguish it from the houses to either side, and of course the little dormer-plus-turret is a real bravura touch; yet like its neighbors, Number 1213 has regularly spaced sash windows and thus attests to the continuing strength of the Georgian building tradition as much as to a growing individualism in city house design. With 1215–29 Buena Vista Street we see attempts to impart more tone, a higher style, to a pair of builder's house rows. These houses of c. 1890 are in the fashionable Richardson Romanesque, their brick fronts veneered in rock-faced stone. Decorative parapets and carved porch capitals contribute to the air of sophistication the builders wished to give, while the porches themselves give a gracious appearance to the aloof stone

1201 Buena Vista Street

fronts. Number 1201, just down the street from these houses, is their contemporary but has pretensions to being a mansion, albeit a very thin mansion: indeed, it is a small-scaled counterpart of the long, narrow Darlington house on Brighton Road, four blocks away. Of the houses north of West North Avenue this is the most pretentious.

In the late 1960s, the Pittsburgh History & Landmarks Foundation defined and named the area the "Mexican War Streets," and launched a neighborhood restoration program that became the first in the nation to benefit a mixed-income, integrated neighborhood. The Mexican War Streets Society, an independent neighborhood organization, now continues the restoration program.

National Register District

Ridge Avenue
Allegheny West

Ridge Avenue was once a street of mansions. The process began at least as long ago as the 1850s; a Greek Revival house of that period survived here until the late 1960s. Italianate, Second Empire, Queen Anne, and Romanesque houses followed in the course of the nineteenth century, some packed close together, some freestanding though in rather restricted grounds. As the twentieth century began, the confidence in Ridge Avenue and its future seemed only to increase. The mining millionaire Henry W. Oliver, the iron-pipe manufacturer Alexander M. Byers, the steelmaker Benjamin F. Jones, Jr., and the ironmaker William P. Snyder built within a block of each other between 1891 and 1911.

The Snyder house of 1911 was the last one of any consequence. Soon, noted residents left Ridge Avenue's urbane but urban environment for country estates. Many of the houses they left behind were converted to business uses or began to deteriorate. In the late 1960s the south block front between Brighton Road and Galveston Avenue was razed for the building of the Community College of Allegheny County; the college also took over the Jones and the Byers-Lyon houses as well as the Western Theological Seminary's Memorial Hall. The remaining Ridge Avenue mansions recall the days when wealth and prestige made a home in Old Allegheny.

B. F. Jones, Jr. house (presently, Jones Hall, Community College of Allegheny County)
Ridge Avenue and Brighton Road, Allegheny West
Rutan & Russell, architects, c. 1908

This, one of the last of the great houses built by the industrial millionaires of Ridge Avenue, was also one of its biggest. It has 42 rooms within and an Elizabethan exterior composed of red brick and ochre terra cotta. The sheer bigness of the place is impressive, though the architects were obviously a little concerned about it. The outline of the main body of the house is softened by buttresses, and the upper windows of the central part are crowned by a heavily modeled frieze; both devices give horizontal emphases that mitigate the height of the construction. The wing is monotonous in its fenestration, but the parapet is bowed upward in three places to give variety.

The owner was a son of Benjamin Franklin Jones, partner and co-founder of the Jones & Laughlin Steel Company, who lived close by in a smaller but still ample Second Empire house.

B. F. Jones, Jr., like many residents of this wealthy area, had a summer estate in Sewickley Heights, about 12 miles away; "Fair Acres" lasted until 1964.

National Register District

Memorial Hall, Western Theological Seminary (presently, West Hall, Community College of Allegheny County)
809 Ridge Avenue, Allegheny West
Thomas Hannah, architect, 1911–12

Terra cotta makes a splashy display in this red-and-cream academic building, ending in a burst of glory on the entrance tower. It is amusing to see how the architect manipulated blocks in several standard sizes to give an effect of randomness to his quoins and window jambs, then absent-mindedly repeated his "random" combinations in adjoining windows. Inside is a peculiar essay in early concrete construction, a circular well surrounded by balconies: a forerunner in miniature of the one at the center of the Union Arcade downtown. The building was to be the central element of a new complex for the Western Theological Seminary, an institution that had been in the neighborhood since 1829. Only a little more than this one building was ever erected.

A fine Tudor-style library and free-standing Tudor tower were demolished in the late 1960s.

National Register District

William Penn Snyder house (presently, Babb, Incorporated)
Ridge and Galveston Avenues, Allegheny West
George S. Orth & Brother, architects, 1911; addition, 1948

An office with an extensive practice in homes for the wealthy was called upon to design what proved to be the last of the great Ridge Avenue houses. The exterior, with its Ionic order, was built in brownstone. Inside, the style was primarily Elizabethan though not completely so. The house had some curiosities of plan. In place of the old-fashioned porte-cochere that projected to shelter the ordinary mansion entrance, there was a motor entrance off Galveston Avenue that admitted cars into the house, then to a six-car garage or to an exit on-to the alley behind. From this motor entrance guests could walk to a mezzanine overlooking a basement ballroom. There was also a central vacuum-cleaning system, with inlets at convenient places in every room; this was a popular device early in the century until fears of explosive mixtures of air and lint caused its abandonment. The annex of 1948 was faced in the original stone and is not apparent.

William Penn Snyder was in the iron brokerage business, and was a partner with Henry W. Oliver in the development of iron mining in the Lake Superior area. He was also proprietor of the Shenango Furnace Company, makers of pig iron.

The Snyders lived in the house until 1920; then the family began to use "Wilpen Hall," their summer home in Sewickley Heights, the year around.

National Register District; Landmarks plaque

Byers-Lyon houses (presently, Byers Hall, Community College of Allegheny County)
901 Ridge Avenue, Allegheny West
Alden & Harlow, architects, 1898

This is in fact a double house, built for the wrought-iron and pipe manufacturer Alexander M. Byers, with a smaller adjoining unit for his daughter and her husband who was the banker J. Denniston Lyon. The style is Flemish Renaissance. The houses are arranged in an L, with cloister-like arcades on a small garden court, bordered with an iron fence and a very elaborate wrought-iron gateway.

National Register District

Chalfant house
915 Ridge Avenue, Allegheny West
C. 1900

Many well-to-do or rich Pittsburghers around 1900 built new houses such as this. The human parallel might be a serious, preoccupied man who dresses correctly for a social occasion without feeling social. The golden-brown Roman brick is a fine material, the porch in an unfluted Grecian Ionic order is very handsome, and the Federal-style ironwork above it is quite delicate. These and other individual features could have been elements of a forthcoming and even witty design. And yet this house is grave in effect as so many large Pittsburgh houses are; the local genius could make Georgian feel like Romanesque. But this is not to disparage the Chalfant house, which has character and invites the passer-by to speculate on the lives that were spent within its slightly brooding depths.

National Register District; Landmarks plaque

Houses
Allegheny West

Immediately north of Ridge Avenue is a small area called Allegheny West or Lincoln-Beech, a portion of the original Allegheny Town's western out-lots beyond the Commons. Western Avenue, which passes through the district, has long been the main street, containing today a mixture of domestic architecture from the latter half of the nineteenth century and commercial buildings from the twentieth. Lincoln and Beech Avenues, running parallel to Western, are much quieter streets, lacking its visual disorder and its pressure of traffic. Demolition as well as commercial development have impaired the integrity of the area — here a cornice gone or windows badly remodeled; there a vacant lot where a large house stood — but there is still character and plenty of good architecture in Allegheny West. This serves as a reminder that early in this century, if its houses were not so grand as those of Ridge Avenue, this was still a very substantial place to live.

Number 934 Western Avenue illustrates the oldest type of house found in the neighborhood: a house of about 1850 in which the new Italianate manner is treated, not in the usual rich and heavy way but with an attenuated lightness that still suggests the spareness and precision of Greek Revival design. The cottage at the rear of 827 Lincoln Avenue dates from 1878, and shows a matured Romanticism in its Gothic windows and its exterior woodwork, which the Victorians would have regarded as Swiss. Numbers 948–50 Beech Avenue were built in 1876 as a speculation or as a boarding house for employees by two partners in a paving company;

934 Western Avenue

each unit of the double house is individualized by a curved, Dutch-looking gable with a Gothic finial, and bright inset tiles add a little extra sparkle to the usual mixture of brick and sandstone. The 1890-period Romanesque front of 848 Beech Avenue, a refacing of a somewhat older house, is very individual in its false gable and especially in its great front arch, half-concealing a trio of windows and a doorway, set in a delicate wooden frame beyond a very shallow porch.

Of the grander houses of the area, two stand out. The Harry Darlington house of 1890 has only a narrow Romanesque front on Brighton Road, facing the West Common, but its Lincoln Avenue front, the side of the house, is very long and tall, showing the effort that the unknown architect had to make to accommodate on an awkward site all the spaces that such a mansion-sized house required. Number 930 Lincoln Avenue, surviving in a block otherwise almost vacant, belonged to a member of the Thaw family, whose wealth came mainly from railroading. The house, now divided into

948-50 Beech Avenue

848 Beech Avenue

827 Lincoln Avenue (rear)

business and residential quarters, was built in the last part of the nineteenth century, apparently in three separate campaigns.

On Beech Avenue is a plain, turn-of-the-century Classical house with literary associations; here the author Mary Roberts Rinehart lived between 1907 and 1911. The stair of this house is said to have been the original circular staircase that gave the name to one of her best-known novels. Another

Darlington house

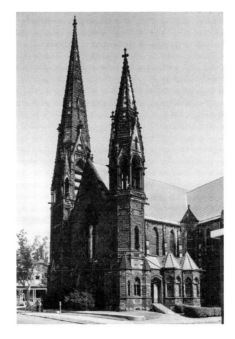

Thaw house

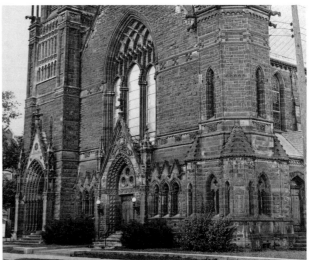

house of literary interest in Allegheny West is the Mid-Victorian Italianate one at 850 Beech Avenue; here, Gertrude Stein — a figure never associated in the public mind with Pittsburgh — was born in 1874. Her family left the area almost at once.

Number 841 Lincoln Avenue was bought by the Pittsburgh History & Landmarks Foundation in 1977, and the Junior League of Pittsburgh restored the house as an example of what could be done in the Allegheny West area. Landmarks still owns the house, which serves as a residence for the Pittsburgh Public Theater traveling personnel.

National Register District

Calvary Methodist Church
Allegheny and Beech Avenues, Allegheny West
Vrydaugh & Shepherd (Kansas City), with T. B. Wolfe, architects, 1893–95

For a Protestant church of the early 1890s, this is unusual both in the elaborateness of its architecture and in being designed in Gothic, not the fashionable Romanesque. It had a wealthy congregation however, and one that desired to build grandly. Therefore, the congregation paid for two spires, much carving that includes gargoyles, windows by Louis Comfort Tiffany — three large ones that were exhibited at the World's Columbian Exposition of 1893 before installation — and woodwork, brasswork, and mosaics befitting the impressive interior. The church, whose spire is conspicuous in distant views of this part of the North Side, makes a dramatic termination to a quiet domestic block of Beech Avenue.

Calvary Methodist's congregation had just come to Allegheny in 1891, after their old church in the Triangle, Christ Methodist, had burned. Another part of the congregation went to the East End, where they built a new Christ Methodist — now First Methodist — Church at Baum Boulevard and Aiken Avenue.

National Register District; Landmarks plaque

185

Emmanuel Episcopal Church
West North and Allegheny Avenues, Allegheny West
Henry Hobson Richardson (Brookline, Mass.), architect, 1885–86

Richardson was commissioned to design Emmanuel Church in 1883 or 1884 but it was only in 1885, after rejection of a more expensive design intended for stone and with a central tower, that his plans were approved and put into execution. Such ornamentation as the building has comes mainly from the treatment of the brickwork. The entrance arches are laid in five rings, with a narrower outer ring: a very conventional way of building an arch in brick. Above these, to the sill level of the upper windows, the bricks are laid in a basket-weave pattern. Other levels in the wall are marked by soldier courses, laid with the bricks on end, and the gable coping is formed by tumbled work, with bricks perpendicular to the gable slope and making tooth-like indentations into the main gable area. At the top is a rounded capstone. And that is all. (Unimpressed by its simplicity, neighbors called Emmanuel the Bake Oven Church.) On the sides, the lower walls slope inward toward sill level, and the sills themselves are connected by a soldier course. This handling of the brickwork, along with a very small amount of rock-faced stone trim, is what really carries the architectural message without. It is the materials and their perceptible solidity that count. The outward flare of the side and apse walls above

window-sill level is not, however, a subtlety of design, as one might expect; Richardson simply underestimated the thrust of the laminated wooden arches that support the roof.

The interior is rather dark beneath the low-set, varnished wooden roof, and was quite simple as built. There is however a marble and mosaic reredos of 1898, designed by Leake & Green. This has its own beauty but seems a little luxurious for such a primitive interior. The three front gable windows are by Tiffany.

National Register District; Landmarks plaque

West End Bridge
Ohio River, between Western Avenue and West Carson Street at Saw Mill Run Boulevard
George S. Richardson of the Allegheny County Department of Public Works, engineer, 1931

One of the handsomest bridges in a county that has perhaps two thousand, and an innovative design for its time. Technically, this is a tied-arch bridge, the 780-foot arch from which the deck is suspended being anchored by ties that run beneath the deck. The trusswork in the arch itself is to keep it from distortion under off-center loads. The cable hangers from the arch were put under tension before the deck was built: one of the first uses of prestressing in the United States. It is best seen from Point State Park, or from the western end of Mount Washington, where the great rise of its arch appears most dramatically.

National Register

Houses
Manchester

After its 1867 annexation by Allegheny, Manchester developed in most of its area as a solid, comfortable residential neighborhood of red brick houses with stone trim and wooden porches, set on an orderly grid of streets laid over an old flood plain, with industry near the Ohio River Shore. Some houses, along West North and Pennsylvania Avenues especially, were detached and villa-like, but many were double houses, uniform row houses, or houses set directly side by side: configurations made possible by the unusual flatness of the land.

1220 West North Avenue

1414 Pennsylvania Avenue

Of the detached houses 1220 West North Avenue is a pleasant late example, with a date somewhere around 1890: a work in what is usually called the Shingle Style, though brick is as much in evidence here as shingles. The very high roof and prominent chimneys symbolize shelter, while the polygonal dormer and tower-like bay window next to it dramatize the view outward from the shelter and add strong sculptural elements. In the round bay window, even the stone transoms and the window panes are curved so as to be in harmony with the basic cylindrical form. Twenty years or more earlier is 1414 Pennsylvania Avenue, a typical Italian villa with front, tower, and side wing set in an echelon pattern and an ample verandah facing the street.

1203-05 West North Avenue

1220-22 Sheffield Street

1203–05 West North Avenue and 1220–22 Sheffield Street illustrate the double houses. Both are from about 1880, and reveal the Late Victorian tendency to give each house individuality in spite of a uniform design, in one case with sharp gabled dormers against a false mansard roof, in the other with miniature hipped roofs rising above the roofline; the Sheffield Street houses are quite unusual in their window canopies, a carryover from the Italian Villa mode that was then obsolete. 1324–26 Sheffield Street are not so much double houses as the first two elements of a house row that was never completed; the stonework of the right-hand house awaits the stonework of an adjoining entrance. The projecting window bays and the false half-timbering in the gables have a British look; houses of very similar appearance were going up in English cities for respectable tradesmen around this same time, the 1880s and 1890s.

The Langenheim house at 1315 Liverpool Street is large, showy, and freestanding though closely surrounded by other buildings: a small city mansion, in fact. Landmarks acquired the house in 1967, at the request of the area residents, when it was in a miserable state of disrepair, and held it for over a decade until a buyer was found who would restore its exterior and adapt its interior for apartments. The original owner was a wholesale grocer, Gustav Langenheim, who may have entrusted its design to his son-in-law Alfred Schwerd, an architect, builder, and manufacturer of architectural woodwork.

Beginning in 1966, the Pittsburgh History & Landmarks Foundation worked with neighborhood residents to create

1324-26 Sheffield Street

Langenheim house

the first historic preservation district in the nation primarily for blacks; the first federally funded historic district program administered by community residents; the first preservation program using Title I urban-renewal funds for the restoration of houses for low- to moderate-income residents; and a series of incentive programs designed to combat displacement and encourage long-time residents to stay and become part of the revitalized community. The Manchester Citizens Corporation now continues the neighborhood restoration effort.

National Register District

Houses
1300 block of Liverpool Street, Manchester
C. 1880 and after

It was the sad spectacle that this block presented in the early 1960s that led to the idea of a preservation organization for Allegheny County, and it is largely because of Landmarks' efforts that the block is generally in good condition today, an outstanding element in a historic neighborhood. The north side of the block is occupied by nine identical double houses in the Second Empire style, all with delicately detailed wooden entrance porches. These, which form the most impressive house row in Pittsburgh, were built in successive campaigns that began some time before 1882.

Across the street the west end begins with a solid five-unit row whose masonry detailing is similar though not identical to that of the houses opposite. Two pairs of houses share very showy wooden porches with arched motifs, spindles, Romanesque capitals, and intricate cast-iron crestings, the dry Mid-Victorian manner of the porches on the north side of the street abandoned. Further east, sobriety sets in; a tame and rather thin Classicism appears in all subsequent porches of the development.

After this comes greater variety: the Romanesque Stifel house of 1885 by Charles M. Bartberger, outwardly picturesque and housing elaborate decorative glass and woodwork; the Langenheim house in a bold if indeterminate style; a little more Second Empire; and a Romanesque house row, stonefronted, boldly gabled, and with continuous front porches. Together both sides of the 1300 block of Liverpool Street form a picture of Victorian middle-class respectability and comfort.

National Register District

Union Methodist Church (presently, New Zion Baptist Church)
Manhattan Street and Pennsylvania Avenue, Manchester
Barr & Moser, architects, 1866–67

Brick is used in a very simple way to create a church of formal dignity. The result could be a clubhouse or a public hall at least as readily as a place of worship but the design is a very handsome one. Only the three curved false gables represent a step too far, impairing the clarity of the design. Inside, the church space is decorated in pressed tin as a result of a remodeling early in the century.

National Register District; Landmarks plaque

Western State Penitentiary (presently, State Correctional Institution)
Doerr Street at the Ohio River, Woods Run
E. M. Butz, architect, 1876–82

A glance at the main cell blocks suggests a local imitation of the architecture of H. H. Richardson, and at one time the suggestion was all the stronger, for until the 1970s the roofline was varied at points with steep hip roofs that had dormers with round-arched windows and little spiky turrets. Richardson, however, was not an influential architect locally when the Penitentiary was under design, and what we see here in fact is a work of Mid-Victorian engineering masonry, faced with stone and ornamented on its publicly visible fronts to do credit to the State. The Warden's House facing the river is in that elaborately picturesque but angular manner of the early 1870s that was to become more supple and integrated as the decade progressed and evolve into the Shingle Style and its masonry equivalent.

Allegheny Observatory
159 Riverview Drive, Perry Hilltop
Thorsten E. Billquist, architect; John Alfred Brashear and James E. Keller, consultants; 1900

Built in light-colored brick and terra cotta, this observatory is clad in a mixed Classical style that includes Greek Ionic columns and distinctively Roman balustrades. Such mixtures could be found in Greece itself in these years, since well-intentioned architects there were attempting to establish the national identity through revival of the ancient architecture; yet they had a nineteenth-century urge to embellish basically Greek designs with features from the Latin world. In Pittsburgh, a sort of return of the Greek Revival took place around 1900; executed in grayish brick and terra cotta, it appeared in several schools and libraries as well as here. Quiet, serious, just a trifle florid at times, it may have been regarded as a specifically intellectual style.

The three domes were built to house two of the old-fashioned refracting telescopes, giant spyglasses of 1860 and 1912 using lenses only, and a reflecting telescope of 1905. The support of this last is a columbarium, housing the ashes of John Brashear and his wife, and of James E. Keller, a former director, and his son. Brashear, a well-known local figure who died in 1920, was an astronomer and maker of scientific instruments who did all the construction and repair work for the Observatory's equipment. His reputation as an astronomer and teacher was such that in 1915 he was officially named "the state's most distinguished man."

National Register; Landmarks plaque

House
1801 Clayton Avenue, Perry Hilltop
C. 1885

This is a house built to see from and to be seen, with its porches and bay windows and its steep tower roof. The siding is unique in the Pittsburgh area: wood grooved to imitate rusticated ashlar. The house commands a view of the Allegheny and Ohio Rivers.

"Heathside Cottage"
Catoma and Myler Streets, Fineview
C. 1860

This kind of outright Gothic Revival is rare in Allegheny County today, and it is quite rare to find it with its vergeboard and other sawn-out wooden trim still present and diamond-paned sash still in the windows. This is an Early Victorian design in spirit rather than a Mid-Victorian one, emphasizing delicacy rather than dignified massiveness, and is very much a borrowing from English Romanticism. The very word "heath" — an open area with wild shrubbery — is English, not American. It suggests the Romantic seclusion this house originally had, looking southward over the growing city of Allegheny from a vantage point 400 feet up.

National Register

Henderson house
Warren and Henderson Streets, Fineview
C. 1860

In detail this imposing, dark sandstone house is Gothic, with some Italianate allusions in its bay window, the window hood above, and the quoins and window surrounds. Seen from the side, where the entrance is, it looks quite Georgian though in its plain, regular fenestration. It has not the fantastic elaboration of the only other large surviving Gothic house in the county, the Singer house in Wilkinsburg, but it is a fortunate survival all the same. It is not far from "Heathside Cottage."

In 1975 the Pittsburgh History & Landmarks Foundation purchased the Henderson house through its revolving fund,

and sold it in 1984 to a development company that has restored its exterior and converted its interior, much altered already, and that of the adjoining carriage house into apartments.

National Register; Landmarks plaque

East Street (or Swindell, or Essen Street) Bridge
Over East Street between North Charles and Essen Streets, East Street Valley
1930

Well known to northbound drivers, the East Street Bridge is a cantilever span with a lower chord in the form of an arch with half-arches at each end. Unlike most trusses, a cantilever truss has an upper chord in tension and a lower chord in compression; this makes possible the two arms that form the ends of the structure. The bridge is 160 feet above the valley and nearly a quarter-mile long.

St. Boniface Church (Roman Catholic)
East and Royal Streets, East Street Valley
A. F. Link, architect, 1925–26

St. Boniface is in a free style, part-Romanesque, part-Byzantine, executed in limestone. Its location at a slight bend in East Street helps make it a specially prominent landmark, although it has always been the grandest construction on this unassuming residential road. Inside is a lavishly decorated space beneath Guastavino tile vaulting. Behind it is a school of 1884, a large but very basic building of brick whose wooden cupola, a paraphrase of the Courthouse tower, is its only notable feature.

For decades this was a neighborhood church, well-attended. But a long, bitterly controversial clearing of land for a major expressway displaced many of the parishioners in the 1960s. Now, however, St. Boniface is more secure. The State has sold it back to the Diocese of Pittsburgh, and the parish itself is strong once again.

National Register; Landmarks plaque

Schiller School
Peralta and Wettach Streets, East Dutchtown
Marion M. Steen, architect, 1939

A fine essay in the use of deep-red textured brickwork, laid to produce zigzag Modernistic ornament. Steen was architect for the Board of Education during the 1930s, and designed a number of school buildings in varieties of the Moderne, all different, all handsomely decorated.

H. J. Heinz Company
Progress Street east of Chestnut Street, East Dutchtown
1896 and after

A bird's-eye view of 1909 shows the buildings of the Heinz Plant, already big after 20 years of growth and with more to come, ranged along a Progress Street that has the air of a grand avenue. Three of the buildings, including the Bottling Building of 1896 which is the oldest now extant, have corner

spires and elevated central panels that say **HEINZ** over and over to the passer-by. Opposite the Administration Building, white terra-cotta and brick Ionic in a complex of brown-brick Romanesque, is a little park with a cubical guardhouse, topped by a cupola with a dome in its turn topped by a smaller cupola, topped finally by an eagle about to take off. Much of this glory is now gone: the spires, the park, the guardhouse, even the Ionic capitals of the Administration Building.

On the other hand the plant has grown, and we can still see the less-fancy but still-ornate additions of the 1910s and 1920s, when architects struggled to harmonize with the sadly unfashionable Richardsonian piles already there. Later, a clean break was made with Albert Kahn's Office Annex, light buff brick and devoid of round arches. Alongside it, in 1958, came an even greater departure: Skidmore, Owings & Merrill's green-glass box of a Research Building. The oldest structure once on the site is gone but extant: the house where Henry J. Heinz had started was floated down from Sharpsburg to the new plant in 1904 as a memento, and was later shipped out to the Greenfield Village Museum at Dearborn, Michigan.

A Stuart Davis mural, *Composition Concrete,* hangs in the lobby of the Research Building.

Henry J. Heinz is well known as one of the early producers of canned and bottled foods. His business began in Sharpsburg, up the Allegheny River, in 1869, then moved to Allegheny in 1889.

Eberhardt & Ober Brewing Company
Troy Hill Road and Vinial Street, East Dutchtown
C. 1880 and after

These are the remains of a large brewery, established at the foot of Troy Hill by two of its prominent residents. The office building of 1897 is quite simple and unassumingly pleasant, with a round corner bay for an entrance. The central building is older and more Victorian, of around 1880 perhaps, with a central tower for the sake of prestige. The northwest wing adjoining is tall, warehouse-like, and minimally ornamented. Across the street from these three stands the two-story, Romanesque, Bottling Department.

The Eberhardt & Ober Brewery began in 1870 when John Ober and William Eberhardt, both brewers as well as brothers-in-law, went into partnership. The firm remained independent until 1899, when it was absorbed into the Pittsburgh Brewing Company. Eventually, both partners were buried, side by side, in similar mausoleums in Allegheny Cemetery.

Ober-Guehl house
Troy Hill Road and Lowrie Street, Troy Hill
1877; additions

This conspicuous Troy Hill house combines the typical Italian Villa formula of gable wall, tower, and side wall in echelon arrangement with the board-framed wall panels of the so-called Stick Style. Extensive one-story additions obscure the original form. At some point some of the surfaces were covered with shingles whose exposed edges are cut in bands of fancy patterns: a treatment commoner to the Shingle Style, with its concern with surfaces, than to the older Stick Style, with its interest in lines.

The house was built for James Dewhurst, who in 1884 sold it to John Ober, a partner in the Eberhardt & Ober Brewery at the foot of Troy Hill. The new owner built a brick stable near by, still standing, with a stone carving of a horse's head above its heavy round arch.

John Ober is remembered for his philanthropies. The Ober Foundation transformed the old Haymarket Square into Ober Park, a green area that in its later days stood between the Boggs & Buhl department store and the Buhl Planetarium.

Rectory, Church of the Most Holy Name of Jesus
1700 Harpster Street, Troy Hill
C. 1875

The window sash is not the original but otherwise this is a perfect example of American Second Empire domestic architecture. Yet in one respect it looks curiously European: where is the front porch? After all, there is a front yard. But this is a neighborhood with a European tradition, and Father

Mollinger, for whom it was built, seems simply not to have wanted one. A ceremonious doorway — which may actually be later than the house — is the more reticent way chosen of greeting the world outside.

Landmarks plaque

St. Anthony's Chapel
1700 Harpster Street, Troy Hill
1880; towers, 1890–91

This is the most interesting building on Troy Hill: a brick Romanesque church fronted in rock-faced sandstone. Although the building campaign went through the years when Richardson Romanesque was in fashion, the style here is used in an attenuated Mid-Victorian way.

The interior is even more remarkable. The Chapel was built by Father Suibertus Gottfried Mollinger, who placed in it his collection of 5,000 holy relics, housed in ornate reliquaries, as well as saints' images and ex-votos. The collection of relics is said to be the largest in the Western Hemisphere. Father Mollinger's parish, that of the Most Holy Name of Jesus, now owns the Chapel and offers public tours. Through the efforts of the parishioners, the Chapel has been steadily restored during the past several years.

Landmarks plaque

PITTSBURGH SOUTH OF THE RIVERS

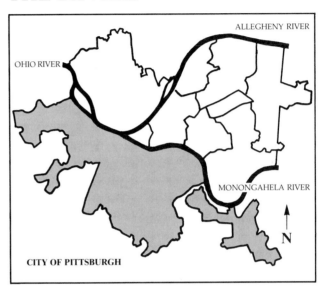

CITY OF PITTSBURGH

The South Side Flats and Slopes: a view down South Seventeenth Street.

Across the Monongahela River from the Triangle rises a 400-foot bluff, now called Mount Washington but originally known as Coal Hill. Pittsburgh owes much to the eight-foot coal seam in this hill, which was first mined in the 1760s, since its development from an 1800-period flatboat town depended on the furnaces and engines that this coal served to fire. The shore at the foot of Coal Hill and the other bluffs along the river began its rapid evolution from farmland to industrial land in 1797 when the glassworks of James O'Hara and Isaac Craig began production opposite the Point. In the next 70 years, four miles of ironworks, glassworks, railroad lines, and tiny boroughs replaced the farms along the river.

Among the Monongahela-shore boroughs were three early nineteenth-century developments of Nathaniel Bedford and his relatives by marriage, the Ormsbys, which are together now known as the South Side Flats. Birmingham, with Bedford Square and its market place at the center, was laid out between South Sixth and South Seventeenth Streets in 1811; East Birmingham lay between South Seventeenth and South Twenty-seventh Streets; and Ormsby extended for a mile-and-a-

193

East Carson Street in the South Side Flats has the city's best grouping of Victorian commercial architecture (right). Below, hillside housing on Volk Way, a pedestrian lane near Kearsage Street, Mount Washington.

half further eastward. Their riverside ironworking plants are now nearly imperceptible as such with the exception of Jones & Laughlin's huge and little-used installation at the eastern end of the Flats, and the local producers of fine glassware that was once famous have all shut down. What remains is a most interesting, intimately scaled neighborhood of Victorian houses, many meticulously kept with flower-planted yards, and churches reflecting a multitude of national origins. And down the neighborhood's center runs East Carson Street with an extraordinary display of Victorian commercial architecture.

South Side residents are proud of their houses and they like the settled quality of life; businesses like the local work ethic and ease of access. The South Side, in fact, arouses a sentiment in Pittsburgh to which the street scenes certainly contribute but which also comes from a good feeling about those who live and work there.

Above the Flats are the South Side Slopes, with more churches among little houses that cling to the hillside, tenuously connected with the neighborhoods above and below by narrow, giddy streets.

Ascending the hills was an early problem that found no easy solution until the advent of the incline. The South Side area eventually acquired 12 inclines, over half of those known to have been in the immediate area of Pittsburgh. Some carried coal from the hillside mine tunnels; others carried pedestrians and vehicles. Only two survive. Of those that are gone, only a vague trace on a hillside or occasional foundations for trestlework survive to recall the impressive structures which opened the hilltops to development.

The edge of Mount Washington has some commerce along Grandview Avenue, especially restaurants which exploit the dramatic view of the rivers and the Triangle. Here and there are fairly tall apartment houses, but the mined-out coal seam, resting on pillars of coal, makes for tricky constructional problems in many places, and much of Grandview Avenue has buildings no more than three stories high; in fact, from below, its silhouette suggests a row of house models ranged on a mantelshelf.

The trolley, beginning in 1888, supplemented the incline, allowing settlement far beyond the brows of the hills, and the back slopes and the adjacent hills of Mount Washington were eventually built up almost completely with detached houses of unassuming design scattered over ridges and hollows. When the South Hills Tunnel opened in 1904, the way was clear for development miles away from the rivers, and Pittsburgh, which had annexed the shore areas in 1872, began annexations of the newly developed neighborhoods. Only Mount Oliver, a borough now totally surrounded by Pittsburgh, escaped. These neighborhoods, so quickly built up, still retain a look of 1900 or 1910: blocky houses of buff, cream-colored, or red brick or white-painted siding, picturesquely disposed over the varied contours of the land. ∎

Pittsburgh & Lake Erie Railroad Terminal (presently, Station Square)
Smithfield Street Bridge and West Carson Street
1897-1918; remodeled, 1976 and after

In 1879 the Pittsburgh & Lake Erie Railroad began operations, breaking a near-monopoly of the Pennsylvania Railroad in the Pittsburgh area. Its first installation on the Monongahela shore, in the industrial settlement beneath Mount Washington known as Sligo, was quite modest, but by 1930 it had taken over almost all the shore land facing the Triangle. While coal hauling was its specialty, it also carried other types of freight and had an extensive passenger operation, and erected buildings large and small alongside its vast yard.

By the late 1960s, though, much of this activity had declined; one proposal was made for conventional redevelopment of this property that would have removed most, if not all, of the buildings. Nothing was done, though, until 1975 when the Pittsburgh History & Landmarks Foundation proposed an adaptive-use project that would save all the historic buildings. Against expert advice and public disbelief, Landmarks proceeded with sub-developers to convert the Freight House of 1897 into a commercial and retail arcade; the Passenger Station of 1901 into the Landmarks Building which houses offices and the Grand Concourse restaurant; the Express House of the early twentieth century into an office building of the same name; the Terminal Annex of 1916, an office building, into the Gatehouse, with modern offices; and the Shovel Transfer Warehouse of 1918 into Commerce Court, with shops, restaurants, and offices.

Recent constructions have included a Sheraton Hotel, the docking facilities and headquarters of the Gateway Clipper excursion fleet, a new parking garage, parking lots, and public open areas with benches, landscaping, and historic artifacts that include railway rolling stock and, as a symbol of the region's past, a Bessemer converter and an ingot mold. New plans are still to be announced for much of the 43-acre site.

An important aspect of the project for Landmarks was to demonstrate its basic urban planning principles as opposed to those used in Allegheny Center, East Liberty, and the Lower Hill: to reuse historic buildings, make vehicular access easy, create humanely scaled open squares and spaces, treat familiar artifacts as sculpture, and utilize the riverfront, heretofore undeveloped in Pittsburgh for such a purpose, as an amenity for people. In addition, the project was based on Landmarks' belief in tapping existing markets in the city and mixing uses in a clean, varied, urban environment. The Allegheny Foundation launched the project with a five million dollar equity grant in 1976, and Station Square has become popular and successful.

National Register; Landmarks plaques

Pittsburgh & Lake Erie Railroad Passenger Station (presently, the Landmarks Building)
One Station Square, south end of Smithfield Street Bridge
William George Burns, architect, 1901; remodeled, 1978–83

At the turn of the century, the P&LE replaced its first small wooden passenger terminal with the present grandiose structure, planned also as company headquarters. Crossman & Sturdy, Chicago decorators, gave the main waiting room a Classical appearance, with imitation-marble columns, carved and varnished woodwork, and a huge fanlight and vault of stained glass, all in the browns, ambers, and greens that appealed to the turn-of-the-century color sense. More modest yet very handsome interiors opened off this great space. Upstairs a small but decorative two-story lobby led to offices with ebonized woodwork and brass hardware that bore the intricate P&LE monogram. Outside was a balloon trainshed whose ultimate length was 700 feet.

In 1978 the first great triumph of the Station Square project came with the opening of the Grand Concourse restaurant, a sympathetic conversion of the old passenger rooms and the adjoining baggage room. In 1983 the office space, which was thoroughly modernized in functioning, yet retained the old ornamental detailing, was reopened. Substantially, the building is in its old form today, with one exception: the trainshed was demolished in the 1930s, and the view from Station Square is now open to the river.

The Landmarks Building now houses the offices of the Pittsburgh History & Landmarks Foundation together with commercial tenants.

National Register; Landmarks plaque

Monongahela Incline
Between West Carson Street and Grandview Avenue at Wyoming Street
John Endres and Samuel Diescher, engineers, 1869-70; rebuilt 1882, 1982-83

Apart from a coal-hauling road elsewhere on Mount Washington, this was the first of Pittsburgh's 20 or more inclines and, with the Duquesne Heights Incline a mile away, it is one of the two survivors. A reconstruction of 1882 gave it a trestle-like structure of wrought iron that was replaced with steel a century later. In 1884 a parallel incline was built immediately to the east to carry wagons and teams; this lasted until 1935. In the latter year, too, the power was converted from steam to electricity.

The West Carson Street station is a reconstruction of c. 1900 in a cheerful Neo-Georgian style (but with a Jacobean lantern on the roof). It was restored inside to approximately its original condition in 1983. The Grandview Avenue station has been remodeled many times and has only vestiges of its Mid-Victorian original design. It is interesting mainly for the control booth, where the oddly out-of-place-looking elevator control and airbrake from the past stand beside the electrical monitors and controls installed in 1983. The cars are entirely new; one of the Victorian cars, with wrought-iron decorative grillework, is preserved at Station Square. The tracks are 635 feet long and rise 367 feet at a 35-degree angle.

The incline is very popular with tourists, and the view from Grandview Avenue, almost 400 feet up, is the most famous one in Pittsburgh.

National Register; Landmarks plaque

W. W. Lawrence Company (Lawrence Paint Building)
1124 West Carson Street
George W. Hogg, builder, 1897

This massive, long-neglected industrial building, once a paint factory, is a reminder of the industry that once crowded the south shore of the Monongahela River opposite the Triangle. It stands in a conspicuous place, across West Carson Street from the Duquesne Heights Incline and almost opposite the Point. For years people have looked at it, admired it, and deplored its deteriorating condition. It is a colossal brick-and-timber construction, with over 100,000 square feet of floor space, ceilings up to 24 feet tall, and six stories, including two below street level.

Duquesne Heights Incline
1197 West Carson Street to 1220 Grandview Avenue
Samuel Diescher, engineer, 1877; rebuilt 1888

The younger of the two inclines still operating in Pittsburgh, this has nonetheless far the oldest rolling stock of any transit system in the county. The original cars of 1877 are still running, their bodies similar to those built for horsecars, with Eastlake interiors of contrasting cherry and birdseye maple with simple incised ornament.

The original track structure of wood and wrought iron was rebuilt wholly in iron in 1888. It is 793 feet long on a 30.5-degree slope, with a 400-foot rise.

The West Carson Street station appears, with its Ionic pilasters, its big round arches, its heavy turned newel posts, its elaborate wrought-iron stair balustrades, and its ochre brick, to be a product of the 1890s. Here, indeed, you step into the past: the flavor of the old industrial city remains untamed, unprettified.

The Grandview Avenue station is a partial restoration of recent years. Its hauling machinery, partly exposed, still uses the old wooden-toothed gear wheels that promote silent running, though the original steam plant was electrified in 1932. The station's waiting room is a pictorial museum of Pittsburghiana and of inclines, aerial tramways, and trolleys around the world.

The incline is operated by a non-profit community group, the Society for the Preservation of the Duquesne Heights Incline.

National Register; Landmarks plaque

Terminal Buildings
East Carson Street and Terminal Way
Charles Bickel, architect, c. 1900

This is an impressive commercial development, reaching from the 400 block of East Carson Street to the Monongahela River and itself reached from the two levels of East Carson and McKean Streets. It contains offices, shops, and most importantly, warehousing. In all there are five buildings, executed in a coppery-brown brick. The architect and the bricklayer worked out a scheme of ornamentation — enough to demonstrate that they cared — but it is obvious that efficiency was the real object. Some of the architectural efforts have been undone in recent years: parapets have had to be reconstructed, and the craftsmanly practice of thinking of how to place each individual brick is long out of date.

St. John the Baptist Ukrainian Catholic Church
East Carson and South Seventh Streets, South Side Flats
1895; enlarged, 1917

This church is a major landmark of the South Side Flats, conspicuous from far away, not only because of its size but also because of its eight lofty onion domes, painted a glossy pale green. The Eastern European presence in Pittsburgh and the industrial areas of the county is manifest in such domes, often to be seen, but this is an extraordinary group, conspicuous in their number, their bright color, and their placement at the entrance to the South Side. The present Seventh Street entrance leads to the original church under a brown-painted Ionic portico in whose pediment is a mosaic of St. John the Baptist.

National Register; Landmarks plaque

Ripley & Company (presently, Salvation Army Adult Rehabilitation Center)
South Ninth and Bingham Streets, South Side Flats
1891

In a more fashion-conscious city, this would be assumed to be a building of the mid-1870s, and even in Pittsburgh it must have seemed old-fashioned. It has a one-fronted design. On South Ninth Street, it is a highly articulated structural skeleton of red brick with sandstone lintels and sills, decorated with bands of richly molded red terra cotta and with a doorway of polished gray granite. The doorway, a low basement entrance, is given an uncertain dignity by a rudimentary pediment at the level of the first-floor window heads, and still more by the raised portion of the corbeled cornice above. At the corner is a round support for an oriel window, now gone. On the Bingham Street side, all this homely but lavish display falls away, and plain industrial construction prevails.

Here, once again, is a work in that unlabeled style based on masonry construction that can be seen at 820 Liberty Avenue in the Triangle. Somehow this spare and hard building is very handsome.

The rare surviving presence of a glassworks structure is fortunate. Into the early twentieth century, the South Side was a famous glassmaking area, especially for tableware. Ripley & Co. was one of the largest, with a diversified production. At the top of the line were engraved-glass and imitation cut and flashed-glass tableware.

National Register District

Pittsburgh Foundry, A. Garrison Foundry Company (presently, Mackintosh-Hemphill Company)
Bingham and South Ninth Streets, South Side Flats
C. 1900

A pair of business buildings of about the same time, built of an unusual light-beige brick and linked by a later construction. The corner building, though very simple, has been carefully studied as a work of architecture. Its hip roof with jutting eaves, the diapering over the second-floor arches, and its good proportions suggest the way a good Philadelphia architect of the 1890s might have handled the problem of a low-budget office building. The other building, more industrial in character, uses rough-surfaced sandstone lintels and sills for textural contrast. The treatment of its arches is very peculiar: they seem unsupported, with the curtain wall falling back at their spring line. The idea was probably to sketch out a Palladian window in minimal terms.

The Pittsburgh Foundry dates back to 1803, progressing from early casting of iron utensils to the making of ordnance in this century. It became the Mackintosh-Hemphill Company in the 1870s.

National Register District

Birmingham Number One (later, Bedford School)
910 Bingham Street, South Side Flats
1850

A big Greek Revival schoolhouse, perhaps the oldest surviving in Pittsburgh. The window arrangement is purely utilitarian with no attempt at architectural effect, at mitigating the impression of a big box, but the gables have nicely executed brick dentils. Originally, each upper floor had eight uniform windows and there were Doric entrance porches. There was also a two-stage belfry and clock tower at one end.

Like a number of other large Victorian schoolhouses in Pittsburgh, this has ceased to be a school. But in its time it was a sign of progress. The apparatus for free, though as yet not compulsory, education had been created by the State Legislature in 1836, in the confident hope that this would create better, as well as more competent, citizens. As is true in this case, the new schoolhouses were usually large and rather factory-like. They constituted fire hazards, with their wooden stairs and floor structure, and were eventually replaced by larger and more modern schools.

National Register District

South Side Market House (presently, South Side Recreation Center)
Bedford Square, South Side Flats
Charles Bickel, architect, 1893; remodeled, 1915, 1950, 1978

As built, this was a Richardson Romanesque work, with four peaked towers in the compulsively picturesque spirit of Late Victorian public architecture. When it was rebuilt in 1915 after a fire, the towers came off, the gable roof was brought down to the eaves on both fronts, and a well-scaled stone cartouche was set into the south front memorializing the new work. This cartouche is the building's one decoration today, set off by swags and surmounted by a bull's head. The Romanesque walls otherwise survive largely as built, industrial rather than civic architecture.

This is one of Pittsburgh's two remaining market houses, and gains extra distinction from being situated at the center of a public square. The buildings that surround it are generally smaller, so that the market has a monumental quality by contrast.

National Register District; Landmarks plaque

Commercial buildings
East Carson Street, South Side Flats

East Carson Street, the main street of the South Side Flats, has a mile-long low-rise commercial district stretching from South Ninth to South Twenty-fourth Streets, which is remarkable for its abundant and vivid Victorian commercial architecture. The street is flanked by nearly continuous building walls of two- to four-story structures. Street level shops are a flourishing mixture of establishments for residents — food and clothing stores, bars, services of all kinds — and new restaurants, antique shops, and artists' studios. The storefronts have often been altered, and altered again. But upper stories generally remain unchanged and striking in their Victorian ornamentation. In some cases, builders repeated basic building designs with slight variations in proportion and ornamentation. Other facades display widely divergent Victorian stylistic variations. And occasional cast iron facades and Classical bank buildings add even greater contrasts.

1201-05 East Carson Street

At 1201-05 East Carson Street, Bedford Square is grandly introduced by a three-story triple Italianate building with a cast-iron arcade on its shop fronts; the strong effect of the repeated round arches makes this one of the most effective designs on the street. At South Fourteenth Street, the old German Savings Deposit Bank, now a branch of Mellon Bank, has the rather ponderous Classicism that prevailed in 1896, when it was constructed; yet its light-gray granite is treated with the crispness and cleanness that suits the material best, with plain surfaces and delicate details in contrast. Another bank, at 1736 East Carson Street, has a softer effect: a Beaux-Arts structure of 1902 that was later lengthened. Here, yellow-gray sandstone appears in contrast with bright-red brick to create rich color rather than the spare monochrome of the German Bank. The few touches of Rococo ornament are very mild accents in the composition, whose true strength, apart from its color, lies in the rhythmic

German Savings Deposit Bank

1736 East Carson Street

1739 East Carson Street

procession of tall arched windows. Facing this bank, at 1739 East Carson Street, is a grandiose cast-iron building in the Second Empire style, probably from the 1870s. We reproduce a slightly out-of-date photograph of it here in order to show its design clearly; partly blocked windows and dark-brown paint have since obscured its lines, though not irreversibly. With its mansard roofs and fancy dormers, the building has the most panache of those in the district. Much humbler, but still quite interesting, are the twin shop fronts at Numbers 2104-06, the oldest in the district and very rare survivors in Pittsburgh from the Greek Revival period. Carefully restored, they now form the front of Le Pommier, one of the new restaurants in the area.

2104-06 East Carson Street

Beginning in 1968, the Pittsburgh History & Landmarks Foundation helped develop an education program to show merchants how business could be increased by restoring commercial shop fronts to their original architectural character. Landmarks also acquired several historic structures and restored them as model properties. Neighborhood restoration efforts continue today through the leadership of several local organizations.

National Register District

First Associated Reformed Church (later, Ninth United Presbyterian Church)
South Fourteenth and Bingham Streets, South Side Flats
1854

This is the oldest datable church building on the South Side Flats, and one of the oldest in Pittsburgh. In general a sober Greek Revival work, sparing in ornament, it has a simple but impressive front with later Gothic openings. The thick piers, framing the panels in which the windows are actually set, establish a strong compositional rhythm.

National Register District; Landmarks plaque

Number Seven Police Station
93 South Thirteenth Street, South Side Flats
Charles Bickel, architect, c. 1900

This former police station has three fronts. Two of these are of warm-gray brick with a matching, richly patterned banding of terra cotta under sheet-metal cornices. The treatment is one that Stanford White used in several New York buildings early in the 1890s, notably the Judson Memorial Church. Architects in this period often enjoyed such intensely detailed surfaces; the Carnegie Library in Lawrenceville is another such example, using very similar terra cotta. The third front, on Uxor Way, is a stable wing of ordinary brick, quite plain except for a frieze of recessed panels. At the time of writing, this building is deserted and boarded up. Some use needs to be found for it. Police station or not, this has a festive exterior, and one can imagine it full of life again, its masonry clean, its metal ornamentation repaired and freshly painted. When such buildings are rehabilitated, it is hard to imagine how they could ever have been neglected.

St. Adalbert's Church (Roman Catholic)
162 South Fifteenth Street, South Side Flats
1889

A massive work in Richardson Romanesque built for a Polish congregation, St. Adalbert's dominates and forms the climactic feature of a narrow, gently sloping street. The most impressive way to see it, however, is from several blocks eastward on Mary Street; from this viewpoint the facade and towers rise above an intervening block of small houses, concluding the vista of a broad but unassuming street with a piece of architectural drama. Next to the church is the rectory, round-arched and in a free style as much Classical as Romanesque.

Landmarks plaque

Christian Moerlein Company beer warehouse (presently, B. M. Kramer & Company, Inc.)
South Twentieth and Sidney Streets, South Side Flats
C. 1915

A handsome commercial building, taking a full block. The urbanity is typical of the Eclectic period, and the bright-red brick with raked-out mortar joints suggests a date around 1915. Such a surface indeed is often found in houses of the time. The brickwork is laid up in Flemish bond, which is unusually labor-intensive since each successive brick is laid in a direction different from its predecessor. Someone took care over this building, plain as it may seem at first. The ground-floor windows have the so-called Florentine tracery, Early Renaissance in origin, popular in the 1850s, rare in the early twentieth century.

Independent Brewery (later, Duquesne Brewery)
South Twenty-first and Jane Streets, South Side Flats
1899 and after

No longer a brewery, this big complex whose buildings range from 1890s Romanesque to 1940s Modernistic survives underused. Its clock, 60 feet across and clearly readable from a half-mile away, is a prominent South Side feature. The tall cooker building which carries the clock is now used by artists and craftsmen, and other buildings in the complex are used for offices, commerce, and light industry. Architecturally, the most interesting building is the original one, built as the Brew House and Stock House as stone plaques indicate. The architecture is all one expects of a brewery: Germanic in a decidedly pre-Bauhaus way, heavy and elaborate. It has been added to in the original spirit and has also received some unfortunate modifications, so that its original symmetry is gone.

Morse School (presently, Morse Gardens)
Sarah and South Twenty-fifth Streets, South Side Flats
T. D. Evans, architect, 1874; additions and alterations, 1984

A big Italianate school, whose tall windows, useful for light and air, give its facade an air of challenge that the forward break of the center augments. The entrance arches are "Florentine": the intradoses, the inner edges, are round, while the extradoses are bluntly pointed. The same design was used for a school in the Strip.

The Housing Authority of the City has made the school the focal element of a 70-unit apartment group. While not restored, the school has been integrated into the complex in a sympathetic manner.

Mission Pumping Station
340 Mission Street, South Side Slopes
Thomas H. Scott, architect, 1910

Isolated partway up the South Side Slopes, big and simple in its design, this is a conspicuous object in the hilly landscape. The main building contained two vertical triple-expansion steam engines with a capacity of seven million gallons a day apiece; the small building housed the boilers. The style, a very quiet Beaux-Arts manner realized in red brick and white terra cotta, has a distant ancestry in French country architecture of the seventeenth and eighteenth centuries. On the main building the original cornice has been removed, and what was probably a tile roof has been replaced by corrugated sheet metal. The same architect designed the similar Aspinwall Pumping Station a few years later.

The station was an element in the newly reformed water system, which drew water from the Allegheny River at Aspinwall, filtered it, and pumped it to reservoirs in Highland Park for distribution to most of the city. The Mission Pumping Station raised the water to storage tanks on the hill above, in the neighborhood of Allentown.

St. Josaphat Church (Roman Catholic)
2304 Mission Street, South Side Slopes
John T. Comes, architect, 1909-16

The need for economy seems to have driven the architect to a terseness of detailing unusual for the earliest part of the twentieth century. The suave porch of composition stone is massive in form and delicate in detailing, and the Baroque tower top of copper is robust in shape; but the body of the church depends on pale-yellow brick forms inlaid in plain red brick for effectiveness, and the sandstone masonry of the basement is of the simplest sort, the kind that might be found in any house. The architect, who could handle elaborate decorative schemes well at St. Agnes', Oakland, or St. Anthony's, Millvale, did equally well with this simpler church. The tower especially is a very handsome feature of the South Side townscape.

The Rectory of St. Michael

The Casino of 1897 does not conform to the swaggering Monte Carlo image suggested by its name; aside from a little religious symbolism at the doorway, it looks like an ordinary plain apartment house of its time. It has been used for various parish activities.

Landmarks plaque

St. Michael the Archangel Church (Roman Catholic) group
South Fifteenth and Pius Streets, South Side Slopes
Charles Bartberger, architect for church, 1857-61

Halfway up the South Side Slopes, an impressive spired church stands with its entourage of buildings, all of red brick against a hillside of trees and frame houses.

The church itself was built for the Passionist Fathers in a simple pre-Richardson Romanesque, derived from medieval Italy but fashionable in the 1850s: an economical, adaptable style that could dignify an industrial building and not be unworthy of a church. Here, a tall, solid tower and tall proportions in the church itself suggest that money was not too restraining an influence. A few concave curves give a touch of Baroque styling that fits in well. Inside are the original German windows and a white marble altar.

The Rectory of 1889 carries on the Romanesque-plus-Baroque idea in a more vivid and worldly way, mixing several styles quite cheerfully and successfully, responding to the heaven-seeking spire of the church with two bulbous domes.

On the opposite side of Pius Street are three buildings. Our Lady of Charity Center and Eudes Institute occupy an impressive, little-ornamented brick building that presents 18 bays of segmental and round arches, is three stories high, and ends in a dormered gambrel roof.

Next to this are the East and West Buildings of South Side Catholic High School. The former, built in 1887, is a mixture of brick of Queen Anne and Romanesque, picturesquely shaped; the latter, once St. Michael's Mädchen Schule, has taller lines and mixes Romanesque and Classical in a way old-fashioned for 1900 when it was built.

St. Paul of the Cross Monastery
143 Monastery Street, South Side Slopes
Charles Bartberger, architect, 1854, 1858-59; additions and alterations

The monastery stands directly uphill from the St. Michael's Church complex, and is in the hands of the Congregation of Passionist Missionaries as St. Michael's long was. Formerly, a hillside garden connected the two institutions, with Stations of the Cross along its winding path. The exterior of the monastery church of 1858-59 is in the Italian-type Romanesque of the mid-nineteenth century, but the original hard lines and surfaces of the front were reworked at some point early in this century to soften the effect and add picturesqueness to the silhouette. The interior is light and cheerful, early Italian Renaissance in cream and gold, with color in the form of medallions painted on the vaults and good Mid-Victorian and early twentieth-century glass. The other parts of the

203

monastery have been added to and altered a number of times with varying artistic success.

The view toward the Triangle and Oakland from in front of the church is one of the best in Pittsburgh.

Landmarks plaque

Houses
Marne Way, Penelope Street, and Simms Street, Mount Washington
Daniel Hilf, builder, c. 1910

A sickle-shaped development on the rear slope of Mount Washington, built by a local contractor for rental. The individual houses are quite plain but make a visual impact through their rhythmic ascent of the sloping streets as series of close-spaced uniform structures. Some of the house rows are of brick, others of wood. The only ornamentation is on one Simms Street row of flat-roofed wooden double houses; these have very modest bracketed cornices on their fronts.

Chatham Village
Virginia Avenue and Bigham Street, Mount Washington
Ingham & Boyd, architects; Stein & Wright (New York), planners; Ralph E. Griswold of Griswold & Kohan Kie, landscape architect; 1932, 1935

In 1929 the Buhl Foundation, located in Pittsburgh, decided to sponsor an experimental for-profit large-scale housing project for limited-income families. For planning they went to Clarence Stein and Henry Wright of New York, already known for their innovative plans for Radburn, New Jersey,

and Sunnyside Gardens, Long Island. Over two years of study resulted in 197 units in an idyllic setting of trees, lawns, and flowers. The gentle Eclectic architecture, realized in medium-red brick with slate roofs, is perhaps more English Georgian than anything else, but a little bit rural French as well. The automobile is kept firmly in its place, relegated to three garage courts on the perimeter. A recreational area lies alongside to the northwest and the original Bigham house of 1844, at the far end of the development, serves as a community center.

Radburn, being started earlier, has had most of the publicity as an example of American "garden city" planning, but Chatham Village has had notice from such well-known students of urban life as Lewis Mumford (". . . one of the high points in site planning and architectural layout . . . its failure to excite even local imitation remains inexplicable . . .") and Jane Jacobs, who found it socially insular, matriarchal, and boring. (Neither has actually lived there.)

South Hills High School
Ruth and Eureka Streets, Mount Washington
Alden & Harlow, architects, 1916-24

On the sort of broad hilltop that in Istanbul would support an Imperial mosque, Pittsburgh has put several of its public schools. So it is here: this massive brown-brick, slightly Gothic high school rises with easy dominance among little houses and looks out over South Hills Junction and the surrounding valley. Its nearby neighbor is another powerful structure, the ventilator building for the Liberty Tunnels.

Liberty Tunnels ventilating plant
201 Secane Avenue, Mount Washington
Stanley L. Roush, architect, 1928

The Liberty Tunnels, or Liberty Tubes as they are usually called, fulfilled a long-felt desire of motorists to get to the South Hills directly rather than by going over or around Mount Washington. Ventilation proved more of a problem than the engineers had calculated, and while the first of the two Tubes was finished in 1922 the opening had to be put off until 1924 while a solution was worked out. In 1928 a mechanical plant with four tall stacks was built over the center of the Tubes. The material is a bright-red brick with limestone detailing, and the style is a bland quasi-Gothic manner. The four great stacks could not have been more fortunately placed from a scenic point of view; their powerful forms thrust upward from the shelf-like spur of the hillside on which the plant stands, in dramatic contrast with the broad valley spaces around them, framing views of distant hillsides, contrasting their simple surfaces with the tiny-looking houses and trees beyond and their vivid redness with the more neutral colors of the landscape.

House
311 Lowenhill Street, Beechview
C. 1850

Board-and-batten siding was apparently introduced in 1834 by the New York architect Alexander Jackson Davis, and was popular for several decades thereafter. Those who have seen it will understand why. Like a row of Lombardy poplars in the front yard, it seems able to turn any construction, however aesthetically empty, into architecture. Its insistent verticals blur the effect of bad proportions, organize haphazard fenestration schemes, create a striking pattern under direct sunlight, and glorify a frame structure as a thing made of wood, making the material tangible through visual means. In this house, Gothic trim romps under the roof, a little ineffectually against the strong rhythm of the battens. Window surrounds in carpenter's Greek Revival fare better, with their broad and large surfaces. Traces of a porch remain on the center of the house; should a compatible new porch be added this would be a very balanced house front, a piece of dignified architecture unique in this neighborhood.

John Frew house
105 Poplar Street, Oakwood
Before 1800; c. 1840

The original stone farmhouse was two-storied, with rubble walls secured at the corners by tall, shallow quoins. A plan of 1936, made for the Western Pennsylvania Architectural Survey, shows only one room on the ground floor with a stair along an end wall. To this, around 1840, a one-and-a-half-story addition of brick was built, five bays wide and with a porch on each side. Perhaps the roof of the stone part was remodeled at the time; in any event the two parts share the same roof, which extends downwards over the broader brick section and its porches. East of the house is a two-story springhouse, sympathetically incorporated into a modern garage and greenhouse structure. Its stonework consists of tall, shallow slabs tied into backup masonry by alternate thin, deep courses: the very facing methods that can be seen on the walls of the Courthouse.

Small and simple though it is, this is one of our handsomest survivors of the Georgian period.

Landmarks plaque

Corliss Street Tunnel
Corliss and West Carson Streets, Esplen
Stanley L. Roush, architect; D. N. Sprague, chief
engineer; 1913-14

Taking Corliss Street under the tracks of the old Pennsylvania
Railroad Panhandle Route, this work of the City of Pittsburgh
was carried out with a Baroque flourish: the concrete portal
imitates a rusticated archway, and above it an overscaled
stone tablet gives name and date to the speeding traffic.
Beneath this is the City escutcheon, decorated with festoons.

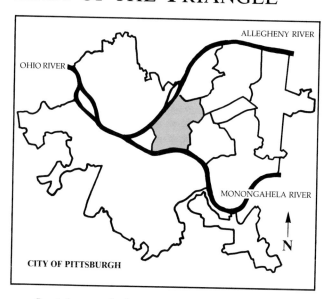

A theater and dance hall from the glory days of black entertainment on the Hill: the New Granada on Centre Avenue.

EAST OF THE TRIANGLE

Just beyond the Triangle two hills present steep slopes to the rivers, meet in a rising valley, and eventually merge. The northern hill, by far the larger, is Herron Hill. The smaller, overlooking the Monongahela River, is the Bluff. The strong contours of the terrain have created a number of separate neighborhoods, each with its own history and character.

For more than a century the Bluff has been the home of two institutions, Duquesne University and Mercy Hospital, and of a dwindling neighborhood of Victorian houses. Institutional expansion has unsettled the place visually, as large buildings both graceful and awkward, as well as parking lots, have replaced the houses and increased the building scale.

The rising valley, which gradually approaches the upper level of the Bluff, is known vaguely as Uptown: an early extension of the original Pittsburgh, full of close-set red brick houses, mostly Italianate, with occasional churches. Into this matrix, along Fifth and Forbes Avenues, commercial buildings and warehouses were inserted be-

Smallman Street in the Strip — unruly with railroad tracks and stone paving — is a corridor for produce markets and leads to St. Stanislaus.

tween 1870 and 1910, so that the original domestic architecture was upstaged by high, ornate facades, and relegated more and more to the side streets. In recent years developers have been restoring and adapting the commercial buildings, even the houses, for offices. Naturally, this renovation activity is most intense closest to town; further east, along Fifth and Forbes Avenues, Uptown blends, along with the eastern part of the Bluff, into Soho, a neighborhood of houses, apartments, and shops where respectability and ruin stand side by side.

Herron Hill's vast, tilted surface is simply known as the Hill. Early in the nineteenth century the Hill was country, with small scattered settlements of varying purpose. It had country estates, working farms, coal mines, and a village of black freedmen. From the middle of the nineteenth century until its end, the city expanded into this area, building over the enormous surface. The Hill became a place of many cultures and many levels of prosperity, where solid middle-class houses and atrocious slums could both be found on close-built streets. In the twentieth century, the older ethnic and Jewish population moved away, and the Hill became largely black, the Harlem of Pittsburgh, the place where the best jazz could be heard but a place also with most of the problems of Harlem. Urban renewal in the 1950s removed virtually all of the Lower Hill, closest to town, in anticipation of a great municipal showpiece of amphitheater, Center for the Arts, and apartment slabs. The grand plan was never full realized, and the Civic Arena and apartment houses that were

built seem lost in a desert of paving and bare ground.

The steep northern face of Herron Hill, looking out over the Allegheny River Valley, contains a little and rather isolated neighborhood called Polish Hill. Its angular and close-built streets are not conspicuous in themselves, but in the church of the Immaculate Heart of Mary, with its Baroque domes, Polish Hill has one of the conspicuous landmarks of the city, visible for miles.

Below Herron Hill is a long, narrow area of the river plain known as the Strip. There is little to recall the intensely active, extremely smoky industrial quarter of a century ago, the promiscuous blend of furnaces, industrial sheds, railroad buildings, houses, and churches that arose under the stimulus of the Allegheny River timber rafts, the Pennsylvania Canal, the Pennsylvania Railroad, and the oil barges drifting down from the north: the Strip where the devastating riots of the Railroad Strike of 1877 took place, where George Westinghouse began his manufacturing operations, and where the first commercial aluminum ingot was poured in 1888. Today this is a pleasingly haphazard and vital district of warehouses and wholesalers, best known for its food markets. Its busiest time is the dead of night when the food is sold in bulk; but by day, the domestic shoppers come in search of the best salami, fruit, vegetables, and fish in the city. This present identity is threatened from time to time by proposals for redevelopment, but the colorful and spontaneous vitality of the Strip should not be heedlessly sacrificed. ■

Administration Building and Chapel, Duquesne University
Bluff and Colbert Streets, the Bluff
1883-84; c. 1900

Duquesne University was founded in 1878 as the Pittsburgh Catholic College of the Holy Ghost, and its five-story Administration Building, sited at the western end of the Bluff, has been a prominent skyline object for a century. The style is that nameless one in which basic masonry construction is used decoratively, to the extent that decoration exists at all. Stone beltcourses at the levels of the window sills and arch springings offer contrast to the verticals of the window openings and the buildings as a whole. The somewhat later Chapel is in the Victorian brick vernacular used equally for ecclesiastical and industrial buildings, though Gothic arches make clear its function as a church.

Armstrong Tunnel
Between the Tenth Street Bridge and Forbes Avenue, Uptown
Stanley L. Roush, architect; Vernon R. Covell of the Allegheny County Department of Public Works, chief engineer; 1926-27

The tunnel portals are constructed in the heaviest and simplest Italian Renaissance style, with cut-stone arches and cornices of an urbane, even bland, character that tempers somewhat the heavy, rock-faced engineering stonework of the rest. This is the end of a long tradition of such stonework; the Liberty Tubes, opened earlier, already had portals of concrete.

The tunnel is 1,300 feet long, and makes a 40-degree change of direction just inside the Forbes Avenue portals to lead properly to the bridge.

Fifth Avenue High School
Fifth Avenue and Miltenberger Street, Uptown
Edward Stotz, architect, 1894

Abandoned, this was for many years a sad sight: the more so because its broad proportions, its generous ornamentation, and its warm, orangeish brick create a genial building. Unlike the Mid-Victorian schoolhouse, which tends to stare you down as you approach, this one seems to invite you to come in and be educated. This, by the way, was the first fireproof school in Pittsburgh. At the time of writing, rehabilitation work is in progress for display space.

Church of the Epiphany (Roman Catholic)
Washington Place and Centre Avenue, the Hill
Edward Stotz, architect, 1902

A red Italian Romanesque church, which with three parochial buildings survived the Lower Hill clearance of 1960. Beside it is Epiphany School of 1910, behind the school is the St. Regis Residence of 1914, and attached to the church at the rear is the Parish House of c. 1900. The church is handsome, and is the more valuable as evidence that this barren hillside was once the location of a neighborhood.

It served as the Roman Catholic cathedral in the 1900s between the time when the second St. Paul's in the Triangle was sold and 1906, when the new St. Paul's in Oakland was consecrated.

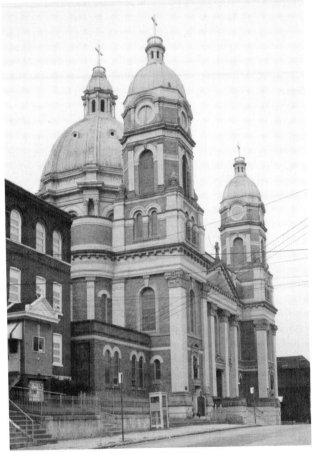

Immaculate Heart of Mary Church (Roman Catholic)

3058 Brereton Street, Polish Hill
William P. Ginther (Akron), architect, 1904

Centered on a domed space 98 feet high inside, this church has the most Baroque silhouette of any in the county, signaling the otherwise-inconspicuous Polish Hill neighborhood for miles. There is spare carving in sandstone. The facade pilasters have Composite capitals. The color contrast between light-gray and medium-brown brick enlivens the masonry. Inside, the church is lavishly furnished in a heavy Classical way characteristic of the 1900s. The same architect designed St. Philip's, Crafton, and St. Mary's Help of Christians, McKees Rocks.

Landmarks plaque

Commercial building

1127 Penn Avenue, the Strip
1892

Applied to commerce, the Richardson Romanesque style attained a remarkable degree of attenuation. In the typical store or loft building, only the front and the rear offered window space, and the need for the maximum area of sash conflicted with the demands of an architectural scheme that offered prestige. In the fashionable Romanesque, the usual solution was one or more giant arcades framing light window and spandrel construction, with a smaller-scaled upper story and a fancy parapet. Such is the case here, though the parapets have an incomplete look, as if false gables were removed at some point.

Sixteenth Street Bridge
Allegheny River between Sixteenth Street and Chestnut Street, the Strip
James G. Chalfant, County engineer; Warren & Wetmore (New York), architects; 1923

Seahorses by Leo Lentelli (New York), leaping off in all directions from beneath armillary spheres, dramatize the crossing of the Allegheny, which at this point is about 700 feet wide. The bridge undertakes this passage in three trussed-arch spans, the longest being 437 feet. Four masonry piers by the architects who completed Grand Central Station bear the Lentelli sculptures and other, very handsome, ornament. The Municipal Art Commission, which had a say in any river bridge design within Pittsburgh, determined both the design and the ornamentation.

National Register

St. Stanislaus Kostka Church (Roman Catholic)
Twenty-first and Smallman Streets, the Strip
Frederick C. Sauer, architect, 1891-92

In the middle of the produce district stands this Romanesque church of darkened red brick with trim in stone that is now painted. The towers were once taller, but the upper parts were removed after weakening by an explosion. The inscription on the central arch, *Ad Majorem Dei Gloriam,* means "To the greater glory of God." Inside, art depicts the religious and secular history of Poland, since this is a Polish Catholic parish, the earliest in Pittsburgh. The church is a prominent sight among the warehouses of the Strip, its decorative architecture in welcome contrast with the plain and time-worn buildings around.

National Register; Landmarks plaque

Armstrong Cork Company
Twenty-third and Railroad Streets, the Strip
Frederick J. Osterling, architect, 1901, 1902; addition, 1913

A trio of massive buff-brick buildings, presently unused. The two long blocks perpendicular to the river are by Frederick J. Osterling, one of the busiest Pittsburgh architects of the 1900 period. Such buildings appear in every city: idled where they were once busy, they challenge those who hate to see them deteriorate or disappear. At the time of writing, there were plans to convert this complex into a business, produce, and retail center.

211

Thirty-seventh Street north of Penn Avenue typifies Lawrenceville's narrow streets.

LAWRENCEVILLE

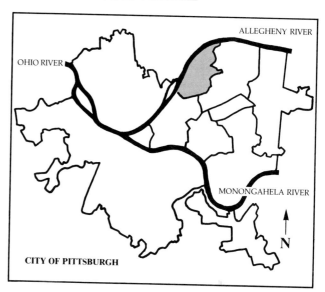

ALLEGHENY RIVER

OHIO RIVER

MONONGAHELA RIVER

N

CITY OF PITTSBURGH

Lawrenceville is a dense but sprawling neighborhood, full of incident and discovery as the South Side Flats are, with a northerly view from its sloping streets toward wooded hills across the Allegheny River that better-known neighborhoods on flat terrain cannot match. Butler Street at its base is busy and commercial; but a block or two away, the somewhat narrow residential streets are calm and solid, and thoroughly Victorian. Red-brick houses are interrupted only by an occasional church or school, or the local branch of the Carnegie Library; institutions seem to prefer the homey obscurity of Lawrenceville's side streets. A visitor gets the impression of a community that keeps itself to itself, is not too interested in publicity, but knows its worth.

Lawrenceville was a development of William B. Foster, father of the song-writer Stephen Collins Foster, who was born there. A broad strip of Foster land was purchased in 1814 by the U.S. Army for the Allegheny Arsenal, the neighborhood's greatest employer and — in an explosion of 1862 — the cause of its worst disaster. The Arsenal, long vanished as an institution, survives in a few taken-for-granted buildings, fragments of the whole, and a few other Lawrenceville buildings which may have been influenced by the Arsenal's design. But it is the ascending strip of land of the upper Arsenal site, now including a high school, park, and County health center from bottom to top, that is the great reminder of the past.

The neighborhood has a potentially attractive small urban space in Doughboy Square, a wedge of land with a statue at Butler Street and Penn Avenue. But Lawrenceville's great open space is found further east on Butler Street, where a slight bend reveals the Gothic gateway and Romantic landscape of Allegheny Cemetery, where trees and tombs seem to stretch into infinity.

A survivor from the Arsenal near Thirty-ninth and Foster Streets.

Pittsburgh Brewing Company
Liberty and Herron Avenues
1888 and after

The last Pittsburgh-owned brewery, producer of the locally popular Iron City Beer, still functions in Lawrenceville. Its most interesting building is the original office block, built of red brick and stone with buff terra-cotta detailing in the uncertain Classical manner of the 1890 period. Other brewery buildings repeat its round arches and its brick corbeling in various ways, but without the same intensity of detail.

Landmarks plaque

Engine Company Number Twenty-five
3343 Penn Avenue
C. 1890

Here is a powerful and apparently incomplete building, a slightly startling incident as one passes along Penn Avenue in Lawrenceville. The right-hand tower is just *half* a tower! Somebody split it down the middle. And it has the windows of a winding stair that rises blindly into a coping. The turrets over the center archway have skillfully corbeled bottoms, but no tops. Something was but is no more, or should have been but never was. The power of what *is*, is considerable, although the great arch over the two fire-engine doors has a crutch-like pier of stone to offset the uncertainty of its abutment.

Pennsylvania National Bank
Penn Avenue and Butler Street
Beezer Brothers, architects, c. 1900

At Doughboy Square, Allen Newman's *Doughboy* of 1921 stands alertly before a small bank building of brownish Roman brick and terra cotta. The bank's style is a simply detailed Beaux-Arts that enlivens and does not overburden the facades. Both the style and color remind one at once of Union Station. The ensemble of bank and statue give a remarkable dignity to an unattractive street scene, and it is to be hoped that a good use will be found some day for the building.

St. Augustine's Church (Roman Catholic)
Thirty-seventh and Bandera Streets
Rutan & Russell, architects; John T. Comes, designer; 1899

St. Augustine's, the second church of the parish, is a notable landmark in Lawrenceville, rising above the housetops. The church is designed in Italian Romanesque, with that style's distinctive jutting hood over a facade sculpture of St. Augustine. Yet it was built for a German parish, which had the right to receive instruction in German. The interior, 58 feet high, has an octagonal lantern at the crossing that rises

215

to 72 feet, and is decorated with stained glass, murals, and marblework. Five altars, including the main altar, are from the original church of 1863.

John T. Comes, the designer, was soon to begin independent practice and become the best-known local architect of Catholic churches and institutional buildings.

McKee house
3600 Penn Avenue
C. 1870

This house has very tenuous associations with the family of Stephen Collins Foster, but only because of some cellar masonry surviving from his birthplace. In fact, it is a very pleasant medium-sized Second Empire house, whose exterior has been carefully restored and whose interior has been converted into apartments, a small art center, and offices for the American Wind Symphony.

A small urn on the front lawn commemorates Foster's birth.

U.S. Marine Hospital (presently, Allegheny County Health Department)
Penn Avenue and Fortieth Street
C. 1900

To obtain some conception of this building's style, one must look at the split curved pediment of the doorway, the window arches with their keystones, and the window sash with their many panes. The conclusion is English, somewhere around 1700, though the flaring eaves with exposed rafter ends have more of a Latin flavor. Indeed, if you try

to label the building's style you are frustrated; this is a genial piece of Eclecticism in the most literal sense. Once a hospital, it was obviously intended to be reassuring: a nice big house rather than a mere institution. The rather broad proportions themselves suggest a relaxed attitude, as does the bright red of the brickwork. The landscaped setting with enormous sycamore trees enhances the effect.

Allegheny Arsenal area
North of Penn Avenue between Thirty-ninth and Fortieth Streets
1814 and after

Allegheny Arsenal once dominated Lawrenceville, an apron of land running downhill from Penn Avenue to the Allegheny River. Two famous names were associated with its early buildings: Benjamin Henry Latrobe, an outstanding early architect, while he was in Pittsburgh setting up a steamboat yard for Robert Fulton, and Thomas Pope, a brilliant engineer. Some of the early buildings may have been built after Latrobe's designs, and Pope may also have had some designs executed. Today only fragments exist. An explosion in 1862 destroyed at least one building, and after the Civil War the Arsenal became less and less important; in 1907 part was given to the City for a park, and in 1926 the rest was sold. In Arsenal Park is an adapted version of the original powder magazine, a massive, low-built stone structure that carries a handsome cast-iron symbolic plaque. Otherwise, the most intact remnant stands near the Washington Crossing Bridge, a Greek Revival building of two stories with Doric pilasters.

Washington Crossing Bridge
Allegheny River at Fortieth Street
Charles S. Davis, County engineer; Janssen & Cocken, architects; 1923

In November 1753, Major George Washington, returning from an unsuccessful debate with the French in Northwest Pennsylvania, attempted to cross the Allegheny River in the Lawrenceville area. He nearly drowned, nearly froze to death, but reached Shannopin's Town, the nearest approach to civilization in the Pittsburgh area. The plate-arch bridge shown here, similar to the Thirty-first Street Bridge downstream in its general design, commemorates this event. The bridge has a Classical dignity that understates its size: the central span is 360 feet and gives 72 feet of clearance above the water. Dimensions on the Thirty-first Street Bridge are similar. The balustrade has metal plates bearing coats-of-arms of historic significance.

Carnegie Library of Pittsburgh, Lawrenceville Branch
279 Fisk Street
Alden & Harlow, architects, 1898

Three years after their Quattrocento Carnegie Library in Oakland was finished, the architects built this neighborhood library on a sloping street of homes in Lawrenceville. The banded arches over the windows have a Low Countries quality about them, especially over such big windows separated by narrow piers. The doorway element of brick and richly figured white terra cotta suggests, however, the free variations on Italian Renaissance architecture that Stanford White was making earlier in the decade. This library, it is believed, was the first in the United States to have a separate children's room. The building is well suited to its setting: monumental as is appropriate, yet rather modest too, and like the neighborhood generally, of red brick.

St. Mary's Church (Roman Catholic) group
300 Forty-sixth Street
James Sylvester Devlin, designer for church, 1873-74; John T. Comes, architect for Chapel of St. Anne, 1921; Carlton Strong, architect for Lyceum, 1913

At the top of a hillside street, ending at a back gate of St. Mary's Cemetery, is a group of buildings that seems set off from the rest of Pittsburgh. St. Mary's Church, designed by the civil engineer who laid out the Cemetery, is plain in form but with a front heavily buttressed and ornamented with elaborate brickwork. The Chapel of St. Anne and a Lyceum are both by architects who were prominent in Catholic church work in the Pittsburgh area. The rectory of c. 1900 is one of those loose, amiable, generally Colonial Revival houses that abound around Pittsburgh, remarkable though for its great depth. St. Mary's School of 1881 is a stern Victorian schoolhouse, three stories high and still with its belfry; the Victorian school, like some other Victorian factories, summoned you for the day with a bell.

The Academy of c. 1850 is Greek Revival of the simplest sort with the exception of a very fancy, delicate cast-iron porch, the sort usually associated with New Orleans or Mobile although once quite common in the industrial North.
Landmarks plaque

217

St. Francis General Hospital
Penn Avenue and Forty-fifth Street
1871 and after; Schmidt, Garden & Erikson (Chicago), architects for Mary Immaculate Hall (presently, Mental Health Center), 1932

Along with older parts in massive 1890s Gothic and 1900s Beaux-Arts, which in themselves are striking, this hospital complex has a remarkable and very large building, visible on its hillside site for miles. Presently the Mental Health Center, it was once a nurses' residence. The detailing is Art Deco, the general effect is Romanesque, and the fantastic bricklaying suggests the sort that avant-garde architects in Amsterdam were calling for around 1920. Here is a building from a moment in architectural history when incongruous forces might contribute to a single design: craftsmen clothing, brick by carefully laid brick, a steel frame; ornament affectedly modern on a tall building with a medieval silhouette.

Allegheny Cemetery

Allegheny Cemetery was the fourth major rural public cemetery established in the United States when it was incorporated in 1844. John Chislett, superintendent of the Cemetery and architect of its Butler Street gateway, designed a Romantic landscape plan of lawns, plantings, and winding roads on the hillside site. The cemetery's original 100 acres have since been trebled to extend to the Penn Avenue entrance.

Victorian Pittsburgh used the cemetery as its primary burial ground, and enjoyed its planned open space as a rare pleasure. A tour of Allegheny Cemetery is still one of the great visual adventures of Pittsburgh, full of the beauty and curiosity that a major Victorian cemetery has to offer. The verdant landscape, the massed obelisks and other monuments of every kind, and the famous Pittsburgh names to be seen throughout — B. F. Jones, Henry W. Oliver, Stephen Foster, Lillian Russell — make for a unique experience. The Cemetery administration knows this, and issues a map and guide for those who want to take the tour.

Butler Street gateway and administration building, Allegheny Cemetery
4734 Butler Street
John Chislett, architect for gateway, 1847; Barr & Moser, architects for administration building, 1868

As well as planning the cemetery, Chislett designed its receiving vault and its lower entrance. The vault is gone, replaced by a larger one of generally similar design, but his very handsome Tudor gateway for the lower entrance remains. The leaf ornament in the spandrels has an Early Victorian softness and lushness — this is not crisp Tudor foliage — but otherwise it has the authentic touch and is very well proportioned besides. The administration building is perhaps — perhaps — not quite as brilliant in its conception, but both have a remarkable mixture of quaintness, repose, and bristling energy. You can see in both either the mellow beauty of the engraving the Cemetery uses on its literature or the perkiness of the little upright turrets on the gateway and the tower with its even tinier turrets.

National Register District

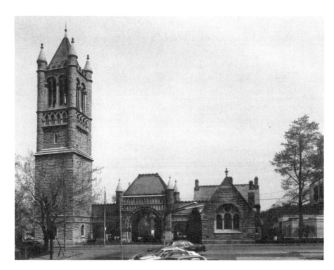

Penn Avenue gateway, Allegheny Cemetery
4715 Penn Avenue
Dull & Macomb, architects, 1887

This tower stands out in a general view of Bloomfield, at whose border it stands, especially now that the gray-granite walls and red tile roof have been cleaned. This is naive Richardson Romanesque, designed when the form of the Courthouse tower was known but before it was completed, and imitating it in a very general way. The openings have wrought ironwork with all the wayward fancy of which the 1880s were capable. Wrought iron had made a return at the beginning of the decade, replacing the more facile cast iron that had dominated architectural ornament since 1840, and architects were eagerly exploiting its distinctive limitations and possibilities, the artistry attainable by the smith rather than the pattern-maker.

The caretaker's house, despite the Victorian granite walls and steep tile roof, is in commonsensical contrast, almost a Georgian design realized a hundred years later.

National Register District

Monuments
Allegheny Cemetery

Allegheny Cemetery's funerary monuments are extremely varied, yet present a more unified effect than they once did. The earliest tombs were of sandstone, marble, even zinc, and it was quite usual for family plots to be surrounded by iron fences. Tightened regulations around the beginning of this century eliminated the fences and other visually distracting auxiliary features and demanded that new tombs be made of materials that would be proof against deterioration. As a result, this is largely a cemetery of granite and bronze, though plenty of weathered sandstone and marble tombs remain.

Wilkins monument

Moorhead mausoleum

The very grandest of the sandstone tombs is the Moorhead mausoleum of 1862, in a remote hollow of Section 26: a Gothic tomb, eroded by time but full of barbaric splendor. The Wilkins monument of 1888 in Section 14 is barbaric in another way; it represents the family of William Wilkins, that brilliant and versatile early Pittsburgher, as a granite tree with severed limbs. Each limb is a family member, memorialized by a bronze plaque on an individual stump. Granite too is the tall mausoleum in Section 1, dating from 1893, of J. B. Ford, founder of the Pittsburgh Plate Glass Company: a hard, challenging edifice accompanied by brooding statuary but with a blaze of warm color inside from stained glass in the rooftop lantern. The Eberhardt and Ober mausoleums, side by side in Section 14 and similar in design, recall the famous brewery at the foot of Troy Hill. These two are of granite, with designs worked out in contrasting matte and glossy finishes; William Eberhardt's, the larger and more elaborate — he was the dominant partner even in death — dates from 1893.

Many of the monuments are now being restored by the Allegheny Cemetery Historical Association.

National Register District

J. B. Ford mausoleum

Eberhardt and Ober mausoleums

The eastern part of Oakland, with Herron Hill to the north.

Oakland

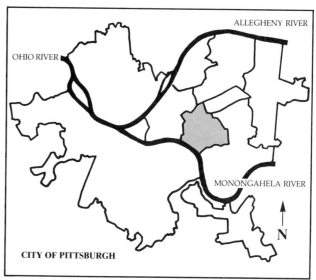

CITY OF PITTSBURGH

At the eastern end of Soho, Fifth Avenue winds upward and eastward in an S-curve, while Herron Hill retreats to form the backdrop of a plateau that extends southward to overlook the Monongahela River. On this plateau about 200 feet above the river, and on the Herron Hill slope behind, a few wealthy Pittsburghers began to build villas early in the nineteenth century. Fifth Avenue, then a country road, was a major route eastward, and the setting was airy, offered good views, and lay well beyond the city and the factories and house rows that were developing on its outskirts. Members of the Third Presbyterian Church downtown so favored this western part of Oakland that it was sometimes called the Third Church Colony.

Horsecar service in 1860, followed by cable traction in 1888 and electric trolley service in 1896, changed the character of the neighborhood. Houses, close-set but very solid and respectable nonetheless, arose along Fifth Avenue and the parallel Forbes Avenue in the area of the villas, while housing and commerce extended eastward and southward into what had once been farmland.

221

Flourishing Eclecticism: the Pittsburgh Athletic Association.

At the eastern end of Oakland, a narrow tract called Bellefield had been platted in 1850 next to the vast acreage of farmland owned by Pittsburgh's most famous expatriate Mary Croghan Schenley. South of Fifth Avenue, Bellefield developed as an unpretentious section of homes on little streets; to the north it was notably more pretentious, with Italianate and Second Empire villas and houses, many by the Philadelphian Isaac Hobbs.

The donation of 300 acres of Schenley land for a major urban park and the consequent donation of the Carnegie Institute suggested that the central part of Oakland was destined for great things, and beginning in 1897 Franklin F. Nicola bought more Schenley acreage for development. One consequence of the land he put on the market was the transfer of the University of Pittsburgh, beginning in 1908, from its Perry Hilltop campus. The Oakland hillside campus of Henry Hornbostel's grand plan was hardly realized at all, but the University made its mark on Oakland with the Cathedral of Learning, begun in 1926 and built into the 1930s, and in its further constructions of the 1950s and 1960s. In its takeover of existing buildings, it continues to make its mark. Carnegie-Mellon University, whose largely Hornbostel campus lies to the east across Junction Hollow, made its mark in a more orderly fashion beginning in 1904.

The villas, meanwhile, yielded to early twentieth-century development. Magee Hospital was built on the plateau land below Forbes Avenue, and in the late 1920s other hospitals began to build on the hillside close to the Pitt Medical School. The first Georgian and Florentine constructions seemed sufficiently gigantic at the time but construction has gone on and on, swallowing up blocks of houses, engulfing the original buildings in annexes, until today the Medical Center, once reasonably gracious, suggests an industrial district with some aesthetic pretensions.

In Bellefield, apartment buildings rose. Beginning with the Bellefield Dwellings of 1902–04, this became Pittsburgh's premier district for apartment living — apartment living, that is, with comfort, in prestigious buildings with careful architectural treatment. Near by, in Schenley Farms, Nicola developed a tightly controlled City Beautiful development of fine houses. Today Schenley Farms' residential streets retain a studied early twentieth-century graciousness in an Oakland subject to an ever-increasing level of activity and spatial demand.

Consequently, the present nature of Oakland is that of a neighborhood assembled from incongruous pieces rather than one that has evolved. Nicola's Civic Center of institutional palaces, his Schenley Farms housing district, the factory-like hospitals, and Pitt's large buildings of varying age and quality are insertions, though sometimes beautiful ones, into a smaller-scaled neighborhood of houses and shops. Along the avenues a few houses survive, though their ground floors are mostly given over to the commercial froth of cheap restaurants and shops that large institutions generate.

But south of Forbes Avenue, the general effect is different. Here are Victorian houses in various states of repair, seedily respectable apartment buildings, little stores, close-built streets that meet at odd angles, and an occasional grand effect such as the open green of Oakland Square or the proscenium-box view up Junction Hollow from North Parkview Avenue. The institutions seem remote, although the hillside hospitals are quite visible to the north and the tapering silhouette of the Cathedral of Learning dominates the horizon.

The history of Schenley Park is intimately connected with that of Oakland, but here the land has escaped the developer's hand. Although it is intensely used for recreational purposes, it extends an arm into the heart of the Civic Center, and has its own incidents of formality — in particular a fine collection of public sculpture — as well as wooded valleys, grassy slopes, and log houses preserved on their original sites, seemingly remote from institutions and close-built streets.

Houses
2701–07 Fifth Avenue and 1–7 Robinson Street
C. 1875

This is a notable row of eight houses, similar though not absolutely uniform in design, whose basic simplicity, a survival of the Georgian tradition, is varied with bay windows, large dormers, and modest Italianate ornament. At this point, Fifth Avenue curves eastward out of Soho, and the lower four houses are set into an echelon formation to follow it. The unified composition is a very pleasant one, well-proportioned and dignified, and makes a good emphatic introduction to Oakland.

Houses
368–82 McKee Place
C. 1920

This is a very unusual house row, white-stuccoed and climbing the gentle slope of the street. One-story front walls, two-story roofs, and highly visible chimneys create an Old World effect that the sight of the original casements, opened in the summertime, would have enhanced. There has been much remodeling since the houses were built, but the row remains impressive.

St. Peter's Episcopal Church
Forbes and Craft Avenues
John Notman (Philadelphia), architect, 1851–52; moved and reconstructed, 1901; Vrydaugh & Wolfe, architects for additions, 1901

Around 1850 the Protestant Episcopal Church in the United States, which was in communion with the Church of England, was under considerable influence from the Ecclesiological Society, a British organization determined to restore the form and instruments of worship to sound medieval practice. The Society had determined that the optimum architectural style, in most cases, was fourteenth-century English Gothic from the Decorated period. This was the style that Notman used for the most part at St. Peter's, though his broach spire is thirteenth-century English. The results, though not elaborate, were refined, and the congregation that sold its land opposite the Courthouse for the construction of the Frick Building, retained and moved the church, re-erecting it stone by stone in Oakland. In the reconstruction, Vrydaugh & Wolfe added a new porch and parish buildings to the rear.

No gift of prophecy attended the choice of a new site. The villas across Forbes Street immediately yielded to a trolley barn, and the middle-class houses and apartment houses near by deteriorated in a few decades. The Boulevard of the Allies, in the early 1920s, ran close by to remove homes and impose a psychological barrier between the church and a large part of Oakland. Yet the handsome old church remains, its spire visible for miles, marking one end of Oakland as the Cathedral of Learning does the other.

Landmarks plaque

House
315 Oakland Avenue
C. 1860

Forlorn at the end of a parking lot stands one of Oakland's best houses. Its porch has lost the brackets it must once have had, but the vergeboards of the front gable and dormer have held on. The style is a mixed one, half-Italianate, half-Gothic. The mixture is typical of the mid-nineteenth century; so is the formula of one building mass with a gable toward the street and an adjacent mass presenting its side. This house, well preserved outside in spite of everything, should be restored and put to distinguished use.

Medical Arts Building
Fifth Avenue and Atwood Street
Maximilian Nirdlinger, architect, 1931–32

The Medical Arts building introduced Oakland to "modern" architecture in the first significant way. Some of the original Modernistic detailing is visible above the ground floor, but the spectacular zigzag effect of the canopies over the shops and of the entrance was destroyed in a remodeling of the 1970s. The lobby, though, retains most of its old detailing.

Iroquois Apartments
Forbes Avenue and Atwood Street
Frederick J. Osterling, architect, 1901

A block-wide expanse of apartments with three light courts on the front, designed in an indeterminate Classical style. A brown brick and lighter gray terra-cotta trim show the prevailing preference at the time for rather dark colors as do the Iroquois' contemporaries the Hotel Schenley and Union Station. Three elaborate entrance halls once led to the interior, while open galleries to the rear connected the service rooms. Built at a time of considerable apartment-house construction, the Iroquois was grander than usual: no homely porches stacked three high, but slightly swelling window bays overlooking Forbes Avenue to create a bold effect from down the street. It shows the same sort of heavy elegance that Osterling put into the Arrott Building downtown. The Iroquois Apartments building has been remodeled for offices.

Forbes National Bank (presently, Mellon Bank)
Fifth Avenue and Oakland Avenue
E. P. Mellon, architect, 1930

Here is a very pleasant Italian Renaissance neighborhood bank, which once had a polychromed beamed ceiling vividly contrasting but stylistically in keeping with the monochrome limestone exterior. The style is that found in several of the medical institutions built near by in the 1930s; Mellon was involved as an architect with some of these. Such a simple and well-studied building is a treat to see. It uses only enough detailing, and most details are of exactly the right size and form. Such buildings are not "exciting," and they can be merely bland, but when they are good they are very good indeed.

Western State Psychiatric Hospital (presently, Western Psychiatric Institute and Clinic)
O'Hara and De Soto Streets
Raymond M. Marlier, architect, 1939–40; addition

Built in a hard-featured Modernistic style of orangeish brick, this mental hospital arose in a neighborhood of academic and medical buildings. The other medical buildings were urbanely Georgian or Italian Renaissance. Perhaps, whatever the style, the architecture was meant as a message to the entering patient: entering a Florentine hospital you will be treated graciously; entering a Modernistic hospital you will be briskly and efficiently fixed.

The Civic Center

The crown of Oakland is the Civic Center that Franklin F. Nicola dreamed of from the time he purchased his first cornfield in 1897, and that others soon helped him realize. Many American cities have planned such splendid places, begun them, and sometimes even largely finished them. Around 1900 the City Beautiful was a common ideal, a place of palaces and avenues, trees and lawns, elegant costumes and carriages. Beggars, broken-down wagons, gangling wooden poles strung with wires had no place there. In such visions they ceased to exist, or existed elsewhere.

Eventually, splendid architecture did surround, almost entirely, that great 14-acre lawn where the Cathedral of Learning rose. The homely, sooty buildings of Victorian Oakland were only a few steps away, but there were points of view from which the spectacle was *almost* perfect. Nor did it involve the cold perfection of a grand avenue. Bigelow Boulevard, the fast road from town that terminated at the entrance to Schenley Park, approached the Civic Center by way of a curve and two right angles and reached Schenley Plaza off-axis. This was eccentric conduct for a City Beautiful boulevard, but this and other irregularities of the street layout encouraged architects to treat each building individually while giving it their best efforts.

First United Presbyterian Church (presently, Bellefield United Presbyterian Church)
Fifth Avenue and Thackeray Street
William Boyd, architect, 1896

A Richardson Romanesque church of sandstone with a low 16-sided central lantern that serves, like the arcaded bow window of the front, to emphasize that this is basically an auditorium. It is a "tower" church, similar in conception to the Shadyside Presbyterian Church of 1889. To the rear is a semicircle of Sunday-school rooms around a space once lighted by a stained-glass dome.

National Register District

University Club
123 University Place
Henry Hornbostel, architect, 1923; addition, 1963

The clubhouse, built of warm-gray brick with limestone detailing, has externally a very generalized Renaissance character that could be English as readily as Italian. Inside, spaces are Tudor, Italian Renaissance and, in the case of the great dining room overlooking the street, Adam. Above the dining room is a dining terrace, an excellent place to view the architecture of the Civic Center. The building is quite dignified, yet is modest too, and has a warm, home-like feeling inside.

Oakland Turnverein (later, various institutions of the University of Pittsburgh)
O'Hara and Thackeray Streets
Kiehnel & Elliott, architects, c. 1912

Built by a German-American gymnastic association, this building passed into the hands of the University of Pittsburgh in less than a decade and has served a variety of purposes ever since. The basic organization is Classical, but the detailing is avant-garde by 1912 standards, with stone doorways and terra-cotta frieze ornamentation of a new sort. The ornament has not the authority of that by Frank Lloyd Wright or Louis Sullivan — it wants to be new but is not quite sure how — yet it does suggest progressive Chicago trends. Treating the second-floor window zone as a broad band gives the whole composition a unity and a horizontal emphasis that it needs.

National Register District

Thaw Hall

Schenley Farms Campus, University of Pittsburgh
Bigelow Boulevard and Parkman Street
Palmer & Hornbostel (New York), planners and original architects; planned 1908

In 1908 the Western University of Pennsylvania, then on Perry Hilltop on the North Side, purchased a hillside cow pasture in Oakland from Franklin F. Nicola and instituted a competition for its development as a new campus. Palmer & Hornbostel's winning master plan was most ambitious, with a great Classical temple at the top and a multitude of lesser buildings flanking a broad descending lawn crisscrossed by a zigzag road and stairs.

Of the great plan that Henry Hornbostel designed, only fragments were built. Thaw Hall of 1908–09, on O'Hara Street opposite the Soldiers' and Sailors' Memorial, is the most

easily seen and the most interesting. Its uncompleted terraced front, ending in a single temple-like pavilion, makes an interesting composition while its richly modeled terra cotta attests to Hornbostel's brilliance with ornament. The cream-colored brick and rough gray granite — probably intended for carving — are good complementary materials; Hornbostel was to use the same materials superbly at the Fine Arts Building at Carnegie Tech a few years later. The brick and the terra cotta were used again in the other buildings erected: the School of Mines, later State Hall, built in 1908–09 and now gone; Mineral Hall of 1912, partway up the hill and notable for its elaborate doorway; and the Medical School, now Pennsylvania Hall, of 1910 at the top of the hill. On the gable of this last is Charles Keck's *Aesculapius* in white terra cotta, modeled with the ancient Egyptian technique of sinking the outline of the figure into the wall surface, then modeling the figure itself in very shallow relief.

To these buildings was added Benno Janssen's severely Grecian Alumni Hall in 1920, and there have been several more recent buildings and annexes.

Allegheny County Soldiers' and Sailors' Memorial
Fifth Avenue and Bigelow Boulevard
Henry Hornbostel of Palmer & Hornbostel (New York), architect, 1907–11

In a competition of 1907 for a County war memorial hall, Hornbostel's design won out over the submissions of such nationally known architects as Ernest Flagg, Cass Gilbert, and Peabody & Stearns, as well as those of prominent local offices. It was built nearly in the form submitted, but the original orientation toward "Grant Boulevard," as Bigelow was then, was sensibly changed on Hornbostel's initiative to take advantage of the long lawn sloping gently to Fifth Avenue. The central mass of light-colored sandstone and terra cotta holds an auditorium for 2,500, with a clerestoried banquet hall above, beneath the pyramidal tiled roof. The spreading base holds two meeting rooms and an ambulatory with cases of military memorabilia, primarily from the Civil War. Charles Keck's *America* sits enthroned over the central doorway, grasping a sheathed sword; on the terrace to the right and left stand a soldier and a sailor of the Civil War by Frederick Cleveland Hubbard, added in 1923.

Except for the landscaping, which is rather plain and fragmentary, the Soldiers' and Sailors' Memorial illustrates Beaux-Arts design in its grandest mode: symmetrical, impressive in massing, rich in detail, Classical in its general lines — the Mausoleum at Halicarnassus was a general model. The great public halls rise above a spreading base of insistent horizontals, outcurved in a welcoming gesture on the Fifth Avenue front in a way that dignifies the small meeting rooms while allowing the ambulatory to pass around the auditorium uninterrupted. Behind this building, Hornbostel's grand hillside campus for the University of Pittsburgh was to have risen.

In the early 1970s, Landmarks became concerned about the physical condition of the building, and under contract with the County Commissioners presented a series of recommendations for its improvement, many of which were adopted.

National Register District; Landmarks plaque

yards, and above the villa-like steps down to Forbes. The materials are brown brick above lower stories of limestone. These are more heedless and utilitarian days for the complex, now used for dormitories, yet the gateways and colonnades remain with their old suave charm.

National Register District

Hotel Schenley (presently, William Pitt Student Union, University of Pittsburgh)
Bigelow Boulevard and Fifth Avenue
Rutan & Russell, architects, 1898

Before its closing in the 1950s this was arguably the most elegant hotel in Pittsburgh: not least because it stood in its own landscaped grounds. Here visiting artists performing at the Syria Mosque a half-block away would stay — Eleanora Duse, in fact, died here — as well as baseball teams playing at Forbes Field, a couple of hundred yards to the south. The design is in the still-tentative Classical manner of the 1890s, executed in brick and terra cotta of a strong tawny shade that suited the taste of Pittsburghers at the time. Inside, the public rooms were spacious and elegant, with a considerable use of marble in the lobby. Conversions in the hotel days were minor: an open portico toward the Boulevard was rebuilt and glazed in as a lounge, and a colonnaded bridge was added to give a connection to the Schenley Apartments when these were opened in the 1920s. In the 1960s, less fortunately, the cornice had to come down. In 1983 the upper floors were gutted and completely reworked inside, while the ground-floor rooms were generally restored and refurnished. The basement was fitted up in a wholly new Post-Modern way and a Corinthian basement colonnade was added on the Forbes Avenue front.

National Register District; Landmarks plaque

Schenley Apartments (presently, Schenley Quadrangle, University of Pittsburgh)
Fifth Avenue opposite Thackeray Street
Henry Hornbostel, architect, 1922

This was Franklin F. Nicola's final speculation, and his home. The Bellefield Company, the developer, printed up a fancy booklet to describe the Apartments: 235 suites, from two to nine rooms in seven units of 10 to 12 floors, the ground floors on Fifth and Forbes Avenues being for stores, and colonnaded and landscaped courts over an underground garage. Meals could be sent up from the Hotel Schenley, and servants could be hired by the hour. The renderings show very nice planting indeed, by the French-looking gateways from Fifth Avenue, along the Doric colonnades of the court-

Cathedral of Learning

Heinz Chapel

Cathedral of Learning campus, University of Pittsburgh
Bigelow Boulevard and Fifth Avenue
Charles Zeller Klauder (Philadelphia), architect; Cathedral of Learning, 1926-37; Heinz Chapel, 1934-38; Stephen Collins Foster Memorial, 1935-37

When John Gabbert Bowman accepted the chancellorship of the University of Pittsburgh in 1921, he found that his university consisted primarily of Hornbostel's few achieved buildings, Benno Janssen's new Alumni Hall, and a great many badly deteriorated wooden barracks from the recent war; and further, that the institution was spectacularly in debt and its creditors out of patience. To say the very least, he took a bold line with the rich and powerful of Pittsburgh. To believe his own account, he must have been one of the most impudent and persuasive diplomats of all time, with a personality and a vision that some very unimpressionable businessmen failed to resist. Having decided to vacate the original hillside site, he persuaded Andrew W. and Richard B. Mellon to give him the 14-acre Frick property near by, around which the Civic Center was growing, and began to push his vision of a great university tower.

When the fifteenth-century Cathedral of Seville was being planned, one of the cathedral chapter urged the construction of a church "so great and of such a kind that those who see it finished shall think that we were mad." Some such Gothic fervor was in Bowman's mind, but his struggle, on the contrary, was to convince everyone that he was sane. A university skyscraper was unheard-of, and the thought of class changes by elevator appalled everyone — reasonably enough, as time would show. Bowman realized that he had to have a plan to display; people had to taste the idea, not merely hear it. He went to Charles Z. Klauder, a sensitive Eclectic architect and a specialist in college design. Klauder reacted coolly, but he and his staff started designing. They tried and tried, and Bowman kept saying that the inspiration was not there; his students must be *inspired* by the building. Temperaments flashed. One evening — this is all Bowman's account — Bowman and Klauder happened to be hearing the Magic Fire Music from *Die Walküre*, and Bowman said that *that* was what he wanted: climax building on climax, leaping ever higher. Klauder and his draftsmen achieved a breakthrough shortly thereafter, an absurd but beautiful tower that Bowman sold to the trustees, the rich donors, the ordinary laboring people, and even the schoolchildren, who were caught up in the growing enthusiasm and gave their dimes to the building campaign.

Seen from a distance, the Cathedral of Learning — so called by a draftsman — rises like solid rock, an irregularly tapering mass 535 feet high. Closer-up, it mingles English Perpendicular and French Flamboyant of the fifteenth century, powerful, ascending lines and delicate detailing. The corners, as they rise, break up again and again as solid stone grows into a multitude of pinnacles; between the corner masses are great traceried arches. Under the textured limestone, though, is a massive steel frame cased in concrete; the tower, it is predicted, will last 300 years. Inside, a ring of 18 ground-floor classrooms, each designed in a different national style as a symbol of Pittsburgh's multinational heritage, surround a great vaulted common room 60 feet high. In the building too are the Greek Revival ballroom from "Picnic House," the old Croghan-Schenley villa, and an eighteenth-century library from a house in Damascus, Syria.

If the Cathedral of Learning was the result of a reverie, the Heinz Chapel, donated by the Heinz family, may have been the product of a dream. Bowman wanted a splendid chapel for his students, and Klauder is rumored to have dreamed of the unique form the chapel took, with an apse at each end and a higher portion, like a pair of transepts, at the center beneath a tall spire. The style is fifteenth-century French Flamboyant again, with windows by Charles Connick of Boston that wash the interior in a gentle purple light. Opinions differ on the chapel. It has been called a frog in a lace nightgown, and its ornamentation has been said to lack the vitality of that in the Cathedral of Learning, to be tired, even senile. Most people, however, would probably react to the chapel with enthusiasm: form, detailing, and all. It is surely much more than a typical product of a slickly professional period of architecture. Interdenominational, it is a favorite wedding church.

Stephen Collins Foster Memorial

The Foster Memorial, with a museum like a polygonal chapter house from a medieval monastery and a small theater, probably has a little less vitality than the other two, yet its detailing is crisp, delicate, and never mechanical. Lithographed sheet music from minstrel shows certainly looks odd inside this vision of fifteenth-century France, but an evocation of Foster's native Lawrenceville or of the Victorian period anywhere was out of the question in the 1930s.

National Register District; Landmarks plaques

Pittsburgh Athletic Association
Fifth Avenue and Bigelow Boulevard
Janssen & Abbott, architects, 1909–11

One of the best buildings in the Civic Center is this clubhouse, built in limestone and a closely matching terra cotta. The style is Venetian Renaissance, with some details traceable to two works of Jacopo Sansovino, the Palazzo Grimiani and the Library of St. Mark in Venice, Italy. A

hipped tile roof finishes off the composition in an appropriate way. Critics have gently reproached the architects for having a strong entablature halfway up, on the grounds that it divides the composition in two: the more so since one Corinthian order stands on another. Yet the facade is strong in its general lines, and its decorative details are good in themselves and well designed for harmony with the whole composition. Under the circumstances, a theoretical fault seems not all that important.

National Register District; Landmarks plaque

Masonic Temple
Fifth and Lytton Avenues
Janssen & Abbott, architects, 1914

A fanciful paraphrase of ancient temple architecture, of limestone with detail work in matching terra cotta. The very tall basement conveys a suitable impression of remoteness from the outside world, and the great doorways are of awesome impressiveness. The Corinthian capitals have an intricate Hellenistic quality. This is very obviously an arcane building, in marked contrast to the openness, almost jollity, of the Pittsburgh Athletic Association next door.

National Register District

Twentieth-Century Club
Bigelow Boulevard and southern end of Parkman Avenue
Janssen & Cocken, architects, 1929–30

An earlier building of 1910 was swallowed up in this Italian Renaissance remodeling of a women's club. The building itself is delicate and rather prim; the wall enclosing the motor entrance is more robust in general, but the urns have their own delicate detailing. Inside, some interiors are Art Deco.

National Register District

Syria Mosque
Bigelow Boulevard north of Fifth Avenue
Huehl, Schmidt & Holmes (Chicago), architects, 1915

This auditorium, built for the Shriners, was long the home of the Pittsburgh Symphony and was used for operas and plays. The architecture is generally Syrian Arabic in two shades of brown brick and terra cotta, with striping that has caused it to be compared to a very large mocha torte. The haughty bronze sphinxes are by Giuseppe Moretti.

National Register District

The Historical Society of Western Pennsylvania
4338 Bigelow Boulevard
Ingham & Boyd, architects, 1912

Although the front of this building carries the three flags that have flown over Western Pennsylvania, the building's style is fifteenth-century Italian Renaissance of the most delicate sort. The materials are white brick and matching terra cotta. Inside, the details are American of the eighteenth and early nineteenth centuries.

The first Pittsburgh attempt at a Historical Society came early, in 1834, but the present society, founded in 1879 and assuming its present name in 1883, was the first such organization to last.

National Register District

Western Pennsylvania School for Blind Children
Bayard Street and North Bellefield Avenue
George S. Orth, architect, 1893–94

The derivation of this unusual facade treatment, a yellowish brick striped with red brick, can only be guessed at. Certainly, the City Hospital at Copenhagen, Denmark, built 30 years before, had had a very similar treatment that may have occurred to an architect who was trying to achieve a striking appearance with institutional economy. The more recent impact of "Ruskin Gothic," which also made quite a feature of striped walls, may have been the inspiration. Or Byzantine architecture for that matter.

When the school moved into its new quarters, it was only a few years old, having been founded with a bequest of 1885.

National Register District

Doorway, First Baptist Church

future. But a second look shows gentle ornament, carving in wood and stone with a half-Gothic, half-Arts-and-Crafts flavor about it, contained in the severe overall composition, and outside a delicately detailed copper flèche rises from the crossing. A third look, for instance at the exterior masonry, shows the subtlety that Goodhue, stimulated by a lavish budget, was prepared to put into a work: verticals that are slightly inclined, stones whose jointing is varied to give a subliminal feeling of life to an otherwise textureless surface.

Inside, limestone arches rise from piers without capitals, and Guastavino tile vaults close the spaces. The nave has very narrow aisles and terminates in a preacher's desk and a wooden screen concealing the baptismal tank. Above, in a loft, is an organ with a stained-glass window behind it, giving a climactic feature. Grisaille glass is used in the nave windows.

National Register District; Landmarks plaque

First Baptist Church
North Bellefield Avenue and Bayard Street
Bertram Grosvenor Goodhue of Cram, Goodhue & Ferguson (New York Office), architect, 1909

Goodhue's treatment of the Modern Gothic his firm so successfully promoted is well shown here. At first glance it is terse, a piece of summarized Gothic that feels modern in its abstention from pinnacles outside and capitals inside, its refusal to be in any way quaint. Its corner masses, gradually falling away as they rise, even anticipate the forms that Moderne skyscrapers were to take some fifteen years in the

Rectory, Bellefield Presbyterian Church (presently, Music Building, University of Pittsburgh)
Fifth and North Bellefield Avenues
Frederick J. Osterling, architect (?), 1891

The tentative attribution to Osterling is based on his having been the architect for the Bellefield Presbyterian Church, for whose pastor this was built. Yet this is a very polished Romanesque design and the church was a very gawky Gothic one: can the swan and the ostrich hatch in the same nest? A long arcaded side porch was later enclosed for a ballroom.

National Register District

Webster Hall
Fifth Avenue and North Dithridge Street
Henry Hornbostel and Eric Fisher Wood, architects, 1925–26

Built as a men's residence club, Webster Hall soon became a regular hotel, and now is a condominium. The exterior style is Italian Romanesque, though the entrance was originally Baroque. Inside, public rooms were French, Spanish, Tudor, Empire, Victorian, and Georgian; little of this Eclectic decoration now remains. The hotel has lost its uppermost cornice as well, but retains much of its exterior distinction all the same, thanks to its location at a turn of the street and its boldly striped wall.

National Register District

St. Paul's Cathedral (Roman Catholic)
Fifth Avenue and North Craig Street
Egan & Prindeville (Chicago), architects, 1903–06;
Edward J. Weber, architect for Synod Hall and Chancery, 1904; Carlton Strong, architect for Rectory, 1926.

The twin spires of St. Paul's Cathedral are prominent, familiar objects on the Oakland skyline, establishing the eastern part of the neighborhood. The two previous cathedrals had been downtown on the site of the Union Arcade, and the move to Oakland was one from an area almost without a remaining resident population to one that was soon to become surrounded by homes. When the decision to build in Oakland was made there *was* no Civic Center, of course: only houses, hillside pastures, and the vague promise of a fine neighborhood that was to be read in the

presence of the Carnegie Institute, Schenley Park, and the Hotel Schenley.

The new cathedral was faced in limestone, which suggested a new spirit in its design, a turning-away from the strong and somber colors of the Victorian past. Yet the actual design was still Victorian in important ways. The new Eclectic architects, who in church architecture were led by Ralph Adams Cram and Bertram Goodhue, tended to think in terms of an overall composition from which the decorative details would grow. The Victorians were more apt to think of the details first, then try to bring them together: this at least is what their actual designs imply. So it is here: the details have a detached quality. There is no true masonry vaulting, and the outer walls lack the flying buttresses one might expect in a five-aisled masonry church, while the piers inside are slender, obviously supporting lighter weights than the vaulted forms suggest. The trend in the future would be toward greater mass inside a church, a feeling of abundant stone or brick supporting the upper walls and the vaults or trusses that covered the space.

Two prominent Pittsburgh Catholic architects have contributed to the cathedral complex: Edward J. Weber in the Synod Hall and Chancery of 1904, which has for the most part a fifteenth-century English look, and Carlton Strong in the Rectory of 1926, in a sophisticatedly simplified Tudor manner.

National Register District; Landmarks plaque

Mellon Institute for Industrial Research, Carnegie-Mellon University
Fifth and South Bellefield Avenues
Janssen & Cocken, architects, 1931–37

While the interiors are in a somewhat-Classical somewhat-Modernistic style, the exterior is resolutely Classical. Perhaps the cornice projects less in proportion to the building height than it would have at one time, but against this we must set 62 monolithic unfluted Ionic columns, 42 feet high, in colonnades on all four sides. A nine-story building — half underground — for scientific research is thus screened by a pure piece of architectural rhetoric, sober in its design, wild in its expense. Stylistically independent of both the exterior and the greater part of the interior is the library, Carolean English of the late seventeenth century, with wood carvings in the manner of Grinling Gibbons.

The Mellon Stuart Company, the contractor, relates that a detailed full-scale mockup of a corner and the nearest two columns was erected for study, and that to erect the columns safely and in their precise positions they were lowered onto carefully placed blocks of ice and allowed to settle.

The Institute was founded in 1913 by Andrew W. and

Richard B. Mellon, who were impressed by the proposal of Robert Kennedy Duncan, a chemistry professor, for industrial research fellowships. Duncan became the first director of the new institute. Its first permanent building of 1915 survives at Thackeray and O'Hara Streets.

National Register District

Young Men's Hebrew Association
315 South Bellefield Avenue
Benno Janssen of Janssen & Cocken, architect, 1924

Of the three buildings presently on this block, the YMHA has a compelling warmth that neither the Board of Education nor the Mellon Institute, with their limestone fronts, can match. The great rusticated arch is of limestone and so are some other details, but this is primarily an essay in brick. A rough-surfaced mulberry-red brick, laid in a "garden-wall" bond that emphasizes horizontals, creates a beautiful textured surface against which the smooth white stone plays. In the uppermost story, special settings of brick in different hues make a quietly colorful frieze. Above is a tiled hip roof. The general effect is Italian Renaissance, but only in a very loose way. Inside, the effect is more Hispanic, with an auditorium ceiling that imitates *artesonado*, the intricate ceiling woodwork of Spain around 1500, in plaster.

National Register District

Board of Education Building
341 South Bellefield Avenue
Ingham & Boyd, architects, 1926–27

The architects were among the most tasteful this area has seen. The Historical Society of Western Pennsylvania, Chatham Village, and the Buhl Planetarium are witnesses to the quality of their work. Here they executed a suave official building in limestone, Italian Renaissance with a few discreet Baroque touches. Inside is a landscaped courtyard of the same quality as the facades.

National Register District

First Congregational Church (presently, St. Nicholas Cathedral)
419 South Dithridge Street
Thomas Hannah, architect, 1904

A Grecian Ionic portico, executed in sandstone, is the grand and appropriate introduction to a church that has belonged to the Greek Orthodox Church since 1923. The exterior, with its big round-arched windows, is not otherwise specifically symbolic, but the interior is rich with paintings and mosaics. Notable inside are the painting in the dome of Christ the Pantocrator (Ruler of All), with its background of gold leaf, and the iconostasis of metal and mosaic, with peacocks finely depicted on the Royal Doors. Further art is to be found within the sanctuary, including a painting of the Mother and Child and a fresco of the Last Supper.

Landmarks plaque

Carnegie Institute
4400 Forbes Avenue
Longfellow, Alden & Harlow (Boston and Pittsburgh), architects for original building, 1892–95; Alden & Harlow, architects for Forbes Avenue section, 1903–07

Mary Croghan Schenley's 1889 gift of the land for Schenley Park prompted Andrew Carnegie to offer the City a cultural institution to stand at the park's main entrance. The present library section that now faces Schenley Plaza was the first built, outwardly a foursquare Italian Renaissance building, dignified but simple, richly carved in only a few places. Only toward Forbes Avenue was it fancy: there the Music Hall bowed forward in a hemicycle flanked by two Venetian campaniles, and the entrance and foyer group in front of it were surmounted by a carved balustrade, two domes, and four lampposts bearing clusters of gaslights so elevated from the street that they must have been intended to be seen rather than to see by.

Inside are calm vaulted corridors, decorated with medallions and leaf ornament by the Bostonian Elmer Ellsworth Garnsey and originally more decorated than now, and a great skylit reading room. The effect of this earlier portion, aside from its indecisive and now-removed Forbes Avenue features, is exactly right for such a public institution: a beauty that comes partly from decorative stonework and bronzework, partly from the simple, placid geometry of the vaulted spaces; a refreshing sense of solidity in the stone walls, oaken bookcases, and heavy, varnished doors with brass hinges; and a home-like feeling too: the rooms are big but make no attempt to overawe the public, and you are comfortable in them. On the unhappy side, however, is the modernization that clutters the entrance and lobby area, destroying its original lucidity.

The Forbes Avenue enlargements begun in 1903 were conceived in a different spirit, one of ostentation, with two complicated entrance pavilions that include Corinthian columns and numerous bronzes by John Massey Rhind (New York). The showiness is typical of the time, and most people see in it the Beaux-Arts style; yet there is a stiffness, a lack of curves anywhere, that suggests rather Imperial Germany. The design would have been unimpressive in Paris, but it might have gone over in Berlin. One of the entrance pavilions leads to a new foyer for the Music Hall, an interior that must be seen to be believed, sumptuous in the truest sense with many kinds of marbles, richly molded bronzework, and heavy plaster; there is a story that Carnegie *demanded* that it cost more than any throne room as a tribute to the sovereign people.

The other entrance leads to the marble stair hall of the original Museum of Art, home of the famous Carnegie International art exhibitions; around the walls are the *Saga of Steel* murals of John White Alexander, which have drawn the sneers of several generations but that sin mostly in being out of fashion. At the center, between the entrances, is a great hall of architectural casts, doorways, windows, pulpits, columns, capitals, and fragments of every sort from the historic architecture of Europe, reproduced in plaster.

The Scaife Gallery addition of 1974 added vastly to the spaces of the Museum of Art.

Humbler, set apart, but very big all the same is the Bellefield Boiler Plant in Junction Hollow below the Institute, a brick industrial building of 1903–07 by Alden & Harlow added to in 1943. Brick, not ashlar, it is a self-respecting construction despite its almost-total lack of decoration. When it was built, the public was invited to inspect the dynamos and engines in the Institute basement, driven by the steam from this boiler house. This was often the case at the time: The Machine was not yet a generative force in culture in any important way, yet modern society was proud of it. Even a boiler house had to be decent if not elegant in a first-class architectural group such as this.

National Register District; Landmarks plaques

Hammerschlag house

Stengel house

4123 Bigelow Boulevard

4309 Parkman Avenue

Houses
Schenley Farms

The northern end of Franklin F. Nicola's massive purchases from the Schenley Estate and the O'Hara family was for houses, and from 1907 on was offered to home buyers on a leasing basis with strict obligations on both sides. Nicola was determined that his residential development would be of high quality from the start, with all utilities buried, a special police force, and the best equipment in every house. Most of the gently rising streets were planted with sycamores, and along these streets very substantial houses rose from the late 1900s through the 1920s. Grant Boulevard, soon to be named Bigelow Boulevard, bisected the area on its way from town to the Civic Center; here, trees by the curb yielded to a more open effect of lawns and flowers. The early houses, respectable as they were, were not as well-designed as those of the 1920s, but all suggested — and continue to suggest — a very comfortable way of living. Both Schenley Farms proper and its uphill fringe, Schenley Farms Heights, retain the air of domestic happiness as conceived early in this century.

Something of the same ruggedness found in the Parkman Avenue retaining wall is present in the house that Henry Hornbostel designed at Bigelow Boulevard and Parkman Avenue. Designed around 1910 for Arthur Hammerschlag, president of the Carnegie Technical Schools that Hornbostel was designing and erecting, it has rubble walls up to the second-floor window sills, and rough brown brick in stack bond — brick literally just stacked — from there to the eaves. This design has the same slightly mannered down-to-earth quality that Hornbostel was putting into the Carnegie Tech dormitories. A similar quality is to be found in Kiehnel & Elliott's Stengel house of c. 1915 at 4136 Bigelow Boulevard. There is more explicit ornament here, and a little allusion to Classical design practice, yet inside and out, in brick and wood, the house expresses the ideals of the Arts and Crafts movement of the twentieth century's first two decades; things are simple and sincere, as if an honest workman with a trained eye had formed and arranged stone, brick, wood, and wrought iron in a harmonious way so that the results were at once humble and sophisticated.

In such a development as Schenley Farms, though, reconsidered old ideas are more commonly found than new ones. Number 4123 Bigelow Boulevard, which appears to be from the 1920s, suggests a small English manor or a prosperous farmhouse of the seventeenth century, fitted with new window sash in the eighteenth; its roof is extended in the front to cover a normal American front porch in the way that its historic model might have had an extended roof to shelter a hay wagon. Number 4309 Parkman Avenue is more

4405 Bigelow Boulevard

manorial with its delicate stone balustrade edging a terrace, yet it has a homely as well as a gentlemanly quality. Number 4405 Bigelow Boulevard, by Louis Stevens, has a grander air, with its limestone facing, its loggia with a polychrome terracotta medallion, its rusticated doorway, and its *altana* that rises above the main roof: an Italian villa looking coolly at Goodhue's mixture of zeal and cunning in the First Baptist Church.

National Register District

Retaining wall
Western bend of Parkman Avenue
C. 1905

Site preparation in the Schenley Farms residential neighborhood required cutting into an outlying part of Herron Hill, so that the house blocks are well below the adjacent hillside campus of the University of Pittsburgh. To retain the earth this handsome wall of typical engineering masonry, a kind of dam, was built. Roughly textured, darkened by the Pittsburgh air, romantically overgrown by plants, following the directional change of Parkman Street with a broad curve, the wall is a poetic feature as well as a necessary one. A stair built into the wall gives access to Centre Avenue properties above the street.

National Register District

Schenley High School
Bigelow Boulevard and Centre Avenue
Edward Stotz, architect, 1915–16

In the two decades since Stotz had designed the Fifth Avenue High School both school plans and school facades had changed. The older school was warm in color and picturesque in detailing; here, the limestone fronts are monochrome and monotonous, relying on good proportions, a few architectural motifs, and the dramatic rounded corners useful in a large building whose perimeter is a scalene triangle. The many windows, though, are expressive in themselves; this was a very large and well-equipped school for its time, and the open utilitarian fronts hint at the complex technology of modern education.

National Register District

Apartment buildings
Bellefield

Directly east of Franklin F. Nicola's Schenley Farms development, including his Civic Center, is Bellefield, whose western boundary is marked by Bellefield Avenue. The name of this narrow district was given by Neville B. Craig, the first recorder of Pittsburgh history, who sold a portion of his farm — "Bellefield" — to developers around 1850.

Bellefield Dwellings

The remarkable aspect of Bellefield is the number of its apartment houses. The oldest is Bellefield Dwellings, Centre and North Bellefield Avenues, built in 1902–04 by Carlton Strong, who had just arrived from New York and was to become one of the best-known architects with Catholic connections. Bellefield Dwellings has a bold red-and-white effect, and a rising effect, that suggests that a mildly avant-garde apartment house from the Morningside Heights area of Manhattan had migrated to a still-pastoral part of Pittsburgh. In the next seven decades other apartment houses followed near by, some pretentious, some dull but adequate. There were those 1915 apartment houses where everything seemed to be white in color and relaxed in mood, and then there were

King Edward Apartments

meaner places, mainly much more recent. The King Edward Apartments of 1914, at North Craig and Bayard Streets, illustrates one solution to the problem of the older apartment house, that of packaging its inhabitants graciously. The window sash is commonsensical Georgian, but the exterior otherwise is early English Renaissance in the easily modeled and not-too-expensive terra cotta much in favor at the time.

Royal York Apartments

Another well-known apartment house stands near by, close to Schenley Farms Heights. This is the Royal York Apartments, 3955 Bigelow Boulevard, designed in 1937 by Frederick Stanton of Chicago: a work of off-white terra cotta and light warm-gray brick in a mild Art Deco style. It is big and urbane, and gets some notice from these facts, but its great feature is a porte-cochere supported on columns of wrought iron and milk glass, lit from within.

Central Catholic High School
4720 Fifth Avenue
Edward J. Weber of Link, Weber & Bowers, architect, 1926–27

A very impressive composition in both size and detailing. The material is a warm bright-red brick, laid with calculated irregularity; into this are set, here and there, bold diaper patterns in a darker brick. This is remarkable: at the time when Victorian architecture was most despised, here is decoration that William Butterfield, one of the boldest and baddest Mid-Victorians, might have designed. The central portion of the High School is exalted in its verticality. The towered faculty house behind is much more home-like; it could be a monastic dormitory in Flanders.

Weber was a respected architect of the 1920s who designed other Catholic structures. Notable for a similar boldness of pattern is St. Colman's School in Turtle Creek.

Landmarks plaque

U.S. Bureau of Mines Building
4800 Forbes Avenue
Henry Hornbostel, architect, 1915

Here, as in the contemporary City-County Building, Modern succinctness and Classical pomp are combined. The base and the great portal are in poured gray concrete with a very slight texture that may be due to weathering rather than design. The walls are in Hornbostel's favorite cream-colored brick. Inside is a grand corridor vaulted in Guastavino tile. Such a building reveals a nice balance between the utilitarianism needed in a structure of laboratories and offices, and the monumentality appropriate to an institution of public significance.

National Register

Hammerschlag Hall

Carnegie Technical Schools (later, Carnegie Institute of Technology; presently, Carnegie-Mellon University)
Tech and Frew Streets
Henry Hornbostel of Palmer & Hornbostel (New York, then Pittsburgh), planner and architect; planned 1904.

In 1900 the Carnegie Technical Schools were founded, and by 1904 they were ready to think of a big, coordinated campus. Palmer & Hornbostel won the resulting competition, and Henry Hornbostel came to Pittsburgh to supervise the execution of his plans and to be the institution's first pro-

Guastavino-tile stair, Baker Hall

College of Fine Arts

Margaret Morrison Carnegie College

fessor of architecture. Over the years his plan was greatly modified and was never fully realized, but one basic idea remained: a double range of buildings on a lawn sloping gently down toward the edge of Junction Hollow, with a building terminating the axis at each end and other buildings close by. The style was a personal kind of Beaux-Arts, quite Classical in some details, quite free in others, with an overall clarity of organization and a simplicity of general form that allowed, nevertheless, for infinite variations of detail. The materials were cream-colored brick, brick of a slightly darker, light-caramel tone, white semi-matte terra cotta, pale-gray granite, and exposed concrete, varied with bands of polychrome terra cotta, and a bronze sheathing for window spandrels and mullions and for cornice brackets. The roofs were covered in a lustrous raven-black tile. An almost-white campus with occasional touches of strong color, theatrically presented. Notable are:

Hammerschlag Hall (formerly Machinery Hall) of 1912, at the edge of Junction Hollow, with its great arches front and back, and its thick chimney surrounded by an arcade. In front, on the Hollow side, the bronze scrollwork from the bow of the armored cruiser *Pittsburgh,* removed in 1909 when the Great White Fleet was painted gray.

The northern and southern ranges, including Porter Hall (formerly Industries Hall) of 1905 and Engineering Hall of 1908, with their wings projecting into the central lawn like stage flats and with their touches of polychrome terra cotta. The corridors in the southern range, where archways strapped in iron-like kiln doors, railings of pipe, and lamp brackets also of pipe strike the technological note.

Baker Hall (formerly Administration Hall) of 1914, with its vaults of raw Guastavino tile and its open-newel stair, gravity-defying, in the same material.

The College of Fine Arts of 1912, with its outer niches that were planned for carving to illustrate five styles of architec-

ture but were never finished, its corridor floors of marble inlaid with the plans of five great buildings, its dean's-office doorway that is a cast from Pierre Puget's portal for the Hôtel de Ville of Toulon, and its vault paintings by J. M. Hewlett that are an illustrated course in art history.

Margaret Morrison Carnegie College of 1906 beside the main campus, with its circular Doric colonnade and polychromed frieze.

The Gymnasium of 1923 behind the main campus, Hornbostel's last work here.

McGill, Boss, Welch, Scobell, and Henderson Halls, early twentieth century dormitories in two rugged, simple treatments that play mildly with color and texture.

Post-Hornbostel buildings are for the most part very dull.

Schenley Park

Edward Manning Bigelow, the new Director of the City's Department of Public Works, determined in the late 1880s that Pittsburgh should have real parks, not just the handful of tiny greens that it had acquired from time to time. He had his eye on the large Oakland property of Mary Croghan Schenley, the rich runaway bride of the 1830s whom "Picnic House" had failed to keep at home and who had been living in England for about 40 years. The southern part of her land was an area of knolls and ravines, a place with the potential for a Romantic park but seemingly not too useful otherwise. And yet, in 1889, a land-development company seemed ready to make her an offer. There is a story of a friend of Bigelow's being roused in the small hours, hustled to New York and on board the same liner that carried the development company's agent, a race through the streets of London, an impassioned plea for the people of Pittsburgh over the Schenley breakfast table, a pledge of 300 acres, and a polite greeting as Bigelow's friend walked out the door and the agent walked in.

The land *was* developed as a Romantic park, with landscape design in part by the Englishman William Falconer. Additional land was added (to a current size of 456 acres), and a casino (primarily a skating rink), band shell, zoo, merry-go-round, auto race track, and horse-racing oval all made temporary appearances. More permanent features are a set of handsome bridges, the Phipps Conservatory, a collection of monuments, and two log cabins which were caught up in the net of park land. In the 1930s, through the Works Progress Administration, the park was laced with stone steps and walls.

For the one hundredth anniversary year of Schenley Park in 1989, the Pittsburgh History & Landmarks Foundation hopes to create interest in a major park restoration. This is Pittsburgh's great urban park.

Neill Log House
East Circuit Road, Schenley Park
C. 1790

Writers on American log architecture distinguish between a log cabin, where the logs are laid still rounded to make what was usually a temporary shelter, and the log house, where the logs were squared and carefully fitted together for durability. Here is a pioneer log house, one of the very few surviving eighteenth-century structures in Pittsburgh. A big chimney offered warmth, and a plank door and small, shuttered windows offered protection in a time when Indians were still a threat to frontier families. The roof is made of overlapping planks. This building was restored by the Pittsburgh History & Landmarks Foundation in 1968 and pioneer furnishings were provided by the Junior League of Pittsburgh. It is open to the public by appointment with Landmarks.

Landmarks plaque

Phipps Conservatory
Schenley Drive between Schenley and Panther Hollow Bridges, Schenley Park
Lord & Burnham (Irvington, N.Y.), designers and builders, 1893; entrance rebuilt, 1960s

Henry Phipps, a partner of Andrew Carnegie, had given a conservatory to Allegheny City and in 1891 he offered one as well to Pittsburgh. The builders were Lord & Burnham, specialists in greenhouse design and construction, who erected the first nine display houses. To these in 1896 were added three more, and in 1900 the City added nine growing houses to the rear. In its final form the public areas centered on a great palm house, at whose very center was a fountain with a copy of Giovanni di Bologna's *Mercury*. From this, three wings led to the sides and the rear, where crosswings branched off from octagonal domed spaces. The entrance to the palm house was originally a stone Romanesque structure, but has been replaced by an expedient modern construction. In time, pools, flower terraces, statues, and trees

239

came to surround the Conservatory. These surroundings are not quite what they once were due to considerations of economy and security, but the greenhouses themselves underwent a thorough restoration and modernization in the late 1970s and early 1980s under the joint supervision of the Pittsburgh History & Landmarks Foundation and the City of Pittsburgh. A volunteer committee was established and its members raised over one million dollars for the restoration of the Conservatory; the City and Federal government added approximately five million dollars.

National Register; Landmarks plaque

Panther Hollow Bridge
Panther Hollow Road, Schenley Park
H. B. Rust, engineer, 1896–97

Technically this is a three-hinged parabolic steel-arch bridge, 360-foot span and 45-foot rise: an arch, then, whose vertical dimension is one-eighth that of its horizontal. Four ribs carry the roadway across the ravine and Panther Hollow Lake. The stone abutments are remarkable for two features: Giuseppe Moretti's bronze sculptures of panthers on pedestals above the pavement and the mason's marks scratched into the rock-faced abutment stones so that stonecutters could be paid for the number of stones cut.

At the same time Rust built the Schenley Bridge, a few hundred yards away, to the same basic design. Crossing Junction Hollow between Carnegie Institute and Carnegie-Mellon University, the Schenley Bridge offers a beautiful, dramatic view of the latter. In the early 1960s it was confidently expected that Junction Hollow would be filled with utilitarian space to serve nearby institutions, but this was not carried through.

Both bridges are in weakened condition but must be restored and retained.

Monuments
Schenley Park

Monuments gravitate to, or are precipitated in, parks, their formal spaces and their sylvan glades. Here are three of the outstanding ones in Schenley Park. The Christopher Lyman Magee Memorial stands on axis with the entrance to the Carnegie Library that is the central element of the original

Christopher Lyman Magee Memorial

Carnegie Institute building. It takes the form of a gray granite stela designed by Henry Bacon (New York) — later, the architect of the Lincoln Memorial in Washington — and a bronze bas-relief by Augustus Saint-Gaudens (Cornish, N.H.), one of the great American sculptors. The figure with the cornucopia has sometimes been called Abundance and sometimes Charity. Magee, a political leader, loved to gain abundance but also wanted to be liked, and the ambiguity of naming seems fitting.

Schenley Memorial Fountain

George Westinghouse Memorial

The Schenley Memorial Fountain of 1918 terminates the axis of Schenley Plaza and stands on the buried bridge that once crossed St. Pierre's Ravine. The bronze sculpture by Victor David Brenner, *A Song to Nature,* illustrates that ''Pan the Earth God answers to the harmony and magic tones sung to the lyre by sweet Harmony.'' The granite basin itself is the design of H. Van Buren Magonigle, an architect who specialized in monumental work and is best remembered for the Liberty Memorial in Kansas City, Missouri. Both artists were New Yorkers. The fountain is incomplete today, four bronze turtles that spewed water into the basin having been stolen.

Finally, the George Westinghouse Memorial rests in the depths of the park at West Circuit and Schenley Drives. This is a very dignified Art Deco work of 1930 by Henry Hornbostel and his partner of later years Eric Fisher Wood, with sculpture by Daniel Chester French (Stockbridge, Mass.) and Paul Fjelde (New York). Fjelde executed bas-reliefs on six panels to illustrate the great industrialist's accomplishments while French did all the rest, including a bas-relief bust of Westinghouse and a statue of a knickered schoolboy of a half-century ago, books in hand, contemplating his role model. Beneath Westinghouse is a diagram of his first air brake, possibly the only mechanical drawing to be so immortalized. The whole memorial has a kind of solemn verve to it, creativity and dignity intimately mixed.

Residential comfort on Morewood Avenue.

SHADYSIDE

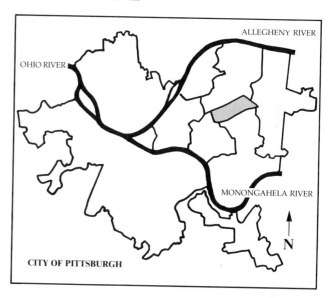

Shadyside stretches eastward from Oakland on flat land between the former Pennsylvania Railroad line to the north and Fifth Avenue to the south. It came into being as a city neighborhood rather slowly despite the stimulus of the railroad after 1852, but the extension of streetcar service from Oakland to East Liberty in 1874 was a help. Shadyside's existing architecture suggests that development began in earnest about 1880 and continued through the 1920s.

The Aikens were early landowners here, and in the 1850s Thomas Aiken erected a country house known as "Shadyside." The name was adopted for the local railroad station and eventually for the whole district. But the name *could* as readily have been devised to promote streetcar-suburb real estate, or been given from simple observation of the area's sylvan streets, so appropriate is it for the neighborhood that developed.

Shadyside acquired associations with gracious living. A rich variety of fine houses on ample lots is found throughout the district, and there are

243

The entrance to the Minnetonka Building, by architect Frederick G. Scheibler, Jr., is an often overlooked feature of the Walnut Street scene.

still a few Fifth Avenue mansions from the Millionaire's-Row days of the early twentieth century. Shadyside also features a collection of short dead-end streets from the early twentieth century with unified residential development. These include Ellsworth Terrace, Colonial Place, and Roslyn Place (1912) which still has wood block street paving. Fashionable shops and restaurants line a quarter-mile stretch of Walnut Street at the neighborhood's very center. But this street scene is actually no more elegant than in any other neighborhood where the shopkeepers have been struck with a mania for remodeling over several decades. In the eastern part of Shadyside, the remodeling mania has also lain heavy on houses, manifest particularly in a grudge against porches and a feeling that bricks ought to be painted: not red as they might be in less-cultured districts, but elephant gray, pale green, beige, or something of the sort. The removal of porches gives the house facades a curious noseless look, and the paint makes them look as if their pores are clogged.

Fortunately, Shadyside has retained many magnificent architectural gestures: picturesque Victorian villas, handsome houses of worship, and early Modern apartment buildings. Pleasant streets abound, and Shadyside remains a green and gracious area.

Church of the Ascension
Ellsworth Avenue and North Neville Street
William Halsey Wood (Newark, N.J.), architect,
1896–98

Wood, always interesting though not always right, designed this Episcopal church a few years after a fantastic submission in the Cathedral of St. John the Divine competition in New York that historians still remember. His Gothic is infinitely tamer here although forcefully introduced by a massive black stone tower modeled after that of a church at Wrexham in Wales. Inside, the walls are brick, once buff, now painted, bearing a heavy wooden roof. The Late Victorian glass is strong and warm in color. A side chapel has a splendid, sinuously carved screen. Some minor alterations to the interior were made by Ralph Adams Cram. The blunt Gothic arches throughout the church are typical of the 1900 period as are the rather broad, squared-off wall masses; this may be because Richardsonian massiveness was still appreciated even as Richardson Romanesque was going out of fashion, or perhaps in order to dissociate this most recent Gothic, in a Classically inclined period, from the gaunt, sharp Mid-Victorian variety.

Landmarks plaque

First Church of Christ Scientist
623 Clyde Street
Solon Spencer Beman (Chicago), architect,
1904–05

As Christian Science spread at the end of the nineteenth century, it cultivated an image of sober good taste that resulted in a collection of Classical churches, undemonstrative but appealing through the high quality of their design and execution. This medium-sized work in Greek Ionic on

a residential side street has the respectability the controversial sect wanted, the dignity and large scale appropriate to a public building, and yet the tact not to overwhelm the houses near by.

Landmarks plaque

Rodef Shalom Congregation
Fifth and Morewood Avenues
Henry Hornbostel of Palmer & Hornbostel (New
York), architect, 1906–07

Hornbostel, who was half-Jewish himself, designed two synagogues for Pittsburgh of which this Reform temple is the earlier and the better-known. There is no specifically Hebraic architectural tradition, and most architects of the early twentieth century faced with the problem of a synagogue would have either adapted Islamic motifs or have treated it as a Classical public hall. Hornbostel was more original. Using his favorite materials, cream-colored brick and terra cotta, he created a compact, massive structure that appears as a simple enclosure of the inner spaces. To dramatize the skyline of the building, yet emphasize the space within, he covered the temple itself with a great Louvre dome of cream-colored terra cotta ribs and green roof tiles. To enliven the brick wall surfaces, he inserted bands of terra cotta that serve as well to tie together details that might otherwise have seemed to drift in such large plain areas. At the

entrance he made very early use of polychrome terra cotta — the glazing technique had just been developed — in frames with mingled geometrical and leaf ornament, and over the central doorway he put a pediment with a menorah against a stained-glass window of leaping flames.

245

Inside, beneath a Guastavino tile vault with a large central skylight, Hornbostel designed a quietly sumptuous interior of mahogany and gilt, focused on an ark in the Ionic order. Lit from above by the skylight, which is framed by lightbulbs, the temple is also lit by six stained-glass windows and blue-and-gold chandeliers.

Rodef Shalom has served two purposes well: as a dignified place of worship and as an ornament to an elegant neighborhood.

National Register; Landmarks plaque

Hillman house
5045 Fifth Avenue
E. P. Mellon, architect, 1924–26

A skeptical look at this house, its proportions especially, suggests its origins. For all practical purposes, this is a house of the 1920s, but the Second Empire style of a half-century before haunts the design, with reason. It began in the late 1870s as a mansion, stiff and symmetrical and made of red brick, for a James Rees: probably the prominent boat- and engine-builder whose works were on the Allegheny River near the Point. In 1919 John Hartwell Hillman, Jr. bought the property and commissioned Benno Janssen to design a wholly new house. Janssen produced a number of sketches — now in the collection of the Pittsburgh History & Landmarks Foundation — but eventually Hillman decided to remodel the house already on the site. E. P. Mellon, architect for such Renaissance buildings as the Forbes National Bank and the Falk Clinic, cased the old house in limestone, covered the mansard roofs in extravagantly irregular slates that speak of the peasant rather than the aristocrat, and added a matching wing. The new style was one of those fusions that a good Eclectic architect could attain, coolly French in the overall impression, British in specific details, eighteenth-century in any case.

Inside, trim and ornament of the Victorian interiors were retained, even copied in new spaces; this was heresy in the Eclectic period, but such heresies do crop up now and then.

Moreland-Hoffstot house
5057 Fifth Avenue
Paul Irwin, architect, 1914

The three fronts of this house that are visible from Fifth Avenue are executed in white terra cotta in a Louis XIV style: a reduced version of McKim, Mead & White's ''Rosecliff'' at Newport, Rhode Island, and more remotely a mixture of themes from the Palace of Versailles and the Grand Trianon in the Palace grounds. The driveway entrance has an iron-and-glass domed marquee, however — an amenity decidedly of the early part of this century. In the 1970s, the fine interior rooms were restored and the house is immaculately maintained.

National Register; Landmarks plaque

Gwinner-Harter house
Fifth and Amberson Avenues
C. 1870; Frederick J. Osterling, architect for remodeling, 1911

A big, gray-painted Second Empire house in well-tended grounds. An early twentieth-century porch, characteristically double-columned in a way that removes some of the air of flimsiness single columns so widely spaced would have had, opposes a strong horizontal to the nervous verticality of the original front. Second Empire was much despised four decades after the height of its fashion, and the new porch at least mitigated the annoyance of its continuing presence. This is one of the oldest survivors of the old Millionaire's Row in this area; only ''Willow Cottage'' at Chatham College is older. It makes a handsome object in its spacious and well-landscaped grounds, and it is to be hoped that it will remain for a long time.

McCook house
Fifth and Amberson Avenues
Carpenter & Crocker, architects, 1906

A typical Rich Man's House in the Elizabethan style popular at the turn of the century. It has the besetting vice of domestic architecture of this period, a compulsion to make every few feet along a facade different from all the rest as if repetition were a proof of artistic laxity. Yet it has some good points too: the use of plain, smooth lintels and transoms that maintain the integrity of the wall despite such a variety of openings; the framing of the right-hand bay window with paired Tuscan columns, which creates a pleasing puzzle as to where the wall is supposed to have gone; and the frisky stringcourse above the second-floor windows that jumps over a third-floor opening and down again.

Shadyside Presbyterian Church
Amberson Avenue and Westminster Place
Shepley, Rutan & Coolidge (Boston), architects, 1889; additions, 1892 and after; Wilson Eyre & McIlvaine (Philadelphia), architects for alterations to interior, 1938

H. H. Richardson's successor firm designed this church, and its form and detailing reveal the level of competence to which the master, then three years dead, had brought his office. This is a "tower" church, probably the first in Pittsburgh.

It was modeled after Richardson's own Trinity Church in Boston of some fifteen years before, and itself inspired a number of local imitations. The interior is basically a preaching space, yet the architects wanted to avoid the old-fashioned, box-like meeting-house plan. The solution was to provide broad and very short nave and transept arms beneath a huge central lantern. The transepts, rather than accommodating altars as they might have in the Middle Ages, thus became part of the principal space and their gabled fronts varied the outline of the building and gave visual support to the lantern with its great pyramidal roof. Whether anyone realized it or not, the blunt cruciform plan recalled that of some early Western Pennsylvania log churches, where transepts added space while giving structural stability.

The interior was entirely remodeled in 1938, in a blander Romanesque than that of the exterior. The sanctuary terminates in a niche-like apse, with a figure of Christ in gold and colored mosaic by Rudolf Scheffler.

National Register; Landmarks plaque

Colonial Place
5141 and 5205 Ellsworth Avenue and Colonial Place
George S. Orth, architect, 1898

Edward B. Alsop, a developer, laid out Colonial Place in 12 lots. The two houses facing on Ellsworth Avenue are blocky three-storied buildings of light-brown brick with sandstone Ionic colonnades that were meant not as entrances, not even probably as porches, but rather as twin fanfares to announce the project. The remainder of the houses are lower, gable-roofed, much more informal, but spacious and gracious all the same.

247

Houses
Shadyside

Shadyside, an almost-flat area with a rail service to town by 1860 and a horsecar service a decade later, was a natural place for a "desirable" residential neighborhood in the late nineteenth century. Around 1900 there were still a few rural sights, like grazing sheep, to be noticed here and there, but the general appearance of the district was urban, with mansions along Ellsworth Avenue to the north, the "Millionaire's Row" of Fifth Avenue to the south, and in between a multitude of detached houses on small properties. Most streets were largely developed by 1925. Today, Shadyside remains rich in houses, particularly west of South Aiken Avenue.

4841 Ellsworth Avenue

424 Shady Avenue

Number 4841 Ellsworth Avenue dates from 1860 and is in the Italianate style that was among the earliest to be used in Shadyside. Its arcaded porch gives it the air of a country villa rather than a city house, as if it were built to afford a view of a river or a great valley rather than a rural road that was destined to become a street. That Italianate persisted is indicated by the house of 1877 at 424 Shady Avenue, at the eastern end of the neighborhood near East Liberty; such rather fancy yet somber architecture is quite common at this end of Shadyside.

The Abbott and Marshall houses of c. 1860 and the Spinelli house of c. 1870 and later are in the center of Shadyside, across St. James Street from each other near Westminster Place. All are Romantic survivors from the pastoral phase of Shadyside, cottages overtaken by the city around 1880.

Abbott and Marshall houses

Spinelli house

They are fairly simple places — though the Spinelli house is complicated by remodelings — with board-and-batten walls and a few elementary Gothic and Italianate forms. The houses are a few years later than the Utopian Evergreen Hamlet of 1851 in Ross Township, but they share the same ideals of quiet seclusion and the same expression of these ideals in design.

The Late Victorian houses that came to the neighborhood were not deterred from a picturesque expression by being on relatively restricted properties, as Numbers 717 and 719 Amberson Avenue make clear. The first of these, from 1884 and to designs by Charles M. Bartberger and E. G. W. Dietrich, is determinedly sophisticated in its interplay of verticals and horizontals with the bold diagonals of roof forms; the sculptural virtuosity of the best Shingle Style architects back east, in Philadelphia and New England, must have inspired such an essay in the art of composition. Number 719, by George S. Orth who was to go on to design mansions, was built in 1886 for a middle-management employee of Henry Clay Frick. It is less obviously organized than Number 717 and less easy to label as to style, but shares its neighbor's studied informality. A book about life in this house around 1900, *The Spencers of Amberson Avenue*, is very illuminating: not least because it reveals how many people were crowded into the house's rooms. In contrast, a very unusual house of 1892, of about the same size and again in the Shingle Style, is to be found at 328 Morewood Avenue. This has a sophisticated simplicity that is quite unique. The

717 *Amberson Avenue*

719 *Amberson Avenue*

328 *Morewood Avenue*

424 *Denniston Street*

5960 *Alder Street*

unknown architect has designed a gabled house and decorated its details, varied its surfaces, in a very minimal way. Whoever he was, he was an unusual Victorian in using just enough detailing to enliven his composition and relying on strong forms and good proportion to do the rest.

Larger houses of the 1890 period were most unlikely to make such quiet statements. The big corner house at 424 Denniston Street blithely mingles Queen Anne, Shingle Style, and Colonial Revival details, and its architect's motto must have been, Never a dull moment. Yet simple, strong forms — two gables, a chimney, a tower, and the porch that was originally wrapped around the tower — dominate and impose order on the minor features. The double house at 5960 Alder Street illustrates the usual consequences of this 1890 picturesqueness. Here, the fancy corbeled chimneys, the gables, tower, and porches are combined in a very effective way: this is a handsome building. Usually, though, the features tend to stray in the composition, to be a mere accumulation of objects intended to dress up the sober red-brick mass of a house.

Toward 1900, greater simplicity set in. At 5023–25 Castleman Street is a double house of a Classical form, very mildly Queen Anne in its pilastered brick dormers but really catching the eye through twin porches in Grecian Ionic

that may in fact be additions to an earlier fabric. The effect is quite elegant, and the absence of railings makes these porticoes rather than porches: raises their tone, as it were. The house at 718 Devonshire Street represents the massive Colonial Revival house type often to be found in Shadyside and the nearby parts of Squirrel Hill. This was built in 1896 to designs by the Boston firm of Peabody & Stearns, who designed other Pittsburgh houses as well. The proportions are not Georgian, but a solid Georgian elegance was certainly

5023-25 Castleman Street

5050 Amberson Place

sunken panels, and an entrance porch of very unusual design. Such experimentation was not to continue; Eclecticism dominated early twentieth-century construction in Shadyside, creating mellow evocations of England or France, or syntheses of both.

718 Devonshire Street

Minnetonka Building
Walnut and Copeland Streets
Frederick G. Scheibler, Jr., architect, 1908

This is a Scheibler commercial and apartment building from two years after the very different Old Heidelberg. Two stories of cream-colored brick with clean-cut window openings rise above tapered square columns of limestone. Few architects anywhere in the world were willingly designing city architecture with such extreme simplicity, and a considerable amount of art glass — in the doorways outside and in, and in the stair skylights — supports the cut stonework in giving the impression that parsimony was not the cause of this general plainness. The curved corner windows, too, imply an experiment in new, pure forms. Calling attention to a rounded corner, and even putting windows in it, suggests Viennese Secession architecture of this time.

The eight apartments are largely in the original condition, with marble-and-brass gas fireplaces with inset ceramic designs.

704 Amberson Avenue

the architects' aim. It was too soon for Pittsburghers to be parted from their porches, and here as in the decades that followed the porch was moved to the side of the house, leaving the front free for architectural display.

While Colonial Revival and the subsequent Neo-Georgian were introducing a formal architecture to Shadyside, some architects were being mildly experimental. Edward J. Weber's house of 1913 at 704 Amberson Avenue is rather like an English farmhouse, with big chimneys and stuccoed walls and with a roof that does not imitate, yet in its form implies, thatch. On Amberson Place, one of the numerous cul-de-sacs in Shadyside, Maximilian Nirdlinger designed a house, again in 1913, that has Classical symmetry and even Classical columns but experiments with varied window rhythms,

Third Presbyterian Church
Fifth and South Negley Avenues
Theophilus Parsons Chandler (Philadelphia),
architect, 1901–03

Chandler, who also designed the present First Presbyterian Church, was one of those architects of wayward imagination that Philadelphia produces every now and then. The supreme effect in this case is inside, where the arches and struts of a cross-gabled double-hammer-beam roof leap about in all directions. But the exterior, with its sinuous Flamboyant tracery, its pinnacles and gables, and its red-and-white stonework, suggests too the work of a lively mind. Behind the church is a stately medieval hall more reposeful in design, a grandiose presence in the domestic streets of Shadyside.
Landmarks plaque

Highland Towers
340 South Highland Avenue
Frederick G. Scheibler, Jr., architect, 1913

Scheibler was generally inclined toward quaintness when the budget permitted, but here he produced one of the earliest, and still one of the best, works of Modern architecture in Pittsburgh. This is a sensitive Modernism, its strong, simple forms realized in a strongly textured golden-brown brick, its windows glazed with small, leaded panes, its spandrels filled with geometrical designs of blue tile on cream-colored stucco. The craftsman, not The Machine, is the presence felt here, notwithstanding the clean lines and the visible concrete work in the courtyard.
National Register; Landmarks plaque

Apartment building
6111 Alder Street
C. 1910

An apartment house that reflects avant-garde trends in Central Europe, though in a stolid Pittsburgh way. The pilasters are crowned with sculptured Art Nouveau impressions of ancient theatrical masks, and the stair windows above the sinuously pedimented entrances have delicate near-Rococo tracery. A big cove cornice, a hollow quarter-round in the tradition of ancient Egypt, makes an emphatic conclusion to the entire building mass.

Alder Court
6112 Alder Street
Henry M. Kropff, architect, 1913

A large Jacobean apartment house, U-shaped in plan, of light-brown brick with terra-cotta detailing. The detailing is not original at all, yet there is a pleasant homelike quality about the building, formed as it is around a garden court. The scale is domestic; the tenants are domiciled, not merely stacked as they are in so many apartment houses.
Landmarks plaque

Captain Alfred E. Hunt Armory
324 Emerson Street
1911; 1916; 1921

Repeated Doric pilasters lend a magnificence, and yet delicacy as well, to a Pennsylvania National Guard artillery armory that has as its neighbors the Alder Court apartment-house and Sacred Heart Church. The great length of the building is broken up by many closely spaced verticals, and the scale is so ambiguous that one is pleasantly unclear whether this is a big building trying to look small or a small building trying to look big. Either way it is a dramatic feature of a quiet neighborhood street.

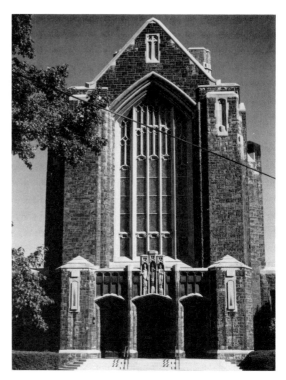

Sacred Heart Church (Roman Catholic)
Shady Avenue and Walnut Street
Carlton Strong, architect; completed by Kaiser, Neal & Reid, architects; 1924–53

In its squared-off corner buttresses, its segmental pointed arches, and its segmental-arched doorways caught between flanking masses, this church shows the influence of Bertram

Goodhue, architect of the First Baptist Church in Oakland. Inside, an unusual and powerful timber roof leads to an east wall painted in muted patterns. A chapel to one side, in fourteenth-century English Gothic, has vaulting bosses in the form of brightly painted escutcheons.

Landmarks plaque

Sellers house (presently, Rectory, Calvary Episcopal Church)
Shady Avenue and Walnut Street
1858

This red-brick house, although now painted, gives a good idea of an early East End mansion. It shows the casual attitude to stylistic purity that the Victorians had; the composition is informal to a degree that seems to call for Gothic detailing — and indeed all the gables once had vergeboards and pinnacles. Yet much of the detailing is Italianate, with characteristic traceried window sash in round-headed windows.

Built by Francis Sellers, this was one of the first mansions in the area, whose settlement was encouraged by the opening of rail service from the Triangle in 1852. It originally stood on a 10-acre estate.

National Register; Landmarks plaque

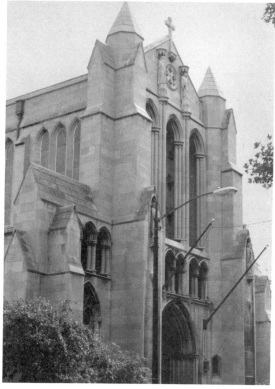

Calvary Episcopal Church
Shady Avenue and Walnut Street
Ralph Adams Cram of Cram, Goodhue & Ferguson (Boston Office), architect, 1906-07

Cram was justly proud of the crossing tower of this church, which bears the most successful spire in the city. The general style is Early English, English Gothic of the early thirteenth-century, but as creatively reworked by an architect who perceived Gothic as a living style and a natural expression of the Christian religion. It should be compared with the nearly contemporary First Baptist Church, in Oakland, by Cram's partner Goodhue. The personalities of the two men, eventually to go their separate ways, are evident in their buildings: Cram the idealist, seldom brilliant but always good and certainly getting his convictions across; Goodhue the artist, using the challenge of a church commission to exercise his compositional wizardry.

Landmarks plaque

Large turn-of-the-century houses on Stratford Avenue in Friendship.

EAST LIBERTY AND VICINITY

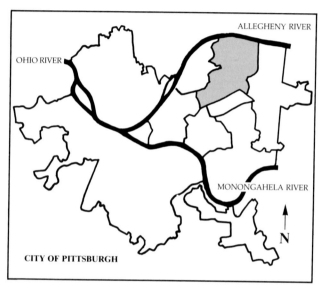

OHIO RIVER

ALLEGHENY RIVER

MONONGAHELA RIVER

N

CITY OF PITTSBURGH

The tower of East Liberty Presbyterian Church marks the traditional crossroads of a neighborhood which still has some of the character of an independent town. Five successive churches have stood on this site since 1819 while a farming hamlet, home of the enterprising Negley family, first developed into a village; then, with the completion of the Pennsylvania Railroad main line in 1852, became a commuter suburb; and in time developed still further, with the successive arrivals of horsecar, cable-car, and trolley lines from the Triangle. By 1910, East Liberty, though part of Pittsburgh since 1868, was like a city itself. Every express stopped at its handsome train station. Penn Avenue was a retail street equal to those of the Triangle, in the process of acquiring a wealth of terra cotta and tile-faced commercial buildings and theaters. On Highland Avenue stood the new 13-story Highland Building, built by Henry Clay Frick to the designs of D. H. Burnham & Company of Chicago. Around this center were streets of houses, apartment buildings, churches, and public institutions.

255

West of East Liberty was the Friendship neighborhood, mainly residential, solidly middle-class, largely Late Victorian. Its southern edge close to East Liberty was defined by Baum Boulevard which already, in 1910, was becoming a gathering place for those who dealt with automobiles: dealers, auto-body builders, filling station proprietors.

North of East Liberty, Highland Avenue ran for a mile to the cheerfully pompous gate piers marking the entrance to Highland Park. The Highland area was mostly residential, a neighborhood of mansions, near-mansions, and very pleasant streets of more modest but ample houses. The park, on land painstakingly acquired by Edward Manning Bigelow, opened to the public in 1893 and had as notable features two large reservoirs and a zoo; the zoo was intentionally sited here to serve as a trolley destination.

By 1960, the business center of East Liberty had declined, and much of the local civic energy had vanished. Planners ruthlessly applied urban renewal in the late 1960s: a circular road around the business center, pedestrian malls, new street furniture, the conventional devices of the time. The Pittsburgh History & Landmarks Foundation opposed these remedies, which attempted to suburbanize what was really a "downtown" area and broke up familiar patterns of human activity. The new plan was, in fact, not a success: demolitions for the circular road exposed the plain, grimy backs of buildings and left vacant spaces; drivers were confused by the parking and traffic layouts;

and the street furniture was visually ineffective. Some of the urban renewal measures were undone in the next two decades, but not before long-established businesses had failed. Today a more conservative approach is being tried, which seeks to preserve existing buildings and rebuild local morale while attracting new businesses. At the time of writing, plans were announced to open the Penn Circle section of Penn Avenue to auto traffic and to rebuild the streets with curbs, parking spaces, and parking meters. ◼

This Modernistic tile facade on Penn Avenue typifies East Liberty's commercial district (above). Below, shingles and stained glass on Sheridan Avenue in Highland.

Regent Theatre
5941 Penn Avenue, East Liberty
Harry S. Bair, architect, 1914

East Liberty's character as almost an independent entity, a commercial center with an identifiable focus and a growing economy, lasted well into the twentieth century. Commercial construction in East Liberty went on through the great terra-cotta period from 1900 to 1930. At the Regent Theatre, Harry S. Bair was not commissioned, in 1914, to design the sort of extravagant picture palace that was common a decade later. Nevertheless, he was already designing in a genre that had matured, and he sought to attract the public with a white facade that had a polychrome frieze and, in the deep entrance, colored tiles depicting European villa scenes. Above the doors were art-glass windows. The very plain marquee is modern.

East Liberty Presbyterian Church
South Highland and Penn Avenues, East Liberty
Cram & Ferguson (Boston), architects, 1931–35

In the center of East Liberty stands this church of cathedral dimensions, one of those colossal architectural gifts that the Mellon family has given to Pittsburgh; this was donated by Richard Beatty and Jennie King Mellon in memory of their mothers.

Cram, recently delighted and inspired by Spanish Gothic, put much of what he had learned into the church itself, and he and his partners designed the elaborate and adjoining church "plant" in a plain fifteenth-century style that would not look out of place anywhere in a large part of Western Europe. The effect, on a large Pittsburgh city block, is of a medieval town clustered around its Great Church. Though building with Presbyterian money, Cram had his mind on older sects — he himself was very high Anglican — and so designed the chancel that at a half-hour's notice could be set up for a Catholic or Anglican High Mass, beneath John Angel's sculptured reredos of the Last Supper. In his memoirs, Cram insists on the structural integrity of the church — like many Gothicists, he demanded that what seemed to be masonry construction *be* masonry construction — but in truth the great tower is framed in steel and concrete. No matter: it is a big, glorious tower, 300 feet high, a reminder that the often-mishandled neighborhood of East Liberty still lives.

Landmarks plaque

Highland Building
121 South Highland Avenue, East Liberty
D. H. Burnham & Co. (Chicago), architects, 1910

Henry Clay Frick, besides building extensively in the Triangle, erected this building at the center of East Liberty. The Highland Avenue front shows a new evolution of the base-shaft-capital formula, though modernization has marred both the base and the upper part of the cornice. Instead of

257

giving the uppermost stories of the building a distinctive treatment, Burnham's designers put a decorated band across the level of the uppermost story, then flared the columns outward into a coved form, almost like a vault seen in longitudinal section. The original molding in which this cove terminated is gone, as is the cheneau that once rested on it to give a scalloped skyline.

This front is in glazed off-white terra cotta and has a strong vertical emphasis, but on the northern front, which originally was less visible, the treatment is much plainer, though, typically of the time, there is a small amount of decorative treatment. Here, the design changes direction; horizontal bands of white terra cotta define the heads and sills of the windows in the buff-brick wall. At the top of this side wall the greater part of the cheneau survives.

Nabisco Brands Bakery
6425 Penn Avenue, East Liberty
1917

The earliest factories in the United States looked like slightly overgrown schoolhouses, complete with belfrys for summoning the employees. Mill buildings soon grew to colossal size though, and many owners sought ways of giving them polite architectural treatment. Here is such an effort, adapted to a frame of steel or reinforced concrete. The skeleton is clothed in red and buff brick, and strips of white terra cotta are used for accent. A rudimentary entablature, broken forward at each column, crowns the building beneath a brick parapet. The building is a familiar East End sight.

In this economically Classical building, Premium Saltines, Ritz Crackers, and Chips Ahoy! are manufactured.

Sixth United Presbyterian Congregation of Pittsburgh (presently, Eastminster United Presbyterian Church)
North Highland Avenue and Penn Circle North, East Liberty
William S. Fraser, architect, 1893

With its rock-faced stone, numerous round arches, and broad proportions, this is a very convincing work of Richardson Romanesque. Unlike many other such churches for denominations that emphasize preaching, there is no big central lantern. Instead there is a spired corner tower, its upper story an octagon with four square turrets. This compositional scheme is probably derived from the towers of Coutances Cathedral in France.

Stevenson Building
South Highland Avenue and Penn Circle South, East Liberty
W. Ross Proctor, architect, 1896

Built for the George K. Stevenson Co., a grocery that remained here until 1977, this building of sandstone and golden-brown Roman brick shows in its simplified Italian Renaissance style the influence of McKim, Mead & White, New York architects who were famous in the 1890s. Little-ornamented, the design is strong, simple, and refined. Its dignified corner entrance gives it the air of a small Victorian bank, not a grocery store.

Landmarks plaque

258

East Liberty Market House (later, Motor Square Garden)
Baum Boulevard and South Beatty Street, East Liberty
Peabody & Stearns (Boston), architects, 1898-1900

A single-story hall of about 40,000 square feet, this served as a public market until 1915 and has been used, fitfully, for spectator sports, exhibition, sales, and business purposes since. The brick is deep yellow and the dome is glazed and quite handsome in its transparency. The future of this, one of only two surviving market halls in Pittsburgh, is uncertain. In 1985 there was a project to remodel the market for retail purposes, with a probability of realization.

National Register; Landmarks plaque

Automobile dealership
Baum Boulevard and Roup Avenue, Friendship
C. 1940

A plain piece of Modernistic, but conspicuous in the crowded Baum Boulevard scene because of its corner tower: a simple but bold touch like this sometimes enlivens an otherwise-drab area. A pulsating light appears in the tower after dark. Baum Boulevard and Beatty Street, which crosses it, have been the home of automobile dealers, and in earlier days of parking garages and automobile body builders, since before 1910.

Christ Methodist Church (presently, First United Methodist Church)
Aiken Avenue between Centre Avenue and Baum Boulevard, Friendship
Weary & Kramer, architects, 1891–93

This is a very large and conspicuous Richardson Romanesque ''tower'' church, whose principal massing is a broadened and simplified version of Richardson's own Trinity Church in Boston. The geometrical power of the basic church, however, is complicated by the entrances and the little arcades at ground level; these are added onto, rather than integrated with, the main body of the building and in themselves are overassertive. Yet the overall boldness of the design and the siting make this a landmark of the most literal sort.

Calvary Methodist Church in the Allegheny West area of the North Side is a sister church in a way; both congregations worshiped in the original Christ Methodist Church until it burned in 1891.

Landmarks plaque

Friendship School
Friendship Avenue and Graham Street, Friendship
Charles M. Bartberger, architect, 1899

Here is a school in the gently sad Classical style found elsewhere in Pittsburgh institutional architecture, the Allegheny Observatory for instance. The materials are a light-brown brick and a warm pale-gray terra cotta, the latter used to execute a Composite order as well as surrounds to all the windows. There is a slight lavishness to the treatment, and yet an air of dignity, that is found for instance in the contemporary work of the New Yorkers McKim, Mead & White. There is a quiet charm about the building, to which its open setting contributes. The broad front windows are the result of an early remodeling.

Fourth United Presbyterian Church (presently, Greater Pittsburgh Christian Temple)
South Pacific and Friendship Avenues, Friendship
C. 1895

Here is Richardson Romanesque, often found in Pittsburgh churches, but of a special sort. The arcaded entrance front with a flanking turret is derived, not from Richardson's churches but from the libraries that he designed for various small New England communities. The big apse-like feature is an Akron-plan Sunday-school arrangement, with classrooms around a central space. The alternation of high and low stonework courses indicates that the stone is a facing: the low courses go into back-up brickwork to anchor the higher courses, which are only a few inches thick. The same treatment is visible on the exterior of the Courthouse. The forms have a telling effect, and the big rounded wall, although so simple in treatment, is the most effective feature of all.

Ursuline Academy (presently, Ursuline Center)
201 South Winebiddle Street, Friendship
1867; Carlton Strong, architect for chapel, gymnasium and sisters' residence, 1913; additions, 1926

An attractive little academic group centered on a mansion of the 1860s, used as a convent and school after 1893 and now a neighborhood center. Winebiddle Street is one of the pleasantest in Pittsburgh, and this is its most interesting feature. The Second Empire house, the nucleus of the group, has a rather bristling effect alongside the quieter medieval forms of the other units, but the contrast is certainly not discordant.

Landmarks plaque

Congregation B'Nai Israel
327 North Negley Avenue, Highland
Henry Hornbostel, with W. S. Fraser, Philip Friedman, and Alexander Sharove, architects, 1923

This very unusual design has all the massive repose usually to be found in synagogue architecture of the early twentieth century, yet its various elements have a mutual independence quite uncommon. A great drum of dark random ashlar, austere and massive as if in response to the steep hillside close behind, terminates in a blind arcade of contrasting lightness. Above, immediately beneath the dome, is a very original band of blue and orange tiles in a diamond pattern, a weightless feature above the weighty stonework. A porch of buff brick and limestone, paraphrasing Brunelleschi's porch to the Pazzi Chapel in Florence, shows the way into the drum. Here again is contrast; the porch, though substantial, lacks the sense of sheer mass found in the stone in which it is set.

Here is a design executed a decade and a half after Hornbostel built Rodef Shalom and a few years before Friedman and Sharove built Poale Zedeck in Squirrel Hill. These two synagogues, 21 years apart, have much more in common with each other than with B'Nai Israel; both are set in undramatic residential neighborhoods, and are light in hue and open in character. The inference is that here the architects wanted a simple and powerful shape that would not be overwhelmed by the hill behind, yet wanted the building to have a cheerful, welcoming quality too.

The interior has been much remodeled, with new stained glass by Jean-Jacques Duval replacing the original clear glass. Some of the original ornament remains, however, especially on the ceiling.

Landmarks plaque

Alpha Terrace
716–740 and 721–743 North Beatty Street, Highland
C. 1889; 1894

Rationalism is sometimes a burden in looking at architecture, and occasionally one owes it to oneself to entertain a willing suspension of disbelief. Here are 25 deep, narrow row houses ranged on both sides of a street, with fronts that are contrived to make them look like little castles and Queen Anne villas. Nothing could be more absurd than to take two building types that are in their nature free-standing and assemble them tightly together in seemingly casual order. Yet there is a relaxed and slightly melancholy charm about Alpha Terrace that overrides rational objections. Somehow the results are evocative; the slight elevation of the house rows above street level, the separation from the street by shallow areas of lawn and terrace, and even the slightly unkempt appearance of the whole place work with the facades themselves to give it a special feeling.

Landmarks plaque

Houses
Highland

Between central East Liberty and Highland Park is a large expanse of houses. A few of the houses are early commuter dwellings that go back to the Mid-Victorian period, but intensive construction dates from the 1890s through the 1920s, the great trolley period. The division between East Liberty and Highland is perceptible, even a little too perceptible: East Liberty is random commerce, housing, and vacant spaces; Highland is more comfortable in character, laissez-faire in architectural style, though most of its homes show a certain ponderous 1900-period dignity.

6021 St. Marie Street

Number 6021 St. Marie Street seems to date from the 1880s, before the area was generally built up. The boxy building as a whole is nothing out of the ordinary, a typical Victorian Italianate enclosure of habitable space with a bracketed cornice. The porch, though, with its short urn-like posts and heavily scalloped brackets, suggests what Americans had done by 1880 with the design reforms urged by Charles Locke Eastlake, an Englishman, around 1870. Eastlake was tired of fancy design and advocated a return to simple craft methods, in woodworking, among other areas. The result, when his writings became fashionable in the United States, was such an orgy of sawing, chamfering, turning, and drilling that Eastlake was disgusted at the style which he had fathered.

Number 830 North Highland Avenue is Richardson Romanesque as the style was often applied in house design. The chimneys and the big hipped roof strive for visual power, but the architect allowed himself to be distracted by details. In the porch columns, every drum of stone retains its personal identity, and the bay window, gable, and dormer of

830 North Highland Avenue

261

935 North Highland Avenue

the front are at best a loose confederation. Such houses are often best enjoyed as one lives in them; one enjoys their spaces, their ornamental details, their views in various directions. Their individual features, even the specific rough forms of their stones, are familiar sights.

930 Sheridan Avenue

A house like 935 North Highland Avenue, with its brick walls neatly laid and its extensive detailing modeled in a matching red terra cotta, is much less random and casual. The style is Flemish Renaissance, a style adopted in the 1890s for houses especially; like the French Renaissance that was fashionable for mansions then, it seemed to offer a compromise between Classical correctness — here present in regular window spacing and overall symmetry — and the domesticity expressed in big roofs and gables. Deviating from symmetry is the masonry porch, which on this corner lot faces both streets. The porch, a deep arcade, offers its own compromise solution to the dilemma created by the American love of such a feature and the requirements of the European style: a cloister inside-out was a way of getting around the problem.

Number 930 Sheridan Avenue, built in 1902, is rare in using a Gothic masonry style. It has the massive look and the low pointed arches common in churches at the time: an air of "muscular Christianity" as the Victorians called it. The hipped roof and the dormers are boldly tiled, so that the scalloped vergeboard below the central dormer gable becomes a little ineffectual, a piping voice feebly raised amid much basso discourse. Over the ground-floor windows are lights of stained glass by J. Horace Rudy.

Johnston house
6349 Jackson Street, Highland
Frederick G. Scheibler, Jr., architect, 1921

This is one of Scheibler's late works, a composition that balances his Modernist tendencies with his Romantic ones. The sheer white walls, stucco on hollow tile, are crisply pierced with large openings, including that at one corner for an upstairs porch. On the other hand, roofs are prominent, even a little overemphasized perhaps, as expressions of the idea of shelter. The entranceway is splayed outward to exaggerate its prominence. And the leaded glass of the windows includes delicate, random-looking plant motifs in stained glass, as if Nature had invaded spaces designed for plain clear glass.

Henius house
1315 Cordova Road, Highland
Frederick G. Scheibler, Jr., architect (?), c. 1918

The photograph given here dates from 1979, several years before a fire that required extensive restoration. Scheibler's fondness for quaint effects suggests him as the architect of this house: Old World carpentry, eyelid dormers, and the same random shingling, curving around the eaves like thatch, that he later used on the Harter house on Beechwood Boulevard.

The slightly wavering lines of the half-timbering could be Scheiblerian; they have a more convincing look than the usual machine-sawn slats, with edges perfectly straight, that most architects and builders applied to their walls as decorative half-timbering.

One of the most interesting things about Scheibler is the diversity of approaches he used to solve his two standard problems, the small-to-medium-sized house and the medium-sized apartment house. Some of the time he would build simply and rationally, supporting his masonry with exposed steel lintels and using neat, plain brickwork. Other times he went all-out for quaintness, as here. In either case the design succeeded.

Bendet house
1321 Cordova Road, Highland
Theodore Eicholz, architect (?), c. 1927

Eclecticism in the late 1920s used the formidable resources that had developed in the building industry to produce architecture, houses especially, of remarkably contrived quaintness. Here, for instance, is a basically simple composition: a gable roof with a chimney and a projecting entrance on one side. Yet the roof is made to curve toward the eaves and sag wearily elsewhere and is pierced by hairpin-shaped dormers of a most unusual sort, while the little entrance bears a candle-snuffer roof as tall as the main roof. The house is executed in rubble, randomly laid brick, clapboards, and slating that is ragged on its exposed edges. The neatness of the clapboard and banded pier on the end wall seems almost a betrayal of the architect's intention to produce an image of a picturesque, time-worn cottage.

Vilsack Row
1659–93 Jancey Street, Morningside
Frederick G. Scheibler, Jr., architect, 1912

Eighteen housing units in three groups on an embankment above the street. Wide, glazed openings, International Style long before such a thing was identified or even greatly extant, alternate with solid brick walls with arched doorways. The crisp contrasts of voids and solids, remarkable in 1912, are still fresh and enjoyable. Some unfortunate remodeling has taken place, visible primarily on the porches.

The design for Vilsack Row was used also for a row at 7124–34 Churchland Street in the Lincoln-Lemington neighborhood.

"Baywood" (presently, King Center)
1251 North Negley Avenue, Highland
C. 1880; additions and alterations, 1890s

Alexander King, owner of this house, was a glass manufacturer and the father-in-law of Richard Beatty Mellon. After Alexander King's death in 1890 his widow remodeled the rather stiff Second Empire house, adding a new wing and a broad, glazed front porch and apparently altering the windows in the tower.

Behind the house, in 1898, King's son Robert Burns King added a feature more notable than the house itself: the "English Parapet" at the edge of the ravine, a mock castle with four small stone towers and a brick keep that served as a storage space. This landscape feature, now largely disappeared, was a folly in the old English sense — an elaborate, showy construction with little or no practical purpose — and, as such, a great rarity in the Pittsburgh area.

Robert Burns King lived on at "Baywood," but promised the City in 1949 that on his death the estate would be available as a public park. He died in 1954, and the house is now a teaching center for the arts and an office for the City's Department of Parks and Recreation.

Gate piers
Highland Avenue and Stanton Avenue entrances,
Highland Park, Highland
Giuseppe Moretti, sculptor, 1896, 1900

Though there were no monumental buildings at the main
entrance to Highland Park, the Parks Department of 1900
left you in no doubt whatever that you had arrived at a very
special place. Two great piers of clustered Ionic columns
terminated Highland Avenue in a very monumental fashion.
From their tops, laurel-wreathed women with babies waved
at you; closer to ground level, half-dressed women raised
torches in salute; and on the nearby balustrades eagles
gestured with their wings. Beyond the gate piers were
decorative beds of flowers and grass, centered on an
ornamental pool with a fountain, and the embankment of
the reservoir beyond was planted in floral designs that might
show stars or portrait heads.

Of this stunning display the gate piers — women, babies,
eagles, and all — survive to amuse and delight the eye.

At the Stanton Avenue entrance, two sculptures of horses
being tamed represent Man subduing the forces of Nature.
Moretti modeled them after sculptures made for a palace at
Marly, France, by the early eighteenth-century sculptor
Guillaume Coustou, but the theme of the horse tamer goes
back to ancient Rome.

264

THE EAST END

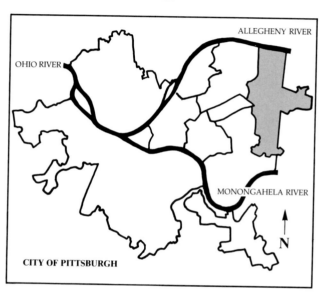

"East End" is a term loosely used by Pittsburghers for an entire group of neighborhoods east of Oakland and north of Squirrel Hill. These neighborhoods were built up on relatively flat land during the latter half of the nineteenth century, and their proximity to the Pennsylvania Railroad main line promoted development. Shadyside, East Liberty, Friendship, and Highland all qualify as parts of the East End.

The remaining neighborhoods further east and north of the railroad are densely developed and modest, but not without episodes of architectural distinction. Two impressive displays of bridge architecture cross Washington Boulevard in the ravine between Larimer and Lincoln-Lemington; and the latter neighborhood has two of the city's lesser-known architectural gems — Engine Company Number Thirty-eight and Lemington School — along Lemington Avenue. Homewood has the large and handsome Holy Rosary Church of Ralph Adams Cram, but it is basically a neighborhood of simple row houses.

In Point Breeze, south of the railroad, spacious planning and architectural elegance prevailed.

A detail from Old Heidelberg in Point Breeze.

265

McPherson Boulevard and Thomas Street were part of the Boulevard Park Plan as laid out in 1885: boulevard streets with grassy islands, lined with very substantial houses. Near by were some of Pittsburgh's greatest mansions such as George Westinghouse's "Solitude" and H. J. Heinz's "Greenlawn." These two are now gone, although the Westinghouse property remains whole as a public park and "Greenlawn" is survived by its carriage house and an elegant metalwork fence along the 7000 block of Penn Avenue. Of the great houses, only Henry Clay Frick's "Clayton" remains, very much as it was, inside and out. "Clayton" remains a large property, but 150 acres of the "back yard" became Frick Park in 1919, and an additional parcel became the site of the Frick Art Museum in 1970.

The East End is also territory of the architect Frederick G. Scheibler, Jr., showing the range of his art from the modest simplicity of row houses in Homewood to the complex composition of Old Heidelberg near the city's eastern border. ▨

Row houses stand ad infinitum on Formosa Way in Homewood.

Larimer School

Larimer Avenue and Winslow Street, Larimer
Ulysses J. L. Peoples, architect, 1896; additions

The outstanding feature of this school was a clock tower like an Italian Romanesque campanile, added in 1904, removed again in the 1950s. Its prominence in the Larimer scene is evident in the primitive painting of *Larimer Avenue Bridge* (1932) by John Kane. The school was built in stages and is a mixture of design approaches from the most matter-of-fact brick construction of the 1890s, vestigially Romanesque, through Italian Romanesque, Palladian, and very simplified 1930s Classical. A richly detailed recessed entryway, which served as the base of the tower, is the most intriguing element.

Pennsylvania Railroad and Lincoln Avenue viaducts

East of Washington Boulevard, Larimer
William H. Brown, chief engineer for Pennsylvania Railroad viaduct, 1902–03; Lincoln Avenue viaduct, 1906

Around 1900 the Pennsylvania Railroad built its bridges of masonry rather than steel trusswork whenever possible, thus acquiring structures that needed little maintenance and were equal to any future loads. This viaduct was part of a new freight line, the Brilliant Cutoff, running from the main line to a junction at Aspinwall. The exterior is typical engineering masonry of the time: heavy, rugged ashlar filled with concrete. Track level was 78 feet above the now-vanished Silver Lake; five arches have an 80-foot span and one other arch a 100-foot span. Through this viaduct another has been threaded to carry Lincoln Avenue across Washington Boulevard; this includes two elliptical stone arches. Both make a very impressive sight, one of the last of its kind to be created. A few years later, concrete would have been used, as in the Larimer Avenue Bridge near by.

Larimer Avenue Bridge

Larimer Avenue over Washington Boulevard, Larimer
T. J. Wilkerson of the City of Pittsburgh Department of Public Works, engineer, 1911–12

Early in the century, interest in concrete increased sharply as its properties became understood and reinforcing systems were devised. The Larimer Avenue Bridge was an early triumph: the second-longest concrete arch in the world at the time with a span of 300 feet, four inches. Slender piers rise from the main arch to end in an arcade beneath the deck; the arches and capitals are probably both merely decorative, a concession to a public used to the masonry tradition. Such

267

bridges continued to be built in the Pittsburgh area into the 1930s. The inherent vice they share, a readiness to decay progressively as concrete falls away to expose reinforcement, which rusts and swells, stripping away more concrete, has led to either demolition or drastic alteration in most cases.

Stanley L. Roush, then City Architect, added handsome decorative lampposts to the bridge.

Engine Company Number Thirty-eight
Lemington Avenue and Missouri Street, Lincoln-Lemington
Kiehnel & Elliott, architects, 1909

An architectural firm that sometimes did experimental work early in the century here produced a firehouse in an advanced manner that owes something to Continental Europe. There seems to be no specific precedent, but the bands of upper-floor windows and the stepped gables of the tower suggest the Netherlands. The materials are yellow-orange glazed brick — unusual itself — stone, and on the tower, stucco.

Lemington School
7060 Lemington Avenue, Lincoln-Lemington
Marion M. Steen, architect, 1937

A buff-brick school with terra-cotta decorations on the projecting auditorium and gymnasium wings and over the central classroom block. The colors are purple, green, red, and blue on an amber background, and the effect is outstanding and unusual, a testimonial both to the potential of terra cotta as a decorative material and to the interest in modern but vivid, individualistic buildings on the part of the Board of Education at the time. Other examples of the latter are the Letsche School on the Hill and the Schiller School in Dutchtown.

268

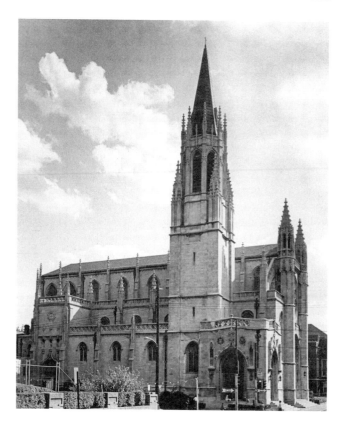

Holy Rosary Church (Roman Catholic)
North Lang Avenue and Kelly Street, Homewood
Ralph Adams Cram of Cram & Ferguson (Boston), architect, 1928

Of Cram's three churches in Pittsburgh, this is the least known. Yet it is a large and handsome building in a kind of synthetic fifteenth-century Continental Gothic that includes a grandiose French Flamboyant rose window and broad wall areas, under a low-pitched roof, that have a Spanish quality. The interior was specifically inspired by the Gothic churches of Barcelona, Spain, with tall, slender piers and high aisles beneath a relatively low clerestory. The corner porch, with crocketed French accolades over the arches, has slightly cambered parapets to hint at gables, but the whole church has the sort of high-shouldered look that Cram always favored in parts of the city where land was exiguous: a boxy office building or apartment house next door could make steep roofs and tall gables look silly, but not such predominantly rectangular forms as these.

Landmarks plaque

Scheibler row houses
Homewood

Frederick G. Scheibler, Jr. built for the most part on a very humble scale: never a skyscraper, never a mansion, never a church. He was an architect for the East End middle class, housing them with such artistry as the budget permitted but apparently willing to build to any budget at all. Highland Towers and Old Heidelberg Apartments stand out in his work by their relative size and their workmanship, yet he also designed simple row houses, matter-of-fact constructions where the mere relationship of voids and solids was nearly all he had.

6926-50 Bennett Street (detail)

An example is 6926-50 Bennett Street in Homewood, built in 1909. Here the front porches are supported on simple, wide-spaced stuccoed piers, arranged to frame *three* bays in front of what are in fact *quartets* of row houses. On the second story, more clearly visible than the first, four flat-headed windows with stuccoed spandrels beneath the sills stand together at the center, and single windows with segmental arches are situated close to the ends. These elements all further the impression of a *single* unified facade. Only the first-story openings and short walls which divide the porch space into four sections reveal that there are four houses here, instead of three, or one.

Inglenook Place

Other Scheibler row house groups in Homewood are located in the 7900 block of Inglenook Place and at 7902-24 Hamilton Avenue. The former group includes some houses which are nearly identical to the Bennett Street houses, and some which are designed in a similar but more straightforward manner. The latter group has projecting sun porches fitted with casements.

Meado'cots
425–47 Rosedale Street and 7817–23 Madeira Street, Homewood
Frederick G. Scheibler, Jr., architect, 1912

Commissioned to design 12 residential units around a courtyard, Scheibler produced a design in buff brick with exposed steel beams to carry the masonry over the openings. The economy is apparent in such materials, as it is in the simplest plank vergeboards to mask the junction between the roofing and the gables, and the absence of ornament, even capitals for the porch columns. Yet gables, chimneys, and porches individualize the units and break up the skyline and perimeter of the construction, and visible roofs with broad eaves state the theme of shelter. "Cot" is an Anglo-Saxon word for a simple home, and in itself states such a theme.

Meado'cots is not in good condition today, and it is to be hoped that the necessary repairs and maintenance will restore it to its former self.

Linwood Apartments
McPherson Boulevard and North Linden Avenue, Point Breeze
Frederick G. Scheibler, Jr., architect, 1907

The Linwood was built the year after the central part of the Old Heidelberg apartments and is similar in a number of details: the porches with tapering wooden posts above a masonry ground floor, the touches of non-historical ornament, and the openings of varying size cut neatly into the cemented wall. Here was a typical six-unit East End apartment house with its characteristic compositional problem of unifying something that in its nature is a duality, and Scheibler forced a measure of unity on the front with a pergola between the porches and a central chimney.
Landmarks plaque

269

Parkstone Dwellings
6937 Penn Avenue, Point Breeze
Frederick G. Scheibler, Jr., architect, 1922

After the Modernism of Highland Towers and the Minnetonka in Shadyside, Scheibler did not go on Towards a New Architecture. Like his San Francisco contemporary Bernard Maybeck, his Modernism was of an undogmatic sort, and he could on the other hand be quite pixyish at times. Here he is very much in a pixyish mood: four little doorways, separated by concrete toadstools, lead to the four housing units. Persian rugs imitated in tile seem to hang from upper porch parapets. Steep roofs of irregular slate cover everything. Inside over the fireplaces are dinosaurs, again in tile.

"Clayton"
Penn and Homewood Avenues, Point Breeze
C. 1870; Frederick J. Osterling, architect for remodeling, 1891-92; additions

In 1882, Henry Clay Frick bought a Mid-Victorian house and entrusted Osterling with a general remodeling. Osterling gave the Penn Avenue and a portion of the Homewood Avenue fronts a chateau-like appearance, with steep roofs and gables, yet saved the airy original porte-cochere and left the less visible portions of the house alone. In these remaining areas, simple additions appear to have been made later. "Clayton" is thus not a thoroughly conceived work of art, as Frick's New York mansion of 20 years later, by Carrere & Hastings, was to be; in the way of many Pittsburgh mansions it impresses the viewer with size and sobriety, an air of massive dignity, rather than by compositional elegance.

Other buildings were erected on the long property, which

ran 1,100 feet back to Reynolds Street; these included a conservatory and, eventually, the Frick Art Museum. After Frick's death in 1919, his daughter Helen Clay Frick inherited the house and maintained it as it was in her father's lifetime; though she lived in New York, she visited occasionally, especially to vote. She died in 1984, willing the house to a private family foundation as a museum.

Old Heidelberg
South Braddock Avenue and Waverly Street, Point Breeze
Frederick G. Scheibler, Jr., architect, 1906; additions, 1908

This is one of Scheibler's best-known and largest works, and one that illustrates both his rationalism and his love of fantasy. He had a commission typical of the 1900s, to add to the rapidly growing stock of three-story apartment buildings in the East End, giving each apartment its own porch. The original structure was to have 12 units, double the usual amount.

Instead of providing the usual box with Classical ornament, Scheibler looked to the advanced pre-Bauhaus architecture of Central Europe, which often experimented with decorative detailing while retaining a Germanic partiality to high roofs. His design emerged as a big gabled structure, simple in its overall form and with windows cut crisply through its cemented walls. The roof plane in front descended in three places to cover projecting porch structures, the one at the center being treated as an entrance pavilion. An inset decorative tile panel and an eyebrow dormer on the center line helped the mass of this pavilion in unifying a building that otherwise would appear as two distinct elements butted together without any real cohesion. The windows, varying as they did in dimensions and placement, were prevented from setting up visual rhythms that would break up the integrity of the wall. To the basic composition Scheibler added mildly innovative ornament, including the famous toadstool relief that gives a fairy-tale effect to what is not in actuality a very fanciful design.

The cottage wings projecting toward the street, also by Scheibler, are much plainer, but their simple masses add strength to the whole composition.

National Register; Landmarks plaque

The Whitehall
East End Avenue and Tuscarora Street, Point Breeze
Frederick G. Scheibler, Jr., architect, c. 1905

A six-unit apartment house, with the customary Pittsburgh porches but without the usual Ionic columns. Relying on proportion for effect, the front has only one fancy touch: the entrance, with its wavering arch that may have had its source in the avant-garde architecture of Hungary.

Landmarks plaque

7721 Abbott Street

Houses
7721–25 Abbott Street, Point Breeze
C. 1875

Three miniature Italian villas form the most interesting remains of a Mid-Victorian development just inside Pittsburgh's eastern boundary. Number 7721 is the most nearly intact, though its porch is a replacement. Number 7723 lost its tower top in a remodeling of 1894.

Squirrel Hill's Beechwood Boulevard features richly textured residential architecture and spacious landscaping.

SQUIRREL HILL, HAZELWOOD, AND ENVIRONS

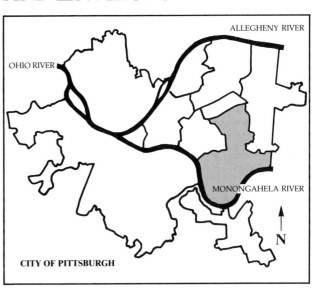

ALLEGHENY RIVER

OHIO RIVER

MONONGAHELA RIVER

N

CITY OF PITTSBURGH

Like Oakland which adjoins it to the west, Squirrel Hill is a neighborhood of diverse elements. The oldest part is its rather steep northern slope, which looks across Fifth Avenue to the flat terrain of Shadyside. The houses here are quite often Late Victorian, always substantial and sometimes in the mansion class. The Woodland Road area, most notably, is like a well-kept park whose most prominent tenant is Chatham College but which contains great houses of the past and the present. Murrayhill Avenue, parallel to Woodland Road, is decidedly middle-class by comparison, but for sheer picturesqueness, it is one of the most enjoyable streets in Pittsburgh. In general, this northern slope is rich in domestic architecture of the 1890 to 1920 period.

Most of Squirrel Hill, however, developed late. It was close to the heart of the enormous area annexed by Pittsburgh in 1868, but its central road, Forbes Avenue, was not an important communication route. It had no commuter rail line and no major industry, and the passengers of the Fifth Avenue streetcar line that passed along its northern edge had the easier alternative of a level walk to homes in Shadyside and East Liberty, where building land was readily available until after 1900. A population map of 1910 shows Squirrel Hill very sparsely settled in most parts, yet at this same time conditions were beginning to change. This was due partly to new electric trolley lines, which were built in anticipation of traffic their presence would generate, and partly to the 1922 opening of the Boulevard of the Allies, offering fuss-free communication with town by way of Schenley Park.

As a result, the neighborhood generally is a product of the 1910-to-1930 period with a number of architectural and scenic variations. Murdoch Farms, north of Forbes Avenue near Schenley Park, is a small 1920s area of conscious elegance, with well-studied English-looking houses among tall trees. Beechwood Boulevard, toward the eastern edge of the neighborhood, is a broad residential street of looping turns, a showplace of the 1910s and 1920s with trees, lawns, and flowers as a setting for comfortable houses.

Shingle Style, Colonial Revival, and Craftsman houses appear in many parts of Squirrel Hill. Yet if there is a typical Squirrel Hill house, it is probably a detached house of about 1925, veneered in artificially roughened brick and given an Old World flavor through gables, a porch with tiny arches, and perhaps an entrance through a miniature tower. Toward Schenley Park, apartment houses also vary the scene, but quaintness at moderate expense is the common theme on most streets.

Most of Murray Avenue and the length of Forbes Avenue that crosses it are active commercial streets, places where one can go for specialty items not found even downtown as well as for the ordinary requirements of a middle-class neighborhood. The rows of shops on Forbes have broad walks with the worldly character of an esplanade,

but Murray is close-built and almost East European, the prevailing Jewish heritage evident in many of the small shops.

South of Squirrel Hill and beyond Greenfield is Hazelwood, looking south and west over a great bend in the Monongahela River. Until shortly before 1900 Hazelwood was an exurb, enjoyed by villa-dwellers for its scenic views, its peace, and its pure air. In 1871, however, the Pittsburgh & Connellsville Railroad which ran along the shore became the final link to Pittsburgh for the Baltimore & Ohio, and a yard and repair shops were established. Around 1900 the Jones & Laughlin Steel Company extended its plant from the foot of Oakland to Hazelwood, installing there a large battery of coke ovens. This was before any attempts were made to control pollutants, and the air was so fouled in a short time that the nearby hillsides were stripped of plant life. The sylvan retreat, the pleasant suburb, became an industrial town. But even now it retains a few old villas and other architectural reminders of its remote past.

The Squirrel Hill Cafe on Forbes Avenue is a handsome Moderne design (above). Below, industry in Hazelwood, both blessing and curse.

McClelland house ("Sunnyledge")
Fifth and Wilkins Avenues, Squirrel Hill
Longfellow, Alden & Harlow (Boston and Pittsburgh), architects (?), 1888

There is some doubt as to the authorship of this house. Richardson Romanesque, it may even be a product of Richardson's own office not previously recognized; the present owner has the 1882 specifications for a now-vanished stable building that appear to stem from there. The traditional attribution is to Longfellow, Alden & Harlow, and since Frank Alden was a Richardson draftsman this would at least constitute a proximity to the master. Certainly, Richardson's best examples are fully absorbed: quiet but not featureless massing, a few well-chosen details, good materials. The vice of getting quaint or fancy — from which Richardson's own office was not exempt — is quite absent here, and though a historian could date the house, give or take a few years, it is hardly "dated" at all; there is not much fad about it.

The interior is not very different from the time when it was built for Dr. James Henderson McClelland, a homeopathic physician: a place of dark, varnished woodwork, with grisaille glass lighting the stair. The current owner is treating the house and its furnishings with great care.

The future of this historic house should be carefully watched, though, since it is in a section of Fifth Avenue favored for development.

Landmarks plaque

Howe Springs
Fifth Avenue opposite South Highland Avenue, Squirrel Hill
C. 1910

This little reinforced-concrete temple, now unused and littered, was once an access to water from springs that ran through the Howe estate on the hillside behind. The triple outlet, long dry, was a welcome stop for cyclists and passersby on summer days, who could enjoy not only a long drink of water but some shade. It would be a shame to see such a picturesque feature disappear, and it now appears that it will be present as a feature of a new development.

Woodland Road
Squirrel Hill

Between Fifth Avenue and Wilkins Avenue is a hilly, wooded area, privately owned including its roads, that has escaped intensive development. Much of the land is owned by Chatham College (originally, Pennsylvania Female College; later, Pennsylvania College for Women), which began in a mansion (now gone), built an academic complex on a high knoll, and then absorbed other mansions that had gathered in the area. Mansions, near-mansions, and comfortable homes from the Eclectic period, the time of real wealth, appear along the winding roads almost casually, and there are important modern houses here as well. But the true glory of Woodland Road is its verdant landscape, which envelops and creates a setting for its architecture.

"Willow Cottage" (later, Gateway House, Chatham College)
Fifth Avenue and Woodland Road, Squirrel Hill
C. 1860

This, the oldest surviving element of Fifth Avenue's "Millionaire's Row," was the gatehouse of the estate of Thomas Howe, whose main house was replaced by "Greystone." "Willow Cottage" is not the typical gatehouse; it is large, and well-enough outfitted that members of the Childs family, relatives of the Howes, lived here at the turn of the century. The style may have been considered Gothic, or possibly Swiss, in Mid-Victorian times. In any case, it remains a charming feature of a street that has lost too much of its old character, and a promising introduction to the parklike area of academic buildings and mansions beyond.

275

"Greystone" (later, Benedum Hall, Chatham College)
East Woodland Road near Fifth Avenue, Squirrel Hill
W. H. Vantine, architect, 1911–12

This was the mansion of Michael Late Benedum, a famous entrepreneur in the oil business who had bought the old Howe estate and razed its Gothic main house. While the 23-room interior contains ornate interiors in the styles of seventeenth- and eighteenth-century England, the exterior is rather homely, an expanded version of a middle-class house. A five-bay porch with doubled Tuscan columns precedes a front with two bay windows beneath a dormered tiled roof. The principal block is symmetrical, but at the rear, where the main entrance is, symmetry is completely given up and windows are pierced through the stone walls wherever is handiest. The masonry imitates that of the demolished Howe house: small, squared, not perfectly regular stones laid in courses of varying heights. The cornice shows a peculiarity of the time, a return to the Italianate practice of using paired brackets of fancy outline.

In front of the house, down a flight of steps, is a large Renaissance fountain in concrete. The steep site, near the lower end of the Woodland Road area, leaves the house just visible from Fifth Avenue.

At the time of writing, it appeared that the steep green setting of "Greystone" and the adjacent "Willow Cottage" would be developed with town houses and a condominium block in a way that would preserve both historic buildings but greatly alter the character of the landscape.

Laughlin house (later, Andrew W. Mellon house; presently, Andrew W. Mellon Hall, Chatham College)
Woodland Road, Squirrel Hill
1897; enlarged after 1917

Curiously never attributed to an architect, this house was built for the Laughlin family of Jones & Laughlin Steel in

1897. It was bought by Andrew Mellon in 1917 and enlarged with tennis courts, bowling alleys, and a large underground pool. It remained in the Mellon family until 1940, when it was given to Chatham College. The style is Early Tudor. An adjoining carriage house, whose roofs are much more prominent than those of the main house and whose style is less correct historically, has much more of a Late Victorian appearance today.

Marshall house (later, Arts and Crafts Center; presently, Pittsburgh Center for the Arts)
Fifth and Shady Avenues, Squirrel Hill
Charles Barton Keen (Philadelphia), architect, 1911–12

Despite its hard, white stucco finish, which is not seventeenth-century, the general design suggests an English house of the Carolean period. This is so especially because of the columned doorway with its curved pediment, the tall, simple chimneys, and the hip roof with simple hip-roofed dormers. Yet it is a suggestion, not an imitation: proportions, finish, and the design of the short porte-cochere block deviate from precedent.

The house has long served as a gallery for local artists' associations, and has become a popular institution of the city. Its location beside Mellon Park, the site of the former Richard Beatty Mellon estate, gives it an especially agreeable setting.

Houses
Squirrel Hill

A population map of 1910 shows most of Squirrel Hill as very thinly settled, and a look at the neighborhood suggests that the parts fairly well built up by then were those nearest Fifth Avenue, the northern boundary. When the neighborhood developed as a whole, shortly thereafter, it developed rapidly with modest Eclectic housing. Brick veneer was typical. Naturally, there were exceptions; a few particularly interesting houses had been pioneers in the neighborhood, and in some places the standard of new construction was higher than elsewhere.

Number 6661 Aylesboro Avenue is quite exceptional, a quasi-medieval house with a sandstone bay window that may well date from 1870. Four bands of random stonework enliven its walls with a sort of barbaric energy, yet this is tamed by a broad dormer and a segmental-arched porch, both very likely added when the house was moved in 1920. Originally it was the office and sexton's house for the near-by Homewood Cemetery. Number 1171 Murrayhill Avenue — this is a picturesque street from top to bottom — is a very sophisticated Shingle Style house from around 1890. We do not know the architect, but he obviously had been looking at — if not creating — the contemporary seaside architecture of New England, and he uses his forms neatly but interestingly. A neighboring house at number 1175 is equally good, and shows how this carefully informal style was evolving into the more symmetrical Colonial Revival. Number 1180 Murrayhill Avenue, the Judge McClung house, is the Colonial Revival as commonly found in Pittsburgh. There are plenty of other examples, but this house has the special distinction of being Willa Cather's residence from 1901 to 1906.

At 5605 Aylesboro Avenue is a house in a style not to be identified, but quite common in the 1900s. It suggests the simplest kind of Victorian Italianate but is broader and more solid, and the wide span of the porch especially varies from the Victorian model, if model it was. The effect is usually solemn, yet there are the fancy touches such as the trails of husks that hang from the capitals. Such houses are not Pittsburgh's alone — they have a Midwestern feeling about them — yet an architect around 1910 said, "If a Pittsburgh man were let alone, that is the kind of house he would have."

One Pittsburgher who was not let alone was John Worthington, whose Elizabethan mansion of stone at 5505 Forbes Avenue was built to designs by Louis Stevens around 1915. The house is now part of Temple Sinai.

6661 Aylesboro Avenue

1171 Murrayhill Avenue

1175 Murrayhill Avenue

5605 Aylesboro Avenue

277

Worthington house

5644-62 Forbes Avenue

1424 Bennington Avenue

An elevated area of Squirrel Hill between Forbes and Fifth Avenues was developed in the 1920s as Murdoch Farms, and now appears as a lovely and rather secluded area of Anglo-French architecture among big trees. Number 1424 Bennington Avenue is very English, something that Sir Edwin Lutyens might have designed for Hampstead Garden Suburb near London. The date is probably around 1925, and though we have no present clues about the architect, Janssen & Cocken would come as no surprise.

5703-39 Forbes Avenue

House groups
5644–62 and 5703–39 Forbes Avenue, Squirrel Hill
C. 1910

Two housing groups facing central courts were built a block apart around the same time and in the same style, the manner now called Arts and Crafts or sometimes Craftsman. Their construction is plain, they are undecorated, there are no visible subtleties of detail, yet enough effort has been made to create variety and picturesqueness. The designer of the 5600-block houses, some of which are known to have existed in 1911, is unknown, but Thomas A. and I. K. Watkins both designed and built those in the 5700 block.

Congregation Poale Zedeck
Shady and Phillips Avenues, Squirrel Hill
Philip Friedman and Alexander Sharove, architects, 1928

At a time when many synagogues were in a more or less Near Eastern style, alluding to the origins of Judaism, Poale Zedeck held to the turn-of-the-century tendency to create a massive Classical exterior. The architects had worked with Hornbostel a few years before at B'Nai Israel, and there is a certain Hornbostelian air to this building, specifically suggesting Rodef Shalom. Here once again are cream-colored brick, gently polychromed terra cotta, and a big arch with a triple entrance beneath. One of the pleasantest features is the skeletal inner archway, a Palladian motif executed in terra cotta of Della Robbia blue with off-white edging. Situated among trees and houses at a slight bend of Shady Avenue, the synagogue has a very attractive site.

Harter house
2557 Beechwood Boulevard, Squirrel Hill
Frederick G. Scheibler, Jr., architect, 1923

Here, Scheibler adopted a practice sometimes found early in this century: that of imitating thatch, with its rounded verges and eaves, in another material. In this case he used blue-green shingles laid with extreme irregularity. The roof now is, unfortunately, in bad condition.

Woods house
4604 Monongahela Street, Hazelwood
C. 1790

A forlorn-looking house in an industrial neighborhood, the Woods house is holding fast because of its simple, solid construction and the absence of any use for the land it occupies. This is one of perhaps five or six eighteenth-century buildings left in Pittsburgh, and with proper grading around it, it would be seen as well-proportioned. Stone voussoirs over the door and lower story windows are the only ornaments.

Episcopal Church of the Good Shepherd
Second Avenue and Johnston Street, Hazelwood
William Halsey Wood (Newark, N.J.), architect, 1891

The smallest of Halsey Wood's three buildings in the county, Good Shepherd has an artfully rustic expression. An industrial town has grown around it, yet with its low walls of rubble and dark-red brick, its prominent roof, and its much-louvered, shingled little tower it announces itself as a simple country church. Such a quality of sophisticated humility, a practice of rejecting pompous gestures and ornamental displays in favor of plain materials and vernacular forms — yet composing these with a very knowing eye — had begun early in the Romantic period and would persist far into the twentieth century.

Landmarks plaque

279

First Hungarian Reformed Church
221 Johnston Street, Hazelwood
Titus De Bobula, architect, 1903–04

A small De Bobula church, at first glance well-proportioned but no more, reveals some interesting details on closer examination. The texture of the doorway arch, crisp and emphatic, turns the ordinary yellow-gray sandstone of this area, for once, into something almost beautiful. The buttresses of the tower rise in a long, steady slope, an Art Nouveau or Beaux-Arts treatment unlike the Gothic practice of setting them back in stages. Finally, and most remarkably, the windows beside the tower are rampant arches, as if the sheer mass of the tower had exerted a gravitational pull on their crowns.

ALONG THE MONONGAHELA

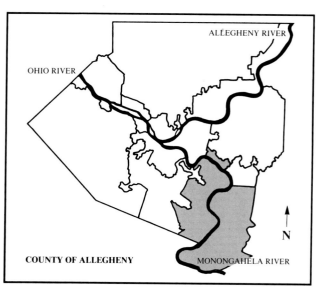

Upriver from the South Side, the Monongahela River turns generally eastward, then turns southward in a series of zigzag bends toward its source in West Virginia, 128 miles from the Pittsburgh Point. The hills advance toward the water's edge, then retreat again. In the narrowest parts, with room only for a road and a rail line, the slopes are wild, trees and shrubs interrupted only by pipelines or electric pylons. But where there is room on the shores there are industrial plants, with towns behind them on the river plains and the slopes beyond.

At first glance this seems to be engineer's, not architect's, country. Blast furnaces up to 300 feet high, giant industrial sheds, machinery of all sizes, billows of steam, bridges, and dams establish a heroic scale, while by contrast the towns behind seem like semi-permanent encampments, hastily called into being a century ago to serve the industrial plants and never fully put in order. Yet a closer look shows architectural works like the Carnegie Libraries of Braddock and Munhall or the cluster of churches in Homestead and Munhall, built to last and indicative of stable,

The Edgar Thomson Works in North Braddock symbolizes the industrial presence in the ''Mon Valley.''

prosperous communities with more on their minds than the making of steel and money.

Before 1870 the industrial valley to be seen today hardly existed. Elizabeth, founded in 1787, West Elizabeth, and a few other places were boat-building centers. Drifting flatboats, coalboats, and even ocean-going vessels whose true careers began at New Orleans were launched from their yards earlier in the century, and later steamers and diesel towboats were built as well. Toward the middle of the century, both mining and navigation were stimulated by a steady and increasing demand for coal: steam coal for domestic hearths, for boilers to drive machinery, and for the locomotives that replaced the earlier wood-burners; metallurgical coal, suitable for coking, to feed the new blast furnaces that were replacing the old, remote charcoal furnaces. Beginning in 1841 a private company canalized the Monongahela, partly for the packet trade, mostly for the coal boats that first drifted, then were driven by sternwheelers, to their markets.

The mines, the boatyards, the navigation, and the occasional small factories in riverside settlements here and there introduced a modest industrial presence to the river above Pittsburgh before 1870. So did the Pittsburgh & Connellsville Railroad on the north shore; when the Pittsburgh & Connellsville came to McKeesport in 1857, that small community of 1795 began to grow, and in 1870 became the home of the large National Tube Works. In 1873, Andrew Carnegie, who already had manufactured steel, built a large Bessemer plant, with a specialty in rail, on a site next to Turtle Creek where the British General Edward Braddock had met his celebrated defeat in 1755. Named the Edgar Thomson Works after the president of the Pennsylvania Railroad, the shipper and best customer for the product, the plant attracted a work force that turned the adjacent village of Braddock's Field into the industrial town of Braddock. In 1873, the Homestead Bank & Insurance Company laid out a little town on the south shore of the river, which it named after itself. In 1879, Andrew Kloman bought land in Homestead for the Pittsburgh Bessemer Steel Company, then sold the plant in 1883 to the Carnegie Phipps Company. In 1884, the Carrie Furnaces — blast furnaces are commonly named after women — were built at Rankin on the north shore to supply smelted iron to customers; eventually it supplied hot metal — molten iron straight from the furnace — to the Homestead plant across the river. In the mid-1880s, George Westinghouse relocated the Union Switch & Signal Company to the semi-rural commuter area of Swissvale, and toward the end of the decade began the move of his other plants to the Turtle Creek Valley, near Braddock and along the Pennsylvania Railroad main line. In 1900, Henry Clay Frick established the St. Clair Furnace and St. Clair Steel Companies nearly opposite Elizabeth; from these grew the town of Clairton, which also became the location of a large coking plant.

Thirty years, then, sufficed to turn this portion of the Monongahela from a shore and hillside area where one settled to farm, mine coal, do a little manufacturing, or merely enjoy the scenery from one's porch into a place of infernal if heroic sights, noises, and smells. Yet areas remained where this industrial intensity never came, or came only in limited ways. West Mifflin Borough, which touches the river at three places, does have large plants on its uplands but is also part-rural, part-suburban, and has accommodated as well the old Curtis-Bettis Airfield of 1925, the Allegheny County Airport, and Kennywood, one of the nation's great amusement parks. Other areas with river frontage, Elizabeth and Forward Townships and Jefferson Borough, have always been rural. Here large untamed spaces and farmhouses from the early nineteenth century still abound. ■

Farmland in the upper Mon Valley: a view from Sunny Side Hollow Road in Forward Township.

Houses
208–14 Hazel Way, West Homestead
C. 1900

These worker's tenements are a rare survival, with their outside stairs leading to open but recessed galleries on the second floor from which the upper rooms are reached. Each of the units is two bays wide and is lighted only from the front and rear.

Mesta house
540 Doyle Avenue, West Homestead
C. 1900

This was the Colonial Revival mansion of George Mesta, founder in 1887 of the Mesta Machine Company. The company's gigantic plant is the most conspicuous sight in West Homestead. It manufactured heavy machinery for steel mills until 1983.

The house is big, decorated, and symmetrical on the front, but still rather artless externally as so many homes of the local rich were. The second floor of the conspicuous side wall has three types of window, for instance, used randomly. The dormers are unusual in being shaped as Palladian windows.

Marrying in late middle age, Mesta was building another home for his wife Perle — later a famous Washington hostess — when he died in 1925.

Homestead High Level Bridge
Monongahela River at Mile 7.25, between Pittsburgh and Homestead
Allegheny County Authority; George S. Richardson, design engineer; J. E. Greiner Company (Baltimore), consulting engineers; 1934–37

In the days before computers the appeal of the so-called continuous truss, passing over more than two points of support and functioning as a single structural member throughout its length, was greatly tempered by the practical impossibility of finding out exactly what was happening under given conditions. The Swiss-born Pittsburgh engineer Ernest M. Wichert devised a simple solution. Instead of having a post rise from each pier, the Wichert truss had a Y-shaped member to which the lower chord of each span was hinged. This slight break in structural continuity permitted easy stress calculation and allowed a measure of control over the forces acting on the structure under any condition of loading or settlement. Wichert is reported by George S. Richardson, who designed the main trusses, to have received a royalty of $25,000 for this first application of his truss. It received limited use thereafter.

St. Mary Magdalene Church (Roman Catholic)
East Tenth Avenue and Amity Street, Homestead
Frederick C. Sauer, architect, 1895

Fronting on a park, St. Mary Magdalene is one of the most conspicuous of the churches that are so numerous in the Homestead-Munhall residential area. Bandings and arches of rock-faced brownstone, a gable wall of ochre brick diapered in red brick, rose windows with richly modeled red

283

terra-cotta surrounds, and doorways in quasi-Richardson-ian stonework add to the display. Inside is a long, dark interior of arches on Corinthian columns and kingpost roof trusses. The adjoining rectory is Romanesque, brick with banded stone arches and some fine leaded glass.

Carnegie Library of Homestead
510 Tenth Avenue, Munhall
Alden & Harlow, architects, 1896–98

Much more than a library, this golden-brown building also houses a concert hall and social and athletic rooms. It stands at the top of a small hillside park, a fine setting for its serene architecture in which Renaissance symmetry is combined with mild Romantic variations of perimeter and roof planes. The library had been promised by Andrew Carnegie in 1889 at the dedication of the Carnegie Library at Braddock; the calm scene today offers no reminder that, before Carnegie fulfilled his promise, the violent Homestead Steel Strike had occurred within sight.

St. John's Cathedral (Byzantine Catholic)
Tenth Avenue and Dickson Street, Munhall
Titus De Bobula, architect, 1903

This is the masterpiece of the little-known but interesting De Bobula, probably the largest and most complex product of his curious art. The style is a sort of Art Nouveau, not the sinuous French or Belgian variety but the blockier sort associated with Italy and Central Europe. With De Bobula's use of the style, as in some Italian Art Nouveau designs, Classical detailing is associated.

The central front has a compressed look, with its upper part seemingly squeezed upward from the pressure of the close-set towers. From bottom to top, it has a rusticated arch, surmounted by a colonnade; then, set back a little, another rusticated arch, a cornice, a plain, neutral story, another cornice, and a crowning colonnade. Despite the open colonnade at the top there is no sense of an upward progression toward a climactic feature. Rather, there is layer upon layer of horizontals. The towers, on the other hand, are resolutely vertical, their corners stepping back, breaking up into sub-corners, then chamfers, and finally terminating in domed tempietti. The vertical thrust is strengthened by tall, narrow archways within which the real openings of the towers are set; their surfaces are complicated, yet visually strengthened, by a mixture of stone and brick; and flat, raised crosses rising from stepped elements add to the three-dimensional effect.

The body of the church is plainer, yet is visually tied to the front by diagonally set corner buttresses above which the cornice itself runs toward the towers on a diagonal.

The adjoining rectory is more commonplacely American of its time save for the porch, where open panels above the Classical columns and the architrave are a very unusual feature with Italian precedents from the 1900 period.

The church, now a cathedral, was built for a Carpatho-Ruthenian parish founded in 1896.

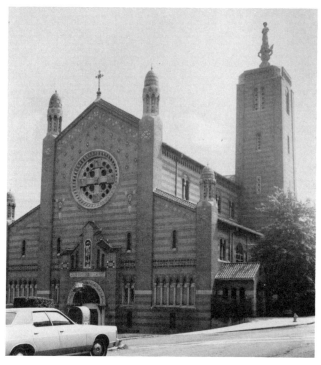

St. Michael Archangel Church (Roman Catholic)
Ninth Avenue and Library Place, Munhall
John T. Comes, architect, 1927

This is one of the largest churches in the Homestead-Munhall area, a work in a free version of Italian Romanesque, in two shades of tan brick, by Pittsburgh's best-known architect of Catholic churches. The congregation that commissioned it was Slovak. On top of the tower, which apparently was designed for a more conventional termination, is Frank Vittor's *St. Joseph the Worker* of 1966. Behind the church are a convent and a rectory, conventional turn-of-the-century buildings that frame the vista of the curious domed belfry of a school within the block.

Union Switch & Signal Company, American-Standard, Inc.
Braddock Avenue by Conrail main line, Swissvale and Edgewood
After 1886; Janssen & Cocken, architects for administration building, 1927

The most interesting element of this large industrial group is the administration building, faced in red brick. In its overall simplicity, with just a few decorative touches such as the crenelated skyline, it suggests the mildly progressive commercial and industrial architecture of Germany in the 1920s. On one side, a covered arched bridge, faced with brick as well, makes a slightly jarring connection with the exposed concrete skeleton of a factory building by the architects Hunting & Davis.

7510 Trevanion Avenue

Houses
7506, 7508, and 7510 Trevanion Avenue, Swissvale
Frederick G. Scheibler, Jr., architect

Three houses by Pittsburgh's creative, ambivalently Modern architect. Number 7510, the Hellmund house, was built in 1915–16, and seems to show a mixture of Germanic rigidity — windows on two stories with an intervening balcony to emphasize the vertical alignment — and Anglo-Saxon informality, derived perhaps from English architecture of the time, in the horizontals of the porte-cochere and the porch.

Its interior is as built, an Arts and Crafts environment of abundant woodwork, tile, and stained glass. It includes a fireplace with openings into both the living and dining rooms: a feature that appears to be derived from Prairie School planning.

285

7508, 7506 Trevanion Avenue

Number 7508, built c. 1917, is a small, simple, and pleasant gambrel-roofed house. Number 7506, from 1905, is the most complex, less obviously organized; it was restored externally in 1981, and the interior is much as it was originally.

Landmarks plaque (7510)

Braddock Carnegie Library and Carnegie Hall
Library Street and Parker Avenue, Braddock
William Halsey Wood (Newark, N.J.), architect for Carnegie Library, 1888; Longfellow, Alden & Harlow (Boston and Pittsburgh), architects for Carnegie Hall, 1893

This was the first of all the world's Carnegie libraries to be dedicated, a few hundred yards from the Edgar Thomson Works, Andrew Carnegie's first major venture in steelmaking. With the 1893 annex, the institution became a community center of a diversified nature; besides the 20,000-volume library it had an 1,100-seat theater, meeting rooms, swimming pool, bath, bowling alley, billiard room, and gymnasium.

William Halsey Wood was a short-lived architect of fantastic ideas that went unrealized and more realizable designs that were executed. Here, he supplied a simple Richardson Romanesque design, symmetrical on the front, with bow windows framing a narrow pavilion with a gable. These carry the most interesting details: cast-iron mullions in the broad first-floor windows and crude, vigorous leaf carvings beneath the cornice. Carnegie Hall is less hearty Romanesque, the product of a firm that was seeing its Renaissance design for the Carnegie Institute to completion; in order to harmonize with the library, Longfellow, Alden & Harlow revived a style they had more or less abandoned. Frank Vittor's World War I Memorial, a figure of Victory from 1922, is a third element

of the group, a light Classical sculpture set against the heavy Romanesque masonry.

In 1983 the Braddock's Field Historical Society acquired the building and, in collaboration with several other groups including the Pittsburgh History & Landmarks Foundation, began a campaign to re-open and find new uses for it. It was then long closed and unwanted in a depressed community with a population only a quarter the size it had been 50 years before. Landmarks completed a major reuse study for the Model Cities Program of the Turtle Creek Valley, but no means to implement it could be found.

National Register; Landmarks plaque

U.S. Post Office
Parker Avenue and Orchard Street, Braddock
Louis A. Simon, designer; James Knox Taylor or Oscar Wenderoth of the U.S. Treasury Department (Washington, D.C.), supervising architect; 1913

The federal presence in a community — manifested usually in a post office — often contrasts markedly with its ordinary buildings. If the government has built for itself rather than renting space, it is almost bound to have done a creditable architectural job, and in the Eclectic past it tended to create palatial pavilions, on a level with banks and passenger stations, that might seem deliberately to one-up the homely buildings around them. Yet citizens were proud of such post offices, not annoyed about them, as public interest in federally sponsored mural projects of the 1930s was to show.

In Braddock, the federal presence *was* in contrast to the surrounding houses. The very delicate detailing is curious, given that the material is limestone. The panels in the piers, the ornament in the spandrels, and the small scale of the balustrade suggest modeling in terra cotta rather than carving in stone, to an extent that raises the question whether some quirky governmental decision substituted the more dignified material after the design was approved.

Church of St. Michael the Archangel (Roman Catholic) (presently, Good Shepherd Church)
Braddock Avenue and Fraser Street, Braddock
Carlton Strong, architect, 1930

This was one of the architect's last works, a church of masonry with a generalized Romanesque feeling and a masonry expression, but also a response to the malaise of architects in the 1930 period about going on with stylistic imitation. The rather tall exterior that culminates in a low-set octagonal lantern has little that can be called decorative, although there is a small open bell tower tucked into an alley

Schwab house
541 Jones Avenue, North Braddock
1890–93

A Richardsonian Romanesque example of company housing at the upper end of the range, this was the house provided for Charles Schwab, the famous superintendent of Carnegie's Edgar Thomson Works, from 1889 to 1892. In the latter year he was transferred to the Homestead Works, where his amiable ways were much needed after the terrible strike. The house stands on a slope, now rather desolate, looking down toward the Monongahela River and the mills. It has simple, powerful forms: one of those dark, brooding places of which a few still survive, inviting one to imagine the life that goes on inside. Year by year, they yield to bland new buildings, or to nothing at all, to vacancy.

Perhaps Frederick J. Osterling, who altered "Clayton" in the East End, provided this similar design. On the other hand, there is some evidence in support of Longfellow, Alden & Harlow, whom Carnegie had praised to Schwab.

side. Inside, the color and texture of brickwork and the simple and powerful curves of the arches and the squinches that bear the lantern are the most telling elements. The chancel, however, is quite frankly and richly decorated. The walls have vine and diaper patterns, and the bracketed ciborium is supported by stone piers representing attenuated, highly stylized angels. These are sculptured in an innovative way associated with the New York architect Bertram Goodhue and his favorite sculptor Lee Lawrie: a very simple mass of stone, from bottom to top, is increasingly broken up into elements that resolve themselves into a conventionalized living being. In this case, the rising and receding masses continue behind the upraised wings of the angels in skyscraper-like forms. Perhaps these, with the very simple arches and the elaborate patterns of the chancel walls, imply that the Church is rooted in tradition yet as modern as today.

House
817 Kirkpatrick Street, North Braddock
C. 1885

An example of upper-rank company housing, rented to U.S. Steel foremen who also received options to purchase. The symmetry of the main building block suggests that all else is additions, including the projecting cubical element, with its stained-glass window, over the porch.

287

Casino

Kennywood Park
4800 Kennywood Boulevard, West Mifflin
1898 and after

There were 13 parks intended as trolley or railroad destinations in Southwestern Pennsylvania in the early part of the century. Kennywood is the outstanding survivor, an orderly, family-type amusement park that today is like a house that several generations have helped to furnish. The gardening, which includes a floral clock, still has a Late Victorian quality regardless of the innovations and changes of nearly nine decades. Even the plants look Victorian. The pavilions are

Carousel

in 1940 Modernistic or styles from before or since. It appears that amusement-park design has an inertia of its own. The Carousel, a big four-row merry-go-round, was built for the Philadelphia Sesquicentennial of 1926 but is in the Baroque tradition, and though the pavilion that shelters it was built when the merry-go-round came here, it has the look of an open-air Shingle Style park shelter of the 1890s; the Casino, the original dining pavilion, looks no older. The Thunderbolt of 1968, judged by connoisseurs to be one of the world's greatest roller-coasters, is still constructed in the primitive bolted-together-white-painted boards manner though it flings you over the edge of a bluff. As you hurtle downwards, the Edgar Thomson steelworks across the river raises austere dark shapes to remind you of the hard work days that made Kennywood a great pleasure for so many through the years.

Landmarks plaques

Allegheny County Airport Terminal
Lebanon Church Road, West Mifflin
Stanley L. Roush, architect, 1931; Henry Hornbostel, architect for additions, 1936

Like other Eclectics, Roush and Hornbostel had occasion to turn their hands to non-historic styles. Here, in something so progressive as an airport, Modernistic seemed appropriate, so Roush created a work in white brick with touches of black, green, and silver, which Hornbostel enlarged using similar detailing. Above the stainless-steel canopy — which may be an early addition — is a semi-hexagonal doorhead, edged with green, black, and silver mosaic, with lavish green tracery: a feature that is Art Deco of a very Parisian sort rather than Modernistic. To each side is an Art Deco urn with medallions bearing images of flight, human and animal.

James D. Van Trump has pointed out that, despite the aggressive newness of the surface style, the ensemble suggests a small Baroque country palace, symmetrical and building up from low side wings to a climactic feature at the center.

The airport was used for commercial flights until 1952, when the Greater Pittsburgh Airport took over this function. It can still accommodate airplanes up to the size of a DC-9, but today handles only private and corporate traffic.

U.S. Post Office
Grant Avenue and Second Street, Duquesne
1900

In the broad proportions of its openings and its Classical ornamentation, this is a good example of turn-of-the-century business architecture. Cleaned and restored, it would be a cheerful feature of the street scene.

McKeesport and Versailles Cemetery
1608 Fifth Avenue, McKeesport
1856 and after

This is a picturesque "rural" cemetery on a hillside, similar in kind to Allegheny Cemetery if less interesting. It suffers in part from being overlooked by a huge and mindlessly designed apartment house. The gateway, though it bears the dedication date of 1856, has decorative carving that suggests the 1880s. The Queen Anne house alongside, though of different materials, is probably a near contemporary.

Bank of McKeesport (presently, McKeesport National Bank)
Fifth Avenue and Sinclair Street, McKeesport
Longfellow, Alden & Harlow (Boston and Pittsburgh), architects (?), 1889-91

Longfellow, Alden & Harlow, who at this same time were designing the Conestoga Building in the Triangle, were recommended for this job by the president of the bank. Though there is no evidence that they got it, some features of both designs are similar: the use of mullion-and-transom windows slightly recessed between structural piers, the presence of arched windows in the uppermost floor, and the feeling that a moment of transition between styles of different character has been reflected in a building design. The Romanesque tendency to glorify masonry as a constructional means is present in the very hard-looking granite corner

column, the rock-faced stone of the basement and quoins, and the mullions and transoms that bind the solids together despite the width of the voids. Yet the level roofline, the regular rhythm of the longer front, and the long, thin Roman brick that minimizes texture are characteristics of the Classical future that was arriving.

In the 1970s the exterior was restored under the guidance of the Pittsburgh History & Landmarks Foundation.

National Register; Landmarks plaque

Lysle Boulevard Bridge
Youghiogheny River at Lysle Boulevard, McKeesport
Allegheny County Authority; George S. Richardson and Eugene Hunting, engineers; 1937-39

The Allegheny County Authority was organized in the mid-1930s as a recipient of federal PWA money. Among other things, the Authority built this two-hinged crescent-arch bridge whose span is about 320 feet. Since only two hinges, at the springing of the arch, were necessary, the parabolic crescent form was exactly right for supporting evenly distributed dead loads and reinforcing the arch against off-center and moving loads. Aside from its ornamental railings, the bridge is undecorated, relying on the inherent grace of the arch for visual effect.

McKeesport Water Filtration Plant
Railroad Street at the Fifteenth Street Bridge, McKeesport
Alexander Potter, engineer, 1907-08; 1925

At the same time that Pittsburgh began filtering its water, McKeesport built a plant for filtering and softening water from the Youghiogheny River. Water was taken from the river beneath the small octagonal Active Intake System Building and piped to the large circular Chemical Treatment Building. After treatment there, it was filtered underground, then sent to the adjacent Pump House, and thence to a reservoir. A fourth building on the site is a chemical-storage plant and power station.

Of the four buildings, the most striking is the Chemical Treatment Building, whose circular plan reflects the radial flow of the water after its arrival from the river. The narrower upper story contains offices and laboratories. The Pump House is also large and impressive, a tile-roofed pavilion in the Beaux-Arts style whose windows, now largely bricked up, were made enormous to ventilate the space once occupied by large, hot reciprocating engines.

Landmarks plaque

Muse house
4222 Third Street, McKeesport
1820; additions, c. 1824 and 1910

To the two-bay original stone house, a three-bay section was added about four years later, giving a typical Georgian house plan with a central hall. The stone is in a lively pattern of random ashlar, roughly axed. Drafts of roughly parallel grooves have been cut around some of the openings and used to outline the adjacent stones. The lintel over the main door has an oval raised medallion, neatly cut with the initials of Fauntley and Catherine Muse, the first owners. Near by is the temple-like springhouse, at 4232 Walnut Street, now used as a home.

Walker house
1026 Third Avenue, Elizabeth Borough
1844

Occasionally in Western Pennsylvania a one-and-a-half-story Greek Revival house survives. Here is a simple but elegant example, built as a summer home for an in-law of the Walker family, which still owns it.

Scott house
Round Hill Park Exhibit Farm, Round Hill Regional Park, Elizabeth Township
1838

At the center of a farm, maintained as an exhibit and containing three barns, the simple but solid Scott house illustrates the most basic sort of Greek Revival. The bricklayer has used the elegant Flemish bond on the front and the cheaper common bond on the other fronts. The practice of making a fine facade toward the road, regardless of the treatment of other fronts, came to Western Pennsylvania as an element of Georgian building practice.

Hutchinson farm
Round Hill Road near Pennsylvania Route 51,
Elizabeth Township
House, 1865

The Georgian building tradition persisted through most of
the nineteenth century in ordinary house construction even
while the fashions in applied ornament changed. Here is the
old formula still vital: rectangular perimeter, gable roof, symmetrical front, sash windows twice as high as wide, disposed
— as was often the case in the eighteenth century — so as
to be paired on each side of the central element. To the simple
brick shell are added an Italianate porch and brackets, delicate
enough to be decorations of the basic geometry, not
distractions.

Allen-Raisner house
Sunny Side Hollow Road, Forward Township
1818–19

This is a handsome late Georgian house, whose delicately
worked doorway includes a decorated fanlight and a curved
pediment, very rare in Georgian architecture in this area. The
orangeish brickwork is laid in Flemish bond on the front and
south gable walls, those most conspicuous from the road,
and in common bond elsewhere. Typically Georgian flat
arches of brick cap the windows.

Van Kirk farm
Round Hill Road and Scenery Drive, Elizabeth
Township
House, c. 1845

This is the main house of a farm, yet its front gives the
appearance of an elegant Greek Revival villa. But it is amusing: should you move around the house, the "architecture"
disappears and ordinary vernacular construction swiftly
comes into view, with pitched roofs and plain walls. The
Georgian way of dressing up a road front and being more
casual about everything else has obviously persisted here.

291

The Westinghouse Bridge and the Westinghouse Electric plant: gateway to the Turtle Creek Valley.

THE TURTLE CREEK VALLEY

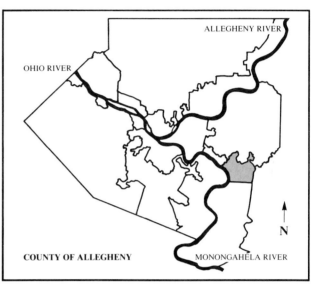

Just upstream from the Edgar Thomson Works in North Braddock, the Monongahela River is joined by a westward-flowing creek whose outlet is nearly concealed by a railroad bridge. This is Turtle Creek, a stream of no great size but one that has worn a deep valley through the hills. Along this valley the Pennsylvania Railroad main line was laid in the early 1850s, determining the role of the valley in the last hundred years as an industrial place.

As so often in the Pittsburgh area, it is the landscape that catches the eye rather than the constructions set against it. The valley floor and the hillsides are occupied by plain wooden houses and commonplace commercial buildings. Yet the large industrial plants that George Westinghouse built along the valley in the late 1880s and early 1890s, the George Westinghouse Memorial Bridge near the mouth of the valley, and a few smaller constructions here and there distinguish the Turtle Creek Valley as a landscape apart.

The first non-Indian settler of the valley is believed to have been John Frazer, a trader who built a cabin near the mouth of the creek in 1748. During the eighteenth century, there was a small

Workers' houses on Larimer Avenue, Turtle Creek.

amount of settlement, mainly agricultural, both in the valley and on the uplands. A military road made during the French and Indian War developed in time into a main road from the East. As elsewhere in the Monongahela Valley area, the early nineteenth-century discovery of coal and the large and increasing demand for coal by local industry effected change. Mines in the hillsides sent coal down by incline to the valley floor for loading into coal boats, which then drifted down the creek into the Monongahela and so to their destinations. Mining, however, did not spoil the scenery to any great extent; in fact, the valley became a resort area around 1850 — with at least one large hotel — served by a plank road from Pittsburgh.

The beginning of Pennsylvania Railroad through service in 1852 along the Turtle Creek Valley and of local operations on the Pittsburgh & Connellsville Railroad along the Monongahela shore in 1857 gave the valley a new character and changed the mode of coal shipment from water to rail. But no trace remains today of Port Perry, a once-busy railroad transit center for coal that flourished in the later nineteenth century on the east side of the mouth of Turtle Creek; its site lies beneath crisscrossing railroad lines.

The decision of George Westinghouse to unite the scattered operations of the Westinghouse Electric & Manufacturing Company in a new plant a

mile up the valley was the major element of a series of events that transformed its lower end from a thinly settled wooded area to a heavily populated series of industrial boroughs. Opened in 1894, the plant occupied 170 acres by 1905, demanding a large labor force. In 1894 too, the Union Railroad, which serves local industry, built a line through the area and eventually made East Pittsburgh, one of the boroughs in which the Westinghouse Electric plant lies, its headquarters. Finally, trolley service at the beginning of this century made the lower Turtle Creek Valley attractive to workers in various industrial installations who were seeking homes.

The upper Turtle Creek Valley developed rapidly as well. In 1889 construction began on the new plant of the Westinghouse Air-Brake Company, and at the same time Westinghouse began construction of a large section of company housing in the newly incorporated borough of Wilmerding. Further up the valley, the railroad workers' towns of Wall and Pitcairn grew in the 1900s around a large rail yard and freight terminal. This facility has since declined, but its broad wedge of land and the memory of its former activity still dominate the surrounding communities.

Today, the observer in the valley is still impressed by the industrial presence. The keen observer may even notice Turtle Creek itself, channeled between factory and rail. ▪

the broadest in this material in the United States. The form is parabolic, the natural form for an evenly loaded arch. The total length is 1,596 feet. By the late 1970s, it was all too apparent that the deck had to be reconstructed, yet the bridge as repaired is very much as before. The entrances have four tall concrete pylons with granite reliefs by Frank Vittor, honoring Westinghouse's development of the Turtle Creek Valley.

National Register; Landmarks plaque

Union Railroad General Offices
666 Linden Avenue, East Pittsburgh
1914

A major architectural problem early in this century was giving a civilized appearance to the large skeleton-framed industrial building, with its big horizontal windows, that had just emerged. A doorway could be given a special surround of stone or terra cotta; spandrels beneath the windows could be faced with brick in fancy bonding; but in general, architecture fled to the parapet, with its uninterrupted wall space and possibilities on the skyline. So it is here: modeled terra cotta that includes lion's masks and friezes of colored tile assist a doorway of Classical character in the decoration of this headquarters for a small industrial railroad.

George Westinghouse Memorial Bridge
U.S. Route 30 over Turtle Creek between East Pittsburgh and North Versailles Township
George S. Richardson and A. D. Nutter of the Allegheny County Department of Public Works, engineers, 1930

Not only does this bridge carry a major highway; it also has served as a triumphal entrance to the Pittsburgh area for rail passengers from the east for half a century. When it was built, its five concrete arches were regarded as a little conservative by European standards, yet the central span of 460 feet was

St. Colman Catholic School
Hunter and Thompson Streets, Turtle Creek
Link, Weber & Bowers, architects, 1928

Contemporary with Central Catholic High School in Oakland and by the same architects, this school's jaunty diapering in sgraffito is even more pronounced than the diapered brickwork of the larger institution. Twin bow windows at either end add to the lively effect. The head of the doorway has a typically Renaissance scallop-shell motif, distorted to fit within a rather tall Gothic arch.

Westinghouse Air Brake Division, American-Standard, Inc., Wilmerding Plant
Airbrake Avenue and Bridge Street, Wilmerding
1890 and after

At one end of the long Westinghouse industrial complex in Turtle Creek Valley is this 35-acre plant, which contains several impressive works of Richardson-influenced Late Victorian industrial architecture. The most interesting is the Machine Shop, with its three long monitor roofs side by side. The outer two roofs have gable ends, now lopsided from the addition of upper space, while the inner one is masked by a kind of false front bearing a tablet. Round and segmental arches, very large as one might expect, pierce the walls to the utmost in a variety that seems capricious until one remembers the problems of arch abutment in a solid-masonry structure. Sloping buttresses flank the side, probably to help sustain the loads of a traveling crane. In the gables, trios of little arches beneath deep corbel tables mark a transition from engineering to architecture in the designer's mind. The

engineering would look better without them. A hip-roofed office building next to the Machine Shop continues the round-arched theme. The Foundry, not readily seen from outside the plant, has a more closed character, with smaller round arches.

Westinghouse Air Brake Company General Office Building (formerly, Library Hall)
Herman Drive and Commerce Street, Wilmerding
1890; Janssen & Cocken, architects for addition, 1927

The Westinghouse Company built the original building, possibly to designs by Frederick J. Osterling, as a public library and community center. This was a philanthropy in the Carnegie manner — immediately after construction of the Braddock Carnegie Library — with a restaurant, library, baths, bowling alleys, and swimming pool. Library Hall burned in 1896 though and was rebuilt as a Westinghouse Air-Brake Company office building, with the reconstructed parts in brick instead of the original random ashlar. Janssen & Cocken's annex is in the chateau spirit of the original, but uses the basic manner in a more sober and orthodox way. The building, halfway up a hillside, is a striking feature, lordly and melancholy, among the trees and commonplace houses.

At the time of publication, the company was willing to donate the building to a non-profit organization that could maintain and use it.

Landmarks plaque

SOUTH OF PITTSBURGH

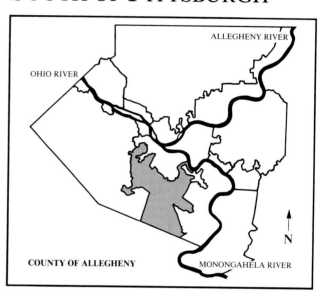

Beginning at Pittsburgh's southwestern edge, a chain of communities runs southward along Chartiers Creek. These have had varied characters: industry and workers' housing in Carnegie, Heidelberg, and Bridgeville; middle-class houses in Ingram and Crafton; and upper-middle-class houses in Thornburg. At Thornburg, members of the Thornburg family, which had owned land along Chartiers Creek since 1791, decided in 1900 to subdivide part of it to create a suburb similar to Tuxedo Park, New York, with informal-looking houses in a wooded setting and good rail access from Pittsburgh. The idea was a success, and today the borough is most visibly a place of rustic houses, Shingle Style or Craftsman, dispersed over the hillside setting.

The South Hills area, however, which extends directly south from Pittsburgh, consists of more uniform suburban development. Before 1904 the terrain of hills and valleys was there but few buildings. The inclines had made the areas overlooking the Monongahela accessible, and trolley cars had begun climbing the South Side Slopes in 1888 for a trip to Mount Oliver a mile and and a half inland, but the area beyond was

Rustic stone and shingles on Hamilton Road typify Thornburg's artful informality.

A South Hills trolley at an intersection in Castle Shannon.

primarily farmland and woods. Only in Castle Shannon, five miles south of the Monongahela, had a serious attempt been made at a South Hills suburb. Around 1870, real-estate promoters went to seemingly fantastic lengths to persuade Pittsburghers to settle on this unpromising land. To render their suburb accessible, they built the Pittsburgh & Castle Shannon Railroad. Travel by this involved a trip to the Carson Street terminal, east of the Smithfield Street Bridge; being hauled in one's coach up a shallow-grade incline; and being pulled by steam locomotive the remainder of the journey, which began with a passage through a 1,700-foot tunnel.

The promoters might have been spared trouble and expense had the electric streetcar been in existence, and the 1904 opening of the South Hills trolley tunnel, running five-eighths of a mile from the Smithfield Street Bridge to the far side of Mount Washington, was a much more effective way of opening up the South Hills. From its elevated southern end at South Hills Junction, trolleys could disperse throughout the hills, running over bridges and along ridges and meeting occasional feeder lines, and builders took quick advantage of the opportunity to build boxy houses, apartment houses, and commercial buildings within an easy walk of the rights-of-way. Their architecture was not sophisticated. There seemed to be no special sense of proportion, no system of design. They built in cream-colored buff brick, made the porch columns Classical, perhaps threw in a suggestion of half-timbering in an occasional unnecessary gable; and somewhere, on the stair or beside the mantelpiece, put windows with art glass. The trolley suburbs of the South Hills are a veritable realm of art glass, in smeary, opalescent colors, intricately geometrical or evoking flowers in May. A design purist can fret over

a street scene in the older suburbs like Dormont or Brentwood, want to tidy up its architecture, make it worthy of the well-kept lawns, the flowers, the trees, and the whole rolling, inhabited landscape. Yet there is a relaxed charm to these places, a feeling of well-being attained in material terms, a pride evident in those well-kept lawns, that makes good architecture no more than the final perfecting touch.

The suburbs have spread greatly since 1928, when the Liberty Bridge was opened to lead from town to the slightly older Liberty Tubes through the hills. The newer suburbs naturally have a character different from that of the older ones. Carried to their very doors, the automobile commuters were able to disperse in a way that was impractical for trolley riders, get well away from main streets, build on larger properties. And while the other architecture of the trolley suburbs tended to be essentially style-less, the newer houses of the 1920s and somewhat later in a community like Mount Lebanon were more subtle, more carefully studied for the most part, full of quaint effects and allusions to Colonial, Cotswold, or Tudor, while the official and commercial buildings of the main street might be discreetly Modernistic. After World War II the expansive trend, long interrupted, resumed, and new tracts of houses, now without much style or character at all, spread over what had been areas of farms and forests.

South Park was a product of the late 1920s and early 1930s, an old farming area given over to serve an increasing population with recreational facilities and the Allegheny County Fairgrounds. The Allegheny County Fair was a popular attraction for many years, but ended in the 1970s, while suburbanization absorbed farmland and expanded the limits of the South Hills and other rapidly developing areas of Allegheny County.

First Presbyterian Church (presently, Ingram Masonic Hall)
West Prospect and Mackin Avenues, Ingram
1899

A prominent building is sometimes imitated in unexpected ways or places. Here is a round, apse-like termination to a church — unusual for the Presbyterians, but possibly accommodating an Akron-plan Sunday-school arrangement. To one side of this is a tower, and to the other what may have been the base of another tower, never built. The very same disposition could be seen in the contemporary Carnegie Institute, where two campanili originally flanked the visible semicircle of the Carnegie Music Hall. In materials — here, a slightly variegated, light-colored brick — details, and proportions, the two buildings are very different, as they are in purpose. Yet the Carnegie Institute's compositional formula gave the unknown architect of the church a hook from which to hang the rather loose features of his design.

House
80 Berry Street, Ingram
C. 1870; alterations and additions, 1968–73

Challenged to give this house a stylistic label its architect would probably have said, "Swiss." It has the far-flung eaves and the solid brackets of a chalet, and a general woodiness of expression. Modern authorities would be more inclined to apply the more recent label Stick Style for the same reason,

especially since wall areas are characteristically marked off into panels by the application of slats. A modern enclosure of a porch and extension of the rear were done with great care and respect.

House
51 Noble Avenue, Crafton
Eli Crum, architect, 1871

There are two curious things about this house. First, it is a log house veneered in brick and stone. The latter, sooty black, is said to have been salvaged from a railroad tunnel. Second, the pungent, intricate detailing of the pediment has been uncovered in recent years; it had been boarded over so that the house presented a bland Classical face to the world. An interesting and sophisticated detail is the extension of the vertical lines of the posts through the entablature with lengths of board and molding. The design in the pediment carries the verticals still further.

St. Philip Church (Roman Catholic)
West Crafton and Broadhead Avenues, Crafton
William P. Ginther (Akron), architect, 1906

This stone church is effectively sited on a hillside and has a single tall tower on one side. The location of the tower is unusual, yet it has important Central European precedents in the Cathedrals of Vienna and Prague. Such a position gives an emphatic central feature to the church but eliminates the

299

structural problems of building it over a crossing. The complex also includes a large school of 1915, built of light-red tapestry brick in the Tudor style; a rectory, also in the Tudor style; and a much plainer convent.

Houses
Thornburg

Thornburg's wooded, hilly terrain, careful planning, and advertising rhetoric — "Pittsburgh's Most Attractive Suburb" — attracted home-builders from the start. While houses of the 1920s and later can be found here, one comes away with the impression of a rather elegant but rustic settlement of the 1905 period, a country place of stone and wood and calculated informality.

Thornburg house

Close to the top of the rise is Frank Thornburg's own house at 1132 Lehigh Road, an open V of coursed rubble and shingles with ample porch areas set in the basic building mass. The focal point is a brick chimney, which functions as an outlet for a fireplace with a large brick hood in the central two-storied hall. It was built in 1905–06 by an architect named MacLaren.

1080 Stanford Road

Less baronial in effect but more conspicuous is the house at 1080 Stanford Road, built in or around 1906 to designs by C. E. Willoughby. White, formal, detached, this house is said to have been modeled after the eighteenth-century Morris-Jumel house in New York City, though it differs from the model in several ways; especially in having an Ionic order instead of a Tuscan one.

Closer to the norm is the "Cobblestone House" at 1137 Cornell Road, probably from around 1905 but carrying on

"Cobblestone House"

the Shingle Style's use of rugged materials and interest in roof planes, with a small amount of Colonial Revival detailing here and there. The cobbles that face the chimney and porch piers are quite unusual.

National Register District

St. Peter and St. Paul Ukrainian Orthodox Greek Catholic Church
Mansfield Boulevard near Walnut Street, Carnegie
Titus De Bobula, architect, 1906

A church by the interesting but obscure De Bobula. The style of the front is novel, sparing in detail, in a blocky sort of Art Nouveau that may have some derivation from contemporary Italian design. The stonework at the base of the central tower builds up very effectively, with the transition from a square element to an octagon handled in a very original paraphrase of eighteenth-century English practice. As usual with Orthodox churches in America the distinctive onion domes are on the front, not distributed around the center as they would be in Russia. The interior was redecorated in 1966.

Landmarks plaque

Andrew Carnegie Free Library
300 Beechwood Avenue, Carnegie
Struthers & Hannah, architects, 1899

Of all the Carnegie Libraries, this is the only one permitted to use the donor's given name. The architects have contrasted the projection of the entrance with the recession of the section above. The windows have the same "Florentine" tracery that Longfellow, Alden & Harlow had used at the Carnegie Institute earlier in the decade. The interior also contains a music hall and Civil War memorial room.

National Register; Landmarks plaque

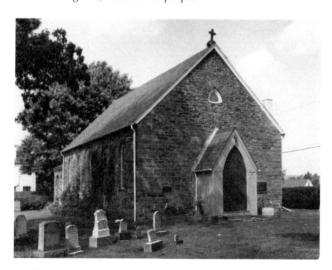

St. Luke's Episcopal Church (presently, Old St. Luke's)
Washington Pike and Church Street, Woodville, Scott Township
1852

This is a primitive church from a time when, to Episcopalians especially, Gothic was apt to be *the* style for a church. Even at the height of the Renaissance, Gothic had never quite died out in northern Europe for ecclesiastical and academic architecture, and in the early nineteenth century American country builders had sometimes combined Greek pilasters with pointed arches in churches. This building was the best a country congregation could do in Southwestern Pennsylvania, while in Pittsburgh the exactly contemporary St. Peter's Church, much more elaborate, expressed the same aspirations with greater means. John Notman, architect of St. Peter's, may have suggested the general design. The porch is a modern reconstruction of one seen in old photographs.

The church and its graveyard fell into disuse, but both have been restored by the Committee to Save St. Luke's, which now, through the Episcopal Diocese of Pittsburgh, holds ecumenical services and opens the church to the public. The Pittsburgh History & Landmarks Foundation offers design and restoration guidance to the Committee to Save St. Luke's.

Landmarks plaque

St. Bernard's Church (Roman Catholic)
311 Washington Road, Mount Lebanon
Comes, Perry & McMullen, architects, 1933–47

This large church, conspicuous on the Mount Lebanon skyline, was actually begun in 1933, but its superstructure waited until 1942 for construction that took until 1947 to complete. The massive early French Gothic style, the richly textured rubble with limestone trim, and the overall air of conviction show it to be a full-blooded design of the Eclectic period that survived to be built well after its time. Churches *were* designed in traditional styles in the 1940s, to be sure, but such an air of confidence about the results had become quite rare. A curious and charming contrast with the rugged stonework comes from the tile roofs, fairy-tale surfaces glazed in random colors, red, green, blue, and others.

Mount Lebanon Municipal Building
710 Washington Road, Mount Lebanon
William H. King, Jr., architect, 1930

Municipal buildings in the 1920s tended to be Classical: Renaissance in its full limestone or marble pomp in the cities, white-and-red Georgian in the suburbs. But now and then a Moderne example appeared as well toward the end of the decade: the image of Progressive Government as opposed to that of the City Fathers, quite possibly. Mount Lebanon chose Modernistic. The doorway, with its diamond-faced stone surround and its bronze relief of *Wisdom in Government*, is mildly allusive to the Renaissance, and the little ziggurat above is monumental in intention. So is the main front, with its steady rhythm of piers. This municipal Modernistic, in short, has much of the traditional solemnity though the specific forms are new. Inside the entrance is a tall reception space, monumental in expression again though scaled to the activities of a borough, with decorative paintings in its upper area.

Arlington Park
Arlington Park Road, Mount Lebanon
1883 and after

This is a cul-de-sac group of 13 houses, most of them originally built in a Gothic or Italianate style, for members of the Arlington Camp Meeting Association of the Methodist Protestant Church of Pittsburgh. The houses have undergone remodelings that have damaged their character, but in some of them original canopies, balconies, brackets, and vergeboards have so far survived. The setting originally was sparsely settled, and a suburb of the trolley and automobile period has grown around it without disturbing it.

Linden Grove
Grove Road and Willow Avenue, Castle Shannon
C. 1890

The Castle Shannon area was the subject, in 1872, of rather frantic efforts by a development company to get Pittsburghers to settle in that part of the South Hills. The problem of access to such an elevated place, in the days before the South Hills trolley tunnel and electric traction, was attacked by having

railroad cars cable-hauled partway up Mount Washington, then attached to locomotives for a conventional rail journey on relatively easy gradients. Buyers were offered a period of free transportation for themselves and building lumber, and two picnic groves, two camp-meeting grounds, and a zoo lured visitors.

Linden Grove, with its dance hall, trolley shelter, sign board, and owner's house, is the most visible reminder of this bygone scheme. The dance hall was not in the original plan, but since the turn of the century the octagonal frame structure has served as a popular objective for trolley riders and local residents. In recent years dances were suspended, and the hall is presently quiet.

Davis house
3423 Brownsville Road, Brentwood
C. 1880

An elaborate porch, decorative brackets, simulated quoins, and decorated window and door heads give an otherwise-simple house touches of elegance. Though not set on a high basement, this house, in its Italianate way, has a similarity to the Federal-style house of Nicholas Way in Edgeworth, another one-and-a-half-story house with a pedimented porch and the air of a villa.

John Work house
Curry Hollow Road, Jefferson Memorial Park, Pleasant Hills
1800

This is an early house of mixed construction, two bays of stone, three bays of squared logs, both parts built apparently at the same time. The relation between the two elements suggests that the house was begun in stone, then completed in logs. The big quoins at the lower part of the front outer corner, diminishing greatly after the sixth course, seem further evidence of an ambitious beginning followed by decreasingly energetic building activity. The projecting chimney in the stone gable wall suggests Virginia practice.

Allegheny County Fairgrounds
Brownsville Road between Corrigan and McCorkle Roads, South Park, South Park Township
Opened 1933

South Park, begun in 1927, was one of the large new County parks, remote from urban areas and planned for automobile access. There were still a considerable number of working farms in the county, and the establishment of a fairgrounds that could also be used for equine sports seemed natural enough. The largest area began as a polo field with grandstands, then was converted to an oval for harness racing with a half-mile track. At one end of this is a barn-like transportation museum of yellow brick. At the other are a circular stable and octagonal blacksmith shop, now privately

operated. Near by are stables and exhibit pavilions, some of frame, some of yellow brick.

South Park calls up associations with Henry Hornbostel. In the Depression years the aging architect had little to design and interested himself in the County Fair. From 1935 to 1939 he was director of Allegheny County Parks, and performed this unaccustomed role with the flamboyance and charm he had brought to the pursuit of his architectural career.

James (or Oliver) Miller house ("Stone Manse")
Stone Manse Drive east of Corrigan Drive, South Park Township
1808; 1830

The Millers, of North Irish origin, were among the earliest settlers in this area. Having sided with the rebels in the Whiskey Rebellion of 1794, the family was reduced, yet James Miller was able to live on in a log house that family had built on its arrival in 1772. In 1808 the lower portion of the present stone house was added by James Miller, and in 1830 his son Oliver replaced the log house with the larger stone section. In 1927 the County bought the property from the Millers of the time.

Now a museum, the Miller house is restored inside and out. It not only illustrates in concrete terms the life of a farming family just after the pioneer period but shows the Georgian architecture of this region in its simplest form: undecorated but orderly and well-proportioned, and with surfaces made interesting by the random patterning and contrasting sizes of the stonework.

National Register; Landmarks plaque

303

A rural survivor: Scratchwell Farm on Oakdale Road in North Fayette Township.

The Western Townships

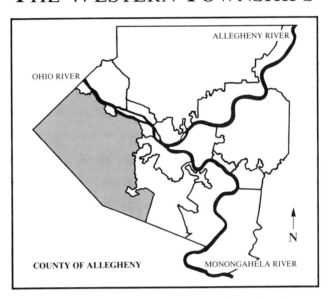

OHIO RIVER
ALLEGHENY RIVER
COUNTY OF ALLEGHENY
MONONGAHELA RIVER
N

Settlement of the western end of Allegheny County south of the Ohio River began in the 1760s, but Indians raided the farms that were established by pioneer families into the 1780s. Even after this menace ended, much of the land remained rather thinly settled. While some construction from the eighteenth century can be found, and an occasional handsome farmhouse or barn from the nineteenth century, man's presence in this area is most evident in other constructions.

Coal mining, which began in the late nineteenth century and continued into the twentieth, has left both worked-out and working mines and ''patches'' of small uniform miners' houses. The Montour Railroad was built in 1878 specifically to haul coal over an 11.5 mile route between the mines of the Imperial Coal Company at Imperial in North Fayette Township to connecting rail lines along the Ohio River in Robinson Township. (It was later extended and absorbed by the Pittsburgh & Lake Erie Railroad.) Oil production was also a major local industry. Oil wells with metalwork derricks are strewn across the landscape; some still

305

operate as do a number of small oil transfer facilities.

Suburbanization since World War II has absorbed farms and erected houses, commercial strips, and office buildings in the western townships. Upper St. Clair Township experienced residential growth early in the century along an interurban trolley line from Pittsburgh to Washington in Washington County. It has since been highly developed in many areas and is now one of Pittsburgh's modern suburbs of choice for the wealthy. But most of the suburbanization in these townships has been stimulated by the Greater Pittsburgh International Airport. This facility has evolved from a few World War II-era U.S. Army airstrips into an international airport which occupies sizeable acreage in both Moon and Findlay Townships. Development spawned by the airport and its access roads has resulted in a rash of suburban office parks and a population increase of over 400 percent in Moon Township alone since 1940.

One of the area's earliest and most significant houses was an early casualty: General John Neville's "Bower Hill," the center of a thousand-acre estate, was burned during the Whiskey Rebellion in 1794. But "Woodville," the predecessor and companion house of "Bower Hill" built by Neville in 1785, survives in Collier Township. Its site is now restricted, but the house remains remarkably unscathed by the 200 years of rebellion, extraction industry, and modern development which have swirled around it. ▪

The National Hill Plan in South Fayette Township survives as an example of mining company housing from early in this century.

Gilfillan farm
Washington Road near Orr Road, Upper St. Clair
Township
House, 1857

The Gilfillans have been in Upper St. Clair since the 1760s. The farm is still in family hands and is still used as a farm despite suburbanization around it, although some of the land has been sold for development. The house shows the break away from the Greek Revival that had been taking place for about a decade and a half. The ground-floor window heads have Greek-looking ornaments over their centers, and the doorway has the typical sidelight-and-overdoor-light framework of an ambitious Greek Revival building. But the front windows are doubled, and the proportions of the houses are spread horizontally in an abandonment of the old Georgian verticality. Vivid paired brackets are positively Italianate, and their use directly under the peaks of the gables, along with the projection of the cornices, suggests an attempt to make the design expressive through ornamental features. This is a late work of a time that was moving from Classical harmony, which had few elements that might challenge the eye, toward fantasy. Around back the windows however are still placidly Georgian of the simplest sort. A big, plain Pennsylvania barn of 1868 and 10 other buildings remain as an example of a large Victorian farm group.

National Register

Barn
2333 Lesnett Road, Upper St. Clair Township
C. 1900

Octagonal barns are a rarity anywhere, though for activities like distributing hay to cows they have practical advantages. Allegheny County may have had more of the type at one time, but this is the only one now in existence.

Walker-Ewing house
Noblestown Road east of Pinkerton Run Road,
Collier Township
C. 1790

Though somewhat modernized inside and out, this two-and-a-half-story log house retains a generally authentic appearance and suggests how such a building can be adapted to present-day needs in a way that respects its antiquity. The house was in the Ewing family until 1973, when the latest owner gave it to the Pittsburgh History & Landmarks Foundation which has improved it and maintains it together with a nearby late Victorian farmhouse.

National Register; Landmarks plaque

John (or Presley) Neville house ("Woodville"; presently, the Neville House)
Washington Pike south of Oakdale Road, Collier Township
1785; additions and alterations

The large steep roof with dormers indicates the preferences of the original owner, General John Neville, for the building customs of his native Virginia. The placement of end chimneys directly within the clapboarded walls is also frequently to be found there. The exterior was originally quite plain and simple in its geometry, but there have been numerous additions. Alterations of 1846 included the trellised porches and Gothic windows in the front dormers and one of the gable walls; the front dormers have gables of a

scalloped, almost Jacobean, appearance. Inside is a good Federal mantelpiece with the delicate woodcarving of the style. As in some other old houses of the United States, the window glass was used as a register of family members and guests, who scratched their names in it with diamonds.

The house passed from John Neville to his son Presley, and thence to other members of the family down to 1973. In 1974 the Pittsburgh History & Landmarks Foundation bought what was left of the estate, which had been reduced and even threatened by public-works projects, for restoration. The Neville House Auxiliary, established with the support of Landmarks in 1976, continues to raise funds for and sponsor events to support the restoration of this historic house.

National Historic Landmark; National Register; Landmarks plaque

Barn
Head of Old North Branch Road, North Fayette Township
C. 1850

This is the only surviving brick barn in Allegheny County: an architecturally rather ambitious one, with its arches and its diamond- and hourglass-pattern ventilator holes. Such barns with brick patterns are almost all confined to South Central Pennsylvania.

Wilson house
Legislative Route 02340 north of North Branch Road, North Fayette Township
1810-12 (?)

Unkempt but charming in its proportions and detailing, this Federal-style house on an English basement has a kinship in its design to the Way house at Edgeworth and the Lightner house in Shaler Township, and it is quite possible that though supposedly older, it dates from the 1830s as they do. The porch may be much newer than the house; certainly the roof, cutting off the old cornice moldings on the front, must be a replacement. Yet the porch is very well proportioned to the house, the result of careful consideration whenever it was built.

DOWN THE OHIO

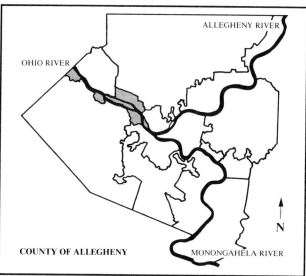

The ethnic presence: the Industrial Bottoms, McKees Rocks.

The Ohio River is one of the most historic rivers of the United States. It was a 981-mile link in the 2,500-mile route, almost wholly by water, that the French of the early eighteenth century contemplated between Quebec and Louisiana. The British victory in the French and Indian War, the formal opening of the Northwest Territory, the defeat of the Indians of the Northeast in 1794, and the Louisiana Purchase of 1803 made the Ohio a grand highway to the West and South, the route of flatboats, keelboats, and from 1811 on, of steamboats. Packet and towboat traffic throve on the Ohio, and even as late as 1980, before the crisis in the steel industry, there was agitation for river locks big enough to accommodate barge tows whose length exceeded that of the largest ocean liners.

And yet the Allegheny County towns along the Ohio have generally been towns by the river rather than river ports. McKees Rocks on the south shore, though strategists *almost* chose it as the site for Fort Pitt in the early 1750s, and though its location was to some extent settled in the

309

Early twentieth-century business architecture at Lincoln and South Fremont Avenues in Bellevue.

eighteenth century, is really a creation of the Pittsburgh & Lake Erie Railroad which began operations through the town in 1879 and located its shops there the next year. Other industry soon gathered as well, and the town attracted the immigrant workers who were coming from Continental Europe in large numbers. The churches of the Industrial Bottoms, next to the river, attest to the variety of cultures represented. Coraopolis, further down the river, was another railroad town, though more residential than McKees Rocks, that was further developed in 1894 by a trolley line that crossed Neville Island.

The conversion of the north shore of the river into a series of suburbs, again beside but not greatly related to the water, came in two principal phases. The Sewickley area — which developed its own special character — lay close to river level, and the opening of the Ohio & Pennsylvania Railroad in 1851 offered such easy access from Allegheny that its conversion from farm area into suburbs happened in a few decades. Closer to Allegheny, the land by the water rose to a hundred-foot elevation, making a daunting climb for rail commuters alighting on the river shore. Here a trolley route, opened around 1900, made the difference; running along the brow of the bluff, the trolley was obviously much more convenient than the railroad. Where villas and small houses had once stood in isolation, middle-class

houses much like those of the South Hills were soon being built in abundance in communities such as Bellevue, Avalon, and Ben Avon.

Between the shores are three islands. Brunot's Island, closest to the Pittsburgh Point, once had a racetrack, but since the turn of the century it has been the location of a series of power stations. Davis Island, small and now deserted, was the location of the first dam on the Ohio, completed in 1885: the first step in a great undertaking that had all but the very end of the river canalized by 1929. Neville Island, just below Davis and five miles long, was covered by gardens in the nineteenth century, producing fruit and vegetables for the Pittsburgh market; then, beginning around 1900, it was industrialized so fully and diversely that today, with the exception of a very small residential area, it looks like a showcase of industrial specimens. The great Dravo boatyard, now closed, and a towboat fleeting area were among the exhibits. There had been a few other boatyards along the Ohio, notably those at Shousetown (now Glenwillard) on the south shore, where the hull of the *Great Republic,* one of the largest Mississippi River sidewheelers, was built in 1867. But the Dravo yard operated on a grand scale, producing towboats and barges on almost an assembly line basis, giving Neville Island an exceptionally intimate contact with the river itself.

Ethnic churches
The Industrial Bottoms, McKees Rocks

Close to the Ohio River and almost isolated from the rest of McKees Rocks is an area called the Industrial Bottoms. A traveler crossing the McKees Rocks Bridge may be intrigued by a row of church towers as he passes above, and tantalized when he tries to double back and approach them. Rising above nearby industry, railroad yards and streets of close-set housing, they are symbols and expressions of the varied ethnic heritage of the industrial workers of the Bottoms.

The nearest of these churches to the bridge is St. Mark's Church (Roman Catholic), built for a Slovak congregation in 1916 to designs by E. B. Lang. The style is Gothic, with a spired tower. Close by is St. Nicholas (Russian) Orthodox Church of 1914, whose front has three onion domes (there are three others elsewhere on the church); inside, beneath a large and elaborate crystal chandelier, is a colorful iconostasis. Both of these churches are on Munson Street.

Nearby, on Ella Street, are two other churches of note: St. Mary's Ukrainian Orthodox Church of 1922, a simplified Byzantine building by Carlton Strong, and Holy Ghost Byzantine Catholic Church of 1917, by John H. Phillips: a curious church with a single domed tower flanked by domed buttresses; its detailing includes a small starburst window, a unique Mexican Baroque touch.

St. Nicholas (Russian) Orthodox Church

St. Mark's Church (Roman Catholic)

St. Mary's Ukrainian Orthodox Church

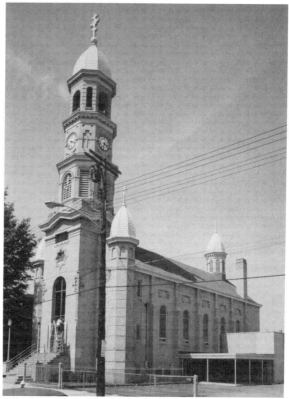

Holy Ghost Byzantine Catholic Church

311

McKees Rocks Bridge
Ohio River at Mile 3.25, between McKees Rocks and Pittsburgh
Vernon R. Covell of the Allegheny County Department of Public Works, chief engineer, 1929–31

Writing around 1960, Carl Condit, a historian of American civil engineering, approved of much that Allegheny County was doing in bridge construction in the 1920s and 1930s, but he could not find it in his heart to like the McKees Rocks Bridge. Expediencies of clearing a river, its banks, a railroad yard, and streets dictated such a variety of bridge structural types in the various spans that he called the whole visual effect "most dissatisfactory." There are indeed 17 spans formed in five different ways. The most notable is the undoubtedly handsome 750-foot river span, a two-hinged steel arch with an enveloping truss that resists off-center loads. The clearance above the river is 40 feet, and the whole bridge length, the greatest in the county, is a little over 4,500 feet. Art Deco pylons bear sculpture by Frank Vittor.

Disunified the total structure may be, yet the overall impression is quite satisfactory. The arch above the river, a graceful shape, is what is really noticed.

St. Francis de Sales Church (Roman Catholic)
Chartiers Avenue and Margaret Street, McKees Rocks
1899

A church of variegated, warm-colored random ashlar, plain except for the triumphal-arch entrance, the four statues above that have a false attic as background, and a red-tiled dome that bears a statue of St. Francis. The design may be modeled after that of Heins & La Farge for St. Matthew's Cathedral in Washington, D.C., its exact contemporary. The white-and-blue interior centers on the inner pendentive dome, supported by paired Corinthian columns.

St. Mary's Help of Christians Church (Roman Catholic)
St. John Street and Church Avenue, McKees Rocks
William P. Ginther (Akron), architect, 1901

This very large church has in its form, size, and setting the air of a cathedral. The very dark, almost black, peculiarly rough brick of the walls is in sharp contrast with trim and ornament of painted composition stone. Besides two entrance towers, complete with spires, there is a stubby flèche over the crossing.

Additional buildings on the large church property include a rectory of the same period with a corner tower and a masonry Gothic porch; a convent of coursed rubble from 1930, designed by Comes, Perry & McMullen in a Romantic manner with some Gothic arches; and a buff-brick school.

Taylor-Wilson Manufacturing Company
Thompson Avenue south of Kennedy Street, McKees Rocks
Robert A. Cummings, engineer, 1905

This is an early reinforced-concrete industrial building, from the period just after the pioneering phase of this structural medium. What reinforcement system was used is not known, but the double lower edge of the beams over each side opening may have a structural basis. Given the starkness of the building, its air of indifference to visual amenity, the same may be true of the big round-arched window at the northern end; it is built as if it were one span of the poured-concrete bridges that were beginning to be constructed around the country.

Preston
Ohio and Orchard Streets, Stowe Township
C. 1900

This settlement of about one hundred frame double houses was begun as a company town for the Pressed-Steel Car Company, complete with its own police force and jail. It is surrounded by railroad and industrial property, but Pressed Steel sold the houses in 1949, and Stowe Township now administers the neighborhood. Many individual houses have been modernized, but the steady repetition of facades, characteristic of a company town, remains.

Repair facility, Lock and Dam Number Two
River Road and Cottage Avenue, Neville Township
C. 1905

Lock and Dam Number Two was built between 1896 and 1906 as part of the system that by 1929 was to have the Ohio River canalized — divided into level pools of water — for almost its entire 981-mile length. The dam was located at Glenfield, close to the point where I-79 now crosses the river. Lock and Dam Number Two was in use until August 1922, when the Emsworth Locks and Dam upstream took over the greater part of its function. This repair facility on Neville Island is a large, sober work of governmental architecture, dignified if not especially graceful. A cantilevered window allowed the state of the dam and its repairs to be observed. This is a rare survivor of the county's river-related architecture.

Coraopolis Bridge (formerly, Sixth Street Bridge, Pittsburgh)
Back channel of the Ohio River at Mile 9.5, between Coraopolis and Neville Township
Theodore Cooper, engineer, 1892; moved, 1927

John Augustus Roebling's suspension bridge at Sixth Street in Pittsburgh was replaced in 1892 by this pair of bowstring trusses, each 440 feet in span. They were designed to take the loads imposed by moving electric streetcars. In 1927, when the fourth bridge on the site was to be constructed, they were jacked up and floated downriver to the back channel of the Ohio alongside Neville Island. Re-erected, they have completed over 90 years of service.

313

Pittsburgh & Lake Erie Railroad Station
Neville Avenue and Mill Street, Coraopolis
Shepley, Rutan & Coolidge (Boston), architects,
1895

This station is by H. H. Richardson's successor firm. Its style
is Richardson Romanesque, and its brownstone and buff
brick are consistent with the style. Richardson himself would
have been bolder in form and scale as his numerous stations
around the Boston suburbs show, but this is a valuable work
of architecture all the same. Like the much later railroad station at Wilkinsburg, it reveals the hand of an accomplished
designer applied to one of the most conspicuous of small-
town building types.

National Register

Shouse house
Main and Bridge Streets, Glenwillard, Crescent
Township
C. 1840; additions

Glenwillard was originally Shousetown, and this was the
house of its founder Peter Shouse, a boat builder who came
here in 1822. The original house was a three-bay construction with a chimney at one end; at a later date, a five-bay
addition with a chimney at each end was added, reproduc-
ing the original details, and the porch that gives the street
front a nearly symmetrical appearance must have been added
later still.

Shousetown was a boat-building area through most of the
nineteenth century, but its grandest moment was probably
in 1867, with the launching of the hull of the *Great Republic*,
designed by Nathan Porter, a relative of Peter Shouse. This,
one of the grandest packets in the Lower Mississippi River
service, was fitted with machinery and cabins at Pittsburgh.

THE SEWICKLEY AREA

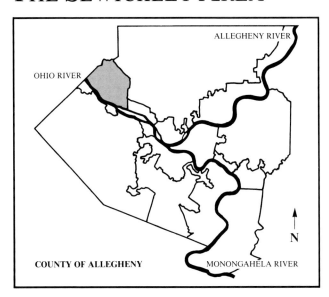

Sewickley, 12 miles down the Ohio River from the Pittsburgh Point, is the focus for an exceptional group of residential boroughs. In this area the hills retreat from the water's edge to leave a fairly broad river plain. The land is easy to build on and in contact with the routes of communication along the river that are closely associated with the area's history.

At first there was an Indian path by the river, which late in the eighteenth century was widened into a road between the towns of Pittsburgh and Beaver. Until the late 1790s, however, there was no settlement on the plain or in the hills, though the Pennsylvania Legislature had surveyed them in 1785 as part of the Depreciation Lands, purchasable with the "depreciation certificates" issued to Revolutionary War veterans as part of their pay. Virginia's claim to Southwestern Pennsylvania, maintained until 1779, and the menace by the Indians, locally ended only in 1792, had discouraged settlement, while land south of the Ohio was more accessible to settlers from the South and was easier to farm. Settlement began in 1797, and as the Beaver Road gained more traffic and as farmers moved into the land along it, what was

A Late Victorian house on Bank Street in Sewickley.

315

Service buildings of a Sewickley Heights estate off Blackburn Road.

to become Sewickley took on the character of a village, while the Edgeworth district a mile further down, halfway between Pittsburgh and Beaver, became a location for small taverns catering to the teamsters.

The opening of service on the Ohio & Pennsylvania (later, the Pennsylvania) Railroad in 1851 started an evolution from a thinly settled place of farms, taverns, and a little commerce into a highly desirable suburban area. Sewickley was incorporated as a borough in 1853, and, while it was a very small borough at first, it was developing rapidly by the mid-1870s as a town of large, comfortable commuter homes with sizeable yards. Immediately to the west was a part of Leet Township generally known as Edgeworth after the Edgeworth female seminary of the 1830s, named for the once-famous Irish novelist Maria Edgeworth. Here were some of the oldest houses of the area, and here came newer houses in the late nineteenth century that were generally even more elegant than those of Sewickley. Edgeworth, like Edgewood east of Pittsburgh, developed a self-awareness and a determination to keep its special character; this led it in 1904 to free itself from Leet Township, which had become industrialized, bury all utility lines, and forbid the interurban trolley line then under construction along the river to pass through.

Above these communities on the river plain, the hills were for a long time thinly settled; they made poor farmland. In the 1890s, though, a number of wealthy citizens of the still independent city of Allegheny perceived that the hills would make a good location for summer estates. Families who wintered in the mansions of Ridge Avenue began to change the character of the place, building estate houses with myriad auxiliary buildings, formal gateways, and curving drives. The move to Sewickley Heights of the Allegheny

Country Club in 1902 confirmed the trend which grew in force through the 1920s. The automobile, which offered independence from the train and the horse-drawn carriage that once met the train at the station, encouraged building in the hills even for year-round occupation, and the gradual decline of the North Side prompted the estate dwellers to make Sewickley Heights their permanent home.

Outside this handsome residential trio of Sewickley, Edgeworth, and Sewickley Heights are other riverside boroughs. East of Sewickley lie Haysville, now signaled by a little street of wooden houses by the river but the location of a large mineral-springs resort hotel in the 1870s, and Osborne, which has its own little houses by the water. West of Edgeworth is the industrial borough of Leetsdale, which is actually of a piece with Ambridge and the other industrial communities of Beaver County that lie beyond.

In these communities some of the best architecture of the county is to be found. The variety is great: sturdy Georgian houses from the early nineteenth century; mansions and villas that have survived in the hills; churches from the Mid-Victorian period on. But the image that predominates is of a substantial house in Sewickley, or a collection of many such houses: not mansions, just nice big upper-middle-class houses of about a century ago or thereabouts, Second Empire, Colonial Revival, or vaguely chateau-like, standing in ample yards, contemplating the world through big windows and the pillars of their porches. These places represent the norm of Victorian living: full of respectability and well-being, counting on good service by the cook, the local merchants, and the Pennsylvania Railroad, free from the dirt and turmoil of places where money is made, but not ostentatious by the standards of the day. ■

Houses
Sewickley

Sewickley has not quite the spaciousness of private properties and the antiquity of individual buildings found in Edgeworth just down the river, but it is a place nonetheless with big old houses in big yards as well as smaller houses with little yards. Although it is located along the Ohio River, it is less a river town than a Victorian railroad suburb beside a river. The second half of the nineteenth century was the time when it flourished, and from that period many excellent houses remain.

422 Frederick Avenue

Number 422 Frederick Avenue is believed to date from slightly before the coming of the Ohio & Pennsylvania Railroad in 1851, the event that caused Sewickley's transformation from hamlet to suburb. The original cottage, later greatly expanded, is the simplest sort of Italianate though with a fancy and rather Gothic porch. Board-and-batten walls stress the vertical lines and enliven the surfaces with light-and-shadow patterns. The leaded window sash, from the Eclectic period, is a later owner's attempt to add quaintness to the rather stiff though pretty design; originally there would have been two-paned wooden sash.

304-22 Peebles Street

The four similar though not identical Italianate houses at 304–22 Peebles Street, beg an explanation. They were built in 1872 by Zehu P. Smith — one for each of his daughters. Although they now have newer porches, they form an unusual and largely intact Victorian ensemble. Three years later, a family named Fleming built a much more sophisticated house at 53 Woodland Road in the so-called Stick Style. In this, wooden surfaces were marked off into panels by applied slats that suggested a building frame, though in fact the real frame was concealed beneath the siding. The presence of a ribbed, stepped chimney at one end, an oriel window jutting from a gable, a mild imitation of half-timbering in the gable peaks, and the use of shingles for siding suggest an architect who was aware of the latest trends of 1875. The shingles were an American substitute

53 Woodland Road

for the flat tiles used in smart English house design as siding, and the other motifs were also fashionably English but only recently in American use. Though the design as a whole still has a Mid-Victorian rigidity of effect, these features were soon to be identified with the Queen Anne style.

Sewickley Borough Municipal Building
Chestnut and Thorn Streets, Sewickley
Charles W. Bier, architect, 1911; addition, 1984

Occasionally an architect early in this century attempted a hybrid Beaux-Arts-Georgian style, as here. The facade is symmetrical and has its windows disposed in a Georgian manner, but each window is rather broad for its height and the sash design compromises between quaintness and utility by having 12 panes above and one below. The entrance and the window above it are not Georgian at all; the division of the window suggests a Greek Revival doorway. The bracketed cornice harks back to Mid-Victorian Italianate: brackets were somewhat in fashion again in the 1910s. The tower, which doubles as a monumental feature and a hose-drying space for the firehouse, has a plausibly Georgian cupola over a very Beaux-Arts cornice. Except on the main front the pattern of openings is very irregular. A curious rear wing, topped by its own little cupola, seems to have been a stable before the fire department was motorized. The plainer modern addition is in clear contrast to the original work though also faced in red brick.

Flatiron Building
Beaver and Division Streets, Sewickley
C. 1875

A local architectural curiosity, and surprisingly the only well-preserved Victorian commercial building in Sewickley. The odd perimeter is caused by the angle of Division Street, laid down on the border between two early land surveys. The Pittsburgh History & Landmarks Foundation acquired and restored the building with community support in the 1970s.
Landmarks plaque

Sewickley Public Library
Thorn and Broad Streets, Sewickley
H. D. Gilchrist, architect, 1923

A dark building of coursed rubble with stone trim, the Sewickley Library is a quiet, reserved, rectangular mass with four corner pavilions. The doorway, with its rusticated jambs and its unusually rounded curved pediment, adds a touch of liveliness, however, and just the necessary amount of urbanity.

Duquesne Light Company substation
Chadwick Street, Sewickley
C. 1935

A Modernistic 12-foot wall of white brick and tile, displaying a colored-tile panel with a cloud-and-flame motif. Set against this is a wrought-iron grille with the figure of a torch-bearer. The mixture of media is very unusual, but a success.

318

Sewickley Presbyterian Church
Beaver and Grant Streets, Sewickley
J. W. Kerr, architect, 1859-61; Rutan & Russell, architects for parish hall, 1914; additions

Six years after Sewickley's incorporation, the Presbyterians could afford to hire a Pittsburgh architect to build a picturesque stone church. The congregation, in fact, was already 20 years old, and had outgrown its first building in 1840. Barr & Moser soon added to the present church with a chapel, designed in 1864 and finished in 1872; Rutan & Russell added the Tudor parish hall in 1914, replacing this chapel; and J. Phillip Davis added the new Gothic Chapel of the Resurrection in 1953. In the parish hall is a mural of the *Faërie Queen* by Hanley Menoch, executed on canvas in a tapestry-like style.

Landmarks plaque

Edgeworth

Just down the Ohio River from Sewickley lies Edgeworth, a spacious residential community with a special character that is emphasized by its situation between Sewickley's mainstreet commerce and Leetsdale's commerce and industry. Edgeworth has always been concerned to control its development and to maintain its natural and social amenities; in 1906, it resisted even the building of a trolley line with success. Edgeworth has some of the most agreeable houses in Allegheny County, including a few that were built not long after white settlers first felt safe from the Indians of the area.

Nicholas Way house
108 Beaver Road, Edgeworth
1838

This is a rare type of Federal-style house in Allegheny County, with its deep pedimented porch leading to a single story over an English basement. The doorway has engaged columns beneath an overdoor light. The front is substantially in the original condition; not so, the back. A similar composition is to be seen in the Lightner house in Shaler Township. Such houses represent an early departure from the local Georgian manner of decorating basic construction in favor of treating the whole building — on its front at least — as a decorative object. The ample porch of temple-like form is not merely a place to sit; it implies that this is the house of a well-to-do, cultured family.

National Register

Walker-Way house
Beaver Road near Quaker Road, Edgeworth
1810–20; rebuilt, 1841; additions and alterations

The original building is the tall three-bay central element, built in 1810: the first brick house between Pittsburgh and Beaver and the second-oldest house in the Sewickley area. To this was added a five-bay section with a long front porch in 1820. The house burned in 1841 and was rebuilt. A two-story porch was added to the original house around 1910, and a rear wing with another two-story porch in 1912. The house thus shows traces of a long, eventful history, during which it has been an inn and a school as well as a family home.

319

Shields Presbyterian Church (presently, Shields Sanctuary of Sewickley Presbyterian Church)
Church Lane and Oliver Road, Edgeworth
J. W. Kerr, architect (?), 1868-69

This is a stone church of refined simplicity, none the worse within for Late Victorian additions. The style is Early English, as the triple lancet windows indicate. Inside, minister, choir, and congregation are united in an almost-intimate space of unpretentious dignity, lighted with Mid-Victorian and 1900-period glass.

The Shields family had been in Western Pennsylvania since about 1800, and lived at "Newington" near by. The congregation, which separated from the Sewickley Presbyterian Church in 1864, named the church after Eliza Leet Shields, who rented the land to the congregation at a very nominal rate.

Landmarks plaque

Shields Mausoleum
Church Lane, Edgeworth
John U. Barr, architect, 1893

Adjacent to the Shields Presbyterian Church, this Gothic mausoleum is unusual in both location and size. It is almost another church in fact, with an impressive bluntly pointed brick barrel vault over a broad central space; the dead are entombed in niches, early Italian Renaissance in style, in the walls. The exterior masonry, narrow and wide courses of a

quartz-like material, suggests a facing of the basic brick construction.

The mausoleum was constructed at the urging of John K. Wilson, related to the Shields family, who deplored the Shields' burial in a neglected cemetery near by.

"Newington"
Shields Lane, Edgeworth
1816; 1823; additions and alterations

"Newington" is a handsome estate that has passed by inheritance from generation to generation since its beginning. It was created by Major Daniel Leet for his married daughter and her husband, Eliza and David Shields. The house has a smaller southern part from 1816 and a northern part from 1823. To the northern part were added two ornate cast-iron porches around 1857 (one removed c. 1900), two mid-Victorian cupolas, and a gable fanlight, c. 1900, replacing an oriel window that was probably an addition itself. The house is surrounded by fine, well-maintained landscaping, apparently to designs of Samuel Parsons in the 1870s with a formal garden of 1910 by Bryan Fleming. On the estate as well are a barn of the 1890s, a smokehouse, a springhouse, a miller's house, a blacksmith's house, and a schoolhouse.

National Register; Landmarks plaque

Bridge
Over Sewickley Creek between Little Sewickley
Creek and Woodland Roads, Edgeworth
Charles Davis, engineer, 1889

This is a carefully thought-out work of architecture as well
as an expedient for getting a minor road over a creek. An
iron truss would have been a possible alternative at the time,
as a wooden covered bridge might have been a few decades
earlier. The choice of a masonry arch, then, may have been
aesthetic.

House
Woodland Road, Edgeworth
Janssen & Cocken, architects, 1928–29

Here is a mansion of a rural French cast, similar to some
found in the Chestnut Hill area of Philadelphia but using
brick instead of the rubble common there. Windows are kept
small to allow the walls to display their color and texture to
the maximum. The roofs have exaggerated pitches — a trait
common enough in Renaissance chateau architecture — but
the extravagant textural roughness of the slating is an excess
typical of the Eclectic period.

Estate buildings
Sewickley Heights

Through most of the nineteenth century, the hilly land above
Sewickley was merely unprofitable farmland and woods, a
place where log houses might linger on for lack of any means
or incentive to replace them. Then, city dwellers began to
rent summer quarters in the town; the practice was
established by the mid-1880s, and soon led to the wealthier
families — many from Allegheny — building for themselves

in the hilly, wooded upland areas. For about half a century,
Sewickley Heights was a place of fine estates reached by
country roads, but by 1940 the greatest period was over.

Many of the estates were subsequently subdivided, and
some of the houses disappeared. The remaining historic landscape is less a matter of estates than of estate fragments:
walls, gates, gatehouses, carriage house/garages, stables,
barns, cottages. But even these have a certain pomp, like
servants in livery.

"Franklin Farm" water tower

The now-decaying water tower of "Franklin Farm," the
B. F. Jones estate, was built around 1900 on a massive stone
base. The tapered shingled tower, whose form suggests a
lighthouse or a windmill, was primarily a mask for the actual tank or standpipe within, but it also had an observation
deck.

Snyder barn

William Penn Snyder's barn, built around the same
time, is a simple but emphatically architectural work, with
its symmetry, its arched doorway that has a token keystone,
its pediment-like gables, and its beltcourse connecting the
heads of the first-floor windows.

"Wilpen Hall"
Waterworks Road, Sewickley Heights
George S. Orth & Brother, architects, 1897-1900

Here is a big, informal stone-and-shingle house, built as the country residence of William Penn Snyder, whose Classical and dignified city house at Ridge and Galveston Avenues still stands. The two houses seem to express different ways of living, appropriate to different occasions. The city house is precise and polished, a setting for formality of conduct. Here a measured relaxation is the theme. The arched windows flank the Classical porch symmetrically. Above, cross-gables impose a rough symmetry on the long front, but on an axis slightly different from that of the entrance. The big roof and the chimneys speak of shelter and comfort, the necessities of life well accommodated.

The interior is spacious, home-like but well-suited to entertaining large numbers. At one end is a huge living room with a stairwell overlooking a billiard space: a Late Victorian combination of functions that is used to create a dramatic space on various levels.

The main house is accompanied by simple but handsome service buildings and smaller houses in the Shingle Style.

geometry, functionally unnecessary, indicates a builder who was taking care to produce a good-looking house. Restoration of log houses is popular these days, and this is a very deserving one.

Lark Inn
Beaver Road and Sycamore Street, Leetsdale
C. 1800

Originally this was the Halfway House, a tavern halfway between Pittsburgh and Beaver. The corners are built up in an ashlar form with large stones, and the remaining masonry is laid for the most part in partial courses. This is one of the very oldest houses in the Sewickley area, and it is fortunate that it has survived so well.

Landmarks plaque

House
Fern Hollow and Hunt Roads, Sewickley Heights
C. 1820

Here is a log house that illustrates the earliest architecture of the county. Both side elevations are the same: symmetrical or very nearly so, with the windows carefully aligned and a door in the center. The chimney is faced in limestone ashlar, and there is a large outside fireplace. Its simple, clean

THE NORTHERN TOWNSHIPS

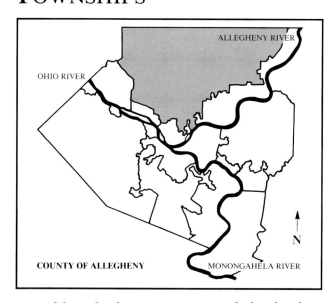

Although the greater part of the land in Allegheny County north of the Ohio and Allegheny Rivers was included in the Depreciation Lands, it was no more eagerly settled before 1795 than Allegheny or the Sewickley area. When the Indian threat ended, however, settlers arrived and agriculture spread over the rolling land. In many parts there are still early log houses and simple masonry farmhouses from the early days.

The settlement that occurred in those first years did not stop at the county line. In 1803 Allegheny's northern neighbor Butler County was organized, and the adjacent Armstrong County was organized in 1805. Butler, Zelienople, and Kittanning were all surveyed in 1803, and beyond these communities lay Franklin and Erie, centers of further settlement.

This northern development meant roads, laid out along the valleys and heading generally northward. Such a road was the old Venango Path, an Indian trail that was converted into a plank road in 1865 and paved for automobiles in 1911; this road, beginning in the central North Side, is today the Perry Highway, U.S. Route 19, ending near

An occasional farmhouse remains even in heavily suburbanized Ross Township, here on Nelson Run Road.

323

Meadville. Another branch of the Venango Path became the Butler Pike which opened in 1822 and passed through Shaler Township. This route survives as Mount Royal Boulevard, a road with a century's worth of interesting houses dating from the early nineteenth to the early twentieth century. Close by and approximately parallel runs the old Butler Plank Road of 1852, now Pennsylvania Route 8 in most places, originating in Etna. This passes through Glenshaw, the settlement where the Shaw family ground grain, made sickles, and mined coal; the road itself was partly a Shaw enterprise.

Railroads have had a lesser influence in these northern townships. The mines of Indiana and West Deer Townships sold coal to the Pittsburgh, Bessemer & Lake Erie Railroad that passed near by. The Western Pennsylvania Railroad (later the Baltimore & Ohio) stimulated Glenshaw's development as a railroad commuter suburb, with Late Victorian houses joining the early Shaw family homesteads. Products as diverse as ice and cut flowers have been produced locally and shipped by rail. But more influential were two interurban trolley lines of 1907: the Butler Short Line that turned inland and northward at Etna and passed near Glenshaw, and the Harmony Short Line that went northwesterly through Ross, McCandless, and Marshall Townships, giving rise in the last of these to Bradford Woods, a sylvan trolley suburb of 1915. The trolleys stimulated commuter settlement and gave the farmers fortunate enough to live near by ready access to town.

Roads and rail lines originating in or near Pittsburgh were not the only means by which the city influenced this part of the county. Reserve Township, adjacent to the Troy Hill section of Allegheny, became a place of summer villas and of cemeteries for Pittsburgh and Allegheny congregations. Evergreen Hamlet and Swan Acres were suburban developments of architecturally distinct character, one 1850s Romantic, the other 1930s Modern. Estates appeared here and there as well. There was, for instance, the spectacular "Hartwood Farms," the Mary Flinn Lawrence estate. And there was "Vosemary Farm," the Pine Township home of Edward Vose Babcock, lumberman and politician, to whom the county owes, among other things, North Park. The park, which lies mainly in McCandless Township, opened in 1927 when that area was still sparsely settled. It was much improved during the 1930s through the Public Works Administration, and now serves as vital open space for a burgeoning suburban population.

Finally, the mineral resources, gas, oil, and especially coal, have left their mark on the area: in Indiana and West Deer Townships in the form of 1900-period company towns near deep-mine portals, in the adjacent Fawn Township in the form of strip mines.

The county townships north of the river are thus an old farming area that has been civilized in some places and violated in others. But there are still areas where the rural character has been only slightly frazzled by suburbanization, and the shape of the land creates beautiful spaces and distant views. ▪

Industry with a rural difference: the greenhouses and workers' cottages of Pittsburgh Cut Flower, Bakerstown-Warrendale Road, Richland Township.

Glenshaw Valley
Shaler Township

Although first developed for small-scale industry, the Glenshaw Valley — apart from the now busy Route 8 — has an almost pastoral character. The flood plain along Pine Creek has the aura of an earlier era with a number of Shaw family houses and the picturesque bell tower of the Glenshaw Valley Presbyterian Church along the largest remaining independent section of the Butler Plank Road. A small grid of streets which backs up to the wooded hillside has a rich collection of late nineteenth- and early twentieth-century houses, particularly along part of Butler Plank Road and the tree-lined Glenshaw Avenue.

Thomas Wilson Shaw house
1526 Butler Plank Road, Glenshaw Valley, Shaler Township
1824; addition, 1830–32

The ell of this house, built by Thomas Wilson Shaw, an eminent doctor and the son of founding settler John Shaw, was a house in itself and still appears as such, with a symmetrical front and a central doorway porch. The front portion, built a half-dozen years later, is of equal size, but here the porch is a four-bayed Grecian Doric composition of square channeled columns with an elegant Greek Revival doorway behind. As in 1824, the bricklayer put up a simple building block; the pomp of the new entrance was the carpenter's work.

Landmarks plaque

House
Glenshaw Avenue and Wilson Street, Glenshaw Valley, Shaler Township
C. 1890

At first glance this seems to be a bungalow, but it has an upper space that erupts through the roof in the form of two gables and two turrets. Quite a plain little house thus takes on the air of a concentrated mansion. The angled chimney suggests diagonally set fireplaces or stoves in room corners.

Isaac Lightner house
Mount Royal Boulevard and Woodland Avenue, Shaler Township
1833

Similar in general appearance to the Nicholas Way house in Edgeworth, the Lightner house also has a Federal-style porch of four Roman Doric columns bearing a windowed pediment; in this case the window has a raised surround with its own little pediment. The front dormers have windows of a segmental-arch form; these are characteristically Federal, whether or not they are part of the original design. There is a detached summer kitchen as well. Despite modernization in 1929 the house exterior, very fortunately, remains substantially as built.

National Register; Landmarks plaque

Shinn-Beall house

DeHaven-Leet house
Mt. Royal Boulevard and Eade Street, Shaler Township
1831 or 1836

A handsome brick farmhouse that gains unusual stateliness from the matching lower wings at its ends. In vernacular guise, this is the county's sole product of the Palladian impulse which created many of the country's great manor houses in similar form — a primary central block with flanking dependencies.

The later doorway shelter, unfortunately, is quite plain; a Greek Revival entrance feature such as may have been present when the house was built would complete the composition. The front of the house is in Flemish bond, with common bond elsewhere. To the rear of one wing is a spacious back porch, and a frame carriage house stands to one side.

Sellers house

Hill-McCallam-Davies house

Hampton house

Evergreen Hamlet
Evergreen Hamlet Road, Ross Township
Hastings & Preiser, surveying and planning, 1851 and after

William Shinn, a lawyer, founded this tiny suburb, originally with five homes on 85 acres, to give middle-class families some of the advantages of country living while allowing reasonable access to places of business. The charter of the Evergreen Association bound the members to certain obligations such as the joint upkeep of a school, yet the houses and their lots were privately owned. The Association lasted only 15 years, but the settlement still has some of the qualities of a Romantic village with which it began. Especially good are the four surviving original houses, the Gothic Hill-McCallam-Davies house (Joseph W. Kerr, architect, 1852) the Shinn-Beall house, Gothic again but of a simpler design; and the very simple and rather Italianate Sellers and Hampton houses: all possibly by Kerr. Unlike the others, which are board-and-batten, the Sellers house has a close-fitting shiplap siding on the front, clapboard elsewhere.

As an early cooperative, Evergreen Hamlet shows a certain socio-economic adventurousness, and its role as a refuge from urban and industrial environment preceded slightly the growth of railroad suburbs, such as East Liberty, Hazelwood, and Sewickley for the same purpose.

National Register; Landmarks plaques

Swan Acres
Swan, Circle, and Wick Drives, Ross Township
1937–38

A dozen houses, none outstanding but offering several interpretations in one place of the concept of Modern architecture as understood here in the late 1930s. The architect or architects are not known but Swan Acres was a development and there was some measure of control over what was built in it, whether for the developer or the buyers. To use innovative styles at all was a bold decision at the time.

Covenanter Presbyterian Church (presently, Depreciation Lands Museum)
4743 South Pioneer Road, Hampton Township
C. 1835

Now a museum of late eighteenth- and early nineteenth-century life, this was built as a church of the simplest type with only a Greek Revival cornice for exterior decoration. The windows have the original glass. The restored Armstrong log house of 1803, moved to the site, is also used for museum purposes.

Sisters of Divine Providence Mother House and La Roche College
9000 Babcock Boulevard, McCandless Township
John E. Kauzor, architect for Mother House, 1927

This large complex, conspicuous in the North Hills, contains a large number of religious and academic buildings clustered around the large, tall Mother House with its chapel. The style of the Mother House is North Italian Romanesque, though the tower with its conical spire may imitate no one of the numerous examples in Italy. The other buildings are generally without character.

Landmarks plaque

Calvert house
2538 Middle Road, Hampton Township
Janssen & Abbott, architects, 1910; addition

Termed a bungalow by the architects, this house in fact had a fully finished bedroom story in the roof. The house, now containing apartments, was originally laid out as three sides of an octagon, with the living room at the center facing northwest so as to take in the summer sunset. Pergolas on cylindrical piers still shade the greater part of the ground story and there is an outside fireplace. Planned with five family bedrooms — one on the ground floor — and two large servants' rooms, this was a spacious house but an unassuming one, designed like some houses then being built in the Philadelphia area. The plans were widely published.

"Hartwood Farms" (presently, Hartwood Acres)
Saxonburg Boulevard, Indiana Township
Alfred W. Hopkins (New York), architect;
house, 1929; stable group, 1926

Here is the largest of the country estates — 639 acres — developed in the Pittsburgh area in the 1920s. It was the property of Mary Flinn Lawrence, daughter of the well-known contractor William Flinn. The main house is typical 1920s Cotswold, an English rural Tudor style expressed in limestone and slate. Learned taste, not original inspiration, is what most rich clients of the time wanted in their homes, and that is what Alfred Hopkins offered. Random-coursed ashlar, slightly irregular roof slating, and leaded windows, some square-paned, some diamond-paned, give a certain variety to a design almost irreproachable as a faithful

"Vosemary Farm"
Babcock Boulevard and Logan Road, Pine Township
C. 1910

This was the summer estate of Edward Vose Babcock. The main house is simple and big, a Colonial Revival structure with a spacious front porch and a broad porte-cochere. There are 11 other outbuildings near the house, plain and unpretentious. A long, low cabana stands neglected behind an oval swimming pool, and there is a rustic garden shelter of untrimmed sticks and poles. The estate once had 700 acres.

Babcock was a lumber millionaire, whose E. V. Babcock & Co. was the world's largest in the production of hardwood. He was mayor of Pittsburgh from 1918 to 1922, and later, as County Commissioner, sponsored creation of the County's North and South Parks. He also had a house on Colonial Place in Shadyside; of the two grandly pillared twin mansions facing Ellsworth Avenue, his is the western one.

"Olive Grange"
Mingo Road south of Valley Road, Marshall Township
C. 1850

The vergeboard, a border of planking that in medieval times hung from the outer edge of a gable roof to shelter the joint between the roof and the wall, was an obvious feature for decorative treatment. Romanticism, rediscovering the Gothic style, took up the vergeboard with enthusiasm. In Swiss chalet architecture, the Romantics found still further expres-

reproduction of the English original. The big stable, garage, and barn group in a nearby hollow is of a humbler material, concrete block, but is quite as picturesqely composed as the house itself. Today, Hartwood Acres is County property, and is used as a cultural and recreational center.

sions of wood, quite notably in the use of sawn-out boards for balustrades and applied ornament. From such sources come the lavish, remarkably intact ornamentation of this house. Most of the ornament is sawn out, but the vergeboards themselves have been carved with chamfers that give an extra richness of effect. The owner takes pride in this unusual house and has it painted to bring out the details.

Barn
Clendenning Road between McMorran and Shepard Roads, West Deer Township
C. 1870

Barn builders indulged their modest fancies in the nineteenth century just as architects did, though their means were more limited. Here, from bottom to top, the carpenter was able to include three types of pointed window heads, though admittedly the lowermost ones, typical carpenter's Greek Revival, are pointed very bluntly.

House
Near Cedar Ridge Road, West Deer Township
C. 1820

Here is an old log house that shows the effect of nearly two centuries of use. There are actually two units, connected by a porch and with a now-enclosed dogtrot, a kind of breezeway, between them. The dogtrot is a vernacular log house form more usually found in Southern states, and this is the only dogtrot house surviving in the county. Only the small unit, which is very small, has a chimney. Some of the logs have been covered with board-and-batten siding, some are exposed. The porch roof is supported partly by turned Late Victorian posts, partly by squared timbers. There is also a barn of round logs covered with vertical boarding.

The property is sited a mile from the nearest road and seems to be deep in Appalachia rather than a few miles from Pittsburgh.

Bridge
Over Bull Creek, west of Bull Creek Road, Fawn Township
"Reno," engineer; Morse Bridge Company (Youngstown), builder; 1878

Victorian bridge engineering tends to be light and rather limber, since human or animal power was usually needed at some point in getting the parts from the fabricating plant to the site. Once there, parts were bolted together or, where rigidity was needed, riveted. This bridge, built the year the Morse company was founded, is a Pratt truss of wrought iron. It is probably the oldest extant metal bridge in the county.

Tarentum on the Allegheny as seen from Westmoreland County.

Up the Allegheny

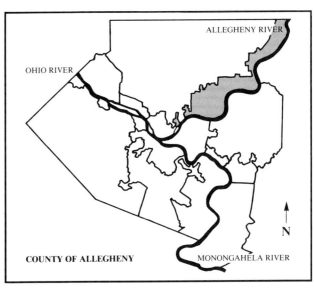

ALLEGHENY RIVER

OHIO RIVER

N

COUNTY OF ALLEGHENY

MONONGAHELA RIVER

The history of the Allegheny River has been markedly different from that of the Monongahela. Though industry has grown up along its bank here and there, especially near Pittsburgh, it has a rather open, rural quality. Pleasure boats are common, and such towboat activity as exists is on a much smaller scale than on the Monongahela. Industrial plants generally take the form of storage tanks, sheds, and small factories rather than the unique, powerful forms of the steel mills. Yet this has been a very busy river, carrying the flatboats of the early nineteenth century on the swollen waters of the spring thaws from remote points of origin, the upstate timber rafts of the mid-nineteenth century, the oil barges of the great boom of the 1860s, and the coalboat bottoms, loaded with simple wood products, that through most of the century went down to Pittsburgh for completion. Where the Monongahela traffic has largely been driven by steam and diesel, the traffic of the Allegheny's great days drifted on water that, before the upstream dams and reservoirs, could run high and fast.

The Pennsylvania Canal, completed in the Pittsburgh area in 1829, ran along the western shore of the Allegheny and contributed to settlement and industrial development in a way that this drifting traffic, largely independent of the shore, did not. Sharpsburg began as a canal port, and Tarentum as a canal port and industrial town. The development of the Western Pennsylvania Railroad in the 1860s and of interurban trolley lines around 1900 further stimulated settlement, with Millvale, Etna, Blawnox, Brackenridge, and Natrona attracting industry and Aspinwall and Cheswick becoming residential towns.

Several Allegheny Valley communities stand out. Millvale is notable not only for St. Anthony's Church, with its Baroque front, but also for St. Nicholas Church, architecturally undistinguished but containing a remarkable set of murals and decorations by Maximilian Vanka portraying the Croatian experience in America. Etna, at one time, was like a Monongahela River town with the Isabella blast furnace in operation until 1954 and Spang, Chalfant & Company, which had evolved from a rolling mill of 1817, manufacturing pipe until 1969. Fox Chapel began early in this century as an area favored for golf clubs and summer homes, acquired a number of estates and a fox hunt in the 1920s, and gradually became a year-round home for many wealthy Pittsburghers. Springdale Borough has the birthplace of biologist and author Rachel Carson, architecturally undistinguished but preserved and operated as a nature study center. Natrona, in Harrison Township, is a riverfront industrial town of narrow close-built streets which has changed little since early in the century owing to its isolated site with industrial plants to either side and a bluff behind. Much of the town is company housing built by the Penn Salt company between 1850 and 1900.

As elsewhere in the county, the landscape demands attention in this valley. But here the landscape has clearly been altered by man, and the path of Pennsylvania Route 28 as it makes its way up river is the result of blasting operations. Nevertheless, the high bluffs, now of naked stone in many places, dominate the surrounding settlement and activity.

Bluffs, railroad, and houses characterize East Deer Township and the entire Allegheny Valley.

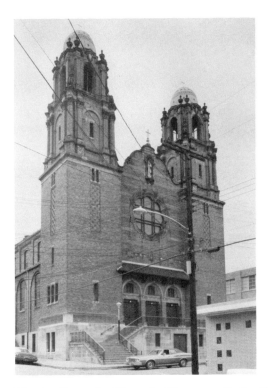

St. Anthony's Church (Roman Catholic)
Howard Street and North Avenue, Millvale
John T. Comes, architect, 1914

Set high to compensate for a sloping street, St. Anthony's displays an impressive front of brown brick and beige terra cotta with bands of colored tile, designed in a free version of Mexican Baroque. The window over the entrance and the tower-tops, with their patterned tile domes, have a full-blooded Mexican look, but the style is not consistent; behind the facade only scalloped gables carry the theme through.

St. Mary's Church (Roman Catholic)
Garnier and Altmayer Streets, Sharpsburg
Peter Dedrichs, architect, 1916

The dominant building of Sharpsburg, St. Mary's is sited in a way that suggests the great church of a small Old World town. Its style is very generally Renaissance, but of no one nation, and its three rose windows are of course less

Renaissance than medieval. A triumphal-arch portal with Composite columns faces the street. At one point the small domes were imperiled but a plea from the Pittsburgh History & Landmarks Foundation to save them was successful.

Aspinwall Pumping Station

City of Pittsburgh Department of Water
226 Delafield Road, Pittsburgh
C. 1907 and after

Into the beginning years of the twentieth century, Pittsburgh drinking water, incredibly, was not treated at all, and the city, drawing its water from the very polluted rivers, was not a healthy place. Filtered water, distributed from this large new intake plant on the Allegheny River beginning in 1908, lowered the incidence of typhoid fever spectacularly, and chemical treatment since has helped still further in preventing contagion.

The Ross Pumping Station of 1907, Rutan & Russell, architects, is the actual intake station. Of golden-brown Roman brick and gray-brown sandstone, it is grandly Beaux-Arts. Such a building was a big shelter for tall steam reciprocating engines, compound or triple-expansion, that might rise 25 or 30 feet from the main floor: impressive mechanical constructions whose slow, unvaried beat was a fine thing to witness. They had to be readily accessible and auxiliary equipment had to be accommodated, and since such engines gave off heat the space they occupied had to be airy. Furthermore, when they were in a government facility, the mood of the time demanded that they be housed with a certain elegance. Hence this grandiose pavilion and other imposing pumping stations of the 1900 period around town.

Also from 1907, and by the same architects, is the Old Administration Building, a handsome Italian villa among the forlorn remains of the old filtration beds it once administered.

The Aspinwall Pumping Station, not far from the Ross, was built in 1913 to designs by Thomas H. Scott, who also designed the Mission Pumping Station on the South Side Slopes. It is built of gray brick, stone, and terra cotta, and distributes the treated water to the Lanpher Reservoir, from which it is relayed elsewhere.

Sauer Buildings
607-717 Center Avenue, Aspinwall
Frederick C. Sauer, architect, 1894-1942

Sauer, an architect, builder, and real-estate developer, spent several decades as a producer of colorless buildings before turning his attention to this hillside property, on which he had already built in a conventional way. He proceeded to remodel and build anew in a primitively fantastic manner, salvaging used materials and ornament, imparting a flimsy quaintness to all but the original house. He was building in a time when quaintness was a selling point in residential construction, yet the impression these buildings gives is not one of commercial calculation; rather, Sauer really seems to have made one of those odd essays in personal expression in building that turn up now and then in some otherwise-staid part of the world. The pride of the place is "Heidelberg," a three-story conversion of a chicken coop into an apartment house.

"Heidelberg"

Ferree house
403 Dorseyville Road, O'Hara Township
C. 1810; remodeled c. 1840 (?)

A curious little Greek Revival house with an inset porch, supported by wooden Doric columns. The original effect may have been one of severely simple elegance, but probably this was always a primitive-looking building that relied on the columns to make a good impression. Inside the porch is a Georgian doorway, raising the possibility that part of the house is older by 20 or 30 years than the present exterior suggests.

"La Tourelle"
8 La Tourelle Lane, Fox Chapel
Janssen & Cocken, architects, 1924

The home of the merchant and philanthropist Edgar J. Kaufmann, who a decade later commissioned Frank Lloyd Wright to design "Fallingwater" in Fayette County. Here as in that more famous house, Kaufmann lived amid rugged materials: brick laid in English bond, artfully irregular roofing slates, fieldstone walls, and flagged and cobbled pavements. The *tourelle* itself is the cylindrical entrance, with its gratuitously steep roof.

Associate Reformed Church (presently, Harmarville United Presbyterian Church)
521 Indianola Road, Harmar Township
1851

This is a very simple Greek Revival country church, with Doric pilasters all around. The cornices and capitals are of wood, the architrave of brick like the pilaster shafts. No water table or bases for the pilasters appear above ground. The interior seems to have its original pews.

Pennsalt housing
Blue Ridge, Greenwich, Wood, Center, Penn, and Federal Streets, Natrona, Harrison Township
1850 and after

The Pennsalt housing district is a prime example of a Western Pennsylvania company town of the mid- and late nineteenth century. The Pennsylvania Salt Manufacturing Company, a chemical works whose principal product was caustic soda, assumed the role of paternalistic landlord and erected about

150 houses and a company store next to its riverfront manufactory. The 16 earliest houses along Federal Street were tiny — 14 by 30 feet with two rooms on each of two floors — but their picturesque steeply pitched roofs and board-and-batten siding gave them the look of "model cottages," intended to attract workers, ameliorate the harshness of industrial conditions, and promote good behavior among workers and their families. There are also later board-and-batten houses, drop-sided houses, brick row houses, and an assortment of other housing types. Two of the brick row houses have been restored by the Pittsburgh History & Landmarks Foundation as an example for current owners.

Pittsburgh and Tarentum Camp Meeting Association
East of Main and Fifth Streets, Harrison Township
C. 1905

Thirty-two cottages stand in a rough oval around an open wooden tabernacle in a rare surviving local instance of a permanent religious revival center. The Methodist group was already established on the land when the original buildings were virtually eliminated by a fire; those seen today are on a new site, and date from 1905 and later. The tabernacle, which has the appearance of a large open picnic shelter, was built to replace the tent originally used; it contains stained glass from a Methodist church formerly on Bingham Street on the South Side. The small, narrow cottages have been remodeled to the extent that no two are now alike. It is interesting to see that some of them, despite being from 1905 or later, are board-and-batten or have Gothic Revival vergeboards on their gables: features more characteristic of 50 years before.

House
2503 Buchanan Road, Harrison Township
C. 1850

If this house is of the mid-1830s, as may be the case, it was refaced later, sometime around 1850. Aside from the paired eaves brackets, the decorative effect depends on ways of using two thicknesses of boarding. The decorative window surrounds are flush with the battens of the walls; the immediate surrounds of the openings are flush with the boards of the siding. The difference in layers is emphasized by the "printer's brace" ogee form on the first-floor window heads.

Burtner house
Burtner Road east of Pennsylvania Route 28, Harrison Township
Philip Burtner, builder, 1818–21

Currently undergoing restoration, the Burtner house will return to its original appearance as the home of a substantial rural citizen of early in the last century. This is a simple, solid house, with little pretense. If the porch, a restoration, has very slightly arched fascias there is almost nothing else to be called ornamental. The rather deep-set windows attest to the thickness of the walls — 30 inches thick in the basement, 18 inches thick at the eaves — whose surfaces have an attractive but practical random pattern of large and small stones.

In 1969 it appeared that the house would be demolished for an access road to an expressway: a plan that aroused public interest in saving it, ill-kept though it was at the time. Important local events had taken place in the house, and it had been the home of an important local citizen, and in 1970 a petition with 2,000 names was submitted to the Governor. He intervened, hours before demolition was to occur, with a reprieve. The access road was realigned, coming near the house but sparing it, and in 1971 a preservation group, Burtner House Restoration, Inc., acquired the house and began its restoration. The Pittsburgh History & Landmarks Foundation was involved in negotiations for both the saving of the Burtner house and the transfer of its title, and now offers its services in the restoration itself.

National Register; Landmarks plaque

EAST OF PITTSBURGH

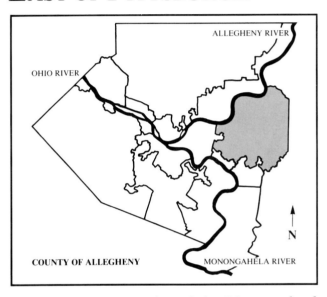

Between Pittsburgh and the Westmoreland County line lies a mixture of communities that together summarize the ways in which the land of Allegheny County has developed.

Should one follow the old Pennsylvania Railroad out of Pittsburgh on its easterly course the first town reached will be Wilkinsburg, once called the Holy City because of its abundance of churches and absence of taverns. It received its distinctive character early in its history thanks to James Kelly, a real-estate dealer who himself was a teetotaler and a man of great local influence in the mid-nineteenth century. It was under his paternalistic hand that the taverns were banned — even though the first building within the present boundaries had been a log tavern — and that the borough was returned to independence after being swept into Pittsburgh's great annexation of 1868. Wilkinsburg has always been a town of modest sufficiency rather than elegance, but has a great house in the Singer mansion of the 1860s.

The railroad then turns south and passes through Edgewood, a borough with its own determined character. Like so many other places on the

Architecture for the Edgewood Idea: Tudor Revival on Beech Avenue.

337

Pennsylvania Railroad, this made an early transition from a farming area to exurb, a place where persons in search of fresh air and a quiet life could make a nightly escape from Pittsburgh. Commuter service began in 1864 and incorporation took place in 1888. In drawing up their boundaries, the people of Edgewood prudently included the greater part of the Union Switch & Signal Company plant that George Westinghouse had established in the area two years before, and thus got an excellent contribution to their tax base; the main entrance, however, they left in the less-fortunate and then-unincorporated Swissvale to the south. They banned other industries and many types of business however, and consolidated their town as a middle-class community of pleasant streets and respectable ways. Early in this century there was talk of the "Edgewood Idea": low taxes, model government, community institutions that offered sociability under the eye of the community. Edgewood had its own church and school, its Civic Club, its Edgewood Club for social purposes, and through these institutions developed a self-sufficiency that promoted the Edgewood Idea.

Of quite a different character is Monroeville, a borough associated with spectacular successes in real-estate development — though not architecture — since the early 1950s. This is the automobile suburb in all its triumph: strip development, shopping centers, office buildings, research facilities, and housing developments, with a population rise in 30 years from 8,000 to 30,000. Yet away from all this, Monroeville retains traces of the Patton Township it once was, with a farming, coal-mining and railroading past.

Between Wilkinsburg and Monroeville lie suburbs in rolling, often wooded country, a mosaic of little boroughs. Churchill, today a prosperous residential suburb, has eighteenth-century roots. One part of it was Bullock Pens, a supply base for the British army and later a veterans' settlement. Forest Hills is associated with Westinghouse Electric and its history. Here KDKA, the country's first commercial radio station, was located in the 1920s, and here too stands the early "atom smasher" of 1938 in the modern Westinghouse Research and Development Center.

North of these suburbs is Penn Hills, also suburbanized but retaining traces of its earlier past in a number of mining "patches" and at least one working coal mine. Two Allegheny River towns adjoin Penn Hills to the north. The nearer is Verona, in the 1860s the location of an engine

house and machine shops for the Allegheny Valley Railroad, and later built up with a mixture of industrial plants near the railroad and the river and of suburban houses on the hillside beyond. Oakmont, adjoining it to the north, has had the same mixed character. The railroad, which the Pennsylvania absorbed, runs at grade along the main street, faced by stores and churches. Here, too, have been light-industrial plants near the river and commuter houses on hillside streets inland; much of the leafy character of the residential area remains.

Finally, Plum Borough is an area of rolling land that is still partly rural though the part near Monroeville has been suburbanized and strip mining has marred the land in some areas. Plum still has examples of early nineteenth-century architecture in primitive country, less because they have been seen as historic treasures than because neither mining nor suburbanization has been extensive.

In general, the area east of Pittsburgh shows the stimulus that a railroad main line could give in the nineteenth century, and road construction in our own time. Where the Pennsylvania main line and the Allegheny Valley Railroad went, commuter and industrial towns grew as the terrain permitted; elsewhere, development awaited the automobile. When this became common, a Monroeville could grow on cheap rural land. ■

A reminder of Patton Township: the Hall Locomotive Shop, Monroeville.

338

Wilkinsburg Pennsylvania Railroad Station
Hay Street at Ross Avenue, Wilkinsburg
Walter H. Cookson, architect, 1916

To eliminate grade crossings in the populous suburb of Wilkinsburg, the Pennsylvania Railroad track level was raised around 1915, necessitating a new station. The new building, limestone with pale-buff brick, is a pleasant gesture to the town, terminating Ross Avenue. The Ionic order between paneled piers and the clock that rises partway above the parapet still have a little of the Beaux-Arts showiness about them, but there would have been much more 10 or even five years before: architectural practice, more and more, was favoring well-schooled good taste, and less and less expressiveness. The basement to one side has its own marqueed entrance, probably a loading dock for Railway Express trucks.

The suburban service to Pittsburgh, and indeed train service of any kind, has long been ended. Yet the station remains as a reminder of the railroad to which Wilkinsburg owed its nineteenth-century development and of the Golden Age of American railroads, which attained their greatest track mileage in the year of this building's erection, 1916.

Landmarks plaque

Singer house
1318 Singer Place, Wilkinsburg
1865

The architect of this lushly Romantic Gothic house is not known, though James D. Van Trump sees J. W. Kerr as a possibility. As with most Victorian architecture, stylistic purity was not a consideration. The walls of coursed rubble have rusticated quoins, very Renaissance, the vergeboards have little turned pendants — Italianate — on their cusps, and the lambrequins and window hoods are of an elaboration beyond anything that an ordinary Gothic Revivalist, let alone any medieval architect, would have used. There is twice the usual amount of everything, except on the relatively restrained porches. Victorian, too, was the private chapel — Singer was an Episcopalian — with a carriage house thriftily installed in its basement. This, unfortunately, was burned in 1976.

This is the handsomest building in Wilkinsburg, and one of the most accomplished works of Victorian Gothic in the county. The present grounds are a small surviving portion of a large estate.

John F. Singer was a steel manufacturer and a partner with Alexander Nimick in Singer, Nimick & Company on the South Side.

National Register

Houses
1330–66 Singer Place, Wilkinsburg
Frederick G. Scheibler, Jr., architect, c. 1912

The floridly Romantic, vertical Singer house has as neighbor a plain, very horizontal, hillside house row by Scheibler. The two are not in strident opposition, but Scheibler's row opposes middle-class bland common sense — and the typical anonymity of builder's housing — to Singer's individualism. This is Scheibler at his most rationalistic, neatly presenting the fundamentals of a row-house design without fancy touches. As in some other of his designs, Scheibler uses casement sash, slightly Old World in effect and allowing more ventilation than sliding sash. Casements were not unheard-of early in the twentieth century but were still rather uncommon.

Western Pennsylvania School for the Deaf
Swissvale Avenue and Walnut Street, Edgewood
After 1892; Alden & Harlow, architects for administration building, 1903

An administration building of 1903 with a tall portico of eight Roman Doric columns graciously dominates a sizeable campus. The remainder of the campus conforms to no one style, though a loose sort of Neo-Georgian is often to be found. The chapel attached to the administration building has windows with so-called Florentine tracery, two round-headed lights with a rondel above.

The Sheltering Arms Home for Aged Protestants (presently, Jane Holmes Residence)
441 Swissvale Avenue, Wilkinsburg
1869; additions

In its time one element of this building has been a home for "wayward girls" and another has been a home for aged couples. The Italianate architecture, sadly calm, is designed with economy in mind. The great porch faces southeast toward the adjoining neighborhood. The two round bays are additions that add a feeling of mass and inner space to the hard, brittle Mid-Victorian exterior.

C. C. Mellor Library and Edgewood Club
Pennwood and West Swissvale Avenues, Edgewood
Edward B. Lee, architect, 1914

This calm, low-set, simple but refined work is unusual for Pittsburgh but echoes contemporary trends elsewhere. The stucco, the hipped tile roofs, and the pergola suggest the simplest sort of country-house architecture then being built in California. On the other hand, pergolas were popular throughout the United States as alternatives to the old-fashioned front porch, offering shade from vines without greatly darkening the rooms behind. Such thick piers were to be found supporting both pergolas and porches in the Philadelphia area, for example.

The Edgewood Club of 1903 expressed the "Edgewood Idea" of amenity and decency in concrete terms. It was founded to enable the young to socialize under the supervision of their elders. The library was begun with Carnegie Foundation money and a gift of books by a citizen at the time of the Club's decision to build the present clubhouse.

Gardner-Bailey house
124 West Swissvale Avenue, Edgewood
1864; additions

This Italianate house, almost a bungalow in its basic form, is one of the oldest houses in Edgewood and the most imaginative. The house is plain in its essential construction, with a doorway and window trim that are still Greek Revival; it is likely that the cupola, the monitor-like construction on the rear wing, the porch, and the ornamentation that put it out of the ordinary were added to the original structure. The simple house thus took on the air of an elegant villa, using Victorian Italianate features just as the Nicholas Way house in Edgeworth, basically similar, had made use of a temple-fronted porch to attain the same purpose in Federal-style terms.

National Register

Linhart homestead
221 Farnsworth Avenue, Wilkins Township
Christin Linhart, builder, c. 1782; addition, 1794

Linhart, one of the earliest settlers in this area and proprietor of a sawmill, built himself a simple log house, later doubled in size for a married daughter. The two-story form seems rather advanced for 1782, raising the possibility of an addition above the original walls. There is a rough symmetry to the completed house, emphasized by the massive stone and brick chimneys at the ends, yet no special attempt has been made to place the windows regularly. Among other things, those of the older section are set higher, and the exposed joist ends on the long walls show that the ground-floor ceiling was higher too; indeed, the upper story is more of a loft, with windows coming almost to floor level.

The house is probably the oldest continuously occupied house in Allegheny County. The window casements and the frame ell to the rear are later work, and so probably is the front porch; yet the house has a pleasant air of great antiquity about it as well as being handsome in itself.

Bullock Pens Church (presently, Beulah Chapel)
Beulah and McCready Roads, Churchill
Williams McCrea, builder, 1837

Although the interior is much changed, the exterior of this simple church is substantially as built. Aside from a few very elementary moldings and a semicircular window in the front gable, the only effort at architecture comes from the Flemish bond of the entrance-front brickwork as opposed to common bond elsewhere.

The cemetery is one of the oldest in Allegheny County. The oldest marked grave dates from 1793. The church and cemetery anchor this twentieth-century suburb in history, so to speak, and Churchill can account itself lucky to have them. So many of our suburbs are all too evidently devoid of a past.

National Register; Landmarks plaque

Crossroads Presbyterian Church (presently, Old Stone Church)
Northern Pike and Stroschen Road, Monroeville
1896; bell tower, 1976

Built of a golden-brown coursed rubble, this is a very simply detailed church but one of sophisticated design nonetheless. Gabled plainly at one end and gabled with a lower slope at the other, the building expands on both sides into broad, hip-roofed polygonal bays. The result is an interplay of roof planes such as the Shingle Style architects of the previous decade had reveled in; with them, the roof might *be* the architecture, and so it is here. The modern bell tower is well placed to add to the play of form; it is a memorial to George Westinghouse and Nikola Tesla, the brilliant inventor who worked for Westinghouse and helped develop the alternating-current system that is standard in modern power transmission.

Landmarks plaque

"Groton" (presently, "Tapawingo")
End of Pike Street, Penn Hills Township
Edward McLaughlin, builder, 1775

This is one of the oldest log houses in Allegheny County, badly in need of repair at the time of writing. It still has mud chinking in the traditional manner, and gun ports in case of Indian attack.

Longue Vue Country Club
Oakwood Road, Penn Hills Township
Janssen & Cocken, architects, 1924–25; additions

There is a nice ambiguity about the style of the original club building. The big chimneys, flush with the gable walls, could be Georgian, yet the overall feeling is that of French rural architecture, a feeling heightened by the use of casement windows. This is the suave rusticity often found in Philadelphia-area architecture of the 1920s, but much less often in Southwestern Pennsylvania; long, slender pieces of rubble in thick mortar, the masonry equivalent of a good

tweed, and above, thick, rough-edged roofing slates. A building as unornamented as any Modern work, it still conveys a lush impression through its picturesque exaggerations of form and texture.

St. Thomas Episcopal Church (presently, St. Paul's Baptist Church)
Second Street and Delaware Avenue, Oakmont
William Kerr, architect, 1874

Many Victorian congregations could afford only wooden churches, but here is an example of how they could achieve dignity nonetheless. The pointed arches are not structural but they say "church." The board-and-batten siding says frankly, "made of wood," and covers the plain walls with a lively pattern of light and shadow that makes other ornament unnecessary. Richard Upjohn, whose Trinity Church in New York City (1839–46) was one of the grandest American churches of its time, designed a number of churches similar to this one and thereby demonstrated that good architecture comes in a wide range of prices.

Oakmont Country Club
Hulton Road, Plum
Edward Stotz, architect for clubhouse, 1904; additions and alterations

Country clubs tend to be sprawling affairs, with a variety of social rooms on the first floor handy to terraces, verandahs, and kitchens and other necessary service areas. Surrounded by golf courses, tennis courts, and other facilities that create large areas of open ground, they are usually low-built and rural in character. Here is an early golf club, noncommittal as to style, shed-dormered on the ends, half-timbered on the entrance front, and with a big American front porch. As with many architect-designed buildings of its period, it strikes an attitude, it presents itself in a certain character. The front as originally designed is symmetrical and perhaps a little prim; yet the decorative half-timbering and the big porch are symbols of informality, relaxation. Perhaps these features hint at a specific degree of relaxation from social formality permissible on these premises.

The 18-hole course, of championship calibre, is regarded by golf historians as a monument in its own right. As designed by Henry C. Fownes in 1903, its hazards penalized careless or incompetent play to an extent unknown on modern courses, and though there have been many modifications, much of the old "penal" quality remains. One sports writer has urged that it be preserved as a national landmark, so evocative is its design of the early years of golf in the United States.

National Register

Church
Coxcomb Hill and Logan's Ferry Roads, Plum
C. 1900

This abandoned church is a mystery, though it may be a Presbyterian church for a Logan's Ferry congregation founded in 1842. A small cemetery, adjoining, has graves of a Stewart family and dates back at least to 1862. The style is primitive and mixed, with a Tuscan portico and angle-topped windows suggesting Gothic arches. In this last detail the church is ahead of its time, since PPG Place in Pittsburgh has exactly the same.

INDEX

Page numbers given in boldface indicate either a separate guide entry for the subject or a specific discussion in the text.